CRITICAL THINKING, READING, AND WRITING
A Brief Guide to Argument

THIRD EDITION

SYLVAN BARNET
Professor of English, Tufts University

HUGO BEDAU
Professor of Philosophy, Tufts University

Bedford/St. Martin's   BOSTON   NEW YORK

For Bedford/St. Martin's
Developmental Editor: Stephen A. Scipione
Production Editors: Karen S. Baart, Stasia Zomkowski
Production Supervisor: Scott Lavelle
Marketing Manager: Karen Melton
Editorial Assistant: Maura Shea
Production Assistants: Coleen O'Hanley, Helaine Denenberg
Copyeditor: Lisa Wehrle
Text Design: Sandra Rigney
Cover Design: Donna Lee Dennison
Composition: Pine Tree Composition, Inc.
Printing and Binding: Haddon Craftsmen, Inc.

President: Charles H. Christensen
Editorial Director: Joan E. Feinberg
Director of Editing, Design, and Production: Marcia Cohen
Managing Editor: Elizabeth M. Schaaf

Library of Congress Catalog Card Number: 98–85189

Manufactured in the United States of America.

2 1 0 9 8
f e d c b

For information, write: Bedford/St. Martin's, 75 Arlington Street, Boston, MA 02116 (617-426-7440)

ISBN: 0–312–17153–6

Acknowledgments

Derek Bok, "Protecting Freedom of Expression on the Campus" (editors' title) from "Protecting Freedom of Expression at Harvard" from *The Boston Globe* (May 25, 1991). Copyright © 1991 by Derek Bok. Reprinted with the permission of the author.

Robert Bork, "Addicted to Health" [editors' title] from *The National Review* (July 28, 1997). Copyright © 1997 by National Review, Inc. Reprinted with the permission of National Review, Inc., 215 Lexington Avenue, New York, NY 10016.

Judy Brady, "I Want a Wife" from *Ms.* (1971). Copyright © 1971 by Judy Brady. Reprinted with the permission of the author.

Lois M. Brenner, "Take the Pain Away" from *The New York Times* (February 21, 1996), "Letters to the Editor." Reprinted with the permission of the author.

Susan Brownmiller, "Let's Put Pornography Back in the Closet" from *Newsday* (1979). Copyright © 1979 by Susan Brownmiller. Reprinted with the permission of the author.

Preface

This book is a text about critical thinking and argumentation—a book about getting ideas, using sources, evaluating kinds of evidence, and organizing material. It also incudes about fifty readings, with a strong emphasis on contemporary arguments. In a moment we will be a little more specific about what sorts of readings we include, but first we want to mention our chief assumptions about the aims of a course that might use *Critical Thinking, Reading, and Writing: A Brief Guide to Argument*.

Probably most students and instructors would agree that, *as critical readers*, students should be able to

- summarize accurately an argument they have read;
- locate the thesis of an argument;
- locate the assumptions, stated and unstated;
- analyze and evaluate the strength of the evidence and the soundness of the reasoning offered in support of the thesis;
- analyze, evaluate, and account for discrepancies among various readings on a topic (for example, explain why certain facts are used or not used, why two sources might interpret the same facts differently).

Probably, too, students and instructors would agree that, *as thoughtful writers*, students should be able to

- imagine an audience, and write effectively for it (by such means as using the appropriate tone and providing the appropriate amount of detail);
- present information in an orderly and coherent way;
- be aware of own assumptions;
- incorporate sources into their own writing, not simply by quoting extensively or by paraphrasing, but also by having digested materials so that they can present it in their own words;
- properly document all borrowings—not merely quotations and paraphrases but also borrowed ideas;
- do all these things in the course of developing a thoughtful argument of their own.

Parts One and Two   Part One (Chapters 1–3) and Part Two (Chapters 4–6) taken together offer a short course in methods of thinking about arguments and in methods of writing arguments. By "thinking" we mean serious analytic thought, including analysis of one's own assumptions (Chapter 1); by "writing" we mean the use of effective, respectable techniques, not gimmicks such as the notorious note a politician scribbled in the margin of the text of his speech: "Argument weak; shout here." For a delightfully wry account of the use of gimmicks, we recommend that you consult "The Art of Controversy," in *The Will to Live,* by the nineteenth-century German philosopher Arthur Schopenhauer. Schopenhauer reminds his reader that a Greek or Latin quotation (however irrelevant) can be impressive to the uninformed, and that one can knock down almost any argument by loftily saying, "That's all very well in theory, but it won't do in practice."

We offer lots of advice about setting forth an argument, but we do not offer instruction in one-upmanship. Rather, we discuss responsible ways of arguing persuasively. We know, however, that before one can write a persuasive argument one must clarify one's own ideas—and that includes arguing with oneself—to find out what one really thinks about a problem. Therefore we devote Chapter 1 to critical thinking, Chapters 2 and 3 to critical reading, and Chapters 4, 5, and 6 to critical writing. These chapters are not all lecturing. Parts One and Two together contain thirty-five readings (three are by students) for analysis and discussion. Moreover, each of the three chapters in Part One contains a casebook, a group of closely related readings. For instance, the casebook in Chapter 1 consists of a newspaper editorial on divorce, followed by five letters that were written in response to the editorial.

All of the essays in the book are accompanied by questions. This is not surprising, given the emphasis we place on asking oneself questions to get ideas for writing. Among the chief questions that writers should ask, we suggest, are such matters as "What is *X*?" and "What is the value of *X*?" (pp. 3–9). By asking such questions—for instance (to look only at these two types of questions), "Is the fetus a person?" or "Is Arthur Miller a better playwright than Tennessee Williams?"—a writer probably will find ideas coming, at least after a few moments of head-scratching. The device of developing an argument by identifying issues is, of course, nothing new; indeed, it goes back to an ancient method of argument used by classical rhetoricians, who proceeded by identifying a *stasis* (an issue) and then asked questions about it: Did *X* do such-and-such? If so, was the action bad? If bad, how bad? (Finding an issue or *stasis*—a position where one stands—by asking questions is discussed in Chapter 5.)

In keeping with our emphasis on writing as well as reading, we raise issues not only of what can roughly be called the "content" of the essays but also of what can (equally roughly) be called the "style"—that is, the ways in which the arguments are set forth. Content and style, of course, cannot finally be kept apart. As Cardinal Newman said, "Thought and meaning are inseparable from each other.... *Style is thinking out into language.*" In our questions we sometimes ask the student to evaluate the effectiveness of the opening paragraph, or to explain a shift in tone from one paragraph to the next, or to characterize the persona of the author as revealed in the whole essay. In short, the book is not designed as an introduction to some powerful ideas (though in fact it is that, too); it is designed as an aid to writing thoughtful, effective arguments on important political, social, scientific, ethical, and religious issues.

The essays reprinted in this book also illustrate different styles of argument that arise, at least in part, from the different disciplinary backgrounds of the various authors. Essays by journalists, lawyers, judges, social scientists, policy analysts, philosophers, critics, activists, and other writers — including undergraduates — will be found in these pages. The authors develop and present their views in arguments that have distinctive features reflecting their special training and concerns. The differences in argumentative styles found in these essays foreshadow the differences students will encounter in the readings assigned in many of their other courses. (Part Three, which offers a philosopher's view, a logician's view, a psychologist's view, a lawyer's view, and a literary critic's view, also reveals differences in argumentative styles.)

Parts One and Two, then, are a preliminary (but we hope substantial) discussion of such topics as *identifying assumptions, getting ideas by means of invention strategies, using sources, evaluating kinds of evidence,* and *organizing material,* as well as an introduction to some ways of thinking.

Part Three "Further Views on Argument" consists of Chapters 7–11. The first of these, Chapter 7, "A Philosopher's View: The Toulmin Model," is a summary of the philosopher Stephen Toulmin's method for analyzing arguments. This summary will assist those who wish to apply Toulmin's methods to the readings in our book. The next chapter, "A Logician's View," offering a more rigorous analysis of deduction, induction, and fallacies than is usually found in composition courses, reexamines from a logician's point of view material already treated briefly in Chapter 3. Chapter 9, with an essay by psychotherapist Carl R. Rogers, complements the discussion of audience, organization, and tone in Chapter 5. Chapter 10, "A Lawyer's View: Steps toward Civic Literacy," introduces students to some basic legal concepts, such as the distinction between civil and criminal cases, and then gives majority and minority decisions in three cases: searching students for drugs, burning the flag, protesting the draft. We accompany these decisions with questions that invite the student to participate in these exercises in democracy. The last chapter in Part Three, "A Literary Critic's View: Arguing about Literature," should help students to see what sorts of things literary critics argue about and *how* they argue. Students can apply what they learn not only to the literary readings that appear in the chapter (poems by Robert Frost and

Andrew Marvell, stories by Kate Chopin and Jean Rhys, and a casebook concerning the national anthem) but also to other literature they may encounter in the course.

WHAT'S NEW TO THE THIRD EDITION

In the first edition of this book we quoted Edmund Burke and John Stuart Mill. Burke said, "He that wrestles with us strengthens our nerves, and sharpens our skill. Our antagonist is our helper." Mill said, "He who knows only his own side of the cause knows little." We can regret the aggressive language in Burke and the sexist language in Burke and Mill, but these two quotations continue to reflect the view of argument that underlies this text. When one writes an argument, one is not setting out to trounce an opponent, and that is partly why such terms as *marshaling evidence, attacking an opponent,* and *defending a thesis* are misleading. True, in television talk shows we see people who have made up their minds and who are concerned only with pushing their own view and brushing aside all other views. But in writing an essay one is engaging in a serious effort to know what one's own ideas are and, having found them, to contribute to a multisided conversation. We learn by listening to others and also by listening to ourselves; we draft a response to something we have read, and in the very act of drafting we may find—if we think critically about the words we are putting down on paper—we are changing (perhaps slightly, perhaps radically) our own position. Even if we do not drastically change our view, the reader at the very least comes to understand why we hold the view we do.

In preparing the third edition we were greatly aided by suggestions from instructors who were using the second edition. In line with their recommendations, in Part One, "Critical Thinking and Reading," we have added checklists to each of the three chapters (checklists for critical thinking, for examining assumptions, for getting started, for examining statistical evidence, and for analyzing an argument), and we have also added casebooks (on divorce, free speech, and bilingual education) to each chapter.

We have also added checklists to Part Two, "Critical Writing," and in the chapter on the research paper we now include advice on using electronic sources. (A new appendix provides a list of World Wide Web sources for the current issues in this book.) We have somewhat heightened the reader's awareness of classical rhetoric by including discussion of topics such as *ethos, logos, pathos, stasis,* and, for that matter, *topos.*

In Part Three, we have increased the number of literary selections in "A Literary Critic's View," and in an effort to increase civic literacy, we have added "A Lawyer's View," with three legal cases (majority and minority opinions). We think that our prefatory material in "A Lawyer's View" concerning such matters as facts and the law and the balancing of interests will help students think not only about the legal cases included in Chapter 10 and in other chapters but also about cases they read in the daily newspaper.

We close with a "Casebook on the State and the Individual," with readings from Sophocles, Plato, and Martin Luther King, Jr.

Note: For instructors who require a text with a large number of essays, a longer edition of this book, *Current Issues and Enduring Questions,* Fifth Edition, is also available. The longer version contains Parts One, Two, and Three (Chapters 1–11) of the present book as well as its own anthology of nearly eighty additional readings.

ACKNOWLEDGMENTS

Finally, it is our pleasant duty to thank those who have strengthened the book by their advice: Lawrence Anderson, Louisiana State University–Shreveport; Evelyn D. Asch, DePaul University; Larry Beason, Eastern Washington University; Donavin Bennes, University of North Dakota; Earnest Cox, Texas Christian University; Ian Crawford, Berry College; Tracy A. Crouch, Stephen F. Austin State University; Ann Ellsworth, University of Washington; Elaine Elmo, Stanley Community College; Larry D. Engel, Rochester Community and Technical College; James M. Ewing, Fresno City College; Jill Fieldkamp, Wartburg College; Karl Fornes, University of Minnesota–Morris; Paula F. Furr, United States Military Academy; Lillis Gilmartin, Sierra Heights College; Eric H. Hobson, St. Louis College of Pharmacy; William T. Hope, Jefferson Technical College; Jane Janssen, Bellevue Community College; K. Kaleta, Rowan College; Cathy Kaye, University of Wisconsin–Milwaukee; Janice Kollity, Riverside Community College; Mary R. Lamb, Texas Christian University; Mary Macaluso, New Mexico Highlands University; Barbara J. McGuire, University of Wisconsin; Jonathan Murrow, West Virginia University; Jeanne Purdy, University of Minnesota–Morris; Lindy J. Rawling, Moorpark College; Ed Reben, Dixie College; Sally Scholz, Purdue University; Christine M. Smith, Butler University; John E. Stowe, Fordham University; Charles Tita, Shaw University; Allen Wall, Chabot College; Eric A. Weil, Shaw University.

We would like especially to thank Janet E. Gardner of the University of Massachusetts, Dartmouth, who revised the research chapter to encompass the latest advice and information on using electronic sources and who prepared the new appendix of Web sites. A timely conversation with Phyllis West of El Camino Community College prompted us to include Sophocles' classic play *Antigone* in the book; our thanks to her as well.

We are also indebted to the people at Bedford/St. Martin's, especially Charles H. Christensen, Joan E. Feinberg, Steve Scipione, Elizabeth M. Schaaf, Karen Baart, Stasia Zomkowski, and Maura Shea, who offered many valuable (and invaluable) suggestions. Intelligent, informed, firm yet courteous, they really know how to think, and how to argue.

Contents

Part Four
A CASEBOOK ON THE STATE
AND THE INDIVIDUAL 383

Part One

CRITICAL THINKING AND READING

1

Critical Thinking

The comedian Jack Benny cultivated the stage personality of a penny-pincher. In one of his skits a stickup man thrusts a gun into Benny's ribs and says, "Your money or your life." Utter silence. The robber, getting no response, and completely baffled, repeats, "Your money or your life." Short pause, followed by Benny's exasperated reply: "I'm *thinking*, I'm *thinking*!"

Without making too much of this gag, we want to point out that Benny is using the word *thinking* in the sense that we use it in *critical thinking*. *Thinking*, by itself, can mean almost any sort of mental activity, from idle daydreaming ("During the chemistry lecture I kept thinking about how I'd like to go camping") to careful analysis ("I'm thinking about whether I can afford more than one week—say two weeks—of camping in the Rockies," or even "I'm thinking about *why* Benny's comment strikes me as funny," or, "I'm thinking about why you find Benny's comment funny and I don't").

In short, when we add the adjective *critical* to the noun *thinking*, we pretty much eliminate reveries, just as we also eliminate snap judgments. We are talking about searching for hidden assumptions, noticing various facets, unraveling different strands, and evaluating what is most significant. (The word *critical* comes from a Greek word, *krinein*, meaning "to separate," "to choose"; it implies conscious, deliberate inquiry.)

THINKING ABOUT DRIVER'S LICENSES AND SCHOOL ATTENDANCE: IMAGINATION, ANALYSIS, EVALUATION

By way of illustration let's think critically about a law passed in West Virginia in 1989. The law provides that although students may drop out of school at the age of sixteen, no dropout younger than eighteen can hold a driver's license.

But what ought we to think of such a law? Is it fair? What is its purpose? Is it likely to accomplish its purpose? Might it unintentionally do some harm, and, if so, can we weigh the potential harm against the potential good? Suppose you had been a member of the West Virginia state legislature in 1989: How would you have voted?

In thinking critically about a topic, we try to see it from all sides before we come to our conclusion. We conduct an argument with ourselves, advancing and then questioning opinions. What can be said *for* the proposition, and what can be said *against* it? Our first reaction may be quite uncritical, quite unthinking: "What a good idea!" or "That's outrageous!" But critical thinking requires us to reflect further, trying to support our position *and also* trying to see the other side. One can almost say that the heart of critical thinking is a *willingness to face objections to one's own beliefs,* a willingness to adopt a skeptical attitude not only toward authority and toward views opposed to our own, but also toward common sense, that is, toward the views that seem obviously right to us. If we assume we have a monopoly on the truth and we dismiss as bigots those who oppose us, or if we say our opponents are acting merely out of self-interest, and we do not in fact analyze their views, we are being critical but we are not engaged in critical thinking.

Critical thinking requires us to use our *imagination,* seeing things from perspectives other than our own and envisioning the likely consequences of our position. (This sort of imaginative thinking—grasping a perspective other than our own, and considering the possible consequences of positions—is, as we have said, very different from daydreaming, an activity of unchecked fantasy.)

Thinking critically involves, along with imagination (so that we can see our own beliefs from another point of view), a twofold activity:

> **analysis,** separating the parts of the problem, trying to see how things fit together; and
>
> **evaluation,** judging the merit of our assumptions and the weight of the evidence in their favor.

If we engage in imaginative, analytic, and evaluative thought, we will have second and third ideas; almost to our surprise we may find ourselves adopting a position that we initially couldn't imagine we would hold. As we think about the West Virginia law, we might find ourselves coming up with a fairly wide variety of ideas, each triggered by the preceding idea but not necessarily carrying it a step further. For instance, we may think X, and then immediately think, "No, that's not quite right. In fact, come to think of it, the opposite of X is probably true." We haven't carried X further, but we have progressed in our thinking.

WRITING AS A WAY OF THINKING

"To learn to write," Robert Frost said, "is to learn to have ideas." But how do we get ideas? One way, practiced by the ancient Greeks and Romans and still regarded as among the best ways, is to consider what the ancients called **topics,** from the Greek word *topos,* meaning "place," as in our word *topography* (a description or representation of a place). For the ancients, certain topics, put into the form of questions, were in effect places where one went to find ideas. Among the classical *topics* were

- definition (What is it?);
- comparison (What is it like or unlike?);
- relationship (What caused it, and what will it cause?);
- testimony (What is said about it, for instance by experts?).

All of these topics or idea-generating places will be treated in detail in later chapters, but here we can touch briefly on a few of them.

If we are talking about the West Virginia law, it's true that we won't get ideas by asking questions concerning definition, but we may generate ideas by asking ourselves if this law is like any other (and, if so, how well did the corresponding law work), and by asking what caused this law, and what it may in turn cause. Similarly, if we go to the topic of testimony, we may want to find out what some students, teachers, parents, police officers, and lawmakers have to say.

If you think you are at a loss for ideas when confronted with an issue (and when confronted with an assignment to write about it), you probably will find ideas coming to you if you turn to the relevant classical topics and begin jotting down your responses. (In classical terminology, you are engaged in the process of **invention** (from the Latin *invenīre,* "to come upon," "to find.") Seeing your ideas on paper—even in the briefest form—will help bring other ideas to mind, and will also help you to evaluate them. For instance, after jotting down ideas as they come and responses to them,

1. you might go on to organize them into two lists, pro and con;
2. next, you might delete ideas that, when you come to think about them, strike you as simply wrong or irrelevant; and
3. then you might develop those ideas that strike you as pretty good.

You probably won't know where you stand until you have gone through some such process. It would be nice if we could make a quick decision and then immediately justify it with three excellent reasons, and could give three further reasons showing why the opposing view is inadequate. In fact, however, we almost never can come to a reasoned decision without a good deal of preliminary thinking.

Consider again the West Virginia law. Here is a kind of inner dialogue that you might engage in as you think critically about it.

The purpose is to give students an incentive to stay in school by making them pay a price if they choose to drop out.

Adolescents will get the message that education really is important.

But, come to think of it, *will* they? Maybe they will see this as just another example of adults bullying young people.

According to a newspaper article, the dropout rate in West Virginia decreased by 30 percent in the year after the bill was passed.

Well, that sounds good, but is there any reason to think that kids who are pressured into staying really learn anything? The *assumption* behind the bill is that if would-be dropouts stay in school, they—and society—will gain. But is the assumption sound? Maybe such students will become resentful, will not learn anything, and may even be so disruptive that they will interfere with the learning of other students.

Notice how part of the job is *analytic,* recognizing the elements or complexities of the whole, and part is *evaluative,* judging the adequacy of all of these ideas, one by one. Both tasks require *imagination.*

So far we have jotted down a few thoughts, and then immediately given some second thoughts contrary to the first. Of course, the counterthoughts might not immediately come to mind. For instance, they might not occur until we reread the jottings, or try to explain the law to a friend, or until we sit down and begin drafting an essay aimed at supporting or undermining the law. Most likely, in fact, some good ideas won't occur until a second or third or fourth draft.

Here are some further thoughts on the West Virginia law. We list them more or less as they arose and as we typed them into a word processor—not sorted out neatly into two groups, pro and con, nor evaluated as you would want to do in further critical thinking of your own. And of course a later step would be to organize the material into some useful pattern. As you read, you might jot down your own responses in the margin.

> Education is <u>not</u> optional, something left for the indi-
>   vidual to take or not to take--like going to a
>   concert, or jogging, or getting annual health
>   checkups, or getting eight hours of sleep each
>   night. Society has determined that it is <u>for the</u>
>   <u>public good</u> that citizens have a substantial educa-
>   tion, so we require education up to a certain age.

> Come to think about it, maybe the criterion of age
>   doesn't make much sense. If we want an educated
>   citizenry, it would make more sense to require
>   people to attend school until they demonstrated
>   competence in certain matters, rather than until
>   they reached a certain age. Exceptions of course
>   would be made for mentally retarded persons, and
>   perhaps for certain other groups.

What is needed is not legal pressure to keep teenagers
    in school, but schools that hold the interest of
    teenagers.

A sixteen-year-old usually is not mature enough to make
    a decision of this importance.

Still, a sixteen-year-old who finds school unsatisfying
    and who therefore drops out may become a perfectly
    useful citizen.

Denying a sixteen-year-old a driver's license may work
    in West Virginia, but it would scarcely work in a
    state with great urban areas, where most high
    school students rely on public transportation.

We earn a driver's license by demonstrating certain
    skills. The state has no right to take away such a
    license unless we have demonstrated that we are
    unsafe drivers.

To prevent a person of sixteen from having a driver's
    license prevents that person from holding certain
    kinds of jobs, and that's unfair.

A law of this sort deceives adults into thinking that
    they have really done something constructive for
    teenage education, but it may work against improv-
    ing the schools. If we are really serious about
    educating youngsters, we have to examine the cur-
    riculum and the quality of our teachers.

Doubtless there is much that we haven't said, on both sides, but we hope
you will agree that the issue deserves thought. (A number of state legislatures are indeed thinking about bills resembling the West Virginia law.)
And if you were a member of the legislature of West Virginia in 1989
you would have *had* to think about the issue.

One other point about this issue: *Today,* if you had to think about the
matter, you might also want to know whether the West Virginia legislation of 1989 is considered a success, and on what basis. That is, you
would want to get answers to such questions as the following:

1. What sort of evidence tends to support the law or tends to sug-
    gest that the law is a poor idea?
2. Did the reduction in the dropout rate continue, or did the reduc-
    tion occur only in the first year following the passage of the law?
3. If indeed students did not drop out, was their presence in school a
    good thing, both for them and for their classmates?

4. Have some people emerged as authorities on this topic? What makes them authorities, and what do they have to say?
5. Has the constitutionality of the bill been tested? With what results?

Some of these questions require you to do **research** on the topic. The questions raise issues of fact, and some relevant evidence probably is available. If you are to arrive at a conclusion in which you can have confidence, you will have to do some research to find out what the facts are.

Even without doing any research, however, you might want to look over the ideas, pro and con, perhaps adding some totally new thoughts, or perhaps modifying or even rejecting (for reasons that you can specify) some of those already given. If you do think a bit further about this issue, and we hope that you will, notice an interesting point about *your own* thinking: It probably is not *linear* (moving in a straight line from A to B to C) but *recursive,* moving from A to C, back to B, or starting over at C and then back to A and B. By zigging and zagging almost despite yourself, you'll get to a conclusion that may finally seem correct. In retrospect it seems obvious; *now* you can chart a nice line from A to B to C—but that was not at all evident to you at the start.

A CHECKLIST FOR CRITICAL THINKING

Attitudes

✓ Does my thinking show imaginative open-mindedness and intellectual curiosity?

  ✓ Am I willing to examine my assumptions?

  ✓ Am I willing to entertain new ideas—both those that I encounter while reading and those that come to mind while writing?

✓ Am I willing to exert myself, for instance to do research in order to acquire information and to evaluate evidence?

Skills

✓ Can I summarize an argument accurately?

✓ Can I evaluate assumptions, evidence, and inferences?

✓ Can I present my ideas effectively—for instance by organizing and by writing in a manner appropriate to my imagined audience?

EXAMINING ASSUMPTIONS

In Chapter 3 we will discuss **assumptions** (normally, unexamined beliefs) in some detail, but here we want to emphasize the importance of *examining* assumptions, both those that you encounter when you read and those that underlie your own essays.

Let's think a bit further about the West Virginia driver's license law. What assumptions did the legislature make in enacting this statute? We earlier mentioned one such assumption: If the law helped to keep teenagers from dropping out of school, then that was a good thing for them and for society in general. Perhaps the legislature made this assumption *explicit* and its advocates defended it on this ground. Perhaps not; maybe the legislature just took this point for granted, leaving this assumption *implicit* (or *tacit*) and unargued, believing that everyone *shared* the assumption. But of course everyone didn't share it, in particular many teenagers who wanted to drop out of school at sixteen and get their driver's license immediately.

Consider, for instance, a newspaper article concerning antisocial activities on campus, ranging from boisterous behavior (including, say, the shouting of racial epithets) to vandalism, theft, and physical violence (perhaps stimulated by excessive drinking), including rape. Until thirty or so years ago, many colleges assumed that they stood *in loco parentis*, "in the place of a parent." What did this mean? Parents would be unlikely to turn over to the police a youngster who struck a sibling or who dipped into a family cookie jar that contained loose change but rather would handle the matter within the family; in similar manner, college administrators would seek to educate offenders, perhaps by reprimands, perhaps by probation or suspension, or in the most severe cases, by expulsion. But the assumption that colleges ought to engage in this sort of quasi-judicial activity when students are alleged to break the law on campus can be questioned. Should colleges be in the business of judging crimes? Or should they let the courts take care of the offenders?

On May 5 and May 6, 1996, the *New York Times* ran a two-part story on the topic of campus discipline. Newspaper stories of this sort are supposed to report the facts, but inevitably they stimulate responses; people want to offer their views on what they have been reading. They may want to argue that the newspaper report was inaccurate, or accurate so far as it went but missed the big issue, or—and here is our point—that it is not enough to report such things, "Something must be done!" One reader of the *Times* story was John Silber, who at that time was president of Boston University. He wrote the following Op-Ed piece (an essay of opinion, printed opposite the editorial page).

As your read Silber's piece, note his assumptions. Does he make any assumptions that you do not share? If so, what are they?

John Silber

Students Should Not Be above the Law

In medieval Europe, there were two parallel court systems: the church's and the king's. The big difference between them was that the church courts did not resort to capital punishment.

In an age when all felonies were capital crimes, the church court was, from the defendants' point of view, considerably more attractive.

Although in theory these courts were limited to clergymen, in practice one proved clerical status by being able to read. And this skill was indulgently tested. One had to read a verse of one's own choosing from the Bible. Hence, the foresighted felon memorized his verse. It assured him of what was known as "benefit of clergy."

This system now seems quaint. But today colleges and universities increasingly tend to circumvent the courts and bury serious criminal cases in their own judicial systems. For instance, a young man at Miami University in Oxford, Ohio, is being allowed to graduate this year even though he was put on "student conduct probation" after he was accused of sexually assaulting an eighteen-year-old freshman who was sleeping.

Colleges have a right to establish judicial codes to assure civility in   5 the classroom, on the campus, and in residences. But the administration of these codes should not give criminals sanctuary from the law.

Yet in many cases administrators successfully press students not to bring criminal behavior to the attention of the police and instead use campus disciplinary proceedings to judge charges of rape, arson, and assault.

No campus court can impose a fine or imprison anyone for a single day. The most serious sanction is expulsion. The penalty for criminal assault is often not much worse than being tossed out of a club.

College judicial systems were originally intended to deal with infractions that were neither felonies nor misdemeanors, perhaps not even torts. And most disciplinary proceedings don't have the basics required for a fair trial: a professional and independent judiciary, enforceable rules of procedure, effective and fairly applied sanctions.

But this is not the most serious problem. Once again, students are receiving special treatment. This treatment was the great scandal of the Vietnam War: The ability to gain entry to and finance college provided a "benefit of clergy" to middle-class young adults who avoided the draft.

Many administrators recoil from the idea that they should oper-   10 ate a collegiate criminal justice system. One can understand why. Outside of law school faculties, few academics have an interest in prosecution.

There is, of course, a simple way for administrators to avoid this entanglement. They can refer all criminal cases to the real criminal justice system. This is their obligation, not merely as administrators but as citizens. (Indeed, there is a name for a citizen who becomes aware of a crime and does not report it: an accessory after the fact.)

Students, predictably, don't like this idea. But in my twenty-five years as a college president, I have heard again and again that students wish to be treated as adults. But I have also heard their repeated demands that they be exempted from the laws of Boston, of Massachusetts, and of the United States.

These two demands are contradictory. Legally, college students are adults. There is, of course, a difference between legal adulthood and substantive adulthood. Some people achieve substantive adulthood at twelve; others never do. But except for the anomaly of the drinking age, everyone can claim legal adulthood at eighteen. And that includes the obligation to be held accountable for criminal behavior—not in juvenile courts or in the even more lenient courts of the academy but in the adult courts.

When colleges and universities usurp the role of the courts, they deny justice to victims. But they also do a terrible wrong to perpetrators, for they deny them entrance into the adult world of responsible action. And in this they fail utterly as educators.

Silber opens his essay by informing the reader about the medieval system of criminal justice, which exempted clerics from the risk of punishments handed out by the criminal courts. By the fourth paragraph we can see the point of this opening; it was to draw a parallel between the assumed unfairness of that medieval practice and (what Silber regards as) the unfair student disciplinary procedures in use by our colleges and universities. Thus, Silber in effect opens his essay on the basis of this crucial assumption:

> It was unfair to give advantages in medieval times to clerics when accused of crimes, and it is no less unfair to give advantages to college students today when they are accused of crimes.

Silber does not argue for this proposition; he does not even assert it explicitly. But he presupposes it as the launching pad for his criticism of today's college disciplinary practices.

In a similar manner, Silber closes his essay with another important assumption:

> College students who are legally adults (eighteen or over) ought to be given the same treatment when accused of crimes as other adults are.

Obviously, college faculty and administrators charged with the responsibility to cope with student misbehavior on campus do not accept this assumption; if they did, the problem that agitates Silber would never have arisen in the first place.

In other places he makes assumptions of no great importance, for instance this one in paragraph 10:

Law school faculties have an interest in prosecution.

Whether or not this proposition is true makes little difference to Silber's overall argument; its role is the minor one of reinforcing Silber's claim (no doubt true) that college and university faculty and administrators are typically very uncomfortable when it comes to disciplinary sanctions for students guilty of serious wrongdoing.

In paragraph 8, Silber draws a contrast between the rough-and-ready disciplinary practices on campus and the strict by-the-rules procedures of the criminal courts. This position might stimulate the reader to wonder whether Silber assumes the following:

College disciplinary practices would be much better if they incorporated the basic procedures that the criminal law requires for a fair trial.

However, by the time the reader reaches paragraph 11 (if not before) it becomes clear that Silber has no interest in this alternative; instead, this is what he assumes:

There are only two alternatives: Either college authorities continue down the current unfair path, or they wash their hands of any attempt to deal with students accused of criminal behavior by turning them over to the mercies of the criminal courts.

The third alternative, of tightening up college disciplinary procedures, is never considered.

In other cases it is not entirely clear just what Silber assumes. He obviously assumes the following:

College disciplinary practices usurp the role of the courts in the criminal justice system.

But does he also assume that this usurpation occurs only occasionally, or does he think that it happens quite often? Silber gives no statistical data to qualify his assumption, and so his readers are left uncertain whether they are worrying about a major problem affecting hundreds of college students every year, or whether Silber is riled up over events of no great frequency.

Do you agree with Silber's assertions

- that it is wrong (para. 6) for college officials in some circumstances to "press students not to bring criminal behavior to the attention of the police and instead use campus disciplinary proceedings to judge charges of rape, arson, and assault"?

- that administrators have an "obligation" (para. 11) to "refer all criminal cases to the real criminal justice system," and that their failure to do so makes them "an accessory after the fact"?

- that (para. 14) "When colleges and universities usurp the role of the courts, . . . they also do a terrible wrong to perpetrators, for they deny them entrance into the adult world of responsible action"?

You may agree or disagree, in whole or in part, with Silber's argument, but it is important to realize that he makes certain assumptions and to think about their implications. For instance, if you agree that administrators who fail to report actions that may later prove to be criminal behavior are "accessories after the fact" (persons who screen or assist felons), are you willing to concede that campus rape crisis centers and other counseling activities may find it impossible to function?

Consider, too, if assumptions allegedly founded on facts are indeed based on facts. Thus, Silber asserts in paragraph 6 that "in many cases administrators successfully press students not to bring criminal behavior to the attention of the police." "Many cases" indicates that he assumes the practice is widespread. If this assumption were questioned, and Silber offered as evidence solely his long experience as a college administrator, would you think that you had to accept the assumption? On the other hand, could you just brush off his assumption as merely the view of one person?

An Op-Ed piece such as Silber's is likely to set readers thinking — not merely thinking about direct replies or refutations but about related issues. For instance, it might stimulate a reader to respond with a letter to the editor, suggesting that college faculty and administrators have a duty to assist young people in understanding what it means to act responsibly, and this duty is not effectively fulfilled by handing them over to the police in borderline cases. Another letter-writer might argue that alcohol is the chief cause of most fraternity-related violence and crime, and colleges need to do more to educate students about drinking. Still another might argue that the real problem is that the *accused* may not get justice because college judicial boards are not restricted to the rules of evidence used by lawyers and judges in court.

One letter-writer was moved by Silber's essay to write about an aspect of the issue that she thought was important and that he had neglected. We reprint this letter here.

Judith H. Christie
What about the Faculty?

To the Editor:

Conspicuously absent from John Silber's argument that colleges not "usurp the role of courts" in dealing with student criminal behavior (Op-Ed, May 9) is any criticism of the manner in which college administrators routinely deal with student complaints of faculty misconduct.

With few exceptions, it has long been the practice of colleges to ignore female students' charges of sexual harassment by male faculty members or to deal with such accusations behind closed doors.

In the rare instances where faculty members are dismissed for sexual harassment, their records do not reflect the reason; that these teachers are free to seek positions at other institutions keeps academia's "dirty little secret" secret.

Faculty members, like students, should be held accountable for their behavior; they, too, are adults and have long enjoyed the "benefit of clergy" exemption Mr. Silber rightly deplores.

- Do you agree that Silber does not raise the point Christie makes?
- Do you think that Christie makes a good point?
- If you do agree that he does not raise her point and that her point is a good one, do you think the omission is a weakness in Silber's essay? Why, or why not?

A CHECKLIST FOR EXAMINING ASSUMPTIONS

✓ What assumptions does the writer's argument presuppose?

✓ Are these assumptions explicit or implicit?

✓ Are these assumptions important to the author's argument, or only incidental?

✓ Does the author give any evidence of being aware of the hidden assumptions in her or his argument?

✓ Would a critic be likely to share these assumptions, or are they exactly what a critic would challenge?

✓ What sort of evidence would be relevant to supporting or rejecting these assumptions?

✓ Are you willing to grant the author's assumptions?
   ✓ If not, why not?

Remember, also, to ask these questions (except the last two) when you are reading your own drafts. And remember to ask yourself why some people may *not* grant *your* assumptions.

A CASEBOOK ON EXAMINING ASSUMPTIONS: Should Divorce Be More Difficult?

Now let's turn to a second issue that is very much in the newspapers because it is very much a part of daily life: divorce. The United States has the world's highest divorce rate, and statisticians estimate that about half of today's marriages will end in divorce. It was not always so. Divorce was fairly unusual in the days when individuals seeking divorce were required to demonstrate the spouse's legally defined intolerable behavior, usually adultery, cruelty, or desertion. But in the 1960s "no-fault" divorce became popular, and today no state requires as a condition of granting a divorce that one party be guilty of a serious fault. It is enough for either party to allege "incompatibility."

No-fault divorce was hailed, perhaps especially by women, as a step forward, but recently it has come under attack. Some feminists argue that high-income husbands can now easily walk away from marriage, impoverishing their wives; some conservatives argue that no-fault divorce is immoral. It has especially come under attack when the couple has a dependent child. For instance, in her book, *It Takes a Village*, Hillary Rodham Clinton says she feels "ambivalent [about divorce] when children are involved." Her worry here is that divorce has a bad effect on children, and one sometimes hears of statistical studies that compare the well-being of children in two-parent families with the well-being of children brought up by one divorced parent. (Incidentally, does this sound like a valid comparison? Or should the comparison be between children of divorced parents and children of parents who, though deeply hostile to each other, for one reason or another remain married?) Some twenty state legislatures are considering proposals to repeal no-fault divorce in cases involving children, and there is now much talk about ways of reducing the divorce rate. We provide a tiny sample of such talk. Before you read any of these writings, however, you may want to find out where you stand on the following issues:

- Should it be harder than it is to get a divorce? In particular, should one party have to demonstrate that the other party is seriously at fault (for example, desertion, physical abuse)? If no fault is alleged, should there be a waiting period, and, if so, how long?

- Should it be harder than it is for couples with dependent children to get a divorce?
- Should there be a two-category system, one for couples without children and one for couples with children?
- In divorces where there are children, is the solution not to tighten the divorce law but to tighten child support laws?
- Should people be required to take a marriage education course before they can get a marriage license?
- Should the Louisiana law of 1997, allowing couples to choose between a no-fault marriage and a "covenant marriage," be enacted by other states? In a covenant marriage, the two participants agree to try to resolve disputes through counseling and to seek divorce only after a mutually agreed-on two-year separation, except for specified circumstances such as adultery, abuse, and imprisonment for a felony.

We begin with an unsigned editorial in the *New York Times*, February 15, 1996, and we follow it with some of the responses printed in subsequent issues.

The *New York Times*
The Divorce Debate

Led by conservative Christian groups, a new movement is afoot to toughen state divorce laws. Its main target is the "no-fault" divorce statutes adopted by every state over the last twenty-five years to make divorces easier, quicker, and less freighted with destructive recrimination.

There are powerful reasons to be alarmed about the impact of family breakups on children, and about the high incidence of poverty in single-parent households. But rolling back the clock to make the legal process of divorce more expensive and acrimonious is not a useful answer.

Supporters of tougher divorce laws complain that the current rules encourage a casual attitude toward the dissolution of marriage. But few people who have lived through a no-fault divorce, especially those with children, would say they took the step lightly.

Even though divorces have jumped about 30 percent in the last twenty-five years, blaming the new laws for a long-term upward trend confuses cause and effect. No-fault divorce was a response to changes already taking place in the family system.

Under the no-fault approach, a divorce is granted even if only one ⁵
spouse wants it. By contrast, a bill just introduced in the Michigan Legislature would deny a divorce when one spouse opposes it unless the
plaintiff could show that a spouse had been physically or mentally abusive, had a problem with alcohol or drugs, had committed adultery, had
deserted the home, or had been sentenced to prison.

The idea is to try to force couples to stay together. But a more likely
consequence would be a return to the perjuries, fabrications, and other
devices required to obtain divorces before no-fault. That would mean yet
more pain for children, as parents slug it out in a prolonged legal blame-
game, wasting scarce family resources in the process.

Another consequence would be to discourage couples from getting
married in the first place—thereby aggravating the already staggering
problem of unwed motherhood and the resulting social and financial
vulnerability of women and children.

The nation should be concentrating on ways to reduce the economic
stresses that experts say contribute both to the high divorce rate and to
the rising number of children born to unmarried couples. Absent fathers
should be required to live up to their child support obligations. But making it more difficult for people to escape a broken marriage seems cruel
and counterproductive.

The first response printed here, an Op-Ed piece by Maggie Gallagher,
does not directly address itself point by point to the preceding editorial,
but clearly it represents an opposing view. Gallagher, a scholar at the Institute for American Values, is the author of *The Abolition of Marriage:
How We Destroy Lasting Love* (1996).

Maggie Gallagher

Why Make Divorce Easy?

For all practical purposes, the debate is over. Almost all Americans
now agree that divorce is harmful to children. Now the question becomes: What, if anything, can we do about the fact that at least half of
our marriages fail?

Get rid of no-fault divorce, say some state legislators in Michigan,
one of several states with an active campaign to reform divorce laws.

Call it a delayed backlash. Unlike some European countries, which impose five-to-seven-year waits for contested no-fault divorces, Americans
in the late '60s and '70s opted for speedy spouse disposal. Almost every
state adopted some version of no-fault divorce, either by eliminating the
need to find marital wrongdoing or by speeding up the divorce process.

In short, no-fault divorce (or more accurately "unilateral divorce") allows one partner to dissolve a marriage at any time, for any reason, or for no reason at all.

No-fault was supposed to remake divorce into a kinder, gentler insti- 5 tution. It hasn't worked out that way. Under no-fault, divorces today are no less angry. In her book *Second Chances*, Judith Wallerstein found that about half of all the couples she studied were still locked in bitter conflict five years after divorcing.

Thanks to no-fault, divorces have also become more common. Between the late '60s and mid-'70s, the likelihood that a couple would divorce in the first five years of marriage jumped by one-third. A recent study in the *Journal of Marriage and the Family* suggests that no-fault pushed up the divorce rate anywhere from 15 to 25 percent.

Supporters of no-fault divorce argue that it strengthens marriage because couples can leave bad marriages and make better ones. But, as the University of Texas demographer Norval Glenn has pointed out, surveys suggest that the opposite has happened. After twenty-five years of no-fault, there are as many unhappy marriages as ever, and far fewer happy ones.

That no-fault divorce has led to a surge in the divorce rate should come as no surprise to anyone who has ever been married. Even the best marriages go through bleak times.

What would happen if courts treated business contracts as they now treat the marriage contract? What if our courts refused to enforce contracts and instead systematically favored the party that wished to withdraw, on the grounds that finding fault was messy, irrelevant, and acrimonious? Under such circumstances, the economy might collapse.

Imposing a five-to-seven-year waiting period for contested no-fault 10 divorces could raise the number of marriages that ultimately succeed while insuring that those who want a quick and easy divorce negotiate with their partners in order to get it.

Law is more than a system of punishments, as Mary Ann Glendon, a Harvard law professor, has pointed out. It is also one way we pass values from one generation to the next. Our divorce laws define what the marriage commitment is.

The purpose of making divorce more difficult is not to torment a couple into staying together but to give weight to the original contract, to put the law on the side of those who say: Wait, think, reconsider. Something of inestimable value—a commitment to love and care for another human being—is about to be lost. Is there really no way the marriage can be saved?

At this point you may want to take a sheet of paper, draw a vertical line down the middle, reread "The Divorce Debate," and in one column jot down a list of the chief points made by the editorial writer. Then reread Gallagher's essay and in the other column jot down her chief points; where she seems to be responding to a point in "The Divorce Debate," put your entry for Gallagher on the same line.

Do you find any shared assumptions? (By the way, one shared assumption of almost all people who publicly discuss the issue, whether they recommend easing or tightening the divorce laws, is that marriage is a good thing. Almost no one who writes on the subject suggests that marriage ought to be done away with.)

Here are four letters that were published in the *New York Times* in the days immediately following the editorial and the Op-Ed piece.

Letters from Patrick G. D. Riley, Lois M. Brenner, Allison Lassieur, and Rebecca Sawyer-Fay

To the Editor:

Re "The Divorce Debate" (editorial, Feb. 15): Nowhere do you mention the constitutional prohibition of laws "impairing the obligation of contracts," found in Article 1, Section 10.

Marriage, in the form recognized throughout the United States, can scarcely be construed as less than a contract binding both parties equally. The Supreme Court has touched on this matter more than once.

In *Dartmouth College v. Woodward,* famously argued by Daniel Webster, Chief Justice John Marshall observed: "When any state legislature shall pass an act annulling all marriage contracts, or allowing either party to annul it, without the consent of the other, it will be time enough to inquire whether such an act be constitutional."

According to the California Court of Appeals, that time arrived in 1888 when the Supreme Court opined that marriage is not a contract. Why not? Because, said the Court in *Maynard v. Hill,* marriage is "more than a contract." The logic of this has raised many an eyebrow.

The Supreme Court refused to revisit the question in 1992 when   5
James Sutherland, whose wife had won a divorce under California's no-fault divorce law, appealed the state court's ruling.

At present, marriage stands as the only contract that one party can nullify without evidence of breach by the other party. What makes this deplorable in the eyes of many is that marriage is sacred, as the state seems to grant when it recognizes the validity of religious marriage.

Patrick G. D. Riley
Wauwatosa, Wis., Feb. 15, 1996

To the Editor:

Re "The Divorce Debate" (editorial, Feb. 15): No-fault has indeed eliminated "perjuries" and "fabrications" in establishing grounds but has failed to dismantle the rest of the divorce meat grinder.

Divorce is more painful, protracted, and costly than ever. Until we make the process more humane, its laws will be vulnerable to "rolling back the clock."

Lois M. Brenner
New York, Feb. 16, 1996
The writer is a matrimonial lawyer.

To the Editor:

Re your Feb. 12 news article on the move to repeal no-fault divorce laws: The problem isn't that divorce is too easy. It's that marriage is.

Anyone, anywhere, for any reason can get married. In some states all that is needed is a justice of the peace and a few dollars. Some states don't even require blood tests.

What if getting married required a more stringent process? If couples had to work for the right to say "I do," more marriages might stay together.

Mandatory counseling that focused on goals would be a start. Required classes on money management and child care, checkups by a physician, counseling on sexual issues, and mandatory prenuptial agreements could help weed out those unions that may be happening for the wrong reasons.

Reinstituting fault divorce won't stop abuse or infidelity. What it will do is force people to drag each other through litigation to end something that should not have begun in the first place.

Allison Lassieur
Damascus, Pa., Feb. 15, 1996

To the Editor:

While not a scholar like Maggie Gallagher (Op-Ed, Feb. 20), I can tell you this: No five-year waiting period or law of any kind would have prevented my husband and me from leaving our former miserable marriages. What a harsher divorce law would have done is render our son illegitimate. When will our leaders stop legislating morality and let us live our lives as best we can?

Rebecca Sawyer-Fay
Hallowell, Me.

You may now want to go back to pages 15–16 and reread (and rethink) your responses to the questions that we asked concerning divorce laws. Has anything said in this six-way conversation caused you to change your mind, at least a little bit? If not, why not? (Religious principles? Experience as the child of divorced parents, or as a divorced person?)

Exercises

1. Think further about the West Virginia law, jotting down pros and cons, and then write a balanced dialogue between two imagined speakers who hold opposing views on the merits of the law. You'll doubtless have to revise your dialogue several times, and in revising your drafts you will find that further ideas come to you. Present *both* sides as strongly as possible. (You may want to give the two speakers distinct characters; for instance, one may be a student who has dropped out and the other a concerned teacher, or one a parent—who perhaps argues that he or she needs the youngster to work full-time driving a delivery truck—and one a legislator. But do not feel that the speakers must present the arguments they might be expected to hold. A student might argue *for* the law, and a teacher *against* it.)

2. With newspaper readers in mind, write (but don't mail) a letter of about 250 words (one double-spaced typed page) setting forth your response to at least one aspect of the arguments concerning divorce. You may want to provide additional evidence to support an argument, or provide counterevidence, or introduce an entirely new issue.

3. Take one of the following topics, and jot down all the pro and con arguments you can think of in, say, ten minutes. Then, at least an hour or two later, return to your jottings and see whether you can add to them. Finally, as in Exercise 1, write a balanced dialogue, presenting each idea as strongly as possible. (If none of these topics interests you, talk with your instructor about the possibility of choosing a topic of your own.) Suggested topics:

   a. Colleges should not award athletic scholarships.
   b. Bicyclists and motorcyclists should be required by law to wear helmets.
   c. High school teachers should have the right to search students for drugs on school grounds.
   d. Smoking should be prohibited in all parts of all college buildings.
   e. College administrators should take no punitive action against students who use racist language or language that offends any minority.
   f. Students should have the right to drop out of school at any age.
   g. In rape trials the names of the alleged victims should not be released to the public.

2

Critical Reading: Getting Started

Some books are to be tasted, others to be chewed, and some few to be chewed and digested.—FRANCIS BACON

ACTIVE READING

In the passage that we quote at the top of the page, Bacon makes at least two good points. One is that books are of varying worth; the second is that a taste of some books may be enough.

But even a book (or an essay) that you will chew and digest is one that you first may want to taste. How can you get a taste—that is, how can you get some sense of a piece of writing *before* you sit down to read it carefully?

Previewing

Even before you read the work you may have some ideas about it, perhaps because you already know something about the **author.** You know, for example, that a work by Martin Luther King, Jr., will probably deal with civil rights. You know, too, that it will be serious and eloquent. On the other hand, if you pick up an essay by Woody Allen you will probably expect it to be amusing. It may be serious—Allen has written earnestly about many topics, especially those concerned with the media—but it's your hunch that the essay will be at least somewhat entertaining and it probably will not be terribly difficult. In short, a reader who has some knowledge of the author probably has some idea of what the writing will be like, and so the reader reads it in a certain mood. Admittedly, most of the authors represented in this book are not widely known, but we give biographical notes that may provide you with some sense of what to expect.

The **place of publication** may also tell you something about the essay. For instance, *The National Review* (formerly edited by William F.

Buckley, Jr.) is a conservative journal. If you notice that an essay on affirmative action was published in *The National Review,* you are probably safe in tentatively assuming that the essay will not endorse affirmative action. On the other hand, *Ms.* is a liberal magazine for women, and an essay on affirmative action published in *Ms.* will probably be an endorsement.

The **title** of an essay, too, may give you an idea of what to expect. Of course a title may announce only the subject and not the author's thesis or point of view ("On Gun Control," "Should Drugs Be Legal?"), but fairly often it will indicate the thesis too, as in "Give Children the Vote" and "Gay Marriages: Make Them Legal." Knowing more or less what to expect, you can probably take in some of the major points even on a quick reading.

Skimming: Finding the Thesis

Although most of the material in this book is too closely argued to be fully understood by merely skimming, still, skimming can tell you a good deal. Read the first paragraph of an essay carefully, because it may announce the author's **thesis** (chief point, major claim), and it may give you some sense of how the argument for that thesis will be conducted. (What we call the thesis can also be called the main idea, or the point, or even the argument, but in this book we use *argument* to refer not only to the thesis statement but also to the entire development of the thesis in the essay.) Run your eye over the rest, looking for key expressions that indicate the author's conclusions, such as "It follows, then, that. . . . " Passages of this sort often occur as the first or last sentence in a paragraph. And of course pay attention to any headings within the text. Finally, pay special attention to the last paragraph because it probably will offer a summary and a brief restatement of the writer's thesis.

Having skimmed the work, you probably know the author's thesis, and you may detect the author's methods—for instance, whether the author supports the thesis chiefly by personal experience, or by statistics, or by ridicule of the opposition. You also have a clear idea of the length and some idea of the difficulty of the piece. You know, then, whether you can read it carefully now, before dinner, or whether you had better put off a careful reading until you have more time.

Reading with a Pencil: Underlining, Highlighting, Annotating

Once you have a general idea of the work—not only an idea of its topic and thesis but also a sense of the way in which the thesis is argued—you can then go back and start reading it carefully.

As you read, **underline** or **highlight** key passages and make **annotations** in the margins (but not in library books, please). Because you are reading actively, or interacting with the text, you will not simply let your eye rove across the page. You will underline or highlight what seem to be the chief points, so that later when you review the essay you can easily locate the main passages. But don't overdo a good thing. If you find yourself underlining or highlighting most of a page, you are probably not thinking carefully enough about what the key points are. Similarly, your marginal annotations should be brief and selective. Probably they will consist of hints or clues, things like "really?," "doesn't follow," "!!!," "???," "good," "compare with Jones," and "check this." In short, in a paragraph you might underline or highlight a key definition, and in the margin you might write "good" or, on the other hand, "?," if you think the definition is fuzzy or wrong. You are interacting with the text, and laying the groundwork for eventually writing your own essay on what you have read.

What you annotate will depend largely on your **purpose.** If you are reading an essay in order to see the ways in which the writer organizes an argument, you will annotate one sort of thing. If you are reading in order to challenge the thesis, you will annotate other things. Here is a passage from an essay entitled "On Racist Speech," with a student's rather skeptical, even aggressive annotations. But notice that at least one of the annotations — "Definition of 'fighting words'" — apparently was made chiefly in order to remind the reader of where an important term appears in the essay. The essay, printed in full on page 39, is by Charles R. Lawrence III, a professor of law at Stanford University. It originally appeared in *The Chronicle of Higher Education* (October 25, 1989), a publication read chiefly by college and university faculty members and administrators.

example of such a policy?

University officials who have formulated <u>policies</u> to respond to incidents of racial harassment have been characterized in the press as "thought police," but such policies generally do nothing more than impose (sanctions) against intentional face-to-face insults. When <u>racist</u> speech takes the form of <u>face-to-face insults</u>, catcalls, or other assaultive speech aimed at an individual or small group of persons, it falls directly within the <u>"fighting words"</u> exception to First Amendment protection. The Supreme Court has held that words which <u>"by their very utterance inflict injury</u> or tend to incite an immediate breach of the peace" are not protected by the First Amendment.

?

example?

What about sexist speech?

Definition of "fighting words"

If the purpose of the First Amendment is to foster the greatest amount of speech, racial insults disserve that purpose. Assaultive racist speech functions as a preemptive strike. The <u>invective is experienced as a blow, not as a proffered idea,</u> and once the blow is struck, it is unlikely that a dialogue will follow. Racial insults are particularly undeserving of First Amendment protection because the perpetrator's <u>intention is not to discover truth</u> or initiate dialogue but to injure the victim. <u>In most situations</u>, members of minority groups realize that they are likely to lose if they respond to epithets by fighting and are forced to remain silent and submissive.

Really? Probably depends on the individual.

Why must speech always seek "to discover truth"?

How does he know?

This, Therefore That

In order to arrive at a coherent thought, or a coherent series of thoughts that will lead to a reasonable conclusion, a writer has to go through a good deal of preliminary effort; and if the writer is to convince the reader that the conclusion is sound, the reasoning that led to the conclusion must be set forth in detail, with a good deal of "This, therefore that," and "If this, then that." The arguments in this book require more comment than President Calvin Coolidge provided when his wife, who hadn't been able to go to church on a Sunday, asked him what the preacher's sermon was about. "Sin," he said. His wife persisted: "What did the preacher say about it?" Coolidge's response: "He was against it."

But, again, when we say that most of the arguments in this book are presented at length and require careful reading, we do not mean that they are obscure; we mean, rather, that the reader has to take the sentences one by one. And speaking of one by one, we are reminded of an episode in Lewis Carroll's *Through the Looking-Glass:*

> "Can you do Addition?" the White Queen asked. "What's one and one and one and one and one and one and one and one and one and one?"
> "I don't know," said Alice. "I lost count."
> "She can't do Addition," the Red Queen said.

It's easy enough to add one and one and one and so on, and Alice can, of course, do addition, but not at the pace that the White Queen sets. Fortunately, you can set your own pace in reading the cumulative thinking set forth in the essays we reprint. Skimming won't work, but slow reading—and thinking about what you are reading—will.

When you first pick up an essay, you may indeed want to skim it, for some of the reasons mentioned on page 23, but sooner or later you have to settle down to read it, and to think about it. The effort will be worthwhile. John Locke, the seventeenth-century English philosopher, said,

> *Reading* furnishes the mind with materials of knowledge; it is *thinking* [that] makes what we read ours. We are of the ruminating kind, and it is not enough to cram ourselves with a great load of collections; unless we chew them over again they will not give us strength and nourishment.

First, Second, and Third Thoughts

Suppose you are reading an argument about pornographic pictures. For the present purpose, it doesn't matter whether the argument favors or opposes censorship. As you read the argument, ask yourself whether "pornography" has been adequately defined. Has the writer taken the trouble to make sure that the reader and the writer are thinking about the same thing? If not, the very topic under discussion has not been adequately fixed, and therefore further debate over the issue may well be so unclear as to be futile. How, then, ought a topic such as this be fixed for effective critical thinking?

It goes without saying that pornography can't be defined simply as pictures of nude figures, or even of nude figures copulating, for such a definition would include not only photographs taken for medical, sociological, and scientific purposes but also some of the world's great art. Nobody seriously thinks pornography includes such things.

Is it enough, then, to say that pornography "stirs lustful thoughts" or "appeals to prurient interests"? No, because pictures of shoes probably stir lustful thoughts in shoe fetishists, and pictures of children in ads for underwear probably stir lustful thoughts in pedophiles. Perhaps, then, the definition must be amended to "material that stirs lustful thoughts in the average person." But will this restatement do? First, it may be hard to agree on the characteristics of "the average person." True, in other matters the law often assumes that there is such a creature as "the reasonable person," and most people would agree that in a given situation, there might be a reasonable response—for almost everyone. But we cannot be so sure that the same is true about the emotional responses of this "average person." In any case, far from stimulating sexual impulses, sadomasochistic pictures of booted men wielding whips on naked women probably turn off "the average person," yet this is the sort of material that most people would agree is pornographic.

Something must be wrong, then, with the definition that pornography is material that "stirs lustful thoughts in the average person." We began with a definition that was too broad ("pictures of nude figures"), but now we have a definition that is too narrow. We must go back to the drawing board. This is not nitpicking. The label "average person" was found to be inadequate in a pornography case argued before the Supreme Court; because the materials in question were aimed at a homosexual audience, it was agreed that the average person would not find them sexually stimulating.

One difficulty has been that pornography is often defined according to its effect on the viewer ("genital commotion," Father Harold Gardiner, S.J., called it, in *Catholic Viewpoint on Censorship*), but different people, we know, may respond differently. In the first half of the twentieth century, in an effort to distinguish between pornography and art—after all, most people don't want to regard Botticelli's *Venus* or Michelangelo's *David* as "dirty"—it was commonly said that a true work of art does not stimulate in the spectator ideas or desires that the real object might stimulate. But in 1956 Kenneth Clark, probably the most influential English-speaking art critic of our century, changed all that; in a book called *The Nude* he announced that "no nude, however abstract, should fail to arouse in the spectator some vestige of erotic feeling."

SUMMARIZING

Perhaps the best thing to do with a fairly difficult essay is, after a first reading, to reread it and simultaneously to take notes on a sheet of paper, perhaps summarizing each paragraph in a sentence or two. Writing a summary will help you

- to understand the contents, and
- to see the strengths and weaknesses of the piece.

Don't confuse a summary with a paraphrase; a **paraphrase** is a word-by-word or phrase-by-phrase rewording of a text, a sort of translation of the author's language into your own. A paraphrase is therefore as long as the original, or even longer; a **summary** is much shorter. Paraphrasing can be useful in helping you to grasp difficult passages; summarizing is useful in helping you to get the gist of the entire essay. (Caution: Do *not* incorporate a summary or a paraphrase into your own essay without acknowledging your source and stating that you are summarizing or paraphrasing.)

Summarizing each paragraph, or each group of closely related paragraphs, will help you to follow the thread of the discourse, and, when you are finished, will provide you with a useful map of the essay. Then, when you reread the essay yet again, you may want to underline passages that you now understand are the author's key ideas—for instance, definitions, generalizations, summaries—and you may want to jot notes in the margins, questioning the logic, or expressing your uncertainty, or calling attention to other writers who see the matter differently.

Here is a paragraph from a 1973 decision of the U.S. Supreme Court, written by Chief Justice Warren Burger, setting forth reasons why the government may censor obscene material. We follow it with a sample summary.

> If we accept the unprovable assumption that a complete education requires the reading of certain books, and the well-nigh universal belief that good books, plays, and art lift the spirit, improve the mind, enrich the human personality, and develop character, can we then say that a state legislature may not act on the corollary assumption that commerce in obscene books, or public exhibitions focused on obscene conduct, have a tendency to exert a corrupting and debasing impact leading to antisocial behavior? The sum of experience, including that of the past two decades, affords an ample basis for legislatures to conclude that a sensitive, key relationship of human existence, central to family life, community welfare, and the development of human personality, can be debased and distorted by crass commercial exploitation of sex. Nothing in the Constitution prohibits a State from reaching such a conclusion and acting on it legislatively simply because there is no conclusive empirical data.

Now for a student's summary. Notice that the summary does *not* include the reader's evaluation or any other sort of comment on the original; it is simply an attempt to condense the original. Notice too that, because its purpose is merely to assist the reader to grasp the ideas of the original by focusing on them, it is written in a sort of shorthand (not every sentence is a complete sentence), though of course if this summary were being presented in an essay it would have to be grammatical.

> Unprovable but acceptable assumption that good books etc. shape character, so that legislature can assume obscene works debase character. Experience lets one conclude that exploitation of sex debases the individual, family, and community. Though no conclusive evidence for this view, Constitution lets states act on it legislatively.

The first sentence of the original, some eighty words, is reduced in the summary to eighteen words. Of course the summary loses much of the detail and flavor of the original: "Good books etc." is not the same as "good books, plays, and art"; and "shape character" is not the same as "lift the spirit, improve the mind, enrich the human personality, and develop character." But the statement in the summary will do as a rough approximation, useful for a quick review. More important, of course, the act of writing a summary forces the reader to go slowly and to think about each sentence of the original. Such thinking may help the reader-writer to see the complexity—or the hollowness—of the original.

The sample summary in the preceding paragraph was just that, a summary; but when writing your summaries, it is often useful to inject your own thoughts ("seems far-fetched," "strong point," "I don't get it"), enclosing them within square brackets, [ ], or in some other way keeping these responses distinct from your summary of the writer's argument. Remember, however, that if your instructor asks you to hand in a summary, it should not contain ideas other than those found in the original piece. You can rearrange these, add transitions as needed, and so forth, but the summary should give the reader nothing but a sense of the original piece.

We don't want to nag you, but we do want to emphasize the need to read with a pencil in hand. If you read slowly and take notes, you will find that what you read will give you the strength and nourishment that Locke spoke of.

Having insisted that although skimming is a useful early step and that the essays in this book need to be read slowly because the writers build one reason upon another, we will now seem to contradict ourselves by presenting an essay that can *almost* be skimmed. Susan Jacoby's essay originally appeared in the *New York Times*, a thoroughly respectable newspaper but not one that requires its readers to linger over every sentence. Still, compared with most of the news accounts, Jacoby's essay requires close reading. When you read the essay you will notice that it zigs and zags, not because Jacoby is careless or wants to befuddle her readers but because she wants to build a strong case to support her point of view, and she must therefore look at some widely held views that she does *not* accept; she must set these forth, and must then give her reasons for rejecting them.

Susan Jacoby

Susan Jacoby (b. 1946), a journalist since the age of seventeen, is well known for her feminist writings. "A First Amendment Junkie" (our title) appeared in a "Hers" column in the New York Times *in 1978.*

A First Amendment Junkie

It is no news that many women are defecting from the ranks of civil libertarians on the issue of obscenity. The conviction of Larry Flynt, publisher of *Hustler* magazine—before his metamorphosis into a born-again Christian—was greeted with unabashed feminist approval. Harry Reems, the unknown actor who was convicted by a Memphis jury for conspiring to distribute the movie *Deep Throat*, has carried on his legal battles with almost no support from women who ordinarily regard themselves as supporters of the First Amendment. Feminist writers and scholars have even discussed the possibility of making common cause against pornography with adversaries of the women's movement—including opponents of the equal rights amendment and "right-to-life" forces.

All of this is deeply disturbing to a woman writer who believes, as I always have and still do, in an absolute interpretation of the First Amendment. Nothing in Larry Flynt's garbage convinces me that the late Justice Hugo L. Black was wrong in his opinion that "the Federal Government is without any power whatsoever under the Constitution to put any type of burden on free speech and expression of ideas of any kind (as distinguished from conduct)." Many women I like and respect tell me I am wrong; I cannot remember having become involved in so many heated discussions of a public issue since the end of the Vietnam War. A feminist writer described my views as those of a "First Amendment junkie."

Many feminist arguments for controls on pornography carry the implicit conviction that porn books, magazines, and movies pose a greater threat to women than similarly repulsive exercises of free speech pose to other offended groups. This conviction has, of course, been shared by everyone—regardless of race, creed, or sex—who has ever argued in favor of abridging the First Amendment. It is the argument used by some Jews who have withdrawn their support from the American Civil Liberties Union because it has defended the right of American Nazis to march through a community inhabited by survivors of Hitler's concentration camps.

If feminists want to argue that the protection of the Constitution should not be extended to *any* particularly odious or threatening form of speech, they have a reasonable argument (although I don't agree with it). But it is ridiculous to suggest that the porn shops on 42nd Street are more disgusting to women than a march of neo-Nazis is to survivors of the extermination camps.

The arguments over pornography also blur the vital distinction be-   5 tween expression of ideas and conduct. When I say I believe unreservedly in the First Amendment, someone always comes back at me with the issue of "kiddie porn." But kiddie porn is not a First Amendment issue. It is an issue of the abuse of power—the power adults have over children—and not of obscenity. Parents and promoters have no more right to use their children to make porn movies than they do to send them to work in coal mines. The responsible adults should be prosecuted, just as adults who use children for back-breaking farm labor should be prosecuted.

Susan Brownmiller, in *Against Our Will: Men, Women and Rape,* has described pornography as "the undiluted essence of antifemale propaganda." I think this is a fair description of some types of pornography, especially of the brutish subspecies that equates sex with death and portrays women primarily as objects of violence.

The equation of sex and violence, personified by some glossy rock record album covers as well as by *Hustler,* has fed the illusion that censorship of pornography can be conducted on a more rational basis than other types of censorship. Are all pictures of naked women obscene? Clearly not, says a friend. A Renoir nude is art, she says, and *Hustler* is trash. "Any reasonable person" knows that.

But what about something between art and trash—something, say, along the lines of *Playboy* or *Penthouse* magazines? I asked five women for their reactions to one picture in *Penthouse* and got responses that ranged from "lovely" and "sensuous" to "revolting" and "demeaning." Feminists, like everyone else, seldom have rational reasons for their preferences in erotica. Like members of juries, they tend to disagree when confronted with something that falls short of 100 percent vulgarity.

In any case, feminists will not be the arbiters of good taste if it becomes easier to harass, prosecute, and convict people on obscenity charges. Most of the people who want to censor girlie magazines are equally opposed to open discussion of issues that are of vital concern to women: rape, abortion, menstruation, contraception, lesbianism — in fact, the entire range of sexual experience from a women's viewpoint.

Feminist writers and editors and filmmakers have limited financial 10 resources: Confronted by a determined prosecutor, Hugh Hefner[1] will fare better than Susan Brownmiller. Would the Memphis jurors who convicted Harry Reems for his role in *Deep Throat* be inclined to take a more positive view of paintings of the female genitalia done by sensitive feminist artists? *Ms.* magazine has printed color reproductions of some of those art works; *Ms.* is already banned from a number of high school libraries because someone considers it threatening and/or obscene.

Feminists who want to censor what they regard as harmful pornography have essentially the same motivation as other would-be censors: They want to use the power of the state to accomplish what they have been unable to achieve in the marketplace of ideas and images. The impulse to censor places no faith in the possibilities of democratic persuasion.

It isn't easy to persuade certain men that they have better uses for $1.95 each month than to spend it on a copy of *Hustler*? Well, then, give the men no choice in the matter.

I believe there is also a connection between the impulse toward censorship on the part of people who used to consider themselves civil libertarians and a more general desire to shift responsibility from individuals to institutions. When I saw the movie *Looking for Mr. Goodbar*, I was stunned by its series of visual images equating sex and violence, coupled with what seems to me the mindless message (a distortion of the fine Judith Rossner novel) that casual sex equals death. When I came out of the movie, I was even more shocked to see parents standing in line with children between the ages of ten and fourteen.

I simply don't know why a parent would take a child to see such a movie, any more than I understand why people feel they can't turn off a television set their child is watching. Whenever I say that, my friends tell me I don't know how it is because I don't have children. True, but I do have parents. When I was a child, they did turn off the TV. They didn't expect the Federal Communications Commission to do their job for them.

I am a First Amendment junkie. You can't OD on the First Amend- 15 ment, because free speech is its own best antidote.

Suppose we want to make a rough summary, more or less paragraph by paragraph, of Jacoby's essay. Such a summary might look something like this. (The numbers refer to Jacoby's paragraphs.)

---

[1]**Hugh Hefner** Founder and longtime publisher of *Playboy* magazine. [Editors' note.]

1. Although feminists usually support the First Amendment, when it comes to pornography many feminists take pretty much the position of those who oppose ERA and abortion and other causes of the women's movement.

2. Larry Flynt produces garbage, but I think his conviction represents an unconstitutional limitation of freedom of speech.

3, 4. Feminists who want to control (censor) pornography argue that it poses a greater threat to women than similar repulsive speech poses to other groups. If feminists want to say that all offensive speech should be restricted they can make a case, but it is absurd to say that pornography is a "greater threat" to women than a march of neo-Nazis is to survivors of concentration camps.

5. Trust in the First Amendment is not refuted by kiddie porn; kiddie porn is not a First Amendment issue but an issue of child abuse.

6, 7, 8. Some feminists think censorship of pornography can be more "rational" than other kinds of censorship, but a picture of a nude woman strikes some women as base and others as "lovely." There is no unanimity.

9, 10. If feminists censor girlie magazines, they will find that they are unwittingly helping opponents of the women's movement to censor discussions of rape, abortion, and so on. Some of the art in the feminist magazine *Ms.* would doubtless be censored.

11, 12. Like other would-be censors, feminists want to use the power of the state to achieve what they have not achieved in "the marketplace of ideas." They display a lack of faith in "democratic persuasion."

13, 14. This attempt at censorship reveals a desire to "shift responsibility from individuals to institutions." The responsibility—for instance, to keep young people from equating sex with violence—is properly the parents'.

15. We can't have too much of the First Amendment.

Jacoby's **thesis,** or major claim, or chief proposition—that any form of censorship is wrong—is clear enough, even as early as the end of her first paragraph, but it gets its life or its force from the **reasons** offered throughout the essay. If we want to reduce our summary even further, we might say that Jacoby supports her thesis by arguing several subsidiary points. We will merely assert them briefly, but Jacoby **argues** them—that is, she gives reasons.

a. Pornography can scarcely be thought of as more offensive than Nazism.
b. Women disagree about which pictures are pornographic.

c. Feminists who want to censor pornography will find that they help antifeminists to censor discussions of issues advocated by the women's movement.

d. Feminist advocates are in effect turning to the government to achieve what they haven't achieved in the free marketplace.

e. One sees this abdication of responsibility in the fact that parents allow their children to watch unsuitable movies and television programs.

If we want to present a brief summary in the form of one coherent paragraph—perhaps as part of our own essay, in order to show the view we are arguing in behalf of or against—we might write something like this summary. (The summary would, of course, be prefaced by a **lead-in** along these lines: "Susan Jacoby, writing in the *New York Times,* offered a forceful argument against censorship of pornography. Jacoby's view, briefly, is . . .".)

> When it comes to censorship of pornography, some feminists take a position shared by opponents of the feminist movement. They argue that pornography poses a greater threat to women than other forms of offensive speech offer to other groups, but this interpretation is simply a mistake. Pointing to kiddie porn is also a mistake, for kiddie porn is an issue involving not the First Amendment but child abuse. Feminists who support censorship of pornography will inadvertently aid those who wish to censor discussions of abortion and rape, or art that is published in magazines such as Ms. The solution is not for individuals to turn to institutions (i.e., for the government to limit the First Amendment) but for individuals to accept the responsibility for teaching young people not to equate sex with violence.

Whether we agree or disagree with Jacoby's thesis, we must admit that the reasons she sets forth to support it are worth thinking about. Only a reader who closely follows the reasoning with which Jacoby buttresses her thesis is in a position to accept or reject it.

Topics for Critical Thinking and Writing

1. What does Jacoby mean when she says she is a "First Amendment junkie"?

2. The essay is primarily an argument against the desire of some feminists to try to censor pornography of the sort that appeals to some heterosexual adult males, but the next-to-last paragraph is about television and children. Is the paragraph connected to Jacoby's overall argument? If so, how?

3. Evaluate the final paragraph as a final paragraph. (Effective final paragraphs are not, of course, all of one sort. Some, for example, round off the essay by echoing something from the opening; others suggest that the reader, having now seen the problem, should think further about it or even act on it. But a good final paragraph, whatever else it does, should make the reader feel that the essay has come to an end, not just broken off.)

4. This essay originally appeared in the *New York Times*. If you are unfamiliar with this newspaper, consult an issue or two in your library. Next, in a paragraph, try to characterize the readers of the paper—that is, Jacoby's audience.

5. Jacoby claims in paragraph 2 that she "believes . . . in an absolute interpretation of the First Amendment." What does such an interpretation involve? Would it permit shouting "Fire!" in a crowded theater even though the shouter knows there is no fire? Would it permit shouting racist insults at blacks or immigrant Vietnamese? Spreading untruths about someone's past? If the "absolutist" interpretation of the First Amendment does permit these statements, does that argument show that nothing is morally wrong with uttering them? (*Does* the First Amendment, as actually interpreted by the Supreme Court today, permit any or all of these claims? Consult your reference librarian for help in answering this question.)

6. Jacoby implies that permitting prosecution of persons on obscenity charges will lead eventually to censorship of "open discussion" of important issues such as "rape, abortion, menstruation, contraception, lesbianism" (para. 9). Do you find her fears convincing? Does she give any evidence to support her claim?

A CHECKLIST FOR GETTING STARTED

✓ Have I adequately previewed the work?

✓ Can I state the thesis?

   If I have jotted down a summary,

   ✓ is the summary accurate?

   ✓ does the summary mention all the chief points?

   ✓ if there are inconsistencies, are they in the summary or the original selection?

   ✓ will the summary be clear and helpful?

A CASEBOOK FOR CRITICAL READING:
Should Some Kinds of Speech Be Curtailed?

Now we present a series of essays that we think are somewhat more difficult than Jacoby's but that address in more detail some of the issues of free speech that she raises. We suggest you read each one through, to get its gist, and then read it a second time, jotting down after each paragraph a sentence or two summarizing the paragraph. Keep in mind the First Amendment to the Constitution, which reads, in its entirety,

> Congress shall make no law respecting an establishment of religion, or prohibiting the free exercise thereof; or abridging the freedom of speech, or of the press; or the right of the people peaceably to assemble, and to petition the government for a redress of grievances.

Susan Brownmiller

Susan Brownmiller (b. 1935), a graduate of Cornell University, is the founder of Women against Pornography, and the author of several books, including Against Our Will: Men, Women, and Rape *(1975). The essay reprinted here is from* Take Back the Night *(1980), a collection of essays edited by Laura Lederer. The book has been called "the manifesto of antipornography feminism."*

Let's Put Pornography Back in the Closet

Free speech is one of the great foundations on which our democracy rests. I am old enough to remember the Hollywood Ten, the screenwriters who went to jail in the late 1940s because they refused to testify before a congressional committee about their political affiliations. They tried to use the First Amendment as a defense, but they went to jail because in those days there were few civil liberties lawyers around who cared to champion the First Amendment right to free speech, when the speech concerned the Communist party.

The Hollywood Ten were correct in claiming the First Amendment. Its high purpose is the protection of unpopular ideas and political dissent. In the dark, cold days of the 1950s, few civil libertarians were willing to declare themselves First Amendment absolutists. But in the brighter, though frantic, days of the 1960s, the principle of protecting unpopular political speech was gradually strengthened.

It is fair to say now that the battle has largely been won. Even the American Nazi party has found itself the beneficiary of the dedicated, tireless work of the American Civil Liberties Union. But—and please notice the quotation marks coming up—"To equate the free and robust exchange of ideas and political debate with commercial exploitation of obscene material demeans the grand conception of the First Amendment and its high purposes in the historic struggle for freedom. It is a misuse of the great guarantees of free speech and free press."

I didn't say that, although I wish I had, for I think the words are thrilling. Chief Justice Warren Burger said it in 1973, in the United States Supreme Court's majority opinion in *Miller v. California*. During the same decades that the right to political free speech was being strengthened in the courts, the nation's obscenity laws also were undergoing extensive revision.

It's amazing to recall that in 1934 the question of whether James   5
Joyce's *Ulysses* should be banned as pornographic actually went before the Court. The battle to protect *Ulysses* as a work of literature with redeeming social value was won. In later decades, Henry Miller's *Tropic* books, *Lady Chatterley's Lover,* and the *Memoirs of Fanny Hill* also were adjudged not obscene. These decisions have been important to me. As the author of *Against Our Will,* a study of the history of rape that does contain explicit sexual material, I shudder to think how my book would have fared if James Joyce, D. H. Lawrence, and Henry Miller hadn't gone before me.

I am not a fan of *Chatterley* or the *Tropic* books, I should quickly mention. They are not to my literary taste, nor do I think they represent female sexuality with any degree of accuracy. But I would hardly suggest that we ban them. Such a suggestion wouldn't get very far anyway. The battle to protect these books is ancient history. Time does march on, quite methodically. What, then, is unlawfully obscene, and what does the First Amendment have to do with it?

In the *Miller* case of 1973 (not Henry Miller, by the way, but a porn distributor who sent unsolicited stuff through the mails), the Court came up with new guidelines that it hoped would strengthen obscenity laws by giving more power to the states. What it did in actuality was throw everything into confusion. It set up a three-part test by which materials can be adjudged obscene. The materials are obscene if they depict patently offensive, hard-core sexual conduct; lack serious scientific, literary, artistic, or political value; and appeal to the prurient interest of an average person—as measured by contemporary community standards.

"Patently offensive," "prurient interest," and "hard-core" are indeed words to conjure with. "Contemporary community standards" are what we're trying to redefine. The feminist objection to pornography is not based on prurience, which the dictionary defines as lustful, itching desire. We are not opposed to sex and desire, with or without the itch, and we certainly believe that explicit sexual material has its place in literature, art, science, and education. Here we part company rather swiftly with old-line conservatives who don't want sex education in the high schools, for example.

No, the feminist objection to pornography is based on our belief that pornography represents hatred of women, that pornography's intent is to humiliate, degrade, and dehumanize the female body for the purpose of erotic stimulation and pleasure. We are unalterably opposed to the presentation of the female body being stripped, bound, raped, tortured, mutilated, and murdered in the name of commercial entertainment and free speech.

These images, which are standard pornographic fare, have nothing to 10 do with the hallowed right of political dissent. They have everything to do with the creation of a cultural climate in which a rapist feels he is merely giving in to a normal urge and a woman is encouraged to believe that sexual masochism is healthy, liberated fun. Justice Potter Stewart once said about hard-core pornography, "You know it when you see it," and that certainly used to be true. In the good old days, pornography looked awful. It was cheap and sleazy, and there was no mistaking it for art.

Nowadays, since the porn industry has become a multimillion dollar business, visual technology has been employed in its service. Pornographic movies are skillfully filmed and edited, pornographic still shots using the newest tenets of good design artfully grace the covers of *Hustler, Penthouse,* and *Playboy,* and the public—and the courts—are sadly confused.

The Supreme Court neglected to define "hard-core" in the *Miller* decision. This was a mistake. If "hard-core" refers only to explicit sexual intercourse, then that isn't good enough. When women or children or men—no matter how artfully—are shown tortured or terrorized in the service of sex, that's obscene. And "patently offensive," I would hope, to our "contemporary community standards."

Justice William O. Douglas wrote in his dissent to the *Miller* case that no one is "compelled to look." This is hardly true. To buy a paper at the corner newsstand is to subject oneself to a forcible immersion in pornography, to be demeaned by an array of dehumanized, chopped-up parts of the female anatomy, packaged like cuts of meat at the supermarket. I happen to like my body and I work hard at the gym to keep it in good shape, but I am embarrassed for my body and for the bodies of all women when I see the fragmented parts of us so frivolously, and so flagrantly, displayed.

Some constitutional theorists (Justice Douglas was one) have maintained that any obscenity law is a serious abridgement of free speech. Others (and Justice Earl Warren was one) have maintained that the First Amendment was never intended to protect obscenity. We live quite compatibly with a host of free-speech abridgements. There are restraints against false and misleading advertising or statements—shouting "fire" without cause in a crowded movie theater, etc.—that do not threaten, but strengthen, our societal values. Restrictions on the public display of pornography belong in this category.

The distinction between permission to publish and permission to dis- 15
play publicly is an essential one and one which I think consonant with First Amendment principles. Justice Burger's words which I quoted above support this without question. We are not saying "Smash the presses" or "Ban the bad ones," but simply "Get the stuff out of our sight." Let the legislatures decide—using realistic and humane contemporary community standards—what can be displayed and what cannot. The courts, after all, will be the final arbiters.

Topics for Critical Thinking and Writing

1. Objecting to Justice Douglas's remark that no one is "'compelled to look'" (para. 13), Brownmiller says, "This is hardly true. To buy a paper at the corner newsstand is to subject oneself to a forcible immersion in pornography, to be demeaned by an array of dehumanized, chopped-up parts of the female anatomy, packaged like cuts of meat at the supermarket." Is this true at your local newsstand, or are the sex magazines kept in one place, relatively remote from the newspapers?

2. When Brownmiller attempts to restate the "three-part test" for obscenity established by the Supreme Court in *Miller v. California*, she writes (para. 7): "The materials are obscene if they depict . . ." and so on. She should have written: "The materials are obscene if and only if they depict . . ." and so on. Explain what is wrong here with her "if," and why "if and only if" is needed.

3. In her next-to-last paragraph, Brownmiller reminds us that we already live quite comfortably with some "free-speech abridgements." The examples she gives are that we may not falsely shout "fire" in a crowded theater, and we may not issue misleading advertisements. Do you think that these widely accepted restrictions are valid evidence in arguing in behalf of limiting the display of what Brownmiller considers pornography? Why, or why not?

4. Brownmiller insists that defenders of the First Amendment, who will surely oppose laws that interfere with the freedom to publish, need not go on to condemn laws that regulate the freedom to "display publicly" pornographic publications. Do you agree? Suppose a publisher insists he cannot sell his product at a profit unless he is permitted to display it to advantage, and so restriction on the latter amounts to interference with his freedom to publish. How might Brownmiller reply?

5. In her last paragraph Brownmiller says that "contemporary community standards" should be decisive. Can it be argued that, because standards vary from one community to another, and from time to time even in the same place, her recommendation subjects the rights of a minority to the

whims of a majority? The Bill of Rights, after all, was supposed to safe-guard constitutional rights from the possible tyranny of the majority.

6. When Brownmiller accuses "the public . . . and the courts" of being "sadly confused" (para. 11), what does she think they are confused about? The definition of "pornography" or "obscenity"? The effects of such literature on men and women? Or is it something else?

Charles R. Lawrence III

Charles R. Lawrence III (b. 1943), author of numerous articles in law jour-nals and coauthor of The Bakke Case: The Politics of Inequality *(1979), teaches law at Stanford University. This essay originally appeared in* The Chronicle of Higher Education *(October 25, 1989), a publica-tion read chiefly by faculty and administrators at colleges and universities. An amplified version of the essay appeared in* Duke Law Journal, *Feb-ruary 1990.*

On Racist Speech

I have spent the better part of my life as a dissenter. As a high school student, I was threatened with suspension for my refusal to participate in a civil defense drill, and I have been a conspicuous consumer of my First Amendment liberties ever since. There are very strong reasons for protecting even racist speech. Perhaps the most important of these is that such protection reinforces our society's commitment to tolerance as a value, and that by protecting bad speech from government regulation, we will be forced to combat it as a community.

But I also have a deeply felt apprehension about the resurgence of racial violence and the corresponding rise in the incidence of verbal and symbolic assault and harassment to which blacks and other traditionally subjugated and excluded groups are subjected. I am troubled by the way the debate has been framed in response to the recent surge of racist inci-dents on college and university campuses and in response to some uni-versities' attempts to regulate harassing speech. The problem has been framed as one in which the liberty of free speech is in conflict with the elimination of racism. I believe this has placed the bigot on the moral high ground and fanned the rising flames of racism.

Above all, I am troubled that we have not listened to the real vic-tims, that we have shown so little understanding of their injury, and that we have abandoned those whose race, gender, or sexual preference con-tinues to make them second-class citizens. It seems to me a very sad irony that the first instinct of civil libertarians has been to challenge even the smallest, most narrowly framed efforts by universities to provide black and other minority students with the protection the Constitution guarantees them.

The landmark case of *Brown v. Board of Education* is not a case that we normally think of as a case about speech. But *Brown* can be broadly read as articulating the principle of equal citizenship. *Brown* held that segregated schools were inherently unequal because of the *message* that segregation conveyed—that black children were an untouchable caste, unfit to go to school with white children. If we understand the necessity of eliminating the system of signs and symbols that signal the inferiority of blacks, then we should hesitate before proclaiming that all racist speech that stops short of physical violence must be defended.

University officials who have formulated policies to respond to inci-   5
dents of racial harassment have been characterized in the press as "thought police," but such policies generally do nothing more than impose sanctions against intentional face-to-face insults. When racist speech takes the form of face-to-face insults, catcalls, or other assaultive speech aimed at an individual or small group of persons, it falls directly within the "fighting words" exception to First Amendment protection. The Supreme Court has held that words which "by their very utterance inflict injury or tend to incite an immediate breach of the peace" are not protected by the First Amendment.

If the purpose of the First Amendment is to foster the greatest amount of speech, racial insults disserve that purpose. Assaultive racist speech functions as a preemptive strike. The invective is experienced as a blow, not as a proffered idea, and once the blow is struck, it is unlikely that a dialogue will follow. Racial insults are particularly undeserving of First Amendment protection because the perpetrator's intention is not to discover truth or initiate dialogue but to injure the victim. In most situations, members of minority groups realize that they are likely to lose if they respond to epithets by fighting and are forced to remain silent and submissive.

Courts have held that offensive speech may not be regulated in public forums such as streets where the listener may avoid the speech by moving on, but the regulation of otherwise protected speech has been permitted when the speech invades the privacy of the unwilling listener's home or when the unwilling listener cannot avoid the speech. Racist posters, fliers, and graffiti in dormitories, bathrooms, and other common living spaces would seem to clearly fall within the reasoning of these cases. Minority students should not be required to remain in their rooms in order to avoid racial assault. Minimally, they should find a safe haven in their dorms and in all other common rooms that are a part of their daily routine.

I would also argue that the university's responsibility for ensuring that these students receive an equal educational opportunity provides a compelling justification for regulations that ensure them safe passage in all common areas. A minority student should not have to risk becoming the target of racially assaulting speech every time he or she chooses to walk across campus. Regulating vilifying speech that cannot be anticipated or avoided would not preclude announced speeches and rallies— situations that would give minority-group members and their allies the chance to organize counterdemonstrations or avoid the speech altogether.

The most commonly advanced argument against the regulation of racist speech proceeds something like this: We recognize that minority groups suffer pain and injury as the result of racist speech, but we must allow this hate mongering for the benefit of society as a whole. Freedom of speech is the lifeblood of our democratic system. It is especially important for minorities because often it is their only vehicle for rallying support for the redress of their grievances. It will be impossible to formulate a prohibition so precise that it will prevent the racist speech you want to suppress without catching in the same net all kinds of speech that it would be unconscionable for a democratic society to suppress.

Whenever we make such arguments, we are striking a balance on 10 the one hand between our concern for the continued free flow of ideas and the democratic process dependent on that flow, and, on the other, our desire to further the cause of equality. There can be no meaningful discussion of how we should reconcile our commitment to equality and our commitment to free speech until it is acknowledged that there is real harm inflicted by racist speech and that this harm is far from trivial.

To engage in a debate about the First Amendment and racist speech without a full understanding of the nature and extent of that harm is to risk making the First Amendment an instrument of domination rather than a vehicle of liberation. We have not known the experience of victimization by racist, misogynist, and homophobic speech, nor do we equally share the burden of the societal harm it inflicts. We are often quick to say that we have heard the cry of the victims when we have not.

The *Brown* case is again instructive because it speaks directly to the psychic injury inflicted by racist speech by noting that the symbolic message of segregation affected "the hearts and minds" of Negro children "in a way unlikely ever to be undone." Racial epithets and harassment often cause deep emotional scarring and feelings of anxiety and fear that pervade every aspect of a victim's life.

Brown also recognized that black children did not have an equal opportunity to learn and participate in the school community if they bore the additional burden of being subjected to the humiliation and psychic assault contained in the message of segregation. University students bear an analogous burden when they are forced to live and work in an environment where at any moment they may be subjected to denigrating verbal harassment and assault. The same injury was addressed by the Supreme Court when it held that sexual harassment that creates a hostile or abusive work environment violates the ban on sex discrimination in employment of Title VII of the Civil Rights Act of 1964.

Carefully drafted university regulations would bar the use of words as assault weapons and leave unregulated even the most heinous of ideas when those ideas are presented at times and places and in manners that provide an opportunity for reasoned rebuttal or escape from immediate injury. The history of the development of the right to free speech has been one of carefully evaluating the importance of free expression and its effects on other important societal interests. We have drawn the line between protected and unprotected speech before without dire results. (Courts have, for example, exempted from the protection of the First Amendment obscene speech and speech that disseminates official secrets, that defames or libels another person, or that is used to form a conspiracy or monopoly.)

Blacks and other people of color are skeptical about the argument 15 that even the most injurious speech must remain unregulated because, in an unregulated marketplace of ideas, the best ones will rise to the top and gain acceptance. Our experience tells us quite the opposite. We have seen too many good liberal politicians shy away from the issues that might brand them as being too closely allied with us.

Whenever we decide that racist speech must be tolerated because of the importance of maintaining societal tolerance for all unpopular speech, we are asking blacks and other subordinated groups to bear the burden for the good of all. We must be careful that the ease with which we strike the balance against the regulation of racist speech is in no way influenced by the fact that the cost will be borne by others. We must be certain that those who will pay that price are fairly represented in our deliberations and that they are heard.

At the core of the argument that we should resist all government regulation of speech is the ideal that the best cure for bad speech is good, that ideas that affirm equality and the worth of all individuals will ultimately prevail. This is an empty ideal unless those of us who would fight racism are vigilant and unequivocal in that fight. We must look for ways to offer assistance and support to students whose speech and political participation are chilled in a climate of racial harassment.

Civil rights lawyers might consider suing on behalf of blacks whose right to an equal education is denied by a university's failure to ensure a nondiscriminatory educational climate or conditions of employment. We must embark upon the development of a First Amendment jurisprudence grounded in the reality of our history and our contemporary experience. We must think hard about how best to launch legal attacks against the most indefensible forms of hate speech. Good lawyers can create exceptions and narrow interpretations that limit the harm of hate speech without opening the floodgates of censorship.

Everyone concerned with these issues must find ways to engage actively in actions that resist and counter the racist ideas that we would have the First Amendment protect. If we fail in this, the victims of hate speech must rightly assume that we are on the oppressors' side.

Topics for Critical Thinking and Writing

1. Summarize Lawrence's essay in a paragraph. (You may find it useful first to summarize each paragraph in a sentence, and then to revise these summary sentences into a paragraph.)

2. In a sentence state Lawrence's thesis (his main point).

3. Why do you suppose Lawrence included his first paragraph? What does it contribute to his argument?

4. Paragraph 7 argues that "minority students" should not have to endure "racist posters, fliers, and graffiti in dormitories, bathrooms, and other common living spaces." Do you think that Lawrence would also argue that straight white men should not have to endure posters, fliers, or graffiti that speak of "honkies" or "rednecks"? On what do you base your answer?

5. In paragraph 8 Lawrence speaks of "racially assaulting speech" and of "vilifying speech." It is easy to think of words that fit these descriptions, but what about other words? Is *Uncle Tom*, used by an African American about another African American who is eager to please whites, an example? Or take the word *gay*. Surely this word is acceptable because it is widely used by homosexuals, but what about *queer* (used by some homosexuals, but usually derogatory when used by heterosexuals)? A third example: There can be little doubt that women are demeaned when males speak of them as *chicks* or *babes*, but are these terms "assaulting" and "vilifying"?

6. Find out if your college or university has a code governing hate speech. If it does, evaluate it. If your college has no such code, imagine that you are Lawrence, and draft one of about 250 words. (See especially his paras. 5, 7, and 14.)

Derek Bok

Derek Bok was born in 1930 in Bryn Mawr, Pennsylvania, and educated at Stanford University and Harvard University, where he received a law degree. From 1971 to 1991 he served as president of Harvard University. The following essay, first published in the Boston Globe *in 1991, was prompted by the display of Confederate flags hung from a window of a Harvard dormitory.*

Protecting Freedom of Expression on the Campus

For several years, universities have been struggling with the problem of trying to reconcile the rights of free speech with the desire to avoid racial tension. In recent weeks, such a controversy has sprung up at Harvard. Two students hung Confederate flags in public view, upsetting students who equate the Confederacy with slavery. A third student tried to protest the flags by displaying a swastika.

These incidents have provoked much discussion and disagreement. Some students have urged that Harvard require the removal of symbols that offend many members of the community. Others reply that such symbols are a form of free speech and should be protected.

Different universities have resolved similar conflicts in different ways. Some have enacted codes to protect their communities from forms of speech that are deemed to be insensitive to the feelings of other groups. Some have refused to impose such restrictions.

It is important to distinguish between the appropriateness of such communications and their status under the First Amendment. The fact that speech is protected by the First Amendment does not necessarily mean that it is right, proper, or civil. I am sure that the vast majority of Harvard students believe that hanging a Confederate flag in public view—or displaying a swastika in response—is insensitive and unwise because any satisfaction it gives to the students who display these symbols is far outweighed by the discomfort it causes to many others.

I share this view and regret that the students involved saw fit to be-   5
have in this fashion. Whether or not they merely wished to manifest their pride in the South—or to demonstrate the insensitivity of hanging Confederate flags, by mounting another offensive symbol in return— they must have known that they would upset many fellow students and ignore the decent regard for the feelings of others so essential to building and preserving a strong and harmonious community.

To disapprove of a particular form of communication, however, is not enough to justify prohibiting it. We are faced with a clear example of the conflict between our commitment to free speech and our desire to foster a community founded on mutual respect. Our society has wrestled with this problem for many years. Interpreting the First Amendment, the Supreme Court has clearly struck the balance in favor of free speech.

While communities do have the right to regulate speech in order to uphold aesthetic standards (avoiding defacement of buildings) or to protect the public from disturbing noise, rules of this kind must be applied across the board and cannot be enforced selectively to prohibit certain kinds of messages but not others.

Under the Supreme Court's rulings, as I read them, the display of swastikas or Confederate flags clearly falls within the protection of the free-speech clause of the First Amendment and cannot be forbidden simply because it offends the feelings of many members of the community. These rulings apply to all agencies of government, including public universities.

Although it is unclear to what extent the First Amendment is enforceable against private institutions, I have difficulty understanding why a university such as Harvard should have less free speech than the surrounding society—or than a public university.

One reason why the power of censorship is so dangerous is that it is   10
extremely difficult to decide when a particular communication is offen-

sive enough to warrant prohibition or to weigh the degree of offensiveness against the potential value of the communication. If we begin to forbid flags, it is only a short step to prohibiting offensive speakers.

I suspect that no community will become humane and caring by restricting what its members can say. The worst offenders will simply find other ways to irritate and insult.

In addition, once we start to declare certain things "offensive," with all the excitement and attention that will follow, I fear that much ingenuity will be exerted trying to test the limits, much time will be expended trying to draw tenuous distinctions, and the resulting publicity will eventually attract more attention to the offensive material than would ever have occurred otherwise.

Rather than prohibit such communications, with all the resulting risks, it would be better to ignore them, since students would then have little reason to create such displays and would soon abandon them. If this response is not possible — and one can understand why — the wisest course is to speak with those who perform insensitive acts and try to help them understand the effects of their actions on others.

Appropriate officials and faculty members should take the lead, as the Harvard House Masters have already done in this case. In talking with students, they should seek to educate and persuade, rather than resort to ridicule or intimidation, recognizing that only persuasion is likely to produce a lasting, beneficial effect. Through such effects, I believe that we act in the manner most consistent with our ideals as an educational institution and most calculated to help us create a truly understanding, supportive community.

Topics for Critical Thinking and Writing

1. Bok sketches the following argument (paras. 8 and 9): The First Amendment protects free speech in public universities and colleges; Harvard is not a public university; therefore Harvard does not enjoy the protection of the First Amendment. This argument is plainly valid. But Bok clearly rejects this conclusion ("I have difficulty understanding why . . . Harvard should have less free speech . . . than a public university"). Therefore, he must reject at least one of the premises. But which one? And why?

2. Bok objects to censorship in order to prevent students from being "offended." He would not object to the campus police preventing students from being harmed. In an essay of 100 words, explain the difference between conduct that is *harmful* and conduct that is (merely?) *offensive*.

3. Bok advises campus officials (and students) simply to "ignore" offensive words, flags, and so forth (para. 13). Do you agree with this advice? Or do you favor a different kind of response? Write a 250-word essay on the theme "How We Ought to Respond to the Offensive Misconduct of Others."

Steven McDonald

Steven McDonald is an associate legal counsel at the Ohio State University. This selection was downloaded from Academe Today, The Chronicle of Higher Education's Web site, on October 28, 1997.

The Laws of Cyberspace: What Colleges Need to Know

Continued incidents of misuse of the Internet on college campuses suggest that we need to reexamine our existing approaches to the problem. For the most part, colleges and universities (much like legislators) have addressed misuse of the Internet as though it were an entirely new issue. In reality, however, it is simply a new form of an old problem: how to handle abuses of free speech and similar types of misconduct.

Hardly anyone uses computers to compute anymore. Instead, we use them to communicate. Every day on our campuses, students and faculty and staff members use our computer systems and networks to disseminate far more text and images than the *New York Times,* far more audio than NPR, and far more video than NBC. They are sending far more electronic mail than paper mail and are engaging in far more electronic discussions than telephone calls. And their electronic messages have a far wider audience than any of the more traditional forms of communications. In effect, people on our campuses are acting as international publishers and broadcasters.

If computer users are engaged in the same kinds of communications as the traditional media are, it should come as no surprise that they also face the same long-standing legal issues and have the same well-settled legal responsibilities and liabilities in connection with those communications that traditional media do. However, few of our users understand themselves to be publishers or broadcasters. At best, only a handful of them are aware of the libel, copyright, obscenity, and other laws applicable to their activities on the Internet—let alone the finer points of "actual malice" doctrine, the Supreme Court's latest pronouncement on the four factors to be considered in analyzing a claim of "fair use," or the scope of "local community standards" in the various jurisdictions through which their racier communications may pass. They also know virtually nothing about the potential legal consequences of violating the applicable laws.

Instead, to the extent that they consider legal issues at all, computer users typically view them through the lens of Internet folklore, which mistakenly conceives of cyberspace as a separate, law-free jurisdiction in which what is permissible is defined solely by the limits of users' technical capabilities. Unfortunately, that view recently has been reinforced by the widespread misconception that the Supreme Court's decision striking down the Communications Decency Act outlawed *all* regulation of the Net.

In fact, while that decision was indeed momentous, all that it really held was that government regulation of the Internet must be consistent with First Amendment principles, and that the C.D.A. was not, because it restricted far more speech than was necessary or appropriate to deal with the problem of minors' access to "indecency." The Supreme Court did not hold that the Internet could not be regulated at all—indeed, it expressly recognized that a more "narrowly tailored" approach to that problem would have been constitutional. Further, the Court certainly did not release computer users from their responsibilities and liabilities under existing, generally applicable laws, such as those governing libel, copyright, and obscenity.

The result of these misconceptions has been that our computer users increasingly, if unknowingly, are engaging in communications that are libelous or obscene, that infringe copyrighted works, and that violate other laws. And because those communications flow through and reside in our computer systems, colleges and universities are being asked and expected to do something about them.

Most commonly, our response to such expectations has been to adopt new, computer-specific codes of conduct, often expressed in long lists of "thou shalt nots." Such codes, however, can do more harm than good: They usually duplicate or conflict with—and therefore sometimes cause confusion about—other applicable laws and institutional policies. Moreover, they can encourage computer users to seek out and exploit the inevitable loopholes; they may infringe upon academic freedom by chilling legitimate expression; and, most important, they can actually increase institutions' liabilities for our users' communications, because they raise expectations about both our ability and our duty to police these communications.

Although the law is not completely settled, what is increasingly clear is that colleges and universities are not liable for an illegal communication solely because they own the system through which that communication flows. We will, of course, always be responsible for the communications of college and university employees on the Internet when they are acting within the scope of their employment. But with respect to the other, "personal" communications on our systems—including, in particular, most student communications—we are liable only when we know, or have good reason to know, of their illegal character but fail to stop them.

Thus, for example, if a student posts a libelous message to our Usenet server and we never learn of it, the student alone will be liable if the message results in a lawsuit. But if we become aware of the existence of the libel on our system, by complaint or any other means, and do nothing about it, we will be liable, along with the student.

The more that we specifically attempt to regulate the content of the personal communications on our systems, the more likely it is that we will be expected to know what that content is, and the more likely it is that we will be held liable for it when it is illegal, whether or not we actually know about the offense. In other words, if we act as if we were newspaper editors, imposing rigid, Internet-specific content guidelines or screening material before it is distributed publicly—or even if we just reserve the right to act in this way—we should not be surprised to find ourselves subjected to the same liabilities as newspapers are for their libelous or other illegal communications. If, however, we act more like a telephone company—that is, simply as the operator of a communications system, the content of which is determined by others—our liability for individuals' personal communications should be reduced.

That is not to say that we should abandon all responsibility. We can and should continue to enforce existing, generally applicable laws and policies in the context of the Internet, just as we would in any other context, when we learn that they have been violated. And, at least for now, the law also appears to require us to investigate in good faith whatever complaints about the legality of our computer users' communications are brought to our attention and—if the complaints are justified—to remove those communications from our systems.

Such after-the-fact enforcement of general laws and policies does not carry with it the legal risks associated with more active editorial control. But because it is impossible, as a practical matter, for us to keep track—let alone control the content—of all of the personal communications on our computer systems, we should be careful not to make it appear that we are doing so by adopting content regulations specific to the Internet.

A more productive approach to the problem of Internet misuse is one that, ironically, we often forget about: education. If, as our experience at the Ohio State University suggests, the primary problem is that our computer users do not understand their legal responsibilities online, rather than that they intend to act maliciously, surely the solution is to teach our users about the relevant legal issues.

For the past year, we have been doing just that at Ohio State. Each quarter, we teach all entering freshmen the basic principles of the laws and university policies relevant to their Internet communications, including libel, copyright, and obscenity laws. These are the areas in which problems arise most frequently, and existing laws and policies already address them quite well. Our main message is: Communications that would be illegal or that would violate university policy in the "off line" world are equally illegal or in violation of university policy when they occur online. We will soon be making our educational materials available to the rest of our computer users as well.

Informal educational efforts also can be extremely effective, particularly when dealing with specific complaints of misuse. Nothing drives home the point so well to those accused of misusing the Internet as a discussion of the concept of *personal* liability—for example, the prospect of as much as $100,000 in statutory damages for a single instance of copyright infringement, as well as a demonstration of how easy it is for a university administrator (or, say, the user's parents and prospective employers) to find a potentially embarrassing communication by means of Web-based search engines such as AltaVista or Deja News. It is only then that some students first understand the consequences of what they may have considered harmless fun.

As part of the same effort, we are also revising our computer-use policy at Ohio State to make it more of an educational tool than a mere list of regulations. To the extent possible, the policy will simply incorporate—and remind our users of—existing relevant laws, policies, and enforcement mechanisms, including our code of student conduct. The policy will include computer-specific rules only to the extent that computers pose unique issues not addressed by existing laws and policies— for example, the need to limit usage so as not to interfere with others' use of the computer resources that are available.

It is still too early to tell how effective our educational approach will be, but the results so far are promising. Our students have seemed eager to learn about "Internet law" (if only because they want to know what they can get away with), and it appears that the number of serious complaints about Internet misuse on our campus is dropping. If that reduction continues, not only should we see a corresponding reduction in potential legal claims against the university, but we will also be able to spend less time and effort on complaints. It seems that with the Internet, as with most things, an ounce of prevention is worth a pound of cure.

Topics for Critical Thinking and Writing

1. McDonald suggests (para. 2) that today's college students and faculties are acting as "international publishers and broadcasters" in their use of computers. Explain whether you think this is a helpful analogy.

2. What does McDonald say are the four factors the Supreme Court has decided must be considered in weighing a claim of "fair use" of printed matter?

3. What was the Supreme Court's holding in the case striking down the constitutionality of the Communications Decency Act?

4. Define each of the following ideas: copyright infringement, libel, obscenity. (Also construct a hypothetical example of each.)

5. Does McDonald believe that university administrations ought to approach the Internet more like newspaper editors or more like telephone operators? Can you tell? Explain why.

6. Consider the educational practices regarding computer use being taught at Ohio State (paras. 14–16). Does your college or university have a similar program? If so, compare it with the one at Ohio State. If not, arrange an interview with your college dean and ask the dean to explain why.

3

Critical Reading: Getting Deeper into Arguments

He that wrestles with us strengthens our nerves, and sharpens our skill. Our antagonist is our helper. —EDMUND BURKE

PERSUASION, ARGUMENT, DISPUTE

When we think seriously about an argument (not name calling or mere rationalization), not only do we hear ideas that may be unfamiliar, but we are also forced to examine closely our own cherished opinions, and perhaps for the first time we really come to see the strengths and weaknesses of what we believe. As John Stuart Mill put it, "He who knows only his own side of the case knows little."

It is customary, and useful, to distinguish between persuasion and argument. **Persuasion** has the broader meaning. To persuade is to win over—whether by giving reasons (that is, by argument) or by appealing to the emotions, or, for that matter, by using torture. **Argument,** one form of persuasion, relies on reason; it offers statements as reasons for other statements. Rhetoricians often use the Greek word **logos,** which merely means "word," to denote this aspect of persuasive writing—the appeal to reason. (The appeal to the emotions is known as **pathos.** Strictly speaking, *pathos* is Greek for "suffering," but it now covers all sorts of emotional appeal, for instance to one's sense of pity or one's sense of patriotism.)

Notice that an argument, in the sense of statements that are offered as reasons for other statements, does not require two speakers or writers who represent opposed positions. The Declaration of Independence is an argument, setting forth the colonists' reasons for declaring their independence. In practice, of course, someone's argument usually advances reasons in opposition to someone else's position or belief. But even if one is writing only for oneself, trying to clarify one's thinking by setting forth reasons, the result is an argument. In a **dispute,** however, two or more people express views that are at odds.

Most of this book is about argument in the sense of the presentation of reasons, but of course reason is not the whole story. If an argument is to be effective, it must be presented persuasively. For instance, the writer's **tone** (attitude toward self, topic, and audience) must be appropriate if the discourse is to persuade the reader. The careful presentation of the self is not something disreputable, nor is it something that publicity agents or advertising agencies invented. Aristotle (384–322 B.C.) emphasized the importance of impressing upon the audience that the speaker is a person of good sense and high moral character. (He called this aspect of persuasion **ethos,** the Greek word for "character," as opposed to *logos,* which we have noted is the word for persuasion by appealing to reason.) We will talk at length about tone, along with other matters such as the organization of an argument, in Chapter 5, but here we deal with some of the chief devices used in reasoning, and we will glance at emotional appeals.

We should note at once, however, that an argument presupposes a fixed **topic.** Suppose we are arguing about Jefferson's assertion, in the Declaration of Independence, that "all men are created equal." Jones subscribes to this statement, but Smith says it is nonsense and argues that one has only to look around to see that some people are brighter than others, or healthier, or better coordinated, or whatever. Jones and Smith, if they intend to argue the point, will do well to examine what Jefferson actually wrote.

> We hold these truths to be self-evident, that all men are created equal: that they are endowed by their Creator with certain unalienable rights; and that among these are life, liberty, and the pursuit of happiness.

There is room for debate over what Jefferson really meant, and about whether he is right, but clearly he was talking about *equality of rights,* and if Smith and Jones wish to argue about Jefferson's view of equality — that is, if they wish to offer their reasons for accepting, rejecting, or modifying it — they will do well first to agree on what Jefferson said or what he probably meant to say. Jones and Smith may still hold different views; they may continue to disagree on whether Jefferson was right, and proceed to offer arguments and counterarguments to settle the point. But only if they can agree on *what* they disagree about will their dispute get somewhere.

REASON VERSUS RATIONALIZATION

Reason may not be our only way of finding the truth, but it is a way we often rely on. The subway ran yesterday at 6:00 A.M. and the day before at 6:00 A.M. and the day before, and so I infer from this evidence that it is also running today at 6:00 A.M. (a form of reasoning known as **induction**). Or: Bus drivers require would-be passengers to present the exact change; I do not have the exact change; therefore I infer I cannot ride on the bus (**deduction**). (The terms *induction* and *deduction* will be discussed shortly.)

We also know that, if we set our minds to a problem, we can often find reasons (not necessarily sound ones, but reasons nevertheless) for almost anything we want to justify. Here is an entertaining example from Benjamin Franklin's *Autobiography:*

> I believe I have omitted mentioning that in my first voyage from Boston, being becalmed off Block Island, our people set about catching cod and hauled up a great many. Hitherto I had stuck to my resolution of not eating animal food, and on this occasion, I considered with my master Tryon the taking of every fish as a kind of unprovoked murder, since none of them had or ever could do us any injury that might justify the slaughter. All this seemed very reasonable. But I had formerly been a great lover of fish, and when this came hot out of the frying pan, it smelt admirably well. I balanced some time between principle and inclination, till I recollected that when the fish were opened I saw smaller fish taken out of their stomachs. Then thought I, if you eat one another, I don't see why we mayn't eat you. So I dined upon cod very heartily and continued to eat with other people, returning only now and then occasionally to a vegetable diet. So convenient a thing it is to be a *reasonable creature,* since it enables one to find or make a reason for everything one has a mind to do.

Franklin of course is being playful; he is *not* engaging in critical thinking. He tells us that he loved fish, that this fish "smelt admirably well," and so we are prepared for him to find a reason (here one as weak as "Fish eat fish, so people may eat fish") to abandon his vegetarianism. (But think: Fish also eat their own young. May we therefore eat ours?) Still, Franklin touches on a truth: If necessary, we can find reasons to justify whatever we want. That is, instead of reasoning we may *rationalize* (devise a self-serving but dishonest reason), like the fox in Aesop's fables who, finding the grapes he desired were out of his reach, consoled himself with the thought they were probably sour.

Probably we can never be certain that we are not rationalizing, but—except when, like Franklin, we are being playful—we can seek to think critically about our own beliefs, scrutinizing our assumptions, looking for counterevidence, and wondering if different conclusions can reasonably be drawn.

SOME PROCEDURES IN ARGUMENT

Definition

Definition, we mentioned in our first chapter, is one of the classical *topics*, a "place" to which one goes with questions; in answering the questions, one finds ideas. When we define, we are answering the question "What is it?," and in answering this question as precisely as we can, we will find, clarify, and develop ideas.

We have already glanced at an argument over the proposition that "all men are created equal," and we saw that the words needed clarification. *Equal* meant, in the context, not physically or mentally equal but something like "equal in rights," equal politically and legally. (And of course "men" meant "men and women.") Words do not always mean exactly what they seem to: There is no lead in a lead pencil, and a standard 2-by-4 is 1⅝ inches in thickness and 3⅜ inches in width.

Definition by Synonym   Let's return, for a moment, to *pornography,* a word that, we saw, is not easily defined. One way to define a word is to offer a **synonym.** Thus, pornography can be defined, at least roughly, as "obscenity" (something indecent). But definition by synonym is usually only a start, because we find that we will have to define the synonym and, besides, very few words have exact synonyms. (In fact, *pornography* and *obscenity* are not exact synonyms.)

Definition by Example   A second way to define something is to point to an example (this is often called **ostensive definition,** from the Latin *ostendere,* "to show"). This method can be very helpful, ensuring that both writer and reader are talking about the same thing, but it also has its limitations. A few decades ago many people pointed to James Joyce's *Ulysses* and D. H. Lawrence's *Lady Chatterley's Lover* as examples of obscene novels, but today these books are regarded as literary masterpieces. Possibly they can be obscene and also be literary masterpieces. (Joyce's wife is reported to have said of her husband, "He may have been a great writer, but . . . he had a very dirty mind.")

One of the difficulties of using an example, however, is that the example is richer, more complex than the term it is being used to define, and this richness and complexity get in the way of achieving a clear definition. Thus, if one cites Lawrence's *Lady Chatterley's Lover* as an example of pornography, a listener may erroneously think that pornography has something to do with British novels or with heterosexual relationships outside of marriage. Yet neither of these ideas is part of the concept of pornography.

We are not trying here to formulate a satisfactory definition of *pornography;* our object is to say that an argument will be most fruitful if the participants first agree on what they are talking about, and that one way to secure such agreement is to define the topic ostensively. Choosing the right example, one that has all the central or typical characteristics, can make a topic not only clear but vivid.

Definition by Stipulation   In arguing, you can legitimately offer a **stipulative definition,** saying, perhaps, that by *Native American* you mean any person with any Native American blood; or you might say, "For the purpose of the present discussion, I mean by a *Native American* any person who has at least one grandparent of pure Native American blood." A stipulative definition is appropriate where no fixed or standard definition is available and where some arbitrary specification is necessary in order to fix the meaning of a key term in the argument. Not everyone may be willing to accept your stipulative definition, and alternatives can probably be defended. In any case, when you stipulate a definition, your audience knows what *you* mean by the term thus defined.

Of course it would *not* be reasonable to stipulate that by *Native American* you mean anyone with a deep interest in North American aborigines. That's just too idiosyncratic to be useful. Similarly, an essay on Jews in America will have to rely on some definition of the key idea. Perhaps the writer will stipulate the definition used in Israel: A Jew is any person with a Jewish mother, or, if not born of a Jewish mother, a person who has formally adopted the Jewish faith. Or perhaps the writer will stipulate another meaning: Jews are people who consider themselves to be Jews. Some sort of reasonable definition must be offered.

To stipulate, however, that by *Jews* you mean "persons who believe that the area formerly called Palestine rightfully belongs to the Jews" would hopelessly confuse matters. Remember the old riddle and the answer: If you call a dog's tail a leg, how many legs does a dog have? Answer: Four. Calling a tail a leg doesn't make it a leg.

Suppose someone says she means by a *Communist* "anyone who opposes the president, does not go to church, and favors a more nearly equal distribution of wealth and property." A dictionary or encyclopedia will tell us that a person is a Communist who accepts the main doctrines of Karl Marx (or perhaps of Marxism-Leninism). For many purposes, we may think of Communists as persons who belong to some Communist political party, by analogy with Democrats and Republicans. Or we may even think of a Communist as someone who supports what is common to the constitutions and governments currently in power in China and Cuba. But what is the point of the misleading stipulative definition of *Communist* given at the beginning of this paragraph, except to cast disapproval on everyone whose views bring them within the definition?

There is no good reason for offering this definition, and there are two goods reasons against it. The first is that we already have perfectly adequate definitions of *Communist,* and one should learn them and rely on them until the need to revise and improve them occurs. The second reason for refraining from using a misleading stipulative definition is that it is unfair to tar with a dirty and sticky brush nonchurchgoers and the rest by calling them derogatory names they do not deserve. Even if it is true that Communists favor more egalitarian distribution of wealth and property, the converse is *not* true: Not all egalitarians are Communists. Furthermore, if something is economically unsound or morally objectionable about such egalitarianism, the only responsible way to make that point is to argue against it.

A stipulation may be helpful and legitimate. Here is the opening paragraph of an essay by Richard B. Brandt titled "The Morality and Rationality of Suicide." Notice that the author first stipulates a definition and then, aware that the definition may strike some readers as too broad and therefore unreasonable or odd, he offers a reason on behalf of his definition:

> "Suicide" is conveniently defined, for our purposes, as doing something which results in one's death, either from the intention of ending one's life or the intention to bring about some other state of affairs (such as relief from pain) which one thinks it certain or highly probable can be achieved only by means of death or will produce death. It may seem odd to classify an act of heroic self-sacrifice on the part of a soldier as suicide. It is simpler, however, not to try to define "suicide" so that an act of suicide is always irrational or immoral in some way; if we adopt a neutral definition like the above we can still proceed to ask when an act of suicide in that sense is rational, morally justifiable, and so on, so that all evaluations anyone might wish to make can still be made.
> — (*A Handbook for the Study of Suicide*, ed. Seymour Perlin)

Sometimes a definition that at first seems extremely odd can be made acceptable, if strong reasons are offered in its support. Sometimes, in fact, an odd definition marks a great intellectual step forward. For instance, recently the Supreme Court recognized that *speech* includes symbolic nonverbal expression such as protesting against a war by wearing armbands or by flying the American flag upside down. Such actions, because they express ideas or emotions, are now protected by the First Amendment. Few people today would disagree that *speech* should include symbolic gestures. (We include an example of controversy over precisely this issue, in Derek Bok's "Protecting Freedom of Expression on the Campus," in Chapter 2.)

An example that seems notably eccentric to many readers and thus far has not gained much support is from page 94 of *Practical Ethics*, in which Peter Singer suggests that a nonhuman being can be a *person*. He admits that "it sounds odd to call an animal a person," but says that it seems so only because of our bad habit of sharply separating ourselves from other species. For Singer, *persons* are "rational and self-conscious beings, aware of themselves as distinct entities with a past and a future." Thus, although a newborn infant is a human being, it is not a person; on the other hand, an adult chimpanzee is not a human being but probably is a person. You don't have to agree with Singer to know exactly what he means and where he stands. Moreover, if you read his essay you may even find that his reasons are plausible and that by means of his unusual definition he has enlarged your thinking.

The Importance of Definitions   Trying to decide on the best way to define a key idea or a central concept is often difficult as well as controversial. *Death,* for example, has been redefined in recent years. Traditionally, a person was dead when there was no longer any heartbeat. But with advancing medical technology, the medical profession has persuaded legislatures to redefine *death* by reference to cessation of cerebral and cortical functions — so-called brain death. Recently, some scholars have hoped to bring clarity into the abortion debate by redefining *life.*

Traditionally, human life begins at birth, or perhaps at viability (the capacity of a fetus to live independently of the uterine environment). Now, however, some are proposing a "brain birth" definition, in the hope of resolving the abortion controversy. A *New York Times* story of November 8, 1990, reported that these thinkers want abortion to be prohibited by law at the point where "integrated brain functioning begins to emerge — about seventy days after conception." Whatever the merits of such a redefinition, the debate is convincing evidence of just how important the definition of certain terms can be.

Last Words about Definition   Since Plato's time, in the fourth century B.C., it has often been argued that the best way to give a definition is to state the *essence* of the thing being defined. Thus, the classic example defines *man* as "a rational animal." (Today, to avoid sexist implications, instead of *man* we would say *human being* or *person*.) That is, the property of *rational animality* is taken to be the essence of every human creature, and so it must be mentioned in the definition of *man*. This statement guarantees that the definition is neither too broad nor too narrow. But philosophers have long criticized this alleged ideal type of definition, on several grounds, one of which is that no one can propose such definitions without assuming that the thing being defined has an essence in the first place — an assumption that is not necessary. Thus, we may want to define *causality*, or *explanation*, or even *definition* itself, but it is doubtful whether it is sound to assume that any of these things has an essence.

A much better way to provide a definition is to offer a set of **sufficient and necessary conditions.** Suppose we want to define the word *circle* and are conscious of the need to keep circles distinct from other geometrical figures such as rectangles and spheres. We might express our definition by citing sufficient and necessary conditions as follows: "Anything is a circle *if and only if* it is a closed plane figure, all points on the circumference of which are equidistant from the center." Using the connective "if and only if" (called the *biconditional*) between the definition and what is being defined helps to force into our consciousness the need to make the definition neither too exclusive (too narrow) nor too inclusive (too broad). Of course, for most ordinary purposes we don't require such a formally precise and explicit definition. Nevertheless, perhaps the best criterion to keep in mind when assessing a proposed definition is whether it can be stated in the "if and only if" form, and whether, if it is so stated, it is true; that is, if it truly specifies *all and only* the things covered by the word being defined.

Definitions can be given by

- synonym,
- example,
- stipulation,
- mentioning the essence, and
- stating necessary and sufficient conditions.

Assumptions

In Chapter 1 we discussed the **assumptions** made by the authors of two essays on campus discipline. But we have more to say about assumptions. We have already said that in the form of discourse known as argument, certain statements are offered as reasons for other statements. But even the longest and most complex chain of reasoning or proof is fastened to assumptions, one or more *unexamined beliefs.* (Even if such a belief is shared by writer and reader, it is no less an assumption.) Benjamin Franklin argued against paying salaries to the holders of executive offices in the federal government on the grounds that men are moved by ambition and by avarice (love of power and of money), and that powerful positions conferring wealth incite men to do their worst. These assumptions he stated, though he felt no need to argue them at length because he assumed that his readers shared them.

An assumption may be unstated. For example, Elizabeth Whelan in her essay on legal prohibition of teenage drinking (p. 83) assumes without explicitly saying so that no matter what the law may be, today's teenagers will consume alcohol and some will do so to excess. A writer, painstakingly arguing specific points, may choose to keep one or more of the assumptions tacit. Or the writer may be as unaware of some underlying assumption as of the surrounding air. For example, Franklin didn't even bother to state another assumption. He assumed that persons of wealth who accept an unpaying job (after all, only persons of wealth could afford to hold unpaid government jobs) will have at heart the interests of all classes of people, not only the interests of their own class. If you think critically about this assumption, you may find reasons to doubt it. Surely one reason we pay our legislators is to make certain that the legislature does not consist only of people whose incomes may give them an inadequate view of the needs of others.

An Example: Assumptions in the Argument Permitting Abortion

1. Ours is a pluralistic society, in which we believe that the religious beliefs of one group should not be imposed on others.

2. Personal privacy is a right, and a woman's body is hers, not to be violated by laws that tell her she may not do certain things to her body.

But these (and other) arguments *assume* that a fetus is not—or not yet—a person, and therefore is not entitled to the same protection against assaults that we are. Virtually all of us assume that it is usually wrong to kill a human being. Granted, we may find instances in which we believe it is acceptable to take a human life, such as self-defense against a would-be murderer. But even here we find a shared assumption, that persons are ordinarily entitled not to be killed.

The argument about abortion, then, usually depends on opposed assumptions: For one group, the fetus is a human being and a potential person—and this potentiality is decisive. But for the other group it is not. Persons arguing one side or the other of the abortion issue ought to be aware that opponents may not share their assumptions.

Premises and Syllogisms

Premises are stated assumptions used as reasons in an argument. (The word comes from a Latin word meaning "to send before," or "to set in front.") A premise thus is a statement set down—assumed—before the argument is begun. The joining of two premises—two statements taken to be true—to produce a conclusion, a third statement, is called a **syllogism** (Greek for "a reckoning together"). The classic example is this:

Major Premise: All human beings are mortal.

Minor Premise: Socrates is a human being.

Conclusion: Socrates is mortal.

Deduction

The mental process of moving from one statement ("All human beings are mortal") through another ("Socrates is a human being") to yet a further statement ("Socrates is mortal") is called **deduction,** from Latin for "lead down from." In this sense, deductive reasoning does not give us any new knowledge, although it is easy to construct examples that have so many premises, or premises that are so complex, that the conclusion really does come as news to most who examine the argument. Thus, the great detective Sherlock Holmes was credited by his admiring colleague, Dr. Watson, with unusual powers of deduction. Watson meant in part that Holmes could see the logical consequences of apparently disconnected reasons, the number and complexity of which left others at a loss. What is common in all cases of deduction is that the reasons or premises offered are supposed to contain within themselves, so to speak, the conclusion extracted from them.

Often a syllogism is abbreviated. Martin Luther King, Jr., defending a protest march, wrote, in "Letter from Birmingham Jail":

> You assert that our actions, even though peaceful, must be condemned because they precipitate violence.

Fully expressed, the argument that King attributes to his critics would be stated thus:

> We must condemn actions (even if peaceful) that precipitate violence.
>
> This action (though peaceful) will precipitate violence.
>
> Therefore we must condemn this action.

An incomplete or abbreviated syllogism in which one of the premises is left unstated, of the sort found in King's original quotation, is called an **enthymeme** (Greek for "in the mind").

Here is another, more whimsical example of an enthymeme, in which both a premise and the conclusion are left implicit. Henry David Thoreau is said to have remarked that "Circumstantial evidence can be very strong, as when you find a trout in the milk." The joke, perhaps intelligible only to people born before 1930 or so, depends on the fact that milk used to be sold "in bulk," that is, ladled out of a big can directly to the customer by the farmer or grocer. This practice was finally prohibited in the 1930s because for centuries the sellers, in order to increase their profit, were known to dilute the milk with water. Thoreau's enthymeme can be fully expressed thus:

> Trout live only in water.
>
> This milk has a trout in it.
>
> Therefore this milk has water in it.

Sound Arguments

The purpose of a syllogism is to *prove* its conclusion from its premises. This is done by making sure that the argument satisfies both of two independent criteria:

> First, all of the premises must be *true*.
>
> Second, the syllogism must be *valid*.

Once these criteria are satisfied, the conclusion of the syllogism is guaranteed. Any such argument is said to prove its conclusion, or, to use another term, is said to be **sound.** Here's an example of a sound argument, a syllogism that proves its conclusion:

> No city in Nevada has a population over 200,000.
>
> Denver has a population over 200,000.
>
> Therefore Denver is not a city in Nevada.

Each premise is **true,** and the syllogism is **valid,** so it proves its conclusion.

But how do we tell in any given case that an argument is sound? We perform two different tests, one for the truth of each of the premises and another for the validity of the argument.

The basic test for the **truth** of a premise is to determine whether what it asserts corresponds with reality; if it does, then it is true, and if it doesn't, then it is false. Everything depends on the content of the premise—what it asserts—and the evidence for it. (In the preceding syllogism, the truth of the premises can be tested by checking population statistics in a recent almanac.)

The test for **validity** is quite different. We define a valid argument as one in which the conclusion follows from the premises, so that if all the premises are true then the conclusion *must* be true, too. The general test for validity, then, is this: If one grants the premises, one must also grant the conclusion. Or to put it another way, if one grants the premises but denies the conclusion, is one caught in a self-contradiction? If so, the argument is valid; if not, the argument is invalid.

The preceding syllogism obviously passes this test. If you grant the population information given in the premises but deny the conclusion, you have contradicted yourself. Even if the population information were in error, the conclusion in this syllogism would still follow from the premises—the hallmark of a valid argument! The conclusion follows because the validity of an argument is a purely formal matter concerning the *relation* between premises and conclusion given what they mean.

One can see this relationship more clearly by examining an argument that is valid but that does *not* prove its conclusion. Here is an example of such a syllogism:

The whale is a large fish.

All large fish have scales.

Therefore whales have scales.

We know that the premises and the conclusion are false: Whales are mammals, not fish, and not all large fish have scales (sharks have no scales, for instance). But where the issue is the validity of the argument, the truth of the premises and the conclusion is beside the point. Just a little reflection assures us that *if* both of these premises were true, then the conclusion would have to be true as well. That is, anyone who grants the premises of this syllogism and yet denies the conclusion has contradicted herself. So the validity of an argument does not in any way depend on the truth of the premises or the conclusion.

A sound argument, as we said, is an argument that passes both the test of true premises and the test of valid inference. To put it another way, a sound argument is one that passes the test of *content* (the premises are true, as a matter of fact) and the test of *form* (its premises and conclusion, by virtue of their very meanings, are so related that it is impossible for the premises to be true and the conclusion false).

Accordingly, an unsound argument, an argument that fails to prove its conclusion, suffers from one or both of two defects. First, not all of the premises are true. Second, the argument is invalid. Usually it is one or both of these defects that we have in mind when we object to someone's argument as "illogical." In evaluating someone's deductive argument, therefore, you must always ask: Is it vulnerable to criticism on the ground that one (or more) of its premises is false? Or is the inference itself vulnerable, because whether or not all the premises are all true, even if they were the conclusion still wouldn't follow?

A deductive argument *proves* its conclusion if and only if *two conditions* are satisfied: (1) All the premises are *true;* (2) it would be *inconsistent to assert the premises and deny the conclusions.*

A Word about False Premises   Suppose that one or more of the premises of a syllogism is false, but the syllogism itself is valid. What does that tell us about the truth of the conclusion? Consider this example:

All Americans prefer vanilla ice cream to other flavors.

Tiger Woods is an American.

Therefore Tiger Woods prefers vanilla ice cream to other flavors.

The first (or major) premise in this syllogism is false. Yet the argument passes our formal test for validity; it is clear that if one grants both premises, one must accept the conclusion. So we can say that the conclusion *follows from* its premises, even though the premises *do not prove* the conclusion. This is not as paradoxical as it may sound. For all we know, the conclusion of this argument may in fact be true; Tiger Woods may indeed prefer vanilla ice cream, and the odds are that he does, because consumption statistics show that *most* (even if not all) Americans prefer vanilla. Nevertheless, if the conclusion in this syllogism is true, it is not because this argument proved it.

A Word about Invalid Syllogisms   Usually, one can detect a false premise in an argument, especially when the suspect premise appears in someone else's argument. A trickier business is the invalid syllogism. Consider this argument:

All crows are black.

This bird is black.

Therefore this bird is a crow.

Let's assume that both of the premises are true. What does this tell us about the truth of the conclusion? Nothing, because the argument is invalid. The *form* of the reasoning, the structure of the argument, is such that its premises (whether true or false) do not guarantee the conclusion. Even if both the premises were true, the conclusion might still be false.

In the preceding syllogism, the conclusion may well be true. It could be that the bird referred to in the second (minor) premise is a crow. But the conclusion might be false, because not only crows are black; ravens and blackbirds are also black. If the minor premise is asserted on the strength of observing a blackbird, then the conclusion surely is false: *This* bird is *not* a crow. So the argument is invalid, since as it stands it would lead us from true premises to accept a false conclusion.

How do we tell, in general and in particular cases, whether a syllogism is valid? As you know, chemists use litmus paper to enable them to tell instantly whether the liquid in a test tube is an acid or a base. Unfortunately, logic has no litmus test to tell us instantly whether an argument is valid or invalid. Logicians beginning with Aristotle have developed techniques that enable them to test any given argument, no matter how complex or subtle, to determine its validity. But the results of their labors cannot be expressed in a paragraph or even a few pages; not for nothing are semester-long courses devoted to teaching formal deductive logic. Apart from advising you to consult Chapter 8 ("A Logician's View"), all we can do here is repeat two basic points.

First, validity of deductive arguments is a matter of their *form* or *structure*. Even syllogisms like the one on Denver on page 59 come in a large variety of forms (256 different ones, to be precise), and only some of these forms are valid. Second, all valid deductive arguments (and only such arguments) pass this test: If one accepts all the premises, then one must accept the conclusion as well. Hence, if it is possible to accept the premises but reject the conclusion (without self-contradiction, of course), then the argument is invalid.

Let us exit from further discussion of this important but difficult subject on a lighter note. Many illogical arguments masquerade as logical. Consider this example: If it takes a horse and carriage four hours to go from Pinsk to Chelm, does it follow that if you have a carriage with two horses you will get there in two hours? In Chapter 8, we discuss at some length other kinds of deductive arguments, as well as **fallacies,** which are kinds of invalid reasoning.

Induction

Whereas the purpose of deduction is to extract the hidden consequences of our beliefs and assumptions, the purpose of **induction** is to use information about observed cases in order to reach a conclusion about unobserved cases. (The word comes from Latin *in ducere,* "to lead into," or "to lead up to.") If we observe that the bite of a certain snake is poisonous, we may conclude on this evidence that another snake of the same general type is also poisonous. Our inference might be even broader. If we observe that snake after snake of a certain type has a poisonous bite, and that these snakes are all rattlesnakes, we are tempted to **generalize** that all rattlesnakes are poisonous.

By far the most common way to test the adequacy of a generalization is to confront it with one or more **counterexamples.** If the counterexamples are genuine and reliable, then the generalization must be false. For example, Ronald Takaki's essay on the "myth" of Asian racial superiority (p. 77) is full of examples that contradict the alleged superiority of Asians; they are counterexamples to that thesis and they help to expose it as a "myth." What is true of Takaki's reasoning is true generally in argumentative writing. We are constantly testing our generalizations against actual or possible counterexamples.

Unlike deduction, induction gives us conclusions that go beyond the information contained in the premises used in their support. Not surprisingly, the conclusions of inductive reasoning are not always true, even when all the premises are true. On page 57 we gave as an example the belief that the subway runs at 6:00 A.M. every day, based on our observation that on previous days it ran at 6:00 A.M. Suppose, following this reasoning, one arrives at the subway platform just before 6:00 A.M. on a given day only to discover after an hour of waiting that there still is no train. What inference should we draw to explain this? Possibly today is Sunday, and the subway doesn't run before 7:00 A.M. Or possibly there was a breakdown earlier this morning. Whatever the explanation, we relied on a sample that was not large enough (a larger sample might have included some early morning breakdowns), or not representative enough (a more representative sample would have included the later starts on holidays).

A Word about Samples   When we reason inductively, much depends on the size and the quality of the sample. We may interview five members of Alpha Tau Omega and find that all five are Republicans, yet we cannot legitimately conclude that all members of ATO are Republicans. The problem is not always one of failing to interview large numbers. A poll of ten thousand college students tells us very little about "college students" if all ten thousand are white males at the University of Texas. Such a sample, because it leaves out women and minority males, obviously is not sufficiently *representative* of "college students" as a group. Further, though not all of the students at the University of Texas are from Texas, or even from the Southwest, it is quite likely that the student body is not fully representative (for instance, in race and in income) of American college students. If this conjecture is correct, even a truly representative sample of University of Texas students would not allow one to draw firm conclusions about American college students.

In short: An argument that uses samples ought to tell the reader how the samples were chosen. If it does not provide this information, it may rightly be treated with suspicion.

Evidence

Induction is obviously of use in arguing. If, for example, one is arguing that handguns should be controlled, one will point to specific cases in which handguns caused accidents, or were used to commit crimes. If one is arguing that abortion has a traumatic effect on women, one will point to women who testify to that effect. Each instance constitutes **evidence** for the relevant generalization.

In a courtroom, evidence bearing on the guilt of the accused is introduced by the prosecution, and evidence to the contrary is introduced by the defense. Not all evidence is admissible (hearsay, for one, is not, even if it is true), and the law of evidence is a highly developed subject in jurisprudence. In the forum of daily life, the sources of evidence are less disciplined. Daily experience, a particularly memorable observation, an unusual event we witnessed—any or all of these may be used as evidence for (or against) some belief, theory, hypothesis, or explanation. The systematic study of what experience can yield is what science does, and one of the most distinctive features of the evidence that scientists can marshal on behalf of their claims is that it is the result of **experimentation.** Experiments are deliberately contrived situations, often quite complex in their technology, designed to yield particular observations. What the ordinary person does with unaided eye and ear, the scientist does, much more carefully and thoroughly, with the help of laboratory instruments.

The variety, extent, and reliability of the evidence obtained in daily life and in the laboratory are quite different. It is hardly a surprise that in our civilization, much more weight is attached to the "findings" of scientists than to the corroborative (much less the contrary) experiences of the ordinary person. No one today would seriously argue that the sun really does go around the earth, just because it looks that way; nor would we argue that because viruses are invisible to the naked eye they cannot cause symptoms such as swellings and fevers, which are quite plainly visible.

Examples

One form of evidence is the **example.** Suppose that we argue that a candidate is untrustworthy and should not be elected to public office. We point to episodes in his career—his misuse of funds in 1994, and the false charges he made against an opponent in 1997—as examples of his untrustworthiness. Or, if we are arguing that President Truman ordered the atom bomb dropped to save American (and, for that matter, Japanese) lives that otherwise would have been lost in a hard-fought invasion of Japan, we point to the stubbornness of the Japanese defenders in battles on the islands of Saipan, Iwo Jima, and Okinawa, where the Japanese fought to the death rather than surrender.

These examples, we say, show us that the Japanese defenders of the main islands would have fought to the end, even though they knew they would be defeated. Or, if we take a different view of Truman's action and argue that the war in effect was already won and that Truman had no justification for dropping the bomb, we can cite examples of the Japanese willingness to end the war, such as secret negotiations in which they sent out peace feelers.

An example is a sample; the two words come from the same Old French word, *essample*, from the Latin *exemplum*, which means "something taken out," that is, a selection from the group. A Yiddish proverb shrewdly says that "'For example' is no proof," but the evidence of well-chosen examples can go a long way toward helping a writer to convince an audience.

In arguments, three sorts of examples are especially common:

1. real events,
2. invented instances (artificial or hypothetical cases), and
3. analogies.

We will treat each of these briefly.

Real Events   In referring to Truman's decision to drop the atom bomb, we have already touched on examples drawn from real events, the battles at Saipan and elsewhere. And we have also seen Ben Franklin pointing to an allegedly real happening, a fish that had consumed a smaller fish. The advantage of an example drawn from real life, whether a great historical event or a local incident, is that its reality gives it weight. It can't simply be brushed off.

On the other hand, an example drawn from reality may not provide as clear-cut an instance as could be wished for. Suppose, for instance, that someone cites the Japanese army's behavior on Saipan and on Iwo Jima as evidence that the Japanese later would have fought to the death in an American invasion of Japan, and would therefore have inflicted terrible losses on themselves and on the Americans. This example is open to the response that in August 1945, when Truman dropped the bomb, the situation was very different. In June and July 1945, Japanese diplomats had already sent out secret peace feelers; Emperor Hirohito probably wanted peace by then; and so on.

Similarly, in support of the argument that nations will not resort to atomic weapons, some people have offered as evidence the fact that since World War I the great powers have not used poison gas. But the argument needs more support than this fact provides. Poison gas was not decisive or even highly effective in World War I. Moreover, the invention of gas masks made it obsolete.

In short, any *real* event is, so to speak, so entangled in its historical circumstances that one may question whether indeed it is adequate or even relevant evidence in the case being argued. In using a real event as an example (and real events certainly can be used), the writer ordinarily must demonstrate that the event can be taken out of its historical context and be used in the new context of argument. Thus, in an argument against any further use in warfare of atomic weapons, one might point to the example of the many deaths and horrible injuries inflicted on the Japanese at Hiroshima and Nagasaki, in the confident belief that these effects of nuclear weapons will invariably occur and did not depend on any special circumstances of their use in Japan in 1945.

Invented Instances   **Artificial** or **hypothetical cases, invented instances,** have the great advantage of being protected from objections of the sort just given. Recall Thoreau's trout in the milk; that was a colorful hypothetical case that nicely illustrated his point. An invented instance ("Let's assume that a burglar promises not to shoot a householder if the householder swears not to identify him. Is the householder bound by the oath?") is something like a drawing of a flower in a botany textbook, or a diagram of the folds of a mountain in a geology textbook. It is admittedly false, but by virtue of its simplifications it sets forth the relevant details very clearly. Thus, in a discussion of rights, the philosopher Charles Frankel says:

> Strictly speaking, when we assert a right for X, we assert that Y has a duty. Strictly speaking, that Y has such a duty presupposes that Y has the capacity to perform this duty. It would be nonsense to say, for example, that a nonswimmer has a moral duty to swim to the help of a drowning man.

This invented example is admirably clear, and it is immune to charges that might muddy the issue if Frankel, instead of referring to a wholly abstract person, Y, talked about some real person, Jones, who did not rescue a drowning man. For then he would get bogged down over arguing about whether Jones *really* couldn't swim well enough to help, and so on.

Yet invented cases have their drawbacks. First and foremost, they cannot be used as evidence. A purely hypothetical example can illustrate a point or provoke reconsideration of a generalization, but it cannot substitute for actual events as evidence supporting an inductive inference. Sometimes such examples are so fanciful, so remote from life that they fail to carry conviction with the reader. Thus the philosopher Judith Jarvis Thomson, in the course of an argument entitled "A Defense of Abortion," asks us to imagine that we wake up one day and find that against our will a celebrated violinist whose body is not adequately functioning has been hooked up into our body, for life-support. Do we have the right to unplug the violinist? Readers of the essays in this book will have to decide for themselves whether the invented cases proposed by various authors are helpful or whether they are so remote that they hinder thought. Readers will have to decide, too, about when they can use invented cases to advance their own arguments.

But we add one point: Even a highly fanciful invented case can have the valuable effect of forcing us to see where we stand. We may say that we are, in all circumstances, against vivisection. But what would we say if we thought that an experiment on one mouse would save the life of someone we love? Or, conversely, if one approves of vivisection, would one also approve of sacrificing the last giant panda in order to save the life of a senile stranger, a person who in any case probably would not live longer than another year? Artificial cases of this sort can help us to see that, well, no, we didn't really mean to say such-and-such when we said so-and-so.

Analogies   The third sort of example, **analogy,** is a kind of comparison. Strictly, an analogy is an extended comparison in which different things are shown to be similar in several ways. Thus, if one wants to argue that a head of state should have extraordinary power during wartime, one can argue that the state at such a time is like a ship in a storm: The crew is needed to lend its help, but the decisions are best left to the captain. (Notice that an analogy compares things that are relatively *un*like. Comparing the plight of one ship to another, or of one government to another, is not an analogy; it is an inductive inference from one case of the same sort to another such case.) Or take another analogy: We have already glanced at Judith Thomson's hypothetical case in which the reader wakes up to find himself or herself hooked up to a violinist. Thomson uses this situation as an analogy in an argument about abortion. The reader stands for the mother, the violinist for the unwanted fetus. Whether this analogy is close enough to pregnancy to help illuminate our thinking about abortion is something that you may want to think about.

The problem with argument by analogy is this: Two admittedly different things are agreed to be similar in several ways, and the arguer goes on to assert or imply that they are also similar in the point that is being argued. (That is why Thomson argues that if something is true of the reader-hooked-up-to-a-violinist, it is also true of the pregnant mother-hooked-up-to-a-fetus.) But of course despite some similarities, the two things which are said to be analogous and which are indeed similar in characteristics A, B, and C, are also different, let's say in characteristics D and E. As Bishop Butler said, about two hundred fifty years ago, "Everything is what it is, and not another thing."

Analogies can be convincing, especially because they can make complex issues simple ("Don't change horses in midstream" of course is not a statement about riding horses across a river, but about choosing leaders in critical times). Still, in the end, analogies can prove nothing. What may be true about riding horses across a stream need not be true about choosing leaders in troubled times, or not true about a given change of leadership. Riding horses across a stream and choosing leaders are, at bottom, different things, and however much these activities may be said to resemble one another, they remain different, and what is true for one need not be true for the other.

Analogies can be helpful in developing our thoughts. It is sometimes argued, for instance — on the analogy of the doctor-patient or the lawyer-client or the priest-penitent relationship — that newspaper and television reporters should not be required to reveal their confidential sources. That is worth thinking about: Do the similarities run deep enough, or are there fundamental differences? Or take another example: Some writers who support abortion argue that the fetus is not a person any more than the acorn is an oak. That is also worth thinking about. But one should also think about this response: A fetus is not a person, just as an acorn is not an oak, but an acorn is a potential oak, and a fetus is a potential person, a potential adult human being. Children, even newborn infants, have rights, and one way to explain this claim is to call attention to their potentiality to become mature adults. And so some people argue that the fetus, by analogy, has the rights of an infant, for the fetus, like the infant, is a potential adult.

While we're on this subject let's consider a very brief comparison made by Jill Knight, a member of the British Parliament, speaking about abortion:

> Babies are not like bad teeth, to be jerked out because they cause suffering.

Her point is effectively put; it remains for the reader to decide whether or not fetuses are *babies;* and, second, if a fetus is not a baby, *why* it can or can't be treated like a bad tooth. And yet a further bit of analogical reasoning, again about abortion: Thomas Sowell, an economist at the Hoover Institute, grants that women have a legal right to abortion, but he objects to the government's paying for abortions:

> Because the courts have ruled that women have a legal right to an abortion, some people have jumped to the conclusion that the government has to pay for it. You have a constitutional right to privacy, but the government has no obligation to pay for your window shades. . . . (*Pink and Brown People,* p. 57)

We leave it to the reader to decide if the analogy is compelling — that is, if the points of resemblance are sufficiently significant to allow one to conclude that what is true of people wanting window shades should be true of people wanting abortions.

Authoritative Testimony

Another form of evidence is **testimony,** the citation or quotation of authorities. In daily life we rely heavily on authorities of all sorts: We get a doctor's opinion about our health, we read a book because an intelligent friend recommends it, we see a movie because a critic gave it a good review, and we pay at least a little attention to the weather forecaster.

In setting forth an argument, one often tries to show that one's view is supported by notable figures, perhaps Jefferson, Lincoln, and Martin Luther King, Jr., or scientists who won the Nobel Prize. You may recall that in the second chapter, in talking about definitions of pornography, we referred to Kenneth Clark. To make certain that you were impressed by his testimony even if you had never heard of him, we described him as "probably the most influential English-speaking art critic of our century." But heed some words of caution:

- Be sure that the authority, however notable, is an authority on the topic in question (a well-known biologist on vitamins, yes, but not on the justice of a war).

- Be sure the authority is not biascd. A chcmist employed by the tobacco industry isn't likely to admit that smoking may be harmful, and a "director of publications" (that means a press agent) for a hockey team isn't likely to admit that watching or even playing ice hockey stimulates violence.

- Beware of nameless authorities: "a thousand doctors," "leading educators," "researchers at a major medical school."

- Be careful in using authorities who indeed were great authorities in their day but who now may be out of date (Adam Smith on economics, Julius Caesar on the art of war, Louis Pasteur on medicine).

- Cite authorities whose opinions your readers will value. William F. Buckley's opinion means a good deal to readers of *The National Review* but not to most feminists. Gloria Steinem's opinion carries weight with many feminists but not much with persons who support traditional family values. If you are writing for the general reader, your usual audience, cite authorities who are likely to be accepted by the general reader.

One other point: *You* may be an authority. You probably aren't nationally known, but on some topics you perhaps can speak with authority, the authority of personal experience. You may have been injured on a motorcycle while riding without wearing a helmet, or you may have escaped injury because you wore a helmet; you may have dropped out of school and then returned; you may have tutored a student whose native language is not English, or you may be such a student and you may have received tutoring. You may have attended a school with a bilingual education program. Your personal testimony on topics relating to these issues may be invaluable, and a reader will probably consider it seriously.

Statistics

The last sort of evidence we will discuss here is quantitative or statistical. The maxim More Is Better captures a basic idea of quantitative evidence. Because we know that 90 percent is greater than 75 percent, we are usually ready to grant that any claim supported by experience in 90 percent of the cases is more likely to be true than an alternative claim supported by experience only 75 percent of the time. The greater the difference, the greater our confidence. Consider an example. Honors at graduation from college are often computed on a student's cumulative grade-point average (GPA). The undisputed assumption is that the nearer a student's GPA is to a perfect record (4.0), the better scholar he or she is, and therefore the more deserving of highest honors. Consequently, a student with a GPA of 3.9 at the end of her senior year is a stronger candidate for graduating summa cum laude than another student with a GPA of 3.6. When faculty members on the honors committee argue over the relative academic merits of graduating seniors, we know that these quantitative, statistical differences in student GPAs will be the basic (even if not the only) kind of evidence under discussion.

Graphs, Tables, Numbers   Statistical information can be marshaled and presented in many forms, but it tends to fall into two main types: the graphic and the numerical. Graphs, tables, and pie charts are familiar ways of presenting quantitative data in an eye-catching manner. To prepare the graphics, however, one first has to get the numbers themselves under control, and for many purposes (such as writing argumentative essays) it is probably more convenient simply to stick with the numbers themselves.

But should the numbers be presented in percentages, or in fractions? Should one report, say, that the federal budget underwent a twofold increase over the decade, or that it increased by 100 percent, or that it doubled, or that the budget at the beginning of the decade was one-half what it was at the end? Taken strictly, these are equivalent ways of saying the same thing. Choice among them, therefore, in an example like this perhaps will rest on whether one's aim is to dramatize the increase (a 100 percent increase looks larger than a doubling) or to play down the size of the increase.

Thinking about Statistical Evidence   Statistics often get a bad name because it is so easy to misuse them, unintentionally or not, and so difficult to be sure that they have been correctly gathered in the first place. (We remind you of the old saw "There are lies, damned lies, and statistics.") Every branch of social science and natural science needs statistical information, and countless decisions in public and private life are based on quantitative data in statistical form. It is extremely important, therefore, to be sensitive to the sources and reliability of the statistics, and to develop a healthy skepticism when confronted with statistics whose parentage is not fully explained.

Consider, for instance, statistics that kept popping up during the baseball strike of 1994. The owners of the clubs said that the average salary of a major-league player was $1.2 million. (The **average** in this case is the result of dividing the total number of salary dollars by the number of players.) The players' union, however, did not talk about the average; rather, the union talked about the **median,** which was less than half of the average, a mere $500,000. (The *median* is the middle value in a distribution. Thus, of the 746 players, 363 earned less than $500,000, 361 earned more, and 22 earned exactly $500,000.) The union said, correctly, that *most* players earned a good deal less than the $1.2 million figure that the owners kept citing; but the $1.2 million average sounded more impressive to the general public, and that is the figure that the guy in the street mentioned when asked for an opinion about the strike.

Here is a more complicated example of the difficulty of interpreting statistics. Violent crime increased in the 1960s and early 1970s, then leveled off, and began to decline in 1981. Did America become more violent for a while, and then become more law-abiding? Bruce Jackson in *Law and Disorder* suggests that much of the rise in the 1960s was due to the baby boom of 1948 to 1952. Whereas in 1960 the United States had only about 11 million people aged twenty to twenty-four, by 1972 it had almost 18 million of them, and it is people in this age group who are most likely to commit violent crimes. The decline in the rate of violent crime in the 1980s was accompanied by a decline in the proportion of the population in this age group—though of course some politicians and law enforcement officers took credit for the reduction in violent crime.

One other example may help to indicate the difficulties of interpreting statistics. According to the San Francisco police department, in 1990 the city received 1,074 citizen complaints against the police. Los Angeles received only half as many complaints in the same period, and Los Angeles has five times the population of San Francisco. Does this mean that the police of San Francisco are much rougher than the police of Los Angeles? Possibly. But some specialists who have studied the statistics not only for these two cities but also for many other cities have concluded that a department with proportionately more complaints against it is not necessarily more abusive than a department with fewer complaints. According to these experts, the more confidence that the citizens have in their police force, the more the citizens will complain about police misconduct. The relatively small number of complaints against the Los Angeles police department thus may indicate that the citizens of Los Angeles are so intimidated and have so little confidence in the system that they do not bother to complain.

We are not suggesting, of course, that everyone who uses statistics is trying to deceive, or even that many who use statistics are unconsciously deceived by them. We mean only to suggest that statistics are open to widely different interpretations and that often those columns of numbers, so precise with their decimal points, are in fact imprecise and possibly even worthless because they may be based on insufficient or biased samples.

A CHECKLIST FOR EVALUATING STATISTICAL EVIDENCE

Regard statistical evidence (like all other evidence) cautiously, and don't accept it until you have thought about these questions:

✓ Was it compiled by a disinterested source? Of course, the name of the source does not always reveal its particular angle (for example, People for the American Way), but sometimes the name lets you know what to expect (National Rifle Association, American Civil Liberties Union).

✓ Is it based on an adequate sample? (A study pointed out that criminals have an average IQ of 91 to 93, whereas the general population has an IQ of 100. The conclusion drawn was that criminals have a lower IQ than the general population. This reading may be accurate, but some doubts have been expressed. For instance, because the entire sample of criminals consisted only of *convicted* criminals, this sample may be biased; possibly the criminals with higher IQs have enough intelligence not to get caught. Or, if they are caught, they are smart enough to hire better lawyers.)

✓ Is the statistical evidence recent enough to be relevant?

✓ How many of the factors likely to be relevant were identified and measured?

✓ Are the figures open to a different and equally plausible interpretation? (Remember the decline in violent crime, for which law enforcement officers took credit.)

Quiz

What is wrong with the following statistical proof that children do not have time for school?

One-third of the time they are sleeping (about 122 days);

One-eighth of the time they are eating (three hours a day, totaling 45 days);

One-fourth of the time is taken up by summer and other vacations (91 days);

Two-sevenths of the year is weekends (104 days).

Total: 362 days—so how can a kid have time for school?

SATIRE, IRONY, SARCASM

In talking about definition, deduction, and evidence, we have been talking about means of rational persuasion. But, as mentioned earlier, there are also other means of persuasion. Take force, for example. If X kicks Y, threatens to destroy Y's means of livelihood, or threatens Y's life, X may persuade Y to cooperate. As Al Capone noted, "You can get more out of people with a gun and a kind word than with just a kind word." One form of irrational but sometimes highly effective persuasion is **satire**—that is, witty ridicule. A cartoonist may persuade viewers that a politician's views are unsound by caricaturing (and thus ridiculing) the politician's appearance, or by presenting a grotesquely distorted (funny, but unfair) picture of the issue.

Satiric artists often use caricature; satiric writers, also seeking to persuade by means of ridicule, often use **verbal irony.** In irony of this sort there is a contrast between what is said and what is meant. For instance, words of praise may be meant to imply blame (when Shakespeare's Cassius says, "Brutus is an honorable man," he means his hearers to think that Brutus is dishonorable), and words of modesty may be meant to imply superiority ("Of course I'm too dumb to understand this problem"). Such language, when heavy-handed, is called **sarcasm** ("You're a great guy," said to someone who will not lend the speaker ten dollars). If it is witty—if the jeering is in some degree clever—it is called irony rather than sarcasm.

Although ridicule is not a form of argument (because it is not a form of reasoning), passages of ridicule, especially verbal irony, sometimes appear in essays that are arguments. These passages, like reasons, or for that matter like appeals to the emotions, are efforts to persuade the hearer to accept the speaker's point of view. For example, in Judy Brady's essay "I Want a Wife" (p. 91), the writer, a woman, cannot really mean that she wants a wife. The pretense that she wants a wife gives the essay a playful, joking quality; her words must mean something other than what they seem to mean. But that she is not merely joking (satire has been defined as "joking in earnest") is evident; she is seeking to persuade. She has a point, and she could argue it straight, but that would produce a very different sort of essay.

EMOTIONAL APPEALS

It is sometimes said that good argumentative writing appeals only to reason, never to emotion, and that any sort of emotional appeal is illegitimate, irrelevant. Logic textbooks may even stigmatize with Latin labels the various sorts of emotional appeal, for instance *argumentum ad populam* (appeal to the prejudices of the mob, as in "Come on, we all know that schools don't teach anything anymore"), and *argumentum ad miseri-cordiam* (appeal to pity, as in "No one can blame this poor kid for stabbing a classmate because his mother was often institutionalized for alcoholism and his father beat him").

True, appeals to emotion may get in the way of the facts of the case; they may blind the audience by, in effect, throwing dust in its eyes or by stimulating tears. A classic example is found in Shakespeare's *Julius Caesar*, when Marc Antony addresses the Roman populace after Brutus, Cassius, and others have assassinated Caesar. The real issue is whether Caesar was becoming tyrannical (as the assassins claim) and would therefore curtail the freedom of the people. Antony turns from the evidence and stirs the mob against the assassins by appealing to its emotions. In the ancient Roman biographical writing that Shakespeare drew on, Sir Thomas North's translation of Plutarch's *Lives of the Noble Grecians and Romans*, Plutarch says that Antony,

> perceiving that his words moved the common people to compassion, . . . framed his eloquence to make their hearts yearn [that is, grieve] the more, and, taking Caesar's gown all bloody in his hand, he laid it open to the sight of them all, showing what a number of cuts and holes it had upon it. Therewithal the people fell presently into such a rage and mutiny that there was no more order kept.

Here are a few extracts from Antony's speeches in Shakespeare's play. Antony begins by asserting that he will speak only briefly:

> Friends, Romans, countrymen, lend me your ears;
> I come to bury Caesar, not to praise him.

After briefly offering some rather insubstantial evidence that Caesar gave no signs of behaving tyrannically (for example, "When that the poor have cried, Caesar hath wept"), Antony begins to play directly on the emotions of his hearers. Descending from the platform so that he may be in closer contact with his audience (like a modern politician, he wants to work the crowd), he calls attention to Caesar's bloody toga:

> If you have tears, prepare to shed them now.
> You all do know this mantle; I remember
> The first time ever Caesar put it on:
> 'Twas on a summer's evening, in his tent,
> That day he overcame the Nervii.
> Look, in this place ran Cassius' dagger through;
> See what a rent the envious Casca made;
> Through this, the well-belovèd Brutus stabbed. . . .

In these few lines Antony first prepares the audience by suggesting to them how they should respond ("If you have tears, prepare to shed them now"), then flatters them by implying that they, like Antony, were intimates of Caesar (he credits them with being familiar with Caesar's garment), then evokes a personal memory of a specific time ("a summer's evening") — not just any old specific time, but a very important one, the day that Caesar won a battle against the Nervii (a particularly fierce tribe in what is now France). In fact, Antony was *not* at the battle, and he did not join Caesar until three years later, but Antony does not mind being free with the facts. His point here is not to set the record straight; rather, it is to stir the mob against the assassins. He goes on, daringly but successfully, to identify one particular slit in the garment with Cassius's dagger, another with Casca's, and a third with Brutus's. Antony of course cannot know which slit was made by which dagger, but his rhetorical trick works. Notice, too, that he arranges the three assassins in climactic order, since Brutus (Antony claims) was especially beloved by Caesar.

> Judge, O you gods, how dearly Caesar loved him!
> This was the most unkindest cut of all;
> For when the noble Caesar saw him stab,
> Ingratitude, more strong than traitor's arms,
> Quite vanquished him. Then burst his mighty heart. . . . (3.2.75–188)

Nice. According to Antony, the noble-minded Caesar — Antony's words have erased all thought of the tyrannical Caesar — died not from the wounds inflicted by daggers but from the heartbreaking perception of Brutus's ingratitude. Doubtless there was not a dry eye in the house. We can all hope that if we are ever put on trial, we have a lawyer as skilled in evoking sympathy as Antony.

The oration is obviously successful in the play and apparently was successful in real life, but it is the sort of speech that prompts logicians to write disapprovingly of attempts to stir feeling in an audience. (As mentioned earlier in this chapter, the evocation of emotion in an audience is called **pathos,** from the Greek word for emotion or suffering.) There is nothing inherently wrong in stimulating our audience's emotions, but when an emotional appeal confuses the issue that is being argued about or shifts the attention away from the facts of the issue, we can reasonably speak of the fallacy of emotional appeal.

No fallacy is involved, however, when an emotional appeal heightens the facts, bringing them home to the audience rather than masking them. If we are talking about legislation that would govern police actions, it is legitimate to show a photograph of the battered, bloodied face of an alleged victim of police brutality. Of course, such a photograph cannot tell the whole truth; it cannot tell us if the subject threatened the officer with a gun or repeatedly resisted an order to surrender. But it can tell us that the victim was severely beaten and (like a comparable description in words) evoke in us emotions that may properly enter into our decision about what sorts of limitations are appropriate. Similarly, an animal rights activist who is arguing that calves are cruelly confined might reasonably tell us about the size of the pen in which the beast—

unable to turn around or even to lie down — is kept. Others may argue that calves don't much care about turning around or have no right to turn around, but the verbal description, which unquestionably makes an emotional appeal, can hardly be called fallacious or irrelevant.

In appealing to emotions then, the important things are

- not to falsify (especially by oversimplifying) the issue, and
- not to distract attention from the facts of the case.

Focus on the facts and concentrate on offering reasons (essentially, statements linked with "because"), but you may also legitimately bring the facts home to your readers by seeking to induce in them the appropriate emotions. Your words will be fallacious only if you stimulate emotions that are not rightly connected with the facts of the case.

**A CHECKLIST FOR ANALYZING
AN ARGUMENT**

✓ What is the writer's thesis? Ask yourself:

  ✓ What claim is being asserted?

  ✓ What assumptions are being made — and are they acceptable?

  ✓ Are important terms satisfactorily defined?

✓ What support is offered on behalf of the claim? Ask yourself:

  ✓ Are the examples relevant, and are they convincing?

  ✓ Are the statistics (if there are any) relevant, accurate, and complete? Do they allow only the interpretation that is offered in the argument?

  ✓ If authorities are cited, are they indeed authorities on this topic, and can they be regarded as impartial?

  ✓ Is this logic — deductive and inductive — valid?

  ✓ If there is an appeal to emotion — for instance, if satire is used to ridicule the opposing view — is this appeal acceptable?

✓ Does the writer seem to you to be fair? Ask yourself:

  ✓ Are counterarguments adequately considered?

  ✓ Is there any evidence of dishonesty or of a discreditable attempt to manipulate the reader?

ARGUMENTS FOR ANALYSIS

Ronald Takaki

Ronald Takaki, the grandson of agricultural laborers who had come from Japan, is professor of ethnic studies at the University of California at Berkeley. He is the editor of From Different Shores: Perspectives on Race and Ethnicity in America *(1987), and the author of (among other writings)* Strangers from a Different Shore: A History of Asian-Americans *(1989). The essay that we reprint appeared originally in the* New York Times, *June 16, 1990, page 21.*

The Harmful Myth of Asian Superiority

Asian Americans have increasingly come to be viewed as a "model minority." But are they as successful as claimed? And for whom are they supposed to be a model?

Asian Americans have been described in the media as "excessively, even provocatively" successful in gaining admission to universities. Asian American shopkeepers have been congratulated, as well as criticized, for their ubiquity and entrepreneurial effectiveness.

If Asian Americans can make it, many politicians and pundits ask, why can't African Americans? Such comparisons pit minorities against each other and generate African American resentment toward Asian Americans. The victims are blamed for their plight, rather than racism and an economy that has made many young African American workers superfluous.

The celebration of Asian Americans has obscured reality. For example, figures on the high earnings of Asian Americans relative to Caucasians are misleading. Most Asian Americans live in California, Hawaii, and New York—states with higher incomes and higher costs of living than the national average.

Even Japanese Americans, often touted for their upward mobility, have not reached equality. While Japanese American men in California earned an average income comparable to Caucasian men in 1980, they did so only by acquiring more education and working more hours.

Comparing family incomes is even more deceptive. Some Asian American groups do have higher family incomes than Caucasians. But they have more workers per family.

The "model minority" image homogenizes Asian Americans and hides their differences. For example, while thousands of Vietnamese American young people attend universities, others are on the streets. They live in motels and hang out in pool halls in places like East Los Angeles; some join gangs.

Twenty-five percent of the people in New York City's Chinatown lived below the poverty level in 1980, compared with 17 percent of the city's population. Some 60 percent of the workers in the Chinatowns of Los Angeles and San Francisco are crowded into low-paying jobs in garment factories and restaurants.

"Most immigrants coming into Chinatown with a language barrier cannot go outside this confined area into the mainstream of American industry," a Chinese immigrant said. "Before, I was a painter in Hong Kong, but I can't do it here. I got no license, no education. I want a living; so it's dishwasher, janitor, or cook."

Hmong and Mien refugees from Laos have unemployment rates that 10 reach as high as 80 percent. A 1987 California study showed that three out of ten Southeast Asian refugee families had been on welfare for four to ten years.

Although college-educated Asian Americans are entering the professions and earning good salaries, many hit the "glass ceiling"—the barrier through which high management positions can be seen but not reached. In 1988, only 8 percent of Asian Americans were "officials" and "managers," compared with 12 percent for all groups.

Finally, the triumph of Korean immigrants has been exaggerated. In 1988, Koreans in the New York metropolitan area earned only 68 percent of the median income of non-Asians. More than three-quarters of Korean greengrocers, those so-called paragons of bootstrap entrepreneurialism, came to America with a college education. Engineers, teachers, or administrators while in Korea, they became shopkeepers after their arrival. For many of them, the greengrocery represents dashed dreams, a step downward in status.

For all their hard work and long hours, most Korean shopkeepers do not actually earn very much: $17,000 to $35,000 a year, usually representing the income from the labor of an entire family.

But most Korean immigrants do not become shopkeepers. Instead, many find themselves trapped as clerks in grocery stores, service workers in restaurants, seamstresses in garment factories, and janitors in hotels.

Most Asian Americans know their "success" is largely a myth. They 15 also see how the celebration of Asian Americans as a "model minority" perpetuates their inequality and exacerbates relations between them and African Americans.

Topics for Critical Thinking and Writing

1. What is the thesis of Takaki's essay? What is the evidence he offers for its truth? Do you find his argument convincing? Explain your answers to these questions in an essay of 500 words.

2. Takaki several times uses statistics to make a point. Do some of the statistics seem more convincing than others? Explain.

3. Consider Takaki's title. To what group(s) is the myth of Asian superiority harmful?

4. Suppose you believed that Asian Americans are economically more successful in America today, relative to white Americans, than African Americans are. Does Takaki agree or disagree with you? What evidence, if any, does he cite to support or reject the belief?

5. Takaki attacks the "myth" of Asian American "success," and thus rejects the idea that they are a "model minority" (recall the opening and closing paragraphs). What do you think a genuine model minority would be like? Can you think of any racial or ethnic minority in the United States that can serve as a model? Explain why or why not in an essay of 500 words.

James Q. Wilson

James Q. Wilson is Collins Professor of Management and Public Policy at the University of California at Los Angeles. Among his books are Thinking about Crime *(1975),* Bureaucracy *(1989),* The Moral Sense *(1993), and* Moral Judgment *(1997). The essay that we reprint appeared originally in the* New York Times Magazine, *March 20, 1994.*

Just Take Away Their Guns

The president wants still tougher gun control legislation and thinks it will work. The public supports more gun control laws but suspects they won't work. The public is right.

Legal restraints on the lawful purchase of guns will have little effect on the illegal use of guns. There are some 200 million guns in private ownership, about one-third of them handguns. Only about 2 percent of the latter are employed to commit crimes. It would take a Draconian, and politically impossible, confiscation of legally purchased guns to make much of a difference in the number used by criminals. Moreover, only about one-sixth of the handguns used by serious criminals are purchased from a gun shop or pawnshop. Most of these handguns are stolen, borrowed, or obtained through private purchases that wouldn't be affected by gun laws.

What is worse, any successful effort to shrink the stock of legally purchased guns (or of ammunition) would reduce the capacity of law-abiding people to defend themselves. Gun control advocates scoff at the importance of self-defense, but they are wrong to do so. Based on a household survey, Gary Kleck, a criminologist at Florida State University, has estimated that every year, guns are used—that is, displayed or fired—for defensive purposes more than a million times, not counting their use by the police. If his estimate is correct, this means that the number of people who defend themselves with a gun exceeds the number of arrests for violent crimes and burglaries.

Our goal should not be the disarming of law-abiding citizens. It should be to reduce the number of people who carry guns unlawfully, especially in places — on streets, in taverns — where the mere presence of a gun can increase the hazards we all face. The most effective way to reduce illegal gun-carrying is to encourage the police to take guns away from people who carry them without a permit. This means encouraging the police to make street frisks.

The Fourth Amendment to the Constitution bans "unreasonable 5 searches and seizures." In 1968 the Supreme Court decided (*Terry v. Ohio*) that a frisk — patting down a person's outer clothing — is proper if the officer has a "reasonable suspicion" that the person is armed and dangerous. If a pat-down reveals an object that might be a gun, the officer can enter the suspect's pocket to remove it. If the gun is being carried illegally, the suspect can be arrested.

The reasonable-suspicion test is much less stringent than the probable-cause standard the police must meet in order to make an arrest. A reasonable suspicion, however, is more than just a hunch; it must be supported by specific facts. The courts have held, not always consistently, that these facts include someone acting in a way that leads an experienced officer to conclude criminal activity may be afoot; someone fleeing at the approach of an officer; a person who fits a drug courier profile; a motorist stopped for a traffic violation who has a suspicious bulge in his pocket; a suspect identified by a reliable informant as carrying a gun. The Supreme Court has also upheld frisking people on probation or parole.

Some police departments frisk a lot of people, but usually the police frisk rather few, at least for the purpose of detecting illegal guns. In 1992 the police arrested about 240,000 people for illegally possessing or carrying a weapon. This is only about one-fourth as many as were arrested for public drunkenness. The average police officer will make *no* weapons arrests and confiscate *no* guns during any given year. Mark Moore, a professor of public policy at Harvard University, found that most weapons arrests were made because a citizen complained, not because the police were out looking for guns.

It is easy to see why. Many cities suffer from a shortage of officers, and even those with ample law-enforcement personnel worry about having their cases thrown out for constitutional reasons or being accused of police harassment. But the risk of violating the Constitution or engaging in actual, as opposed to perceived, harassment can be substantially reduced.

Each patrol officer can be given a list of people on probation or parole who live on that officer's beat and be rewarded for making frequent stops to insure that they are not carrying guns. Officers can be trained to recognize the kinds of actions that the Court will accept as providing the "reasonable suspicion" necessary for a stop and frisk. Membership in a gang known for assaults and drug dealing could be made the basis, by statute or Court precedent, for gun frisks.

The available evidence supports the claim that self-defense is a legiti- 10 mate form of deterrence. People who report to the National Crime Survey that they defended themselves with a weapon were less likely to lose property in a robbery or be injured in an assault than those who did not defend themselves. Statistics have shown that would-be burglars are threatened by gun-wielding victims about as many times a year as they are arrested (and much more often than they are sent to prison) and that the chances of a burglar being shot are about the same as his chances of going to jail. Criminals know these facts even if gun control advocates do not and so are less likely to burgle occupied homes in America than occupied ones in Europe, where the residents rarely have guns.

Some gun control advocates may concede these points but rejoin that the cost of self-defense is self-injury: Handgun owners are more likely to shoot themselves or their loved ones than a criminal. Not quite. Most gun accidents involve rifles and shotguns, not handguns. Moreover, the rate of fatal gun accidents has been declining while the level of gun ownership has been rising. There are fatal gun accidents just as there are fatal car accidents, but in fewer than 2 percent of the gun fatalities was the victim someone mistaken for an intruder.

Those who urge us to forbid or severely restrict the sale of guns ignore these facts. Worse, they adopt a position that is politically absurd. In effect, they say, "Your government, having failed to protect your person and your property from criminal assault, now intends to deprive you of the opportunity to protect yourself."

Opponents of gun control make a different mistake. The National Rifle Association and its allies tell us that "guns don't kill, people kill" and urge the Government to punish more severely people who use guns to commit crimes. Locking up criminals does protect society from future crimes, and the prospect of being locked up may deter criminals. But our experience with meting out tougher sentences is mixed. The tougher the prospective sentence the less likely it is to be imposed, or at least to be imposed swiftly. If the Legislature adds on time for crimes committed with a gun, prosecutors often bargain away the add-ons; even when they do not, the judges in many states are reluctant to impose add-ons.

Worse, the presence of a gun can contribute to the magnitude of the crime even on the part of those who worry about serving a long prison sentence. Many criminals carry guns not to rob stores but to protect themselves from other armed criminals. Gang violence has become more threatening to bystanders as gang members have begun to arm themselves. People may commit crimes, but guns make some crimes worse. Guns often convert spontaneous outbursts of anger into fatal encounters. When some people carry them on the streets, others will want to carry them to protect themselves, and an urban arms race will be underway.

And modern science can be enlisted to help. Metal detectors at air- 15
ports have reduced the number of airplane bombings and skyjackings to nearly zero. But these detectors only work at very close range. What is needed is a device that will enable the police to detect the presence of a large lump of metal in someone's pocket from a distance of ten or fifteen feet. Receiving such a signal could supply the officer with reasonable grounds for a pat-down. Underemployed nuclear physicists and electronics engineers in the post-cold-war era surely have the talents for designing a better gun detector.

Even if we do all these things, there will still be complaints. Innocent people will be stopped. Young black and Hispanic men will probably be stopped more often than older white Anglo males or women of any race. But if we are serious about reducing drive-by shootings, fatal gang wars and lethal quarrels in public places, we must get illegal guns off the street. We cannot do this by multiplying the forms one fills out at gun shops or by pretending that guns are not a problem until a criminal uses one.

Topics for Critical Thinking and Writing

1. If you had to single out one sentence in Wilson's essay as coming close to stating his thesis, what sentence would that be? Why do you think it states, better than any other sentence, the thesis of the essay?

2. In his third paragraph Wilson reviews some research by a criminologist purporting to show that guns are important for self-defense in American households. Does the research as reported show that displaying or firing guns in self-defense actually prevented crimes? Or wounded aggressors? Suppose you were also told that in households where guns may be used defensively, thousands of innocent people are injured, and hundreds are killed—for instance, children who find a loaded gun and play with it. Would you regard these injuries and deaths as a fair trade-off? Explain. What does the research presented by Wilson really show?

3. In paragraph 12 Wilson says that people who want to severely restrict the ownership of guns are in effect saying, "'Your government, having failed to protect your person and your property from criminal assault, now intends to deprive you of the opportunity to protect yourself.'" What reply might an advocate of severe restrictions make? (Even if you strongly believe Wilson's summary is accurate, try to put yourself in the shoes of an advocate of gun control, and come up with the best reply that you can.)

4. Wilson reports in paragraph 7 that the police arrest four times as many drunks on the streets as they do people carrying unlicensed firearms.

Does this strike you as absurd, reasonable, or mysterious? Does Wilson explain it to your satisfaction?

5. In his final paragraph Wilson grants that his proposal entails a difficulty: "Innocent people will be stopped. Young black and Hispanic men will probably be stopped more often than older white Anglo males or women of any race." Assuming that his predictions are accurate, is Wilson's proposal therefore fatally flawed and worth no further thought, or (to take the other extreme view) do you think that innocent people who fall into certain classifications will just have to put up with frisking, for the public good?

6. In an essay of no more than 100 words, explain the difference between the "reasonable-suspicion test" and the "probable-cause standard" that the courts use in deciding whether a street frisk is lawful. (You may want to organize your essay into two paragraphs, one on each topic, or perhaps into three if you want to use a brief introductory paragraph.)

7. Wilson criticizes both gun control advocates and the National Rifle Association for their ill-advised views. In an essay of 500 words, state his criticisms of each side and explain whether and to what extent you agree.

Elizabeth M. Whelan

Elizabeth M. Whelan is president of the American Council on Science and Health. This selection appeared in the May 29, 1995, issue of Newsweek.

Perils of Prohibition

My colleagues at the Harvard School of Public Health, where I studied preventive medicine, deserve high praise for their recent study on teenage drinking. What they found in their survey of college students was that they drink "early and . . . often," frequently to the point of getting ill.

As a public-health scientist with a daughter, Christine, heading to college this fall, I have professional and personal concerns about teen binge drinking. It is imperative that we explore *why* so many young people abuse alcohol. From my own study of the effects of alcohol restrictions and my observations of Christine and her friends' predicament about drinking, I believe that today's laws are unrealistic. Prohibiting the sale of liquor to responsible young adults creates an atmosphere where binge drinking and alcohol abuse have become a problem. American teens, unlike their European peers, don't learn how to drink gradually, safely, and in moderation.

Alcohol is widely accepted and enjoyed in our culture. Studies show that moderate drinking can be good for you. But we legally proscribe alcohol until the age of twenty-one (why not thirty or forty-five?). Christine and her classmates can drive cars, fly planes, marry, vote, pay taxes, take out loans, and risk their lives as members of the U.S. armed forces. But laws in all fifty states say that no alcoholic beverages may be sold to anyone until that magic twenty-first birthday. We didn't always have a national "twenty-one" rule. When I was in college, in the mid-'60s, the drinking age varied from state to state. This posed its own risks, with underage students crossing state lines to get a legal drink.

In parts of the Western world, moderate drinking by teenagers and even children under their parents' supervision is a given. Though the per capita consumption of alcohol in France, Spain, and Portugal is higher than in the United States, the rate of alcoholism and alcohol abuse is lower. A glass of wine at dinner is normal practice. Kids learn to regard moderate drinking as an enjoyable family activity rather than as something they have to sneak away to do. Banning drinking by young people makes it a badge of adulthood—a tantalizing forbidden fruit.

Christine and her teenage friends like to go out with a group to a   5 club, comedy show, or sports bar to watch the game. But teens today have to go on the sly with fake IDs and the fear of getting caught. Otherwise, they're denied admittance to most places and left to hang out on the street. That's hardly a safer alternative. Christine and her classmates now find themselves in a legal no man's land. At eighteen, they're considered adults. Yet when they want to enjoy a drink like other adults, they are, as they put it, "disenfranchised."

Comparing my daughter's dilemma with my own as an "underage" college student, I see a difference—and one that I think has exacerbated the current dilemma. Today's teens are far more sophisticated than we were. They're treated less like children and have more responsibilities than we did. This makes the twenty-one restriction seem anachronistic.

For the past few years, my husband and I have been preparing Christine for college life and the inevitable partying—read keg of beer— that goes with it. Last year, a young friend with no drinking experience was violently ill for days after he was introduced to "clear liquids in small glasses" during freshman orientation. We want our daughter to learn how to drink sensibly and avoid this pitfall. Starting at the age of fourteen, we invited her to join us for a glass of champagne with dinner. She'd tried it once before, thought it was "yucky" and declined. A year later, she enjoyed sampling wine at family meals.

When, at sixteen, she asked for a Mudslide (a bottled chocolate-milk-and-rum concoction), we used the opportunity to discuss it with her. We explained the alcohol content, told her the alcohol level is lower when the drink is blended with ice and compared it with a glass of wine. Since the drink of choice on campus is beer, we contrasted its potency with wine and hard liquor and stressed the importance of not drinking on an empty stomach.

Our purpose was to encourage her to know the alcohol content of what she is served. We want her to experience the effects of liquor in her own home, not on the highway and not for the first time during a college orientation week with free-flowing suds. Although Christine doesn't drive yet, we regularly reinforce the concept of choosing a designated driver. Happily, that already seems a widely accepted practice among our daughter's friends who drink.

We recently visited the Ivy League school Christine will attend in the 10 fall. While we were there, we read a story in the college paper about a student who was nearly electrocuted when, in a drunken state, he climbed on top of a moving train at a railroad station near the campus. The student survived, but three of his limbs were later amputated. This incident reminded me of a tragic death on another campus. An intoxicated student maneuvered himself into a chimney. He was found three days later when frat brothers tried to light a fire in the fireplace. By then he was dead.

These tragedies are just two examples of our failure to teach young people how to use alcohol prudently. If eighteen-year-olds don't have legal access to even a beer at a public place, they have no experience handling liquor on their own. They feel "liberated" when they arrive on campus. With no parents to stop them, they have a "let's make up for lost time" attitude. The result: binge drinking.

We should make access to alcohol legal at eighteen. At the same time, we should come down much harder on alcohol abusers and drunk drivers of all ages. We should intensify our efforts at alcohol education for adolescents. We want them to understand that it is perfectly OK not to drink. But if they do, alcohol should be consumed in moderation.

After all, we choose to teach our children about safe sex, including the benefits of teen abstinence. Why, then, can't we—schools and parents alike—teach them about safe drinking?

Topics for Critical Thinking and Writing

1. Whelan states (para. 3), "Studies show that moderate drinking can be good for you." Ask a reference librarian to help you find out more about these studies. How do they define "moderate drinking"? How does Whelan?

2. In paragraph 3 Whelan speaks, with a touch of mockery in her voice, about "that magic twenty-first birthday." Of course there is nothing magical about this birthday, but if an age must be set, what should the age be? Whelan points out that at eighteen one can vote, serve in the armed forces, drive, and so forth. Does it follow that one age should be set for all activities? Should eighteen be the "magic" age? Why, or why not?

3. Whelan says (para. 6) that her daughter's college generation is far more "sophisticated" than hers was in the mid-1960s. Does she offer any evidence to support this claim? What evidence (if any) could you cite concerning the difference in sophistication between your generation and that of your parents?

4. Also in paragraph 6 Whelan says that "today's teens . . . have more responsibilities than we did." Do you think such a statement can be verified? Explain.

5. Whelan ends her essay by arguing that if teachers, parents, and other authority figures can teach teenagers about "safe sex," then they certainly can teach them about "safe drinking." Do you think the parallel is a good one? Why, or why not?

6. Whelan relates in some detail how she and her husband introduced their daughter to the pleasures of moderate alcohol consumption. In an essay of 250 to 500 words, compare and contrast their daughter's experience with your own. Argue for one course or the other or for some entirely different course.

Robert H. Bork

Robert H. Bork (b. 1927) taught at Yale Law School, resigned to serve as Solicitor General of the United States, and was then appointed to the U.S. Court of Appeals. He is now a resident scholar at the American Enterprise Institute, Washington, D.C. This selection appeared in the July 28, 1997, issue of The National Review.

Addicted to Health

When moral self-righteousness, greed for money, and political ambition work hand in hand they produce irrational, but almost irresistible, policies. The latest example is the war on cigarettes and cigarette smokers. A proposed settlement has been negotiated among politicians, plaintiffs' lawyers, and the tobacco industry. The only interests left out of the negotiations were smokers', who will be ordered to pay enormous sums with no return other than the deprivation of their own choices and pleasures.

It is a myth that today's Americans are a sturdy, self-reliant folk who will fight any officious interference with their liberties. That has not been true at least since the New Deal. If you doubt that, walk the streets of any American city and see the forlorn men and women cupping their hands against the wind to light cigarettes so that they can get through a few more smokeless hours in their offices. Twenty-five percent of Americans smoke. Why can't they demand and get a compromise rather than accepting docilely the exile that employers and building managers impose upon them?

The answer is that they have been made to feel guilty by self-righteous nonsmokers. A few years back, hardly anyone claimed to be seriously troubled by tobacco smoke. Now, an entire class of the morally superior claim to be able to detect, and be offended by, tobacco smoke several offices away from their own. These people must possess the sense of smell of a deer or an Indian guide. Yet they will happily walk through suffocating exhaust smoke from buses rather than wait a minute or two to cross the street.

No one should assume that peace will be restored when the last cigarette smoker has been banished to the Alaskan tundra. Other products will be pressed into service as morally reprehensible. If you would know the future, look to California — the national leader in health fanaticism. After a long day in Los Angeles flogging a book I had written, my wife and I sought relaxation with a drink at our hotel's outdoor bar. Our anticipation of pleasure was considerably diminished by a sign: "Warning! Toxic Substances Served Here." They were talking about my martini!

And martinis *are* a toxic substance, taken in any quantity sufficient 5 to induce a sense of well-being. Why not, then, ban alcohol or at least require a death's head on every martini glass? Well, we did once outlaw alcohol; it was called Prohibition. The myth is that Prohibition increased the amount of drinking in this country; the truth is that it reduced it. There were, of course, some unfortunate side effects, like Al Capone and Dutch Schultz. But by and large the mobsters inflicted rigor mortis upon one another.

Why is it, then, that the end of Prohibition was welcomed joyously by the population? Not because alcohol is not dangerous. Not because the consumption of alcohol was not lessened. And not in order to save the lives of people with names like Big Jim and Ice Pick Phil. Prohibition came to an end because most Americans wanted to have a drink when and where they felt like it. If you insist on sounding like a law-and-economics professor, it ended because we thought the benefits of alcohol outweighed the costs.

That is the sort of calculation by which we lead our lives. Automobiles kill tens of thousands of people every year and disable perhaps that many again. We could easily stop the slaughter. Cars could be made with a top speed of ten miles an hour and with exteriors the consistency of marshmallows. Nobody would die, nobody would be disabled, and nobody would bother with cars very much.

There are, of course, less draconian measures available. On most highways, it is almost impossible to find anyone who observes the speed limits. On the theory of the tobacco precedent, car manufacturers should be liable for deaths caused by speeding; after all, they could build automobiles incapable of exceeding legal speed limits.

The reason we are willing to offer up lives and limbs to automobiles is, quite simply, that they make life more pleasant (for those who remain intact) — among other things, by speeding commuting to work, by making possible family vacations a thousand miles from home, and by lowering the costs of products shipped from a distance. The case for regulating automobiles far more severely than we do is not essentially different from the case for heavy regulation of cigarettes or, soon, alcohol.

But choices concerning driving, smoking, and drinking are the sort 10 of things that ought to be left to the individual unless there are clear, serious harms to others.

The opening salvo in the drive to make smoking a criminal act is the proposed settlement among the cigarette companies, plaintiffs' lawyers, and the states' attorneys general. We are told that the object is to protect teenagers and children (children being the last refuge of the sanctimonious). But many restrictions will necessarily affect adults, and the tobacco pact contains provisions that can only be explained as punishment for selling to adults.

The terms of the settlement plainly reveal an intense hatred of smoking. Opposition to the pact comes primarily from those who think it is not severe enough. For example, critics say the settlement is defective in not restricting the marketing of cigarettes overseas by American tobacco companies. Connecticut's attorney general, Richard Blumenthal, defended the absence of such a provision: "Given our druthers we would have brought them to their knees all over the world, but there is a limit to our leverage." So much for the sovereignty of nations.

What the settlement does contain is bad enough. The pact would require the companies to pony up $60 billion; $25 billion of this would be used for public-health issues to be identified by a presidential panel and the rest for children's health insurance. Though the purpose of the entire agreement is punitive, this slice is most obviously so.

The industry is also required to pay $308 billion over twenty-five years, in part to repay states for the cost of treating sick smokers. There are no grounds for this provision. The tobacco companies have regularly won litigation against plaintiffs claiming injury on the grounds that everybody has known for the past forty years that smoking can cause health problems. This $308 billion, which takes from the companies what they have won in litigation, says, in effect, that no one assumed the risk of his own behavior.

The provision is groundless for additional reasons. The notion that 15 the states have lost money because of cigarettes ignores the federal and state taxes smokers have paid, which cover any amount the states could claim to have lost. Furthermore, a percentage of the population dies early from smoking. Had these people lived longer, the drain on Medicare and Medicaid would have been greater. When lowered pension and Social Security costs are figured in, it seems certain that government is better off financially with smoking than without it. If we must reduce the issue to one of dollars, as the attorneys general have done, states have profited financially from smoking. If this seems a gruesome and heartless calculation, it is. But don't blame me. The state governments advanced the financial argument and ought to live with its consequences, however distasteful.

Other provisions of the settlement fare no better under the application of common sense. The industry is to reduce smoking by teenagers by 30 percent in five years, 50 percent in seven years, and 60 percent in ten years. No one knows how the industry is to perform this trick. But if those goals are not met, the industry will be amerced $80 million a year for each percentage point it falls short. The settlement assumes teenage smoking can be reduced dramatically by requiring the industry to conduct an expensive antismoking advertising campaign, banning the use of people and cartoon characters to promote cigarettes, and similar tactics. It is entirely predictable that this will not work. Other countries have banned cigarette advertising, only to watch smoking increase. Apparently the young, feeling themselves invulnerable, relish the risk of smoking. Studies have shown, moreover, that teenagers are drawn to smoking not because of advertising but because their parents smoke or because of peer pressure. Companies advertise to gain or maintain market share among those who already smoke.

To lessen the heat on politicians, the pact increases the powers of the Food and Drug Administration to regulate tobacco as an addictive drug, with the caveat that it may not prohibit cigarette smoking altogether before the year 2009. The implicit promise is that the complete prohibition of cigarettes will be seriously contemplated at that time. In the meantime, the FDA will subject cigarettes to stricter and stricter controls on the theory that tobacco is a drug.

Another rationale for prohibiting or sharply limiting smoking is the supposed need to protect nonsmokers from secondhand smoke. The difficulty is that evidence of causation is weak. What we see is a possible small increase in an already small risk which, as some researchers have pointed out, may well be caused by other variables such as misclassification of former smokers as nonsmokers or such lifestyle factors as diet.

But the tobacco companies should take little or no comfort from that. Given today's product-liability craze, scientific support is unnecessary to successful lawsuits against large corporations.

The pact is of dubious constitutionality as well. It outlaws the adver- 20 tising of a product it is legal to sell, which raises the problem of commercial speech protected by the First Amendment. The settlement also requires the industry to disband its lobbying organization, the Tobacco Institute. Lobbying has traditionally been thought to fall within the First Amendment's guarantee of the right to petition the government for the redress of grievances.

And who is to pay for making smoking more difficult? Smokers will have the price of cigarettes raised by new taxes and by the tobacco companies' costs of complying with the settlement. It is a brilliant strategy: Smokers will pay billions to have their pleasure taken away.

But if the tobacco settlement makes little sense as public policy, what can be driving it to completion? The motivations are diverse. Members of the plaintiffs' bar, who have signally failed in litigation against tobacco to date, are to be guaranteed billions of dollars annually. The states' attorneys general have a different set of incentives. They are members of the National Association of Attorneys General, NAAG, which is commonly, and accurately, rendered as the National Association of Aspiring Governors.

So far they have got what they wanted. There they are, on the front pages of newspapers all over the country, looking out at us, jaws firm, conveying images of sobriety, courage, and righteousness. They have, after all, done battle with the forces of evil, and won—at least temporarily.

Tobacco executives and their lawyers are said to be wily folk, however. They may find ways of defeating the strictures laid upon them. It may be too soon to tell, therefore, whether the tobacco settlement is a major defeat or a victory for the industry. In any case, we can live with it. But whenever individual responsibility is denied, government control of our behavior follows. After cigarettes it will be something else, and so on *ad infinitum.* One would think we would have learned that lesson many times over and that we would have had enough of it.

Topics for Critical Thinking and Writing

1. Bork refers to smokers as "ordered to pay" (para. 1) for the privilege of smoking and as enduring "exile" (para. 2) from their places of work if they want to enjoy a smoke. With these words, does Bork misrepresent the facts of the matter? Why, or why not?

2. Bork implies that today's "self-righteous nonsmokers" will "happily walk" through exhaust fumes without a second thought (para. 3). Interview six nonsmokers among your friends and ask them whether, in all honesty, Bork's generalization applies to their behavior. In any case, what evidence, if any, does Bork seem to have for his generalization?

3. In an essay of 500 words, explain whether you agree or disagree with Bork when he says "The case for regulating automobiles far more severely than we do is not essentially different from the case for heavy regulation of cigarettes or, soon, alcohol" (para. 9).

4. Bork evidently believes that cigarette smoking does not cause "clear, serious harms to others" (para. 10)—that is, to nonsmokers—or he would favor its prohibition. In an essay of 500 words, explain why you believe he is either right or wrong about the harm smoking causes nonsmokers.

5. Using the resources of your library, find out what the current status is of the "proposed settlement among the cigarette companies, plaintiffs' lawyers, and the states' attorneys general" (para. 11). How, if at all, does it differ from the provisions Bork describes?

6. Explain whether you agree with Bork that, given all the evidence currently available, the "government is better off financially with smoking than without it" (para. 15).

7. Bork invokes a slippery slope objection to the proposed tobacco settlement, suggesting in paragraphs 4 and 24 that soon after cigarettes, some other products will go on trial as "morally reprehensible." Is this just a scare tactic, or do you think he is right?

Judy Brady

Born in San Francisco in 1937, Judy Brady married in 1960 and two years later earned a bachelor's degree in painting at the University of Iowa. Active in the women's movement and in other political causes, she has worked as an author, an editor, and a secretary. The essay reprinted here, written before she and her husband separated, appeared originally in the first issue of Ms. *in 1971.*

I Want a Wife

I belong to that classification of people known as wives. I am A Wife. And, not altogether incidentally, I am a mother.

Not too long ago a male friend of mine appeared on the scene fresh from a recent divorce. He had one child, who is, of course, with his ex-wife. He is looking for another wife. As I thought about him while I was ironing one evening, it suddenly occurred to me that I, too, would like to have a wife. Why do I want a wife?

I would like to go back to school so that I can become economically independent, support myself, and, if need be, support those dependent upon me. I want a wife who will work and send me to school. And while I am going to school I want a wife to take care of my children. I want a wife to keep track of the children's doctor and dentist appointments. And to keep track of mine, too. I want a wife to make sure my children eat properly and are kept clean. I want a wife who will wash the children's clothes and keep them mended. I want a wife who is a good nurturant attendant to my children, who arranges for their schooling, makes sure that they have an adequate social life with their peers, takes them to the park, the zoo, etc. I want a wife who takes care of the children when they are sick, a wife who arranges to be around when the children need special care, because, of course, I cannot miss classes at school. My wife must arrange to lose time at work and not lose the job. It may mean a small cut in my wife's income from time to time, but I guess I can tolerate that. Needless to say, my wife will arrange and pay for the care of the children while my wife is working.

I want a wife who will take care of *my* physical needs. I want a wife who will keep my house clean. A wife who will pick up after my children, a wife who will pick up after me. I want a wife who will keep my clothes clean, ironed, mended, replaced when need be, and who will see to it that my personal things are kept in their proper place so that I can find what I need the minute I need it. I want a wife who cooks the meals, a wife who is a *good* cook. I want a wife who will plan the menus, do the necessary grocery shopping, prepare the meals, serve them pleasantly, and then do the cleaning up while I do my studying. I want a wife who will care for me when I am sick and sympathize with my pain and loss of time from school. I want a wife to go along when our family takes a vacation so that someone can continue to care for me and my children when I need a rest and change of scene.

I want a wife who will not bother me with rambling complaints   5
about a wife's duties. But I want a wife who will listen to me when I feel the need to explain a rather difficult point I have come across in my course of studies. And I want a wife who will type my papers for me when I have written them.

I want a wife who will take care of the details of my social life. When my wife and I are invited out by my friends, I want a wife who will take care of the babysitting arrangements. When I meet people at school that I like and want to entertain, I want a wife who will have the house clean, will prepare a special meal, serve it to me and my friends, and not interrupt when I talk about things that interest me and my friends. I want a wife who will have arranged that the children are fed and ready for bed before my guests arrive so that the children do not bother us. I want a wife who takes care of the needs of my guests so that they feel comfortable, who makes sure that they have an ashtray, that they are passed the hors d'oeuvres, that they are offered a second helping of the food, that their wine glasses are replenished when necessary, that their coffee is served to them as they like it. And I want a wife who knows that sometimes I need a night out by myself.

I want a wife who is sensitive to my sexual needs, a wife who makes love passionately and eagerly when I feel like it, a wife who makes sure that I am satisfied. And, of course, I want a wife who will not demand sexual attention when I am not in the mood for it. I want a wife who assumes the complete responsibility for birth control, because I do not want more children. I want a wife who will remain sexually faithful to me so that I do not have to clutter up my intellectual life with jealousies. And I want a wife who understands that *my* sexual needs may entail more than strict adherence to monogamy. I must, after all, be able to relate to people as fully as possible.

If, by chance, I find another person more suitable as a wife than the wife I already have, I want the liberty to replace my present wife with another one. Naturally, I will expect a fresh, new life; my wife will take the children and be solely responsible for them so that I am left free.

When I am through with school and have a job, I want my wife to quit working and remain at home so that my wife can more fully and completely take care of a wife's duties.

My God, who *wouldn't* want a wife?   10

Topics for Critical Thinking and Writing

1. If one were to summarize Brady's first paragraph, one might say it adds up to "I am a wife and a mother." But analyze it closely. Exactly what does the second sentence add to the first? And what does "not altogether incidentally" add to the third sentence?

2. Brady uses the word *wife* in sentences where one ordinarily would use *she* or *her*. Why? And why does she begin paragraphs 4, 5, 6, and 7 with the same words, "I want a wife"?

3. In her second paragraph Brady says that the child of her divorced male friend "is, of course, with his ex-wife." In the context of the entire essay, what does this sentence mean?

4. Complete the following sentence by offering a definition: "According to Judy Brady, a wife is . . ."

5. Try to state the essential argument of Brady's essay in a simple syllogism. (*Hint:* Start by identifying the thesis or conclusion you think she is trying to establish, and then try to formulate two premises, based on what she has written, that would establish the conclusion.)

6. Drawing on your experience as observer of the world around you (and perhaps as husband, wife, or ex-spouse), do you think Brady's picture of a wife's role is grossly exaggerated? Or is it (allowing for some serious playfulness) fairly accurate, even though it was written in 1971? If grossly exaggerated, is the essay therefore meaningless? If fairly accurate, what attitudes and practices does it encourage you to support? Explain.

7. Whether or not you agree with Brady's vision of marriage in our society, write an essay (500 words) titled "I Want a Husband," imitating her style and approach. Write the best possible essay, and then decide which of the two essays — yours or hers — makes a fairer comment on current society. Or, if you believe Brady is utterly misleading, write an essay titled "I Want a Wife," seeing the matter in a different light.

8. If you feel that you have been pressed into an unappreciated, unreasonable role — built-in babysitter, listening post, or girl (or boy or man or woman) Friday — write an essay of 500 words that will help the reader to see both your plight and the injustice of the system. (*Hint:* A little humor will help to keep your essay from seeming to be a prolonged whine.)

A CASEBOOK FOR ANALYSIS:
Does Bilingual Education Make Sense?

Diane Ravitch

Diane Ravitch (b. 1938) has taught history and education at Teacher's College, Columbia University, and has served as assistant secretary of education. She is now a senior research scholar at New York University and a senior fellow at the Brookings Institution. We reprint an essay that originally appeared in the New York Times, *September 5, 1997, and we follow it with letters written in response.*

First Teach Them English

The Bilingual Education Act of 1968 was intended to help Hispanic children learn English. But nearly thirty years later, it is clear that bilingual education has been a dismal failure.

The United States Department of Education recently reported a dropout rate of 30 percent for Hispanics between the ages of sixteen and twenty-four, more than double the dropout rate for blacks or whites in the same age group. The report also found that Hispanic students who spoke English well were far less likely to drop out than those who did not.

In 1994, a New York City Board of Education study showed that more than 90 percent of the students who started bilingual education in the sixth grade were unable to pass an English-language test after three years of bilingual instruction. The students most likely to languish in bilingual classes for four or more years were Hispanic.

Despite the failure of bilingual education, the President and Congress have agreed to increase federal financing for it to $354 million. That's double the amount spent in 1996, and it will trigger even more spending at the state and local levels.

Moreover, the New York State Education Department is expanding 5 such programs. In June, the state issued new guidelines for students from English-speaking Caribbean nations who speak or understand a Creole language. Many students from countries like Jamaica, Barbados, Antigua, and the Bahamas will be routed into bilingual classes if they score in the bottom 40 percent on an English-language test. The state has listed nearly two dozen distinct Creole languages—including Leeward Islands Creole, Kokoy, Papiamento, and Bermudian Creole—that must be taught when at least twenty students who speak the language are in the same building and the same grade.

If these students had never left their countries they would have been instructed in English, which is the official language of the Caribbean nations identified by the state in this bizarre initiative. Now that they are residents of New York, they will be taught in their native patois.

Apparently, the purpose of this state initiative is not to help students learn English but to maintain their culture. If this is so, then their parents should be told about the poor track record of bilingual education and asked if they want their children enrolled in such a program. Those who want their children to learn English should be allowed to withhold consent. Under existing regulations, parents must navigate an elaborate bureaucratic process to withdraw children from bilingual education.

If schools really want to teach English to children with limited proficiency, they can look to the Middlebury College Language Schools' intensive summer immersion program as a model. Students sign a pledge to communicate only in the new language. By summer's end, they are as fluent as someone who has just completed a first-year college course.

Structured immersion, as this approach is called, works so well that it is used exclusively by the Defense Language Institute in Monterey, Calif., where the Pentagon teaches twenty-four different languages to more than three thousand students each year. Last year, the City University of New York established six English-immersion centers, in which students study English intensively for twenty-five hours a week to prepare them for college-level classes. Many students in the university's English immersion program are New York public school graduates whose language skills are so poor that they are not ready for college.

The United States should not be an English-only society. We should 10 encourage the study of foreign languages in schools and universities. But unless students are fluent in English, they will not have a fair chance of graduating from high school, going to college, and getting good jobs. All students should learn two languages. In this society, one of them must be English.

Ravitch's essay evoked the following responses, all of which were printed in the *New York Times* on September 9, 1997.

Letters from Kendall A. King,
Jeffrey O. Jones, Lisa M. Garcia,
Mathilda Holzman, and Judith D. Wallach

To the Editor:

Re "First Teach Them English" (Op-Ed, Sept. 5): While Diane Ravitch is right about the high dropout rate among Hispanic students, the conclusion she draws is wrong. The problem is not that students receive too much bilingual education but that they receive too little high-quality bilingual instruction.

Good bilingual education programs teach English. They also allow children to keep up with English-speaking peers by teaching reading, writing, and content in the first language. Contrary to popular belief, a 1995 Education Department study found that less than half of the nation's youngest students classified as having limited English proficiency received reading and math instruction in their native language.

Yet there is substantial evidence that school use of the native language not only has positive academic benefits but also lowers dropout rates. Those children who benefit from academic instruction in their native language are significantly more likely to enroll in college.

Kendall A. King
New York, Sept. 6, 1997
The writer is an assistant professor, department of teaching and learning,
N.Y.U. School of Education.

To the Editor:

Diane Ravitch (Op-Ed, Sept. 5) cites a Department of Education study showing that Hispanic students who spoke English well were far less likely to drop out than those who did not. Contrary to Ms. Ravitch, this only confirms the importance of bilingual education.

A case in point is Miguel, a high school boy I mentored for some years. Miguel arrived in the Bronx from a rural town in the Dominican Republic at age fifteen speaking little English. A diligent student who in the Dominican Republic walked miles to school each day, here he was unable to understand those around him or to express his thoughts.

"In my country, I was smart," he told me in frustration.

Enrolled in a New York City high school, he studied English as a second language. While he learned this new tongue, he also had Spanish-language classes in subjects like math and chemistry. Today Miguel speaks English fluently and is a college freshman.

Jeffrey O. Jones
New York, Sept. 6, 1997

To the Editor:

Diane Ravitch (Op-Ed, Sept. 5) cites the dropout rates of Hispanic students as proof that bilingual education has failed. That Hispanic students with low English proficiency drop out at higher rates than Hispanic students with high English proficiency has been proved in education studies to result from differences in socioeconomic status.

Students with low English proficiency are most often children of immigrant parents who have been in this country for a short period of time. The parents tend to have less education and income than parents of Hispanic students born in the United States.

Ms. Ravitch suggests immersion programs as a preferred alternative to bilingual education. Most studies agree that how students adapt to the school environment has a lasting effect on success. Immersion can only make this adaptation more traumatic for non-English-speaking students, suggesting grave consequences for their future educational success.

Lisa M. Garcia
Washington, Sept. 5, 1997

The writer is an intern in education policy at the Rand Corporation.

To the Editor:

I agree with Diane Ravitch (Op-Ed, Sept. 5) that bilingual education has been a dismal failure and that we need to help immigrants become fluent in English and complete high school. I do not agree that structured immersion is a solution.

Ms. Ravitch, in advocating immersion in the new language, seems to have in mind people who are educated in their native language and who need only transfer their native-language literacy to English. While this may be true of the Russian and Asian immigrants in Lexington, Mass., where I live, it is not true of most immigrants who live in the poor neighborhoods of Boston, where I have worked.

When I was living in Paris in 1979, I found a system that worked well. All immigrant children in a neighborhood, whatever their native language, attended the same school. The language of instruction was French and the children were motivated to acquire it. As soon as a child became literate enough to participate in the regular class of French children at his grade level, he was transferred.

Mathilda Holzman
Medford, Mass., Sept. 5, 1997

The writer is professor emeritus of child development, Tufts University.

To the Editor:

Diane Ravitch (Op-Ed, Sept. 5) is right. All students need to know English as well as another language. But that is true only if they want to participate in the life of the community at large, not if their interest is limited to an insular subculture.

The underlying message of the bilingual model is that the particular group with which one identifies is the only one that matters, so why prepare to participate in a heterogeneous society? This is the postmodern message of which Jean Bethke Elshtain, in "Democracy on Trial," writes: "To the extent that there is a *we* in this world of *I*'s, it is that of the discrete group with whom the *I* identifies."

We are stuck in a fragmented world that Ms. Elshtain describes as "a world of many *I*'s who form a *we* only with others exactly like themselves." That being the case, why bother to learn to communicate with those with whom there is no commonality?

Judith D. Wallach
New York, Sept. 5, 1997

Topics for Critical Thinking and Writing

1. Cite the evidence that Ravitch relies on when she concludes that "bilingual education has been a dismal failure" (para. 1). Can you think of any evidence that would contradict her conclusion? Does the letter by Kendall King seriously undermine her view? The letter from Jeffrey Jones? Why, or why not?

2. Can you think of any reasonable explanation for why, as Ravitch reports it, Caribbean natives at home are taught in English, whereas if they come to New York "they will be taught in their native patois" (para. 6)?

3. What is Ravitch's alternative to continuing to fund bilingual education?

4. What is "structured immersion" in foreign-language teaching? Why is it an effective method of instruction? How might Ravitch respond to the criticism in Lisa Garcia's letter? Mathilda Holzman's letter?

5. Ravitch opposes making the United States "an English-only society" (para. 10). List three advantages and three disadvantages of such a development. Which side has the better of the argument, in your judgment?

6. Ravitch favors "the study of foreign languages in [our] schools and universities" (para. 10). How might she reply to the criticism in Judith Wallach's letter?

Part Two

CRITICAL WRITING

4

Writing an Analysis
of an Argument

ANALYZING AN ARGUMENT

Examining the Author's Thesis

Most of your writing in other courses will require you to write an analysis of someone else's writing. In a course in political science you may have to analyze, say, an essay first published in *Foreign Affairs,* perhaps reprinted in your textbook, that argues against raising tariff barriers to foreign trade; or a course in sociology may require you to analyze a report on the correlation between fatal accidents and drunk drivers under the age of twenty-one. Much of your writing, in short, will set forth reasoned responses to your reading, as preparation for making an argument of your own.

Obviously you must understand an essay before you can analyze it thoughtfully. You must read it several times—not just skim it—and (the hard part) you must think about it. Again, you'll find that your thinking is stimulated if you take notes and if you ask yourself questions about the material. Notes will help you to keep track of the writer's thoughts and also of your own responses to the writer's thesis. The writer probably *does* have a thesis, a point, and if so, you must try to locate it. Perhaps the thesis is explicitly stated in the title or in a sentence or two near the beginning of the essay or in a concluding paragraph, but perhaps you will have to infer it from the essay as a whole.

Notice that we said the writer *probably* has a thesis. Much of what you read will indeed be primarily an argument; the writer explicitly or implicitly is trying to support some thesis and to convince you to agree with it. But some of what you read will be relatively neutral, with the argument just faintly discernible—or even with no argument at all. A work may, for instance, chiefly be a report: Here are the data, or here is what X, Y, and Z said; make of it what you will. A report might simply state how various ethnic groups voted in an election. In a report of this sort, of course, the writer hopes to persuade readers that the facts are correct, but no thesis is advanced, at least not explicitly or perhaps even consciously; the writer is not evidently arguing a point and trying to change our minds. Such a document differs greatly from an essay by a political analyst who presents similar findings in order to persuade a candidate to sacrifice the votes of this ethnic bloc in order to get more votes from other blocs.

Examining the Author's Purpose

While reading an argument, try to form a clear idea of the author's **purpose.** Judging from the essay or the book, was the purpose to persuade, or was it to report? An analysis of a pure report (a work apparently without a thesis or argumentative angle) on ethnic voting will deal chiefly with the accuracy of the report. It will, for example, consider whether the sample poll was representative.

Much material that poses as a report really has a thesis built into it, consciously or unconsciously. The best evidence that the prose you are reading is argumentative is the presence of two kinds of key terms:

> **transitions that imply the drawing of a conclusion:** *therefore, because, for the reason that, consequently;*
>
> **verbs that imply proof:** *confirms, accounts for, implies, proves, disproves, is (in)consistent with, refutes, it follows that.*

Keep your eye out for such terms and scrutinize their precise role whenever they appear. If the essay does not advance a thesis, think of a thesis (a hypothesis) that it might support or some conventional belief that it might undermine.

Examining the Author's Methods

If the essay advances a thesis, you will want to analyze the strategies or methods of argument that allegedly support the thesis.

> Does the writer quote authorities? Are these authorities really competent in this field? Are equally competent authorities who take a different view ignored?
>
> If statistics are used, are they appropriate to the point being argued? Can they be interpreted differently?
>
> Does the writer build the argument by using examples, or analogies? Are they satisfactory?
>
> Are the writer's assumptions acceptable?

Are all relevant factors considered? Has the author omitted some points that you think should be discussed? For instance, should the author recognize certain opposing positions, and perhaps concede something to them?

Does the writer seek to persuade by means of ridicule? If so, is the ridicule fair—is it supported also by rational argument?

In writing your analysis, you will want to tell your reader something about the author's purpose and something about the author's **methods.** It is usually a good idea at the start of your analysis—if not in the first paragraph then in the second or third—to let the reader know the purpose (and thesis, if there is one) of the work you are analyzing, and then to summarize the work briefly.

Next you will probably find it useful (your reader will certainly find it helpful) to write out *your* thesis (your evaluation or judgment). You might say, for instance, that the essay is impressive but not conclusive, or is undermined by convincing contrary evidence, or relies too much on unsupported generalizations, or is wholly admirable, or whatever. Remember, because your paper is itself an argument, it needs its own thesis.

And then, of course, comes the job of setting forth your analysis and the support for your thesis. There is no one way of going about this work. If, say, your author gives four arguments (for example: an appeal to common sense, the testimony of authorities, the evidence of comparisons, an appeal to self-interest), you may want to take up these four arguments in sequence. Or you may want to begin by discussing the simplest of the four, and then go on to the more difficult ones. Or you may want first to discuss the author's two arguments that you think are sound and then turn to the two that you think are not. And, as you warm to your thesis, you may want to clinch your case by constructing a fifth argument, absent from the work under scrutiny but in your view highly important. In short, the organization of your analysis may or may not follow the organization of the work you are analyzing.

Examining the Author's Persona

You will probably also want to analyze something a bit more elusive than the author's explicit arguments: the author's self-presentation. Does the author seek to persuade readers partly by presenting himself or herself as conscientious, friendly, self-effacing, authoritative, tentative, or in some other light? Most writers do two things: They present evidence, and they present themselves (or, more precisely, they present the image of themselves that they wish us to behold). In some persuasive writing this **persona** or **voice** or presentation of the self may be no less important than the presentation of evidence.

In establishing a persona, writers adopt various rhetorical strategies, ranging from the use of characteristic words to the use of a particular form of organization. For instance, the writer who speaks of an opponent's "gimmicks" instead of "strategy" is trying to downgrade the opponent and also to convey the self-image of a streetwise person. On a larger scale, consider the way in which evidence is presented and the kind of evidence offered. One writer may first bombard the reader with facts and then spend relatively little time drawing conclusions. Another may rely chiefly on generalizations, waiting until the end of the essay to bring the thesis home with a few details. Another may begin with a few facts and spend most of the space reflecting on these. One writer may seem professorial or pedantic, offering examples of an academic sort; another, whose examples are drawn from ordinary life, may seem like a regular guy. All such devices deserve comment in your analysis.

The writer's persona, then, may color the thesis and help it develop in a distinctive way. If we accept the thesis, it is partly because the writer has won our goodwill.

The author of an essay may, for example, seem fair minded and open minded, treating the opposition with great courtesy and expressing interest in hearing other views. Such a tactic is, of course, itself a persuasive device. Or take an author who appears to rely on hard evidence such as statistics. This reliance on seemingly objective truths is itself a way of seeking to persuade—a rational way, to be sure, but a mode of persuasion nonetheless.

Especially in analyzing a work in which the author's persona and ideas are blended, you will want to spend some time commenting on the persona. Whether you discuss it near the beginning of your analysis or near the end will depend on your own sense of how you want to construct your essay, and this decision will partly depend on the work you are analyzing. For example, if the author's persona is kept in the background, and is thus relatively invisible, you may want to make that point fairly early, to get it out of the way, and then concentrate on more interesting matters. If, however, the persona is interesting—and perhaps seductive, whether because it seems so scrupulously objective or so engagingly subjective—you may want to hint at this quality early in your essay, and then develop the point while you consider the arguments.

Summary

In the last few pages we have tried to persuade you that, in writing an analysis of your reading, you must do the following:

1. Read and reread thoughtfully. Writing notes will help you to think about what you are reading.
2. Be aware of the purpose of the material to which you are responding.

We have also tried to point out these facts:

3. Most of the nonliterary material that you will read is designed to argue, or to report, or to do both.
4. Most of this material also presents the writer's personality, or voice, and this voice usually merits attention in an analysis. An essay on, say, nuclear war, in a journal devoted to political science, may include a voice that moves from an objective tone to a mildly ironic tone to a hortatory tone, and this voice is worth commenting on.

Possibly all this explanation is obvious. There is yet another point, though, equally obvious but often neglected by students who begin by writing an analysis and end up by writing only a summary, a shortened version of the work they have read:

5. Although your essay is an analysis of someone else's writing, and you may have to include a summary of the work you are writing about, your essay is *your* essay. The thesis, the organization, and the tone are yours. Your thesis, for example, may be that although the author is convinced she has presented a strong case, her case is far from proved. Your organization may be deeply indebted to the work you are analyzing, but it need not be. The author may have begun with specific examples and then gone on to make generalizations and to draw conclusions, but you may begin with the conclusions. Similarly, your tone may resemble your subject's (let's say the voice is Courteous Academic), but it will nevertheless have its own ring, its own tone of (say) urgency, or caution, or coolness.

AN ARGUMENT, ITS ELEMENTS, AND A STUDENT'S ANALYSIS OF THE ARGUMENT

Stanley S. Scott

Stanley S. Scott (1933–1992) was vice president and director of corporate affairs of Philip Morris Companies Inc. This essay originally appeared on December 29, 1984, in the Op-Ed page of the New York Times.

Smokers Get a Raw Deal

The Civil Rights Act, the Voting Rights Act, and a host of antidiscrimination laws notwithstanding, millions of Americans are still forced to sit in the back of planes, trains, and buses. Many more are subject to segregation in public places. Some are even denied housing and employment: victims of an alarming—yet socially acceptable—public hostility.

This new form of discrimination is based on smoking behavior.

If you happen to enjoy a cigarette, you are the potential target of violent antismokers and overzealous public enforcers determined to force their beliefs on the rest of society.

Ever since people began smoking, smokers and nonsmokers have been able to live with one another using common courtesy and common sense. Not anymore. Today, smokers must put up with virtually unenforceable laws regulating when and where they can smoke—laws intended as much to discourage smoking itself as to protect the rights of nonsmokers. Much worse, supposedly responsible organizations devoted to the "public interest" are encouraging the harassment of those who smoke.

This year, for example, the American Cancer Society is promoting 5 programs that encourage people to attack smokers with canisters of gas, to blast them with horns, to squirt them with oversized water guns, and burn them in effigy.

Harmless fun? Not quite. Consider the incidents that are appearing on police blotters across America:

In a New York restaurant, a young man celebrating with friends was zapped in the face by a man with an aerosol spray can. His offense: lighting a cigarette. The aggressor was the head of a militant antismoker organization whose goal is to mobilize an army of two million zealots to spray smokers in the face.

In a suburban Seattle drugstore, a man puffing on a cigarette while he waited for a prescription to be filled was ordered to stop by an elderly customer who pulled a gun on him.

A twenty-three-year-old lit up a cigarette on a Los Angeles bus. A passenger objected. When the smoker objected to the objection, he was fatally stabbed.

A transit policeman, using his reserve gun, shot and fatally wounded a man on a subway train in the Bronx in a shootout over smoking a cigarette.

The basic freedoms of more than 50 million American smokers are at risk today. Tomorrow, who knows what personal behavior will become socially unacceptable, subject to restrictive laws and public ridicule? Could travel by private car make the social engineers' hit list because it is less safe than public transit? Could ice cream, cake, and cookies become socially unacceptable because their consumption causes obesity? What about sky diving, mountain climbing, skiing, and contact sports? How far will we allow this to spread?

The question all Americans must ask themselves is: Can a nation that has struggled so valiantly to eliminate bias based on race, religion, and sex afford to allow a fresh set of categories to encourage new forms of hostility between large groups of citizens?

After all, discrimination is discrimination, no matter what it is based on.

Let's examine Scott's essay with an eye to identifying those elements we mentioned earlier in this chapter (pp. 101–04) that deserve notice when examining *any* argument: the author's *thesis, purpose, methods,* and *persona.* And, while we're at it, let's also notice some other features of Scott's essay that will help us appreciate its effects and evaluate its strengths and weaknesses. All this will put us in a better position to write an evaluation or to write an argument of our own confirming, extending, or rebutting Scott's argument.

Title   Scott starts off with a bang—no one likes a "raw deal," and if that's what smokers are getting, then they probably deserve better. So, already in his title, Scott has made a plea for the reader's sympathy. He has also indicated something about his *topic* and his *thesis,* and (in the words "raw deal") something of his *persona;* he is a regular guy, someone who does not use fancy language but who calls a spade a spade.

Thesis   What is the basic *thesis* Scott is arguing? By the end of the second paragraph his readers have a good idea, and surely by paragraph 7, they can state his thesis explicitly, perhaps in these words: *Smokers today are victims of unfair discrimination.* Writers need not announce their thesis in so many words, but they ought to have a thesis, a point they want to make, and they ought to make it evident fairly soon—as Scott does.

Purpose   There's really no doubt that Scott's *purpose* in this essay is to *persuade* the reader to adopt his view of the plight of today's smokers. This amounts to trying to persuade us that his thesis (stated above) is *true.* Scott, however, does not show that his essay is argumentative or persuasive by using any of the key terms that normally mark argumentative prose. He doesn't call anything his "conclusion," none of his statements is labeled "my reasons" or "my premises," and he doesn't connect any clauses or sentences with a "therefore" or a "because."

But this doesn't matter. The argumentative nature of his essay is revealed by the *judgment* he states in paragraph 2: Smokers are experiencing undeserved discrimination. This is, after all, his thesis in brief form.

Any author who has a thesis as obvious as Scott does is likely to want to persuade his readers to agree with it. To do that, he needs to try to *support* it; accordingly, the bulk of the rest of Scott's essay constitutes just such support.

Method   Scott's principal method of argument is to cite a series of *examples* (introduced by para. 6) in which the reader can see what Scott believes is actual discrimination against smokers. This is his *evidence* in support of his thesis. (Ought we to trust him here? He cites no sources for the events he reports. On the other hand, these examples sound plausible, and so we probably shouldn't demand documentation for them.) The nature of his thesis doesn't require experimental research or support from recognized authorities. All it requires is some *reported instances* that can properly be described as "harassment" (para. 4, end). Scott of course is relying here on an *assumption:* Harassment is unfair discrimination—but few would quarrel with that assumption.

Notice the *language* in which Scott characterizes the actions of the American Cancer Society ("blast," "squirt," "burn"—all in para. 5). He chose these verbs deliberately, to convey his disapproval of these actions and subtly to help the reader disapprove of them, too.

Another distinctive feature of Scott's method of argument is found in paragraph 7, after the examples. Here, he drives his point home by using the argumentative technique known as *the thin end of the wedge.* (We discuss it later on p. 285. The gist of the idea is that just as the thin end of the wedge makes a small opening that will turn into a larger one, so a small step may lead to a large step. The idea is also expressed in the familiar phrase, "Give him an inch and he'll take a mile.") Scott here argues that tolerating discrimination today against a vulnerable minority (smokers) could lead to tolerating widespread discrimination against other minorities (mountain climbers) tomorrow—perhaps even a minority that includes the reader. (Does he exaggerate by overstating his case? Or are his examples well chosen and plausible?)

Notice, finally, the role that *rhetorical questions* play in Scott's argument. (A **rhetorical question,** such as Scott's "How far will we allow this to spread?" in para. 7, is a question to which no answer is expected, because only one answer can reasonably be made.) Writers who use a rhetorical question save themselves the trouble of offering further evidence to support their claims; the person asking the rhetorical question assumes the reader understands and agrees with the questioner's unstated answer.

Persona   Scott presents himself as a no-nonsense defender of the rights of a beleaguered minority. This may add little or nothing to the soundness of his argument, but it surely adds to its persuasive effect. By presenting himself as he does—plain-speaking but righteously indignant—Scott effectively jars the reader's complacency (surely, all the good guys *oppose* smoking—or do they?), and he cultivates at least the reader's grudging respect (we all like to see people stand up for their rights, and the more unpopular the cause the more we respect the sincere advocate).

Closing Paragraph   Scott ends with one of those seeming platitudes that tolerates no disagreement—"discrimination is discrimination," thus making one last effort to enlist the reader on his side. We say "seeming platitudes," because, when you come to think about it, of course not all discrimination is morally objectionable. After all, what's unfair with "discriminating" against criminals by punishing them?

Consider a parallel case, that popular maxim "Business is business." What is it, really, but a disguised claim to the effect that *in business, unfair practices must be tolerated or even admired.* But as soon as this sentiment is reformulated by removing its disguise as a tautology, its controversial character is immediately evident. So with Scott's "discrimination is discrimination"; it is designed to numb the reader into believing that all discrimination is *objectionable* discrimination. The critic might reply to Scott in the same vein: There is discrimination, and there is discrimination.

Let's turn now to a student's analysis of Scott's essay—and then to our analysis of the student's analysis.

Tom Wu

English 2B

Professor McCabe

March 13, 1998

                Is All Discrimination Unfair?

        Stanley S. Scott's "Smokers Get a Raw
Deal," though a poor argument, is an extremely
clever piece of writing. Scott writes clearly
and he holds a reader's attention. Take his
opening paragraph, which evokes the bad old days
of Jim Crow segregation, when blacks were forced
to ride at the back of the bus. Scott tells us,
to our surprise, that there still are Americans
who are forced to ride at the back of the bus.
Who, we wonder, are the people who are treated
so unfairly--or we would wonder, if the title of
the essay hadn't let us make an easy guess. They
are smokers. Of course most Americans detest
segregation, and Scott thus hopes to tap our
feelings of decency and fair play, so that we
will recognize that smokers are people too, and
they ought not to be subjected to the same evil
that blacks were subjected to. He returns to
this motif at the end of his essay, when he
says, "After all, discrimination is discrimination, no matter what it is based on." Scott is,
so it seems, on the side of fair play.

        But "discrimination" has two meanings. One
is the ability to make accurate distinctions,
as in "She can discriminate between instant
coffee and freshly ground coffee." The second
meaning is quite different: an act based on
prejudice, as in "She does not discriminate
against the handicapped," and of course this is

Scott's meaning. Blacks were the victims of discrimination in this second sense when they were forced to sit at the back of the bus simply because they were black, not because they engaged in any action that might reasonably be perceived as offensive or harmful to others. That sort of segregation was the result of prejudice; it held people accountable for something (their color) over which they had no control. But smokers voluntarily engage in an action which can be annoying to others (like playing loud music on a radio at midnight, with the windows open), and which may have effects that can injure others. In pursuing their "right," smokers thus can interfere with the rights of others. In short, the "segregation" and "discrimination" against smokers is in no way comparable to the earlier treatment of blacks. Scott illegitimately—one might say outrageously—suggests that segregating smokers is as unjust, and as blindly prejudiced, as was the segregating of blacks.

Between his opening and his closing paragraphs, which present smokers as victims of "discrimination," he cites several instances of smokers who were subjected to violence, including two smokers who were killed. His point is, again, to show that smokers are being treated as blacks once were, and are in effect subjected to lynch law. The instances of violence that he cites are deplorable, but they scarcely prove that it is wrong to insist that people do not have the unrestricted right to smoke in

public places. It is clearly wrong to assault
smokers, but surely these assaults do not
therefore make it right for smokers to subject
others to smoke that annoys and may harm.

Scott's third chief argument, set forth in
the third paragraph from the end, is to claim
that if today we infringe on "the basic freedoms of more than 50 million American smokers"
we will perhaps tomorrow infringe on the freedom of yet other Americans. Here Scott makes an
appeal to patriotism ("basic freedoms," "American") and at the same time warns the reader
that the reader's innocent pleasures, such as
eating ice cream or cake, are threatened. But
this extension is preposterous: Smoking undoubtedly is greatly bothersome to many nonsmokers, and may even be unhealthy for them;
eating ice cream cannot affect onlookers. If it
was deceptive to classify smokers with blacks,
it is equally deceptive to classify smoking
with eating ice cream. Scott is trying to tell
us that if we allow smokers to be isolated, we
will wake up and find that we are the next who
will be isolated by those who don't happen to
like our habits, however innocent. The nation,
he says, in his next-to-last paragraph, has
"struggled so valiantly [we are to pat ourselves on the back] to eliminate bias based on
race, religion, and sex." Can we, he asks, afford to let a new bias divide us? The answer,
of course, is that indeed we should discriminate, not in Scott's sense, but in the sense of
making distinctions. We discriminate, entirely

Wu 4

properly, between the selling of pure food and
of tainted food, between law-abiding citizens
and criminals, between licensed doctors and unlicensed ones, and so on. If smokers are a serious nuisance and a potential health hazard,
it is scarcely un-American to protect the innocent from them. That's not discrimination (in
Scott's sense) but is simply fair play.

AN ANALYSIS OF THE STUDENT'S ANALYSIS

Tom Wu's essay seems to us to be excellent, doubtless the product of a good deal of thoughtful revision. Of course he does not cover every possible aspect of Scott's essay—he concentrates on Scott's reasoning and he says very little about Scott's style—but we think that, given the limits of 500 to 750 words, he does a good job. What makes the student's essay effective? We can list the chief reasons:

- The essay has a title that is of at least a little interest, giving a hint of what is to follow. A title such as "An Analysis of an Argument" or "Scott on Smoking" would be acceptable, certainly better than no title at all, but in general it is a good idea to try to construct a more informative or a more interesting title that (like this one) arouses interest, perhaps by stirring the reader's curiosity.

- The author identifies his subject (he names the writer and the title of his essay) early.

- He reveals his thesis early. His topic is Scott's essay; his thesis or point is that it is clever but wrongheaded. Notice, by the way, that he looks closely at Scott's use of the word *discrimination*, and that he defines this word carefully. Defining terms is often essential in argumentative essays. Of course Scott did *not* define the word, probably because he hoped his misuse of it would be overlooked.

- He takes up all of Scott's main points.

- He uses a few brief quotations, to let us hear Scott's voice and to assure us that he is staying close to Scott, but he does not pad his essay with long quotations.

- The essay has a sensible organization. The student begins with the beginning of Scott's essay, and then, because Scott uses the opening motif again at the end, touches on the end. The writer is not skipping around; he is taking a single point (a "new discrimination" is upon us) and following it through.

- He turns to Scott's next argument, that smokers are subjected to violence. He doesn't try to touch on each of Scott's four examples— he hasn't room, in an essay of 500 to 750 words—but he treats their gist fairly.

- He touches on Scott's next point, that no one will be safe from other forms of discrimination, and shows that it is both a gross exaggeration and, because it equates utterly unlike forms of behavior, a piece of faulty thinking.

- He concludes (without the stiffness of saying "in conclusion") with some general comments on discrimination, thus picking up a motif he introduced early in his essay. His essay, like Scott's, uses a sort of frame, or, changing the figure, it finishes off by tying a knot that was begun at the start. He even repeats the words "fair play," which he used at the end of his first paragraph, and neatly turns them to his advantage.

- Notice, finally, that he sticks closely to Scott's essay. He does not go off on a tangent and talk about the harm that smokers do to themselves. Because the assignment was to analyze Scott's essay

---

A CHECKLIST FOR AN ESSAY ANALYZING AN ARGUMENT

✓ In your opening paragraph (or opening paragraphs) do you give the reader a good idea of what your essay will be doing? Do you identify the essay you will discuss, and introduce your subject?

✓ Is your essay fair? Does it face all of the strengths (and weaknesses) of the argument?

✓ Have you used occasional quotations, in order to let your reader hear the tone of the author, and in order to insure fairness?

✓ Is your analysis effectively organized? Probably you can't move through the original essay paragraph by paragraph, but have you created a coherent structure for your own essay?

✓ If the original essay relies partly on the writer's tone, have you sufficiently discussed this matter?

✓ Is your own tone appropriate?

(rather than to offer his own views on smoking) he confines himself to analyzing the essay.

Exercise

Take one of the essays not yet discussed in class, or an essay assigned now by your instructor, and in an essay of 500 words analyze and evaluate it.

ARGUMENTS FOR ANALYSIS

Rita Kramer

Rita Kramer, the author of At a Tender Age: Violent Youth and Juvenile Justice *(1988) and other books, published this article in the* Wall Street Journal *(May 27, 1992).*

Juvenile Justice Is Delinquent

Anyone who reads newspapers or watches TV is familiar with scenes of urban violence in which the faces of those who rob and rape, maim and kill get younger and younger. On the streets, in the subways, and even in the schools, juvenile crime has taken on a character unthinkable when the present justice system was set up to deal with it. That system, like so many of the ambitious social programs designed in the '60s, has had unintended results. Instead of solving society's ills, it has added to them.

The juvenile justice system now in place in most parts of the country is not very different from New York's Family Court. Originally conceived to protect children (defined by different states as those under age sixteen, seventeen, or eighteen) who ran afoul of the law, it was designed to function as a kind of wise parent providing rehabilitation.

The 1950s delinquent, who might have been a shoplifter, a truant, or a car thief, would not be treated like an adult criminal. He was held to be, in the wording of the New York statute, "not criminally responsible . . . by reason of infancy." He would be given a hearing (not a trial) closed to the press and public and the disposition (not a sentence) would remain sealed, so the juvenile would not be stigmatized by youthful indiscretion. The optimistic belief was that under the guidance of social workers he would undergo a change of character.

It was a dream destined to become a nightmare. In the early 1960s, the character of juvenile court proceedings underwent a radical transformation. Due process was interpreted to grant youthful "respondents" (not defendants) not only the services of a lawyer, but also the protections the criminal justice system affords adults, who are liable to serious penalties if found guilty.

In the hands of Legal Aid Society lawyers (and sometimes sympa-   5
thetic judges), the juvenile system focuses on the minutiae of procedural technicalities at the expense of fact-finding, in order to achieve the goal of "getting the kid off." The question is not whether a teenage boy has beaten up a homeless old man, shot a storekeeper, or sodomized a little girl. He may even admit the act. The question is whether his admission can be invalidated because a police officer forgot to have him initial his responses to the Miranda warnings in the proper place or whether the arresting officer had probable cause to search him for the loaded gun that was found on him.

It has become the lawyer's job not only to protect his young client from punishment, but from any possibility of rehabilitation in the system's various facilities. The best interests of the child or adolescent have been reinterpreted to mean his legal rights, even when the two are in opposition. He now has the right to continue the behavior that brought him into the juvenile court, which he leaves with the knowledge that his behavior had no real negative consequences to him.

Even when there are consequences, they are mild indeed, a fact not lost on his peers. Eighteen months in a facility that usually has TV, a basketball court, and better food and medical care than at home is the worst that all but the most violent repeat offenders have to fear in New York. The system, based on a person's age and not his crimes, fails either to restrain or retrain him.

As juvenile courts were changing, so were juvenile criminals. As recently as the early '70s, the majority of cases before children's and family courts were misdemeanors. In New York City, the most common charge was "jostling," pickpocketing without physical contact. By 1991, robbery—a charge that involves violence against people—had outpaced drug-related offenses as the largest category of crimes by juveniles. Between 1987 and 1991, the fastest-growing crime by juveniles was loaded gun possession, and metal detectors and spot police checks had become routine in some inner-city high schools.

Cases of violent group assault—"kids" causing serious physical injury "for fun"—had increased dramatically. Predatory behavior was becoming a form of entertainment for some of the urban young, white as well as black and Hispanic. Last year, according to Peter Reinharz, chief of New York City's Family Court Division, 85 percent of the young offenders brought into Family Court were charged with felonies. "These are dangerous people," Mr. Reinharz says. "We hardly ever see the nonviolent any more."

Nationwide figures compiled by the FBI's Uniform Crime Reporting   10
Program in 1990 showed the highest number of arrests of youth for violent offenses—homicide, armed robbery, rape, aggravated assault—in the more than twenty-five years that the statistics have been compiled. Juvenile arrest rates, after rising steadily from the mid-1960s through

the 1970s, remained relatively constant until the 1989–90 statistics revealed a 26 percent increase in the number of youths arrested for murder and non-negligent manslaughter, while arrests for robbery had increased by 16 percent, and those for aggravated assault by 17 percent.

But the system still defines juveniles as children rather than as criminals, a distinction that makes little sense to their victims or to the rest of the public. Family Court turns the worst juvenile offenders over to the adult system for trial, but they are still sentenced as juveniles.

When anything does happen it's usually so long after the event, so short in duration, and so ineffective that it's no wonder the young men who rob, maim, rape, and terrorize don't perceive those actions as having any serious consequences. Eighty percent of chronic juvenile offenders (five or more arrests) go on to adult criminal careers.

Is it possible to change these young criminals? And what should be done to protect the community from them?

The first necessity is legislation to open juvenile court proceedings to the public and the press. It makes no sense to protect the privacy of those who are a palpable menace to their neighbors or scruple about "stigmatizing" them. A repeat offender should know the authorities will make use of his past record in deciding what to do with him next time. At present, a young habitual criminal is born again with a virgin record when he reaches the age to be dealt with by the adult system.

Opening court records would also make it possible to undertake   15
follow-up studies to find out what works and what doesn't in the various detention facilities and alternative programs designed to rehabilitate. Taxpayers have a right to know what outcomes they are getting for the $85,000 a year it costs to keep a juvenile offender in a secure facility in New York state.

Intervention should occur early, while there is still time to try measures that might make a difference. First offenders should be required to make restitution to their victims or perform community service. A second arrest should be followed by stronger measures. For those who have families who undertake to be responsible for them, there should be intensive supervision by well-trained probation officers with manageable caseloads. For those who require placement out of the home, it should include intensive remedial schoolwork and practical training in some job-related skill. The youth should remain long enough for such efforts to have some hope of proving effective.

Sanctions should be swift and sure. Once arrested, a court appearance should follow without delay, preferably on the same day, so that there is a clear connection made between behavior and its consequences. Placement in appropriately secure institutions, locked away from the community for definite periods of time, should be the immediate and inevitable response to repeated acts of violence. And incarceration should involve some form of work that helps defray its cost to the community, not just a period of rest and recreation. Young criminals should know that is what they can expect.

A growing cadre of violent teenage boys are growing up with mothers who are children and no resident fathers. What they need most of all is structure and supervision. We may not be able to change attitudes, but we can change behavior. While there is no evidence that any form of therapy can really change a violent repeat offender into someone with empathy for others, it has been demonstrated that the one thing that can result in impulse control is the certainty of punishment.

The present system actually encourages the young to continue their criminal behavior by showing them that they can get away with it. No punishment means a second chance at the same crimes. A significant number of boys arrested for violent crimes were out on parole at the time of the arrest.

They think of the system as a game they can win. "They can't do 20 nothing to me, I ain't sixteen yet" is a repeated refrain in a system that breeds contempt for the law and for the other institutions of society. It is time to acknowledge its failure and restructure the system so that "juvenile justice" ceases to be an oxymoron. We owe it to the law-abiding citizens who share the streets and schools with the violent few to protect the rights of the community and not just those of its victimizers.

Topics for Critical Thinking and Writing

1. In her fifth paragraph Kramer indicates her distress with a system that allows a guilty juvenile to be released because the police failed to comply with some details. But the requirement that police comply with details was generated by police misconduct. If adults can be released because the police fail to act according to all of the standard procedures, why shouldn't juveniles also be released?

2. Kramer says (para. 6) that the current juvenile justice system has made it the defendant's lawyer's job "to protect his young client . . . from any possibility of rehabilitation." Explain her reasoning.

3. Kramer says (para. 7) that if a youthful offender is put away, it is "in a facility that usually has TV, a basketball court, and better food and medical care than at home." Let's assume she is right. Why do you suppose the government provides TV, a basketball court, and better food and medical care than the youth probably has at home? If you were running things, what would you change? Would you, for instance, do away with television sets, or provide medical care that is below the standard? Explain.

4. "But the system," Kramer says in paragraph 11, "still defines juveniles as children rather than as criminals, a distinction that makes little sense to their victims." Does she have a point here? Or might it also be said that of course the victims are distressed, but the feelings of the victims are irrelevant to a society that is trying to deal intelligently and humanely with youthful offenders? Explain.

5. In paragraph 18 Kramer says that "it has been demonstrated that the one thing that can result in impulse control is the certainty of punishment." She offers no evidence. Do you take her statement on trust? Or because it seems self-evident? Or do you assume it is true because it is a principle that guides your own life? Or what? Explain.

6. Kramer says (para. 19): "The present system actually encourages the young to continue their criminal behavior by showing them that they can get away with it." What evidence, if any, does she offer to support this sentence? If she does not support it, should she have, or is it self-evident?

7. In her final paragraph Kramer indicates that the reason we must reform the system is "to protect the rights of the community." Earlier in the essay, however, she also indicated the desirability of helping youthful offenders to reform their conduct. What do you make of the fact that she does not continue this point into her final paragraph?

8. Kramer reports a sudden increase (26 percent) in violent crimes by juveniles in the years 1989–90. If your library receives the FBI's annual *Uniform Crime Reports* or the *Sourcebook of Criminal Justice Statistics*, consult one of these sources and determine whether in the years since 1990 juvenile crime has continued to increase, has leveled off, or has decreased.

9. In paragraph 18 Kramer mentions the "growing cadre of violent teenage boys . . . growing up with . . . no resident fathers." She ends this paragraph insisting on the "certainty of punishment" for such boys. Why do you suppose she doesn't instead recommend measures to punish the fathers for neglecting their sons?

10. List the measures Kramer recommends to decrease juvenile crime. Does she cite any evidence to show that these reforms really would reduce such crime? Can you think of reasons to believe in or to doubt their efficacy?

Jeff Jacoby

Jeff Jacoby is a columnist for the Boston Globe, *where this essay was originally published on February 20, 1997.*

Bring Back Flogging

Boston's Puritan forefathers did not indulge miscreants lightly.

For selling arms and gunpowder to Indians in 1632, Richard Hopkins was sentenced to be "whipt, & branded with a hott iron on one of his cheekes." Joseph Gatchell, convicted of blasphemy in 1684, was ordered "to stand in pillory, have his head and hand put in & have his toung drawne forth out of his mouth, & peirct through with a hott iron." When Hannah Newell pleaded guilty to adultery in 1694, the court ordered "fifteen stripes Severally to be laid on upon her naked back at the Common Whipping post." Her consort, the aptly named Lambert Despair, fared worse: He was sentenced to 25 lashes "and that on the next Thursday Immediately after Lecture he stand upon the Pillory for . . . a full hower with Adultery in Capitall letters written upon his brest."

Corporal punishment for criminals did not vanish with the Puritans — Delaware didn't get around to repealing it until 1972 — but for all relevant purposes, it has been out of fashion for at least 150 years. The day is long past when the stocks had an honored place on the Boston Common, or when offenders were publicly flogged. Now we practice a more enlightened, more humane way of disciplining wrongdoers: We lock them up in cages.

Imprisonment has become our penalty of choice for almost every offense in the criminal code. Commit murder; go to prison. Sell cocaine; go to prison. Kite checks; go to prison. It is an all-purpose punishment, suitable — or so it would seem — for crimes violent and nonviolent, motivated by hate or by greed, plotted coldly or committed in a fit of passion. If anything, our preference for incarceration is deepening — behold the slew of mandatory minimum sentences for drug crimes and "three-strikes-you're-out" life terms for recidivists. Some 1.6 million Americans are behind bars today. That represents a 250 percent increase since 1980, and the number is climbing.

We cage criminals at a rate unsurpassed in the free world, yet few of   5 us believe that the criminal justice system is a success. Crime is out of control, despite the deluded happy talk by some politicians about how "safe" cities have become. For most wrongdoers, the odds of being arrested, prosecuted, convicted, and incarcerated are reassuringly long. Fifty-eight percent of all murders do *not* result in a prison term. Likewise 98 percent of all burglaries.

Many states have gone on prison-building sprees, yet the penal system is choked to bursting. To ease the pressure, nearly all convicted felons are released early — or not locked up at all. "About three of every four convicted criminals," says John DiIulio, a noted Princeton criminologist, "are on the streets without meaningful probation or parole supervision." And while everyone knows that amateur thugs should be deterred before they become career criminals, it is almost unheard of for judges to send first- or second-time offenders to prison.

Meanwhile, the price of keeping criminals in cages is appalling — a common estimate is $30,000 per inmate per year. (To be sure, the cost to society of turning many inmates loose would be even higher.) For tens of thousands of convicts, prison is a graduate school of criminal studies: They emerge more ruthless and savvy than when they entered. And for many offenders, there is even a certain cachet to doing time — a stint in prison becomes a sign of manhood, a status symbol.

But there would be no cachet in chaining a criminal to an outdoor post and flogging him. If young punks were horsewhipped in public after their first conviction, fewer of them would harden into lifelong felons. A humiliating and painful paddling can be applied to the rear end of a crook for a lot less than $30,000—and prove a lot more educational than ten years' worth of prison meals and lockdowns.

Are we quite certain the Puritans have nothing to teach us about dealing with criminals?

Of course, their crimes are not our crimes: We do not arrest blasphe- 10 mers or adulterers, and only gun control fanatics would criminalize the sale of weapons to Indians. (They would criminalize the sale of weapons to anybody.) Nor would the ordeal suffered by poor Joseph Gatchell— the tongue "peirct through" with a hot poker—be regarded today as anything less than torture.

But what is the objection to corporal punishment that doesn't maim or mutilate? Instead of a prison term, why not sentence at least some criminals—say, thieves and drunk drivers—to a public whipping?

"Too degrading," some will say. "Too brutal." But where is it written that being whipped is more degrading than being caged? Why is it more brutal to flog a wrongdoer than to throw him in prison—where the risk of being beaten, raped, or murdered is terrifyingly high?

The *Globe* reported in 1994 that more than two hundred thousand prison inmates are raped each year, usually to the indifference of the guards. "The horrors experienced by many young inmates, particularly those who . . . are convicted of nonviolent offenses," former Supreme Court Justice Harry Blackmun has written, "border on the unimaginable." Are those horrors preferable to the short, sharp shame of corporal punishment?

Perhaps the Puritans were more enlightened than we think, at least on the subject of punishment. Their sanctions were humiliating and painful, but quick and cheap. Maybe we should readopt a few.

Topics for Critical Thinking and Writing

1. When Jacoby says (para. 3) that today we are more "enlightened" than our Puritan forefathers, because where they used flogging "We lock them up in cages," is he being ironic? Explain.

2. Suppose you agree with Jacoby; explain precisely (1) what you mean by *flogging* (does Jacoby explain what he means?) and (2) how much flogging is appropriate for the crimes of housebreaking, rape, robbery, and murder.

3. In an essay of 250 words, explain why you think that flogging would be more (or less) degrading and brutal than imprisonment.

4. At the end of his essay Jacoby draws to our attention the terrible risk of being raped in prison as an argument in favor of replacing imprisonment with flogging. Do you think he mentions this point at the end because he believes it is the strongest or most persuasive of all those he mentions? Why, or why not?

5. It is often said that corporal punishment does not have any effect or, if it does, the effect is the negative one of telling the recipient that violence is an acceptable form of behavior. But suppose it were demonstrated that the infliction of physical pain reduced at least certain kinds of crimes, perhaps shoplifting, or unarmed robbery. Should we adopt the practice?

6. Jacoby draws the line (para. 11) at punishment that would "maim or mutilate." Why draw the line here? Some societies punish thieves by amputating a hand. Suppose we knew that this practice really did seriously reduce theft. Should we adopt it? How about adopting castration (surgical or chemical?) for rapists? For child molesters?

Katha Pollitt

Katha Pollitt (b. 1949) often writes essays on literary, political, and social topics for The Nation, *a liberal journal that on January 30, 1995, published the essay that we reprint here. Some of Pollitt's essays have been collected and published in a volume called* Reasonable Creatures *(1994). Pollitt is also widely known as a poet; her first collection of poems,* Antarctic Traveller *(1982), won the National Book Critics Circle award for poetry.*

It Takes Two: A Modest Proposal for Holding Fathers Equally Accountable

"You start out with the philosophy that you can have as many babies as you want . . . if you don't ask the government to take care of them. But when you start asking the government to take care of them, the government ought to have some control over you. I would say, for people like that, if they want the government to take care of their children I would be for something like Norplant, mandatory Norplant."

What well-known politician made the above remarks? Newt Gingrich? Jesse Helms? Dan Quayle? No, it was Marion Barry, newly installed Democratic mayor of our nation's capital, speaking last November to Sally Quinn of the *Washington Post.* The same Marion Barry whose swearing-in on January 2 featured a poetry reading by Maya Angelou, who, according to the *New York Times,* "drew thunderous applause when she pointed at Mr. Barry and crooned: 'Me and my baby, we gonna shine, shine!'" Ms. Angelou sure knows how to pick them.

One of my neighbors told me in the laundry room that it wasn't very nice of me to have mentioned Arianna Huffington's millions when we "debated" spirituality and school prayer on *Crossfire* the other day. So I won't belabor Mayor Barry's personal history[1] here. After all, the great

---

[1] **Mayor Barry's personal history** Marion Barry served six months in prison for possessing drugs.

thing about Christianity, of which Mayor Barry told Ms. Quinn he is now a fervent devotee, is that you can always declare yourself reformed, reborn, and redeemed. So maybe Mayor ("Bitch set me up") Barry really is the man to "bring integrity back into government," as he is promising to do.

But isn't it interesting that the male politicians who go all out for family values—the deadbeat dads, multiple divorcers, convicted felons, gropers, and philanderers who rule the land—always focus on women's behavior and always in a punitive way? You could, after all, see the plethora of women and children in poverty as the fruits of male feckless-ness, callousness, selfishness, and sexual vanity. We hear an awful lot about pregnant teens, but what about the fact that 30 percent of fathers of babies born to girls under sixteen are men in their twenties or older? What about the fact that the condom is the only cheap, easy-to-use, ef-fective, side-effectless nonprescription method of contraception—and it is the male partner who must choose to use it? What about the 50 per-cent of welfare mothers who are on the rolls because of divorce—i.e., the failure of judges to order, or husbands to pay, adequate child support?

Marion Barry's views on welfare are shared by millions: Women 5 have babies by parthenogenesis or cloning, and then perversely demand that the government "take care of them." Last time I looked, taking care of children meant feeding, bathing, and singing the Barney song, and mothers, not government bureaucrats, were performing those tasks. It is not the mother's care that welfare replaces, but the father's cash. Newt Gingrich's Personal Responsibility Act is directed against unmarried moms, but these women are actually assuming a responsibility that their babies' fathers have shirked. It's all very well to talk about orphanages, but what would happen to children if mothers abandoned them at the rate fathers do? A woman who leaves her newborn in the hospital and never returns for it still makes headlines. You'd need a list as thick as the New York City phone book to name the men who have no idea where or how or who their children are.

My point is not to demonize men, but fair's fair. If we've come so far down the road that we're talking about mandatory Norplant, about starving women into giving up their kids to orphanages (Republican ver-sion) or forcing young mothers to live in group homes (Democratic ver-sion); if *The Bell Curve* coauthor Charles Murray elicits barely a peep when he suggests releasing men from financial obligations to out-of-wedlock children; and if divorced moms have to hire private detectives to get their exes to pay court-awarded child support, then it's time to en-sure that the Personal Responsibility Act applies equally to both sexes. For example:

1. A man who fathers a child out of wedlock must pay $10,000 a year or 20 percent of his income, whichever is greater, in child sup-port until the child reaches twenty-one. If he is unable to pay, the

government will, in which case the father will be given a workfare (no wage) job and a dorm residence comparable to those provided homeless women and children—i.e., curfews, no visitors, and compulsory group-therapy sessions in which, along with other unwed fathers, he can learn to identify the patterns of irresponsibility that led him to impregnate a woman so thoughtlessly.

2. A man who fathers a second child out of wedlock must pay child support equal to that for the first; if he can't, or is already on workfare, he must have a vasectomy. A sample of his sperm will be preserved so he can father more children if he becomes able to support the ones he already has.

3. Married men who father children out of wedlock or in sequential marriages have the same obligations to all their children, whose living standards must be as close to equal as is humanly possible. This means that some older men will be financially unable to provide their much-younger trophy wives with the babies those women often crave. Too bad!

4. Given the important role played by fathers in everything from up- 10 ping their children's test scores to teaching them the meaning of terms like "wide receiver" and "throw weight," divorced or unwed fathers will be legally compelled to spend time with their children or face criminal charges of child neglect. Absentee dads, not overburdened single moms, will be legally liable for the crimes and misdemeanors of their minor children, and their paychecks will be docked if the kids are truant.

5. In view of the fact that men can father children unknowingly, all men will pay a special annual tax to provide support for children whose paternity is unknown. Men wishing to avoid the tax can undergo a vasectomy at state expense, with sperm to be frozen at personal expense (Republican version) or by government subsidy (Democratic version).

As I was saying, fair's fair.

Topics for Critical Thinking and Writing

1. In paragraph 5 Pollitt sums up what she says is a common view of welfare: "Women have babies by parthenogenesis or cloning, and then perversely demand that the government 'take care of them.'" What absurdity is she calling to our attention?

2. In paragraph 4 Pollitt cites three important facts for her argument pointing to "male . . . selfishness" as a chief cause of women on welfare. Consult some reliable source—a word with the reference librarian will probably help guide you to the right place—and verify at least one of these facts.

3. In paragraph 5 Pollitt mentions "Newt Gingrich's Personal Responsibility Act." With the assistance of your college's librarian, locate the text, or at least a summary, of this proposed law. Then look up the Republi-

cans' *Contract with America*, edited by Ed Gillespie and Bob Schellhas (1994), and check out what is described there as the Family Reinforcement Act. How do these two proposed laws differ?

4. Reread the first five paragraphs. Do you think that Pollitt has helped you to think about a problem? Or has she muddied the waters? Explain.

5. Pollitt declares not only once but twice (paras. 6 and 12) that "fair's fair." People also sometimes say "business is business." Both expressions look like more tautologies (needless repetitions), explaining or justifying nothing—yet they aren't really tautologies at all. What do you think is the rhetorical or persuasive function of such expressions?

6. Do you think that any of Pollitt's five proposals might become law? If not, why not, and, further, what *is* her purpose in offering them?

7. If you have read Jonathan Swift's "A Modest Proposal" (p. 151), explain why Pollitt echoes Swift's title in her own title.

David Cole

David Cole, a professor at Georgetown University Law Center, is a volunteer staff attorney for the Center for Constitutional Rights. This essay originally appeared in The Nation *on October 17, 1994.*

Five Myths about Immigration

For a brief period in the mid-nineteenth century, a new political movement captured the passions of the American public. Fittingly labeled the "Know-Nothings," their unifying theme was nativism. They liked to call themselves "Native Americans," although they had no sympathy for people we call Native Americans today. And they pinned every problem in American society on immigrants. As one Know-Nothing wrote in 1856: "Four-fifths of the beggary and three-fifths of the crime spring from our foreign population; more than half the public charities, more than half the prisons and almshouses, more than half the police and the cost of administering criminal justice are for foreigners."

At the time, the greatest influx of immigrants was from Ireland, where the potato famine had struck, and Germany, which was in political and economic turmoil. Anti-alien and anti-Catholic sentiments were the order of the day, especially in New York and Massachusetts, which received the brunt of the wave of immigrants, many of whom were dirt-poor and uneducated. Politicians were quick to exploit the sentiment: There's nothing like a scapegoat to forge an alliance.

I am especially sensitive to this history: My forebears were among those dirt-poor Irish Catholics who arrived in the 1860s. Fortunately for them, and me, the Know-Nothing movement fizzled within fifteen years. But its pilot light kept burning, and is turned up whenever the American public begins to feel vulnerable and in need of an enemy.

Although they go by different names today, the Know-Nothings have returned. As in the 1850s, the movement is strongest where immigrants are most concentrated: California and Florida. The objects of prejudice are of course no longer Irish Catholics and Germans; 140 years later, "they" have become "us." The new "they" — because it seems "we" must always have a "they" — are Latin Americans (most recently, Cubans), Haitians, and Arab Americans, among others.

But just as in the 1850s, passion, misinformation and shortsighted 5 fear often substitute for reason, fairness, and human dignity in today's immigration debates. In the interest of advancing beyond know-nothingism, let's look at five current myths that distort public debate and government policy relating to immigrants.

America is being overrun with immigrants. In one sense, of course, this is true, but in that sense it has been true since Christopher Columbus arrived. Except for the real Native Americans, we are a nation of immigrants.

It is not true, however, that the first-generation immigrant share of our population is growing. As of 1990, foreign-born people made up only 8 percent of the population, as compared with a figure of about 15 percent from 1870 to 1920. Between 70 and 80 percent of those who immigrate every year are refugees or immediate relatives of U.S. citizens.

Much of the anti-immigrant fervor is directed against the undocumented, but they make up only 13 percent of all immigrants residing in the United States, and only 1 percent of the American population. Contrary to popular belief, most such aliens do not cross the border illegally but enter legally and remain after their student or visitor visa expires. Thus, building a wall at the border, no matter how high, will not solve the problem.

Immigrants take jobs from U.S. citizens. There is virtually no evidence to support this view, probably the most widespread misunderstanding about immigrants. As documented by a 1994 A.C.L.U. Immigrants' Rights Project report, numerous studies have found that immigrants actually *create* more jobs than they fill. The jobs immigrants take are of course easier to see, but immigrants are often highly productive, run their own businesses, and employ both immigrants and citizens. One study found that Mexican immigration to Los Angeles County between 1970 and 1980 was responsible for 78,000 new jobs. Governor Mario Cuomo reports that immigrants own more than 40,000 companies in New York, which provide thousands of jobs and $3.5 billion to the state's economy every year.

Immigrants are a drain on society's resources. This claim fuels many of 10 the recent efforts to cut off government benefits to immigrants. However, most studies have found that immigrants are a net benefit to the economy because, as a 1994 Urban Institute report concludes, "immigrants generate significantly more in taxes paid than they cost in services received." The Council of Economic Advisers similarly found in 1986 that "immigrants have a favorable effect on the overall standard of living."

Anti-immigrant advocates often cite studies purportedly showing the contrary, but these generally focus only on taxes and services at the local or state level. What they fail to explain is that because most taxes go to the federal government, such studies would also show a net loss when applied to U.S. citizens. At most, such figures suggest that some redistribution of federal and state monies may be appropriate; they say nothing unique about the costs of immigrants.

Some subgroups of immigrants plainly impose a net cost in the short run, principally those who have most recently arrived and have not yet "made it." California, for example, bears substantial costs for its disproportionately large undocumented population, largely because it has on average the poorest and least educated immigrants. But that has been true of every wave of immigrants that has ever reached our shores; it was as true of the Irish in the 1850s, for example, as it is of Salvadorans today. From a long-term perspective, the economic advantages of immigration are undeniable.

Some have suggested that we might save money and diminish incentives to immigrate illegally if we denied undocumented aliens public services. In fact, undocumented immigrants are already ineligible for most social programs, with the exception of education for schoolchildren, which is constitutionally required, and benefits directly related to health and safety, such as emergency medical care and nutritional assistance to poor women, infants, and children. To deny such basic care to people in need, apart from being inhumanly callous, would probably cost us more in the long run by exacerbating health problems that we would eventually have to address.

Aliens refuse to assimilate, and are depriving us of our cultural and political unity. This claim has been made about every new group of immigrants to arrive on U.S. shores. Supreme Court Justice Stephen Field wrote in 1884 that the Chinese "have remained among us a separate people, retaining their original peculiarities of dress, manners, habits, and modes of living, which are as marked as their complexion and language." Five years later, he upheld the racially based exclusion of Chinese immigrants. Similar claims have been made over different periods of our history about Catholics, Jews, Italians, Eastern Europeans, and Latin Americans.

In most instances, such claims are simply not true; "American cul- 15 ture" has been created, defined, and revised by persons who for the most part are descended from immigrants once seen as anti-assimilationist. Descendants of the Irish Catholics, for example, a group once decried as separatist and alien, have become Presidents, senators, and representatives (and all of these in one family, in the case of the Kennedys). Our society exerts tremendous pressure to conform, and cultural separatism rarely survives a generation. But more important, even if this claim were true, is this a legitimate rationale for limiting immigration in a society built on the values of pluralism and tolerance?

Noncitizen immigrants are not entitled to constitutional rights. Our government has long declined to treat immigrants as full human beings, and nowhere is that more clear than in the realm of constitutional rights. Although the Constitution literally extends the fundamental protections in the Bill of Rights to all people, limiting to citizens only the right to vote and run for federal office, the federal government acts as if this were not the case.

In 1893 the executive branch successfully defended a statute that required Chinese laborers to establish their prior residence here by the testimony of "at least one credible white witness." The Supreme Court ruled that this law was constitutional because it was reasonable for Congress to presume that nonwhite witnesses could not be trusted.

The federal government is not much more enlightened today. In a pending case I'm handling in the Court of Appeals for the Ninth Circuit, the Clinton Administration has argued that permanent resident aliens lawfully living here should be extended no more First Amendment rights than aliens applying for first-time admission from abroad—that is, none. Under this view, students at a public university who are citizens may express themselves freely, but students who are not citizens can be deported for saying exactly what their classmates are constitutionally entitled to say.

Growing up, I was always taught that we will be judged by how we treat others. If we are collectively judged by how we have treated immigrants—those who would appear today to be "other" but will in a generation be "us"—we are not in very good shape.

Topics for Critical Thinking and Writing

1. What are the "five current myths" about immigration that Cole identifies? Why does he describe them as "myths" (rather than "errors," "mistakes," or "falsehoods")?

2. In an encyclopedia or other reference work in your college library, look up the Know-Nothings. What, if anything, of interest do you learn about the movement that is not mentioned by Cole in his opening paragraphs (1 to 4)?

3. Cole attempts to show how insignificant the immigrant population really is (in paras. 7 and 13) because it is such a small fraction (8 percent in 1990) of the total population. Suppose someone said to him, "That's all very well, but 8 percent of the population is still 20 million people—far more than the 15 percent of the population during the years from 1870 to 1920." How might he reply?

4. Suppose Cole is right, that most illegal immigration results from over-staying visitor and student visas (para. 8). Why not pass laws prohibiting foreign students from studying here, since so many abuse the privilege? Why not pass other laws forbidding foreign visitors?

5. Cole cites a study (para. 9) showing that Mexican immigration in Los Angeles County in the decade 1970–80 "was responsible for 78,000 new jobs." Suppose it were also true that this immigration was responsible for 78,000 other Mexican immigrants who joined criminal gangs or were otherwise not legally employed. How might Cole respond?

6. Cole admits (para. 12) that in California, the large population of undocumented immigrants imposes "substantial costs" on taxpayers. Docs Cole offer any remedy for this problem? Should the federal government bear some or all of these extra costs that fall on California?

7. Cole thinks that "cultural separatism" among immigrants "rarely survives a generation" (para. 15). His evidence? Look at the Irish Catholics. But suppose someone argued that this is weak evidence: Today's immigrants are not Europeans, they are Asian and Hispanic; they will never assimilate to the degree that European immigrants did—their race, culture, religion, and the trend toward "multiculturalism" all block the way. How might Cole reply?

8. Do you think that immigrants who arc not citizens and not applying for citizenship ought to be allowed to vote in state and local elections (the Constitution forbids them to vote in federal elections, as Cole points out in para. 16)? Why, or why not? How about illegal immigrants?

Janet Radcliffe Richards

Janet Radcliffe Richards is lecturer in philosophy in England on the central faculty of the Open University, where she specializes in ethics, philosophy of science, and applied philosophy. The essay reprinted here was published in the Newsletter of the Voluntary Euthanasia Society of Scotland *in September 1994.*

Thinking Straight and Dying Well

Presumably you would not have invited me to give this lecture unless you had thought I was on your side; and this puts us from the start in a situation of intellectual and moral danger. People are inclined to be very tolerant of arguments that seem to support conclusions they already accept.

It is easy to think of this fact as just another symptom of the well-known irrationality of our species, but oddly enough, what appears as irrationality is often a sign of a deeper, underlying rationality. When people are careless about facts, or play fast and loose with logic, this is often because they are trying to make it seem (to themselves as well as others) as though various ideas to which they are strongly committed can be made to fit together. Think, for instance, of someone who refuses to give to a charity, asserting (without any investigation of the matter) that charities waste all the money given to them. Pretty obviously, the invented fact is there to allow the person to reach the desired conclusion (not giving money) without having to make an undesirable admission (not being generous).

This is a useful thing to bear in mind in any area where there are strong passions. They are breeding grounds for twisted arguments and invented facts, and identifying these not only clarifies the issues and sharpens political argument; it also offers important indications of what the real motivations are. This applies potentially as much to our own arguments as to our opponents', and provides a method of real progress in moral enquiry. But here I want to concentrate on arguments against euthanasia.

And the first thing to do is to qualify the little I have already said. I have referred to *sides* and *the euthanasia debate*, and *arguments against euthanasia*. But this is just where the trouble starts. A moment's thought shows that the word "euthanasia" is applied to a wide range of actions; not only the ones counted as voluntary euthanasia, but also such things as turning off life support machines, killing defective babies, and not trying to save the lives of people who are senile or badly damaged in accidents.

These are all different, and there is no reason to presume they must 5 be morally identical. Inevitably, however, whenever there is a single word people will tend to think of it as denoting a single thing, and this is always dangerous. In particular, people who think of themselves as against whatever it is will often pounce on arguments that seem to work against the most troubling cases, and wave them around as if they were objections to all.

The first thing to do, therefore, is to pull the issue out of the impressionistic blur produced by the word "euthanasia," and make sure that each issue is analyzed in its own right. We must make sure that the clearest cases are not weakened by spurious association with more difficult ones. And, of course, the other way round. We must not allow any relatively straightforward cases to disguise the difficulty of others.

Since this is a voluntary euthanasia society I shall keep to the range of issues that come up only under that heading. That will be more than enough to be going on with.

THE BASIC ISSUE:
MAKING SUICIDE POSSIBLE

Slippery slopes. Two years ago there occurred the much-publicized case of Dr. Cox, who eventually gave in to the pleadings of a patient in desperate, terminal pain, and who wanted to die. This led to the usual rush of public alarm. Euthanasia must not be allowed, it was protested, because if we gave doctors the right to kill we should be off on a slippery slope, turning off life support machines, clearing geriatric wards, and moving inexorably towards Hitlerian extermination camps. Hitler is always the bogey at the bottom of the slope; an awful warning to anyone tempted to set out on it. Dr. Cox was forced, like Galileo, to recant.

But the issue brought up by this case has nothing to do with allowing doctors to decide whom to kill. It is, quite differently, that of whether people trapped by disability or institutions should be denied the freedom the rest of us have to commit suicide. Many people are simply not able to kill themselves; and it is, incidentally, a striking fact that the very helplessness which makes suicide impossible does itself provide some of the most rational grounds for wanting to die. The present law, which does not forbid suicide, nevertheless ensures that such people must stay alive, because no one else may help them to do what they cannot do alone.

But, say the objectors, at this point it ceases to be suicide and be- 10
comes killing; and killing is wrong. But once again, it cannot be presumed that everything describable by a single word must fall into a single moral category.

Normally we regard it as charitable and generous when people put their own powers at the disposal of the powerless, to enable them to do what they otherwise could not, and we see this as morally quite different from doing the same things against their will. If your aunt whose fingers are crippled with arthritis cannot put the sugar in her tea, and you do it for her, we do not hesitate to distinguish it from malicious tea-sweetening (as from Cicely to Gwendolen in *The Importance of Being Earnest*). Why, then, if you get the pills she wants to make her escape from life, or manipulate the syringe because she cannot do it herself, should we put this in the same moral category as doing those things against her will? In any other case such a conflation would scream out its absurdity; and so it should in this one.

If assisting the suicide of the helpless is killing, we must insist that there are different kinds of killing, and that this kind bears no moral resemblance at all to murder, or even to justifiable forms of killing without consent.

When the matter is put this way, it provides an indication of what really lies behind the objections. When do we say that it is wrong to help other people to do what they want to do, but cannot? Only, surely, when what they want is itself wrong. You would not feel that kindness to your arthritic aunt should extend to putting poison on her behalf into her neighbor's tea. Surely, therefore, anyone who thinks it wrong to assist the suicide of the helpless must think suicide itself wrong. Conversely, if the law does not forbid suicide, it has no justification for its seeing the assisting of suicide as different from the assisting of anything else.

So we can start the clarification of the issues by resolutely detaching this most fundamental case—the desperate situation of people who want to die but cannot kill themselves—from anything else to which the label of euthanasia may have become attached. And when this is done, and (obviously most important) proper safeguards are in place to make sure that what is going on really is assisted suicide and not murder, the slippery-slope idea stands exposed for the irrelevance it is. There is no slope. Suicide is not a thing there is any danger of anyone's getting into a habit of.

Making life worth living. Needless to say, however, that will 15 not be the end of the argument, even when it is clear that the issue is the limited one of freedom to commit suicide. One of the commonest symptoms of deeply rooted attitudes, held not because of the arguments offered in their defense but for other, unstated, reasons, is the speed with which refuted arguments are replaced by others.

The next familiar line of argument is that euthanasia of this sort should not be necessary; that we should instead be making people's lives worth living, by controlling their pain and making them feel valued. And this argument is a good piece of strategy, because no one is going to rush in and deny that we should be doing these things. It also tends to divert supporters of euthanasia into arguments about the extent to which it is possible to control pain, when what they should really be doing is exposing this maneuver as a fudge of the first order, and a particularly dangerous one. To see this, all that is needed is a steady eye for the point at issue. It is claimed that we should make life worth living for the suffering, and *implied* that this is a reason for not allowing help with suicide. But how can a claim that something should not be needed be regarded as a reason for saying it should be forbidden? You might just as well say that because all children should learn to read at school, we should prohibit adult literacy classes.

If we could reliably make everyone's life worth living, no one would want to die, and laws preventing assistance would have no purpose. Conversely, to the extent that they have a purpose, *precisely* what they achieve is to force continuing life on people whose sufferings we have not managed to prevent. The claim that we should prevent suffering is being used to defend a law whose main effect is to perpetuate it.

This is a clear case of an argument so outrageously bad that it could not possibly be thought to work by anyone not already convinced of the conclusion on quite other grounds. It seems obvious, once again, that its proponents really disapprove of suicide altogether, but are unwilling to face the fact that this may mean forcing people to remain alive in agony.

To put the matter even more starkly, the prevention of suicide achieves nothing for the sufferers, but it does mean the rest of us can avoid having forced on our attention the knowledge of how many people there are who would rather be dead, and can more easily forget them. I do not think for a moment that that is the motive of the people who argue in this way, but it is the effect. Anyone who really wants to make people's lives worth living should be glad to allow suicide, as a reminder of the extent of failure.

The dangers of coercion. The final objection I want to consider 20 against allowing assistance with suicide is increasingly common, and widely accepted as conclusive. It is that if euthanasia were allowed, we could never be sure it was truly voluntary. Relatives and doctors might make people feel unwanted, or even (though I have not actually heard this suggested) leave them in more pain than necessary to coerce them into choosing death. And even if this did not happen, people might still feel burdensome and under an obligation to choose to go. We must therefore keep the option closed.

This issue is more complicated than the previous two, and there is no quick answer on the euthanasia side. But what can be shown is that the other side is even less entitled to its own quick answer.

It is necessary to get the form of the problem clear. We should not be thinking about wards full of old people and wondering what their relations would do if we decided to institute voluntary euthanasia. Rather the question is, for everyone in a democracy, about the kinds of institutions we should prefer to live by. Would we, individually, choose to live in a society which forbade voluntary euthanasia altogether, to protect ourselves from the risk of being put under pressure to choose it?

It is certainly true that making things impossible is one way to prevent our being coerced into doing them. This is a well understood maneuver (see, for instance, Thomas Schelling in *The Strategy of Conflict*). On the other hand, it is not one to be adopted lightly. Usually it is absurd to give up an option completely in order to avoid the chance of being put under pressure to use it in a particular way; you would hardly think of giving up the freedom to choose whom to marry in order to avoid the danger of being put under pressure to make the wrong choice. Such decisions can be made only through careful risk analysis, involving estimates of how bad the various possible outcomes are, and how likely they are to come about. How likely is it that our relatives would start putting pressure on us? Is it a severe enough danger to justify the sacrifice of the freedom to opt out if we are in terrible pain?

There is no algorithm for calculations of this sort, but a few comments may help to put the matter in perspective.

First, although this line of argument does not seem to be motivated 25 by a straightforward opposition to suicide, I think in fact it must be. Anyone who can see the anti-euthanasia conclusion as immediate and obvious, rather than as difficult and to be reached only after much agonizing, is willing to give up the suicide option to avoid any risk at all that anyone will be put under pressure to take it. No one who thought the option intrinsically valuable could give it up so quickly. And for anyone who would like to keep it, the case for giving it up need seem nothing like as strong.

For one thing, it is not at all obvious that allowing suicide will make it more likely that people are put under pressure to take that option. It could work quite the other way: Relatives and hospitals might become so afraid of being accused of driving anyone to euthanasia that they become assiduous in their attempts to prevent it. Until we try, we shall not know.

Furthermore, there is no reason to think of these probabilities, whatever they are, as fixed. We could try to influence them in various ways. Perhaps hospitals might deliberately develop a culture in which euthanasia was regarded as a failure, and patients were persuaded not to choose it. (Though that would, of course, create pressures the other way.)

And, finally, a most important point. If different people might have different preferences in this context, we should consider whether it might be possible to let people choose their own risks. Even if suicide were allowed, I do not see why people who did not want the risk of pressure could not (say) sign an anti-suicide pledge, and join societies and churches committed to the repudiation of this option.

That kind of possibility does, indeed, seem to me to settle the issue. But even if it does not, it still seems clear that we need not be bullied by what is widely regarded as a knock-down argument against euthanasia, but which, without the hidden presupposition that suicide is never morally acceptable, is nothing of the sort.

SECOND ISSUE: EASING DEATH

So far I have discussed only one part of the voluntary euthanasia 30
issue, that of making death possible for people who cannot choose to die, and considered three common arguments against it. But of course there are other issues, and a closely related one is that of making death pleasant. For many people suicide is not actually impossible, but can be achieved only by painful or distressing means. Many of us think everyone should have access to the means of dying painlessly.

The usual objection is that this makes suicide too easy, and people will do away with themselves during passing bouts of depression. That, however, confuses ease and pleasantness. Most of us probably think there should be a waiting time, perhaps longer for young people than old, and other safeguards. But that is quite compatible with making death painless for anyone who can show they really want it.

But still, it will be said, to make death less unpleasant is to make it more attractive, and more people will choose it than otherwise would have done. Surely we should keep death unattractive in order to discourage suicide?

If this sounds plausible, consider it in more detail. Think of life as measured against a scale of satisfaction, and each person as fixing a point on that scale at which life becomes not worth living. If we want to prevent people choosing suicide when they reach that point, there are two ways of doing it. One is to make life better, so that it rises again above the crisis point. The other is to make death so unpleasant that things have to get even worse before death becomes an attractive option. Either of these, therefore, would prevent suicides.

But why, exactly, do we want to prevent suicide? What is bad about it? Some people think it bad in itself, and probably as sinful; others think the ground for regret is that anyone's life should be not worth living. If you want to prevent suicide for this second reason, only the first way of proceeding—improving people's lives—makes any sense. Preventing suicide by making death unpleasant does not make anyone's life one scrap more worth living; it just gives them a reason to live with more misery.

In other words, the now-familiar background assumption appears 35 again, in yet another disguise. To oppose allowing people the means of painless suicide is to regard suicide as bad in itself, and to be discouraged whether life is worth living or not.

THIRD ISSUE: ADVANCE DIRECTIVES

Finally, many of us would like to be able to specify that if we became so ill or damaged that we could not make any wishes known, we should be actively killed. This is quite different from saying that everyone in a coma or irreversibly damaged by a stroke should be done away with; that is related, but it needs separate argument. Here the claim is only that we should be allowed to decide for ourselves. What reason could anyone offer for saying that we should not?

The usual line of argument here is that we can never be sure. We cannot be sure that the coma will not be emerged from, or that a new treatment will not be found. Furthermore, we cannot be sure about the state of mind of someone unable to communicate, and who may have undergone a change of mind since writing the directive.

All these arguments, however, make the same presuppositions. They all presuppose that in case of doubt we should err on the side of caution, and that caution means not killing unless we are absolutely certain. Since we can never be certain, we should never risk killing.

But this is another case where risk analysis is needed, and many of us would assess the situation in quite the opposite way. The worst imaginable outcome is not being killed when we might (conceivably) have changed our minds but be unable to say so; far worse than that would be the *unutterable horror* of being trapped for years in a dreadful, degrading existence, unable even to communicate a wish to escape. The same applies to the risk of dying when a cure might be found, as compared with that of being kept alive and its not being found.

This seems to me so clear that it seems also relevant to the involun- 40 tary euthanasia issue: Surely in any case of doubt it would be better to risk killing quickly someone who might not want to die than to leave in such an appalling existence someone who might want to. But the voluntary case seems quite unanswerable, because this is not a matter that needs to be settled for everybody or nobody. It is something that people can choose for themselves, and it seems quite outrageous that they should not be allowed to.

Once again, the opposition to this kind of euthanasia clearly has nothing to do with respect for choices and fears about mistakes. It must arise from a general conviction that no one should be able to choose to die; or at least, to have anyone else's assistance in doing so.

So it seems to me that all the standard arguments against the different forms of voluntary euthanasia are not only seriously mistaken, but mistaken in ways that could not deceive anyone in neutral contexts. The situation seems to be the one I described at the outset. Deep feelings that these things are wrong accompany a wish to justify them (at least in public) in terms that seem more humane and enlightened than a simple opposition to suicide, and the arguments are a valiant attempt to reconcile the irreconcilable. If this were better understood, I think it might be much easier to overcome the continuing resistance to voluntary euthanasia.

DOCTORS AND DYING

Finally, one note on a rather different matter. Advocates of euthanasia often seem to take for granted the idea that it can be justified only by terminal illness and intolerable pain. But this is odd, because there could be innumerable good reasons for wanting to die. Hopeless disability, simple old age that made impossible all the things that gave life purpose, or just not wanting to waste on a nursing home the money you hoped to leave to your children or VESS,[1] might make it perfectly rational to wish to die. Why should we think some reasons, but not others, adequate for euthanasia?

My suspicion is that the idea of confining voluntary euthanasia to cases of terminal illness arises partly from political realism, but even more from assumptions about where doctors fit into all this.

A common line of argument against euthanasia is that doctors 45 should be committed to preserving life. Other people say that their duty of care should be understood more broadly than this, and that there is a

---

[1]VESS Voluntary Euthanasia Society of Scotland. [Editors' note.]

duty to end suffering, even by death, when life is declining and has nothing more to offer. But even these people rarely go so far as to say that doctors should help anyone who simply wants to die.

Obviously any society needs to decide the use its doctors may make of their powers. However, there is no reason why their role, whatever it is, should define the boundaries of euthanasia. There are two aspects to being a doctor: technical knowledge, and a set of commitments about the use that may be made of it. But these two are separable; and even though we might agree that there were certain things doctors should not do, that would not be a reason for saying that no one else should do it either. The means of suicide could be available elsewhere.

If this possibility is widely overlooked, that may be another consequence of the way the euthanasia issue has been seen as the question of what doctors should be allowed to do to people. Voluntary euthanasia is anyway not about allowing doctors to decide when anyone shall die, but about the permissibility of providing technical help for people who are not adequately equipped themselves. But if technical help is the issue, it need not come from doctors at all, and voluntary euthanasia need not be limited to cases of pain and imminent death.

We can see the issue for what it is: the idea that an essential element of a good life is the freedom to leave it in peace and with dignity.

Topics for Critical Thinking and Writing

1. Write a 250-word summary of the main points of Richards's essay.

2. Richards mentions what she calls "the invented fact" (para. 2). What, if any, invented facts about euthanasia does she identify in the course of her essay?

3. Richards mentions having discussed "three common arguments against" voluntary euthanasia (para. 30). What are these three arguments?

4. Formulate as precisely as you can the "slippery slope" argument to which Richards alludes (para. 8). What is her view about this argument as applied to euthanasia? Richards says (para. 14), "Suicide is not a thing there is any danger of anyone's getting into a habit of." But does this show that *assisting* another to suicide is not something that an unscrupulous doctor might get into the habit of doing?

5. Richards reasons (para. 13) that "if the law does not forbid suicide, it has no justification for [making illegal] the assisting of suicide." Suppose someone objected, saying, "Well, if we were to abolish laws against prostitution, that doesn't mean we have to abolish laws against pimping and keeping a brothel." How might Richards reply?

6. Evaluate Richards's analogy in paragraph 16: Prohibiting euthanasia because it isn't needed is like prohibiting adult literacy classes because children ought to learn to read in school.

7. Richards refers (in para. 20) to worries over whether suicide is ever "truly voluntary." What do you think is required for an act to be truly voluntary?

8. Richards says (para. 24), "There is no algorithm for calculations of this sort." What is an "algorithm," and why do you think she asserts there is none of the required sort?

9. Richards refers (in para. 33) to an imaginary scale to measure the value or worth one attaches to going on living, and supposes that each of us might fix a point on that scale when our own "life becomes not worth living." In fifty words, write out what for you would make you conclude that your life was no longer "worth living."

10. Richards seems (in para. 35) to think that suicide is *not* "bad in itself," although it might be quite bad if unnecessary, or bad for other reasons. Can you think of any reasons why one might disagree with her, believing that suicide indeed is bad in itself?

11. In your library, look up (in *Facts on File* or some other source) the activities during the 1990s of Dr. Jack Kevorkian, famous for his role in making physician-assisted suicide a headline issue. Would Richards approve of what Kevorkian has done? Why, or why not?

Peter Singer

Educated at the University of Melbourne and at Oxford, Peter Singer (b. 1946) has taught at Oxford and now teaches at Monash University in Australia. He has written on a variety of ethical issues, but he is especially known for caring about the welfare of animals.

This essay originally appeared in the New York Review of Books *(April 5, 1973), as a review of* Animals, Men and Morals, *edited by Stanley and Roslind Godlovitch and John Harris.*

Animal Liberation

I

We are familiar with Black Liberation, Gay Liberation, and a variety of other movements. With Women's Liberation some thought we had come to the end of the road. Discrimination on the basis of sex, it has been said, is the last form of discrimination that is universally accepted and practiced without pretense, even in those liberal circles which have long prided themselves on their freedom from racial discrimination. But one should always be wary of talking of "the last remaining form of discrimination." If we have learned anything from the liberation movements, we should have learned how difficult it is to be aware of the ways in which we discriminate until they are forcefully pointed out to us. A liberation movement demands an expansion of our moral horizons, so that practices that were previously regarded as natural and inevitable are now seen as intolerable.

Animals, Men and Morals is a manifesto for an Animal Liberation movement. The contributors to the book may not all see the issue this way. They are a varied group. Philosophers, ranging from professors to graduate students, make up the largest contingent. There are five of them, including the three editors, and there is also an extract from the unjustly neglected German philosopher with an English name, Leonard Nelson, who died in 1927. There are essays by two novelist/critics, Brigid Brophy and Maureen Duffy, and another by Muriel the Lady Dowding, widow of Dowding of Battle of Britain fame and the founder of "Beauty without Cruelty," a movement that campaigns against the use of animals for furs and cosmetics. The other pieces are by a psychologist, a botanist, a sociologist, and Ruth Harrison, who is probably best described as a professional campaigner for animal welfare.

Whether or not these people, as individuals, would all agree that they are launching a liberation movement for animals, the book as a whole amounts to no less. It is a demand for a complete change in our attitudes to nonhumans. It is a demand that we cease to regard the exploitation of other species as natural and inevitable, and that, instead, we see it as a continuing moral outrage. Patrick Corbett, Professor of Philosophy at Sussex University, captures the spirit of the book in his closing words:

> We require now to extend the great principles of liberty, equality, and fraternity over the lives of animals. Let animal slavery join human slavery in the graveyard of the past.

The reader is likely to be skeptical. "Animal Liberation" sounds more like a parody of liberation movements than a serious objective. The reader may think: We support the claims of blacks and women for equality because blacks and women really are equal to whites and males — equal in intelligence and in abilities, capacity for leadership, rationality, and so on. Humans and nonhumans obviously are not equal in these respects. Since justice demands only that we treat equals equally, unequal treatment of humans and nonhumans cannot be an injustice.

This is a tempting reply, but a dangerous one. It commits the non- 5 racist and nonsexist to a dogmatic belief that blacks and women really are just as intelligent, able, etc., as whites and males — and no more. Quite possibly this happens to be the case. Certainly attempts to prove that racial or sexual differences in these respects have a genetic origin have not been conclusive. But do we really want to stake our demand for equality on the assumption that there are no genetic differences of this kind between the different races or sexes? Surely the appropriate response to those who claim to have found evidence for such genetic differences is not to stick to the belief that there are no differences, whatever the evidence to the contrary; rather one should be clear that the claim to equality does not depend on IQ. Moral equality is distinct from factual equality. Otherwise it would be nonsense to talk to the equality of human beings, since humans, as individuals, obviously differ in intelligence and almost any ability one cares to name. If possessing greater intelligence does not entitle one human to exploit another, why should it entitle humans to exploit nonhumans?

Jeremy Bentham expressed the essential basis of equality in his famous formula: "Each to count for one and none for more than one." In other words, the interests of every being that has interests are to be taken into account and treated equally with the like interests of any other being. Other moral philosophers, before and after Bentham, have made the same point in different ways. Our concern for others must not depend on whether they possess certain characteristics, though just what that concern involves may, of course, vary according to such characteristics.

Bentham, incidentally, was well aware that the logic of the demand for racial equality did not stop at the equality of humans. He wrote:

> The day *may* come when the rest of the animal creation may acquire those rights which never could have been withholden from them but by the hand of tyranny. The French have already discovered that the blackness of the skin is no reason why a human being should be abandoned without redress to the caprice of a tormentor. It may one day come to be recognized that the number of the legs, the villosity of the skin, or the termination of the *os sacrum,* are reasons equally insufficient for abandoning a sensitive being to the same fate. What else is it that should trace the insuperable line? Is it the faculty of reason, or perhaps the faculty of discourse? But a full-grown horse or dog is beyond comparison a more rational, as well as a more conversable animal, than an infant of a day, or a week, or even a month, old. But suppose they were otherwise, what would it avail? The question is not, Can they *reason?* nor Can they *talk?* but, Can they *suffer?*[1]

Surely Bentham was right. If a being suffers, there can be no moral justification for refusing to take that suffering into consideration, and, indeed, to count it equally with the like suffering (if rough comparisons can be made) of any other being.

So the only question is: Do animals other than man suffer? Most people agree unhesitatingly that animals like cats and dogs can and do suffer, and this seems also to be assumed by those laws that prohibit wanton cruelty to such animals. Personally, I have no doubt at all about this and find it hard to take seriously the doubts that a few people apparently do have. The editors and contributors of *Animals, Men and Morals*

---

[1]*The Principles of Morals and Legislation,* ch. XVII, sec. 1, footnote to paragraph 4. [All notes are the author's unless otherwise specified.]

seem to feel the same way, for although the question is raised more than once, doubts are quickly dismissed each time. Nevertheless, because this is such a fundamental point, it is worth asking what grounds we have for attributing suffering to other animals.

It is best to begin by asking what grounds any individual human has for supposing that other humans feel pain. Since pain is a state of consciousness, a "mental event," it can never be directly observed. No observations, whether behavioral signs such as writhing or screaming or physiological or neurological recordings, are observations of pain itself. Pain is something one feels, and one can only infer that others are feeling it from various external indications. The fact that only philosophers are ever skeptical about whether other humans feel pain shows that we regard such inference as justifiable in the case of humans.

Is there any reason why the same inference should be unjustifiable 10 for other animals? Nearly all the external signs which lead us to infer pain in other humans can be seen in other species, especially "higher" animals such as mammals and birds. Behavioral signs—writhing, yelping, or other forms of calling, attempts to avoid the source of pain, and many others—are present. We know, too, that these animals are biologically similar in the relevant respects, having nervous systems like ours which can be observed to function as ours do.

So the grounds for inferring that these animals can feel pain are nearly as good as the grounds for inferring other humans do. Only nearly, for there is one behavioral sign that humans have but nonhumans, with the exception of one or two specially raised chimpanzees, do not have. This, of course, is a developed language. As the quotation from Bentham indicates, this has long been regarded as an important distinction between man and other animals. Other animals may communicate with each other, but not in the way we do. Following Chomsky,[2] many people now mark this distinction by saying that only humans communicate in a form that is governed by rules of syntax. (For the purposes of this argument, linguists allow those chimpanzees who have learned a syntactic sign language to rank as honorary humans.) Nevertheless, as Bentham pointed out, this distinction is not relevant to the question of how animals ought to be treated, unless it can be linked to the issue of whether animals suffer.

This link may be attempted in two ways. First, there is a hazy line of philosophical thought, stemming perhaps from some doctrines associated with Wittgenstein, which maintains that we cannot meaningfully attribute states of consciousness to beings without language. I have not seen this argument made explicit in print, though I have come across it in conversation. This position seems to me very implausible, and I doubt

---

[2]**Chomsky** Noam Chomsky (b. 1928), a professor of linguistics and the author of (among other books) *Language and Mind* (1972). [Editors' note.]

that it would be held at all if it were not thought to be a consequence of a broader view of the significance of language. It may be that the use of a public, rule-governed language is a precondition of conceptual thought. It may even be, although personally I doubt it, that we cannot meaningfully speak of a creature having an intention unless that creature can use a language. But states like pain, surely, are more primitive than either of these, and seem to have nothing to do with language.

Indeed, as Jane Goodall points out in her study of chimpanzees, when it comes to the expression of feelings and emotions, humans tend to fall back on nonlinguistic modes of communication which are often found among apes, such as a cheering pat on the back, an exuberant embrace, a clasp of hands, and so on.[3] Michael Peters makes a similar point in his contribution to *Animals, Men and Morals* when he notes that the basic signals we use to convey pain, fear, sexual arousal, and so on are not specific to our species. So there seems to be no reason at all to believe that a creature without language cannot suffer.

The second, and more easily appreciated way of linking language and the existence of pain is to say that the best evidence that we can have that another creature is in pain is when he tells us that he is. This is a distinct line of argument, for it is not being denied that a non-language-user conceivably could suffer, but only that we could know that he is suffering. Still, this line of argument seems to me to fail, and for reasons similar to those just given. "I am in pain" is not the best possible evidence that the speaker is in pain (he might be lying) and it is certainly not the only possible evidence. Behavioral signs and knowledge of the animal's biological similarity to ourselves together provide adequate evidence that animals do suffer. After all, we would not accept linguistic evidence if it contradicted the rest of the evidence. If a man was severely burned, and behaved as if he were in pain, writhing, groaning, being very careful not to let his burned skin touch anything, and so on, but later said he had not been in pain at all, we would be more likely to conclude that he was lying or suffering from amnesia than that he had not been in pain.

Even if there were stronger grounds for refusing to attribute pain to those who do not have a language, the consequences of this refusal might lead us to examine these grounds unusually critically. Human infants, as well as some adults, are unable to use language. Are we to deny that a year-old infant can suffer? If not, how can language be crucial? Of course, most parents can understand the responses of even very young infants better than they understand the responses of other animals, and sometimes infant responses can be understood in the light of later development.

This, however, is just a fact about the relative knowledge we have of our own species and other species, and most of this knowledge is simply

15

---

[3]Jane van Lawick-Goodall, *In the Shadow of Man* (Houghton Mifflin, 1971), p. 225.

derived from closer contact. Those who have studied the behavior of other animals soon learn to understand their responses at least as well as we understand those of an infant. (I am not referring to Jane Goodall's and other well-known studies of apes. Consider, for example, the degree of understanding achieved by Tinbergen from watching herring gulls.[4]) Just as we can understand infant human behavior in the light of adult human behavior, so we can understand the behavior of other species in the light of our own behavior (and sometimes we can understand our own behavior better in the light of the behavior of other species).

The grounds we have for believing that other mammals and birds suffer are, then, closely analogous to the grounds we have for believing that other humans suffer. It remains to consider how far down the evolutionary scale this analogy holds. Obviously it becomes poorer when we get further away from man. To be more precise would require a detailed examination of all that we know about other forms of life. With fish, reptiles, and other vertebrates the analogy still seems strong, with molluscs like oysters it is much weaker. Insects are more difficult, and it may be that in our present state of knowledge we must be agnostic about whether they are capable of suffering.

If there is no moral justification for ignoring suffering when it occurs, and it does occur in other species, what are we to say of our attitudes toward these other species? Richard Ryder, one of the contributors to *Animals, Men and Morals,* uses the term "speciesism" to describe the belief that we are entitled to treat members of other species in a way in which it would be wrong to treat members of our own species. The term is not euphonious, but it neatly makes the analogy with racism. The nonracist would do well to bear the analogy in mind when he is inclined to defend human behavior toward nonhumans. "Shouldn't we worry about improving the lot of our own species before we concern ourselves with other species?" he may ask. If we substitute "race" for "species" we shall see that the question is better not asked. "Is a vegetarian diet nutritionally adequate?" resembles the slaveowner's claim that he and the whole economy of the South would be ruined without slave labor. There is even a parallel with skeptical doubts about whether animals suffer, for some defenders of slavery professed to doubt whether blacks really suffer in the way whites do.

I do not want to give the impression, however, that the case for Animal Liberation is based on the analogy with racism and no more. On the contrary, *Animals, Men and Morals* describes the various ways in which humans exploit nonhumans, and several contributors consider the defenses that have been offered, including the defense of meat-eating mentioned in the last paragraph. Sometimes the rebuttals are scornfully dismissive, rather than carefully designed to convince the detached critic.

[4]N. Tinbergen, *The Herring Gull's World* (Basic Books, 1961).

This may be a fault, but it is a fault that is inevitable, given the kind of book this is. The issue is not one on which one can remain detached. As the editors state in their Introduction:

> Once the full force of moral assessment has been made explicit there can be no rational excuse left for killing animals, be they killed for food, science, or sheer personal indulgence. We have not assembled this book to provide the reader with yet another manual on how to make brutalities less brutal. Compromise, in the traditional sense of the term, is simple unthinking weakness when one considers the actual reasons for our crude relationships with the other animals.

The point is that on this issue there are few critics who are genuinely 20 detached. People who eat pieces of slaughtered nonhumans every day find it hard to believe that they are doing wrong; and they also find it hard to imagine what else they could eat. So for those who do not place nonhumans beyond the pale of morality, there comes a stage when further argument seems pointless, a stage at which one can only accuse one's opponent of hypocrisy and reach for the sort of sociological account of our practices and the way we defend them that is attempted by David Wood in his contribution to his book. On the other hand, to those unconvinced by the arguments, and unable to accept that they are merely rationalizing their dietary preferences and their fear of being thought peculiar, such sociological explanations can only seem insultingly arrogant.

II

The logic of speciesism is most apparent in the practice of experimenting on nonhumans in order to benefit humans. This is because the issue is rarely obscured by allegations that nonhumans are so different from humans that we cannot know anything about whether they suffer. The defender of vivisection cannot use this argument because he needs to stress the similarities between man and other animals in order to justify the usefulness to the former of experiments on the latter. The researcher who makes rats choose between starvation and electric shocks to see if they develop ulcers (they do) does so because he knows that the rat has a nervous system very similar to man's, and presumably feels an electric shock in a similar way.

Richard Ryder's restrained account of experiments on animals made me angrier with my fellow men than anything else in this book. Ryder, a clinical psychologist by profession, himself experimented on animals before he came to hold the view he puts forward in his essay. Experimenting on animals is now a large industry, both academic and commercial. In 1969, more than 5 million experiments were performed in Britain, the vast majority without anesthetic (though how many of these involved pain is not known). There are no accurate U.S. figures, since there is no federal law on the subject, and in many cases no state law either. Estimates vary from 20 million to 200 million. Ryder suggests that 80 million may be the best guess. We tend to think that this is all for vital medical research, but of course it is not. Huge numbers of animals are used in university departments from Forestry to Psychology, and even more are used for commercial purposes, to test whether cosmetics can cause skin damage, or shampoos eye damage, or to test food additives or laxatives or sleeping pills or anything else.

A standard test for foodstuffs is the "LD50." The object of this test is to find the dosage level at which 50 percent of the test animals will die. This means that nearly all of them will become very sick before finally succumbing or surviving. When the substance is a harmless one, it may be necessary to force huge doses down the animals, until in some cases sheer volume or concentration causes death.

Ryder gives a selection of experiments, taken from recent scientific journals. I will quote two, not for the sake of indulging in gory details, but in order to give an idea of what normal researchers think they may legitimately do to other species. The point is not that the individual researchers are cruel men, but that they are behaving in a way that is allowed by our speciesist attitudes. As Ryder points out, even if only 1 percent of the experiments involve severe pain, that is 50,000 experiments in Britain each year, or nearly 150 every day (and about fifteen times as many in the United States, if Ryder's guess is right). Here then are two experiments:

> O. S. Ray and R. J. Barrett of Pittsburgh gave electric shocks to the feet of 1,042 mice. They then caused convulsions by giving more intense shocks through cup-shaped electrodes applied to the animals' eyes or through pressure spring clips attached to their ears. Unfortunately some of the mice who "successfully completed Day One training were found sick or dead prior to testing on Day Two." [*Journal of Comparative and Physiological Psychology*, 1969, vol. 67, pp. 110–116]
>
> At the National Institute for Medical Research, Mill Hill, London, W. Feldberg and S. L. Sherwood injected chemicals into the brains of cats—"with a number of widely different substances, recurrent patterns of reaction were obtained. Retching, vomiting, defecation, increased salivation and greatly accelerated respiration leading to panting were common features." . . .
>
> The injection into the brain of a large dose of Tubocuraine caused the cat to jump "from the table to the floor and then straight into its cage, where it started calling more and more noisily whilst moving about restlessly and jerkily . . . finally the cat fell with legs and neck flexed, jerking in rapid clonic movements, the condition being that of a major [epileptic] convulsion . . . within a few seconds the cat got up, ran for a few yards at high speed, and fell in another fit. The whole process was repeated several times within the next ten minutes, during which the cat lost faeces and foamed at the mouth."

This animal finally died thirty-five minutes after the brain injection. [*Journal of Physiology*, 1954, vol. 123, pp. 148–167]

There is nothing secret about these experiments. One has only to 25 open any recent volume of a learned journal, such as the *Journal of Comparative and Physiological Psychology*, to find full descriptions of experiments of this sort, together with the results obtained—results that are frequently trivial and obvious. The experiments are often supported by public funds.

It is a significant indication of the level of acceptability of these practices that, although these experiments are taking place at this moment on university campuses throughout the country, there has, so far as I know, not been the slightest protest from the student movement. Students have been rightly concerned that their universities should not discriminate on grounds of race or sex, and that they should not serve the purposes of the military or big business. Speciesism continues undisturbed, and many students participate in it. There may be a few qualms at first, but since everyone regards it as normal, and it may even be a required part of a course, the student soon becomes hardened and, dismissing his earlier feelings as "mere sentiment," comes to regard animals as statistics rather than sentient beings with interests that warrant consideration.

Argument about vivisection has often missed the point because it has been put in absolutist terms: Would the abolitionist be prepared to let thousands die if they could be saved by experimenting on a single animal? The way to reply to this purely hypothetical question is to pose another: Would the experimenter be prepared to experiment on a human orphan under six months old, if it were the only way to save many lives? (I say "orphan" to avoid the complication of parental feelings, although in doing so I am being overfair to the experimenter, since the nonhuman subjects of experiments are not orphans.) A negative answer to this question indicates that the experimenter's readiness to use nonhumans is simple discrimination, for adult apes, cats, mice, and other mammals are more conscious of what is happening to them, more self-directing, and, so far as we can tell, just as sensitive to pain as a human infant. There is no characteristic that human infants possess that adult mammals do not have to the same or a higher degree.

(It might be possible to hold that what makes it wrong to experiment on a human infant is that the infant will in time develop into more than the nonhuman, but one would then, to be consistent, have to oppose abortion, and perhaps contraception, too, for the fetus and the egg and sperm have the same potential as the infant. Moreover, one would still have no reason for experimenting on a nonhuman rather than a human with brain damage severe enough to make it impossible for him to rise above infant level.)

The experimenter, then, shows a bias for his own species whenever he carries out an experiment on a nonhuman for a purpose that he would not think justified him in using a human being at an equal or lower level of sentience, awareness, ability to be self-directing, etc. No one familiar with the kind of results yielded by these experiments can have the slightest doubt that if this bias were eliminated the number of experiments performed would be zero or very close to it.

III

If it is vivisection that shows the logic of speciesism most clearly, it is 30 the use of other species for food that is at the heart of our attitudes toward them. Most of *Animals, Men and Morals* is an attack on meat eating—an attack which is based solely on concern for nonhumans, without reference to arguments derived from consideration of ecology, macrobiotics, health, or religion.

The idea that nonhumans are utilities, means to our ends, pervades our thought. Even conservationists who are concerned about the slaughter of wildfowl but not about the vastly greater slaughter of chickens for our tables are thinking in this way—they are worried about what we would lose if there were less wildlife. Stanley Godlovitch, pursuing the Marxist idea that our thinking is formed by the activities we undertake in satisfying our needs, suggests that man's first classification of his environment was into Edibles and Inedibles. Most animals came into the first category, and there they have remained.

Man may always have killed other species for food, but he has never exploited them so ruthlessly as he does today. Farming has succumbed to business methods, the objective being to get the highest possible ratio of output (meat, eggs, milk) to input (fodder, labor costs, etc.). Ruth Harrison's essay "On Factory Farming" gives an account of some aspects of modern methods, and of the unsuccessful British campaigns for effective controls, a campaign which was sparked off by her *Animal Machines* (London: Stuart, 1964).

Her article is in no way a substitute for her earlier book. This is a pity since, as she says, "Farm produce is still associated with mental pictures of animals browsing in the fields . . . of hens having a last forage before going to roost. . . ." Yet neither in her article nor elsewhere in *Animals, Men and Morals* is this false image replaced by a clear idea of the nature and extent of factory farming. We learn of this only indirectly, when we hear of the code of reform proposed by an advisory committee set up by the British government.

Among the proposals, which the government refused to implement on the grounds that they were too idealistic, were: *"Any animal should at least have room to turn around freely."*

Factory farm animals need liberation in the most literal sense. Veal 35 calves are kept in stalls 5 feet by 2 feet. They are usually slaughtered when about four months old, and have been too big to turn in their stalls for at least a month. Intensive beef herds, kept in stalls only proportionately larger for much longer periods, account for a growing percentage of beef production. Sows are often similarly confined when pregnant, which, because of artificial methods of increasing fertility, can be most of the time. Animals confined in this way do not waste food by exercising, nor do they develop unpalatable muscle.

"A dry bedded area should be provided for all stock." Intensively kept animals usually have to stand and sleep in slatted floors without straw, because this makes cleaning easier.

"Palatable roughage must be readily available to all calves after one week of age." In order to produce the pale veal housewives are said to prefer, calves are fed on an all-liquid diet until slaughter, even though they are long past the age at which they would normally eat grass. They develop a craving for roughage, evidenced by attempts to gnaw wood from their stalls. (For the same reason, their diet is deficient in iron.)

"Battery cages for poultry should be large enough for a bird to be able to stretch one wing at a time." Under current British practice, a cage for four or five laying hens has a floor area of 20 inches by 18 inches, scarcely larger than a double page of the *New York Review of Books*. In this space, on a sloping wire floor (sloping so the eggs roll down, wire so the dung drips through) the birds live for a year or eighteen months while artificial lighting and temperature conditions combine with drugs in their food to squeeze the maximum number of eggs out of them. Table birds are also sometimes kept in cages. More often they are reared in sheds, no less crowded. Under these conditions all the birds' natural activities are frustrated, and they develop "vices" such as pecking each other to death. To prevent this, beaks are often cut off, and the sheds kept dark.

How many of those who support factory farming by buying its produce know anything about the way it is produced? How many have heard something about it, but are reluctant to check up for fear that it will make them uncomfortable? To nonspeciesists, the typical consumer's mixture of ignorance, reluctance to find out the truth, and vague belief that nothing really bad could be allowed seems analogous to the attitudes of "decent Germans" to the death camps.

There are, of course, some defenders of factory farming. Their arguments are considered, though again rather sketchily, by John Harris. Among the most common: "Since they have never known anything else, they don't suffer." This argument will not be put by anyone who knows anything about animal behavior, since he will know that not all behavior has to be learned. Chickens attempt to stretch wings, walk around, scratch, and even dustbathe or build a nest, even though they have never lived under conditions that allowed these activities. Calves can suffer from maternal deprivation no matter at what age they were taken from their mothers. "We need these intensive methods to provide protein for a growing population." As ecologists and famine relief organizations know, we can produce far more protein per acre if we grow the right vegetable crop, soy beans for instance, than if we use the land to grow crops to be converted into protein by animals who use nearly 90 percent of the protein themselves, even when unable to exercise.

There will be many readers of this book who will agree that factory farming involves an unjustifiable degree of exploitation of sentient creatures, and yet will want to say that there is nothing wrong with rearing animals for food, provided it is done "humanely." These people are saying, in effect, that although we should not cause animals to suffer, there is nothing wrong with killing them.

There are two possible replies to this view. One is to attempt to show that this combination of attitudes is absurd. Roslind Godlovitch takes this course in her essay, which is an examination of some common attitudes to animals. She argues that from the combination of "animal suffering is to be avoided" and "there is nothing wrong with killing animals" it follows that all animal life ought to be exterminated (since all sentient creatures will suffer to some degree at some point in their lives). Euthanasia is a contentious issue only because we place some value on living. If we did not, the least amount of suffering would justify it. Accordingly, if we deny that we have a duty to exterminate all animal life, we must concede that we are placing some value on animal life.

This argument seems to me valid, although one could still reply that the value of animal life is to be derived from the pleasures that life can have for them, so that, provided their lives have a balance of pleasure over pain, we are justified in rearing them. But this would imply that we ought to produce animals and let them live as pleasantly as possible, without suffering.

At this point, one can make the second of the two possible replies to the view that rearing and killing animals for food is all right so long as it is done humanely. This second reply is that so long as we think that a nonhuman may be killed simply so that a human can satisfy his taste for meat, we are still thinking of nonhumans as means rather than as ends in themselves. The factory farm is nothing more than the application of technology to this concept. Even traditional methods involve castration, the separation of mothers and their young, the breaking up of herds, branding or earpunching, and of course transportation to the abattoirs and the final moments of terror when the animal smells blood and senses danger. If we were to try rearing animals so that they lived and died without suffering, we should find that to do so on anything like the scale of today's meat industry would be a sheer impossibility. Meat would become the prerogative of the rich.

I have been able to discuss only some of the contributions to this 45 book, saying nothing about, for instance, the essays on killing for furs and for sport. Nor have I considered all the detailed questions that need to be asked once we start thinking about other species in the radically different way presented by this book. What, for instance, are we to do about genuine conflicts of interest like rats biting slum children? I am not sure of the answer, but the essential point is just that we *do* see this as a conflict of interests, that we recognize that rats have interests too. Then we may begin to think about other ways of resolving the conflict — perhaps by leaving out rat baits that sterilize the rats instead of killing them.

I have not discussed such problems because they are side issues compared with the exploitation of other species for food and for experimental purposes. On these central matters, I hope that I have said enough to show that this book, despite its flaws, is a challenge to every human to recognize his attitudes to nonhumans as a form of prejudice no less objectionable than racism or sexism. It is a challenge that demands not just a change of attitudes, but a change in our way of life, for it requires us to become vegetarians.

Can a purely moral demand of this kind succeed? The odds are certainly against it. The book holds out no inducements. It does not tell us that we will become healthier, or enjoy life more, if we cease exploiting animals. Animal Liberation will require greater altruism on the part of mankind than any other liberation movement, since animals are incapable of demanding it for themselves, or of protesting against their exploitation by votes, demonstrations, or bombs. Is man capable of such genuine altruism? Who knows? If this book does have a significant effect, however, it will be a vindication of all those who have believed that man has within himself the potential for more than cruelty and selfishness.

Topics for Critical Thinking and Writing

1. In his fourth paragraph Singer formulates an argument on behalf of the skeptical reader. Examine that argument closely, restate it in your own words, and evaluate it. Which of its premises is most vulnerable to criticism? Why?

2. Singer quotes with approval (para. 7) Bentham's comment, "The question is not, Can they *reason?* nor Can they *talk?* but, Can they *suffer?*" Do you find this argument persuasive? Can you think of any effective challenge to it?

3. Singer allows that although developed linguistic capacity is not necessary for a creature to have pain, perhaps such a capacity is necessary for "having an intention" (para. 12). Do you think this concession is correct? Have you ever seen animal behavior that you would be willing to describe or explain as evidence that the animal has an intention to do something, despite knowing that the animal cannot talk?

4. Singer thinks that the readiness to experiment on animals cuts out the ground for believing that animals don't suffer pain (see para. 21). Do you agree with this reasoning?

5. Singer confesses (para. 22) to being made especially angry "with my fellow men" after reading the accounts of animal experimentation. What is

it that aroused his anger? Do such feelings, and the acknowledgment that one has them, have any place in a sober discussion about the merits of animal experimentation? Why, or why not?

6. What is "factory farming" (paras. 32–40)? Why is Singer opposed to it?

7. To the claim that there is nothing wrong with "rearing and killing animals for food," provided it is done "humanely," Singer offers two replies (paras. 42–44). In an essay of 250 words summarize them briefly and then indicate whether either persuades you, and why or why not.

8. Suppose someone were to say to Singer: "You claim that capacity to suffer is the relevant factor in deciding whether a creature deserves to be treated as my moral equal. But you're wrong—the relevant factor is whether the creature is *alive*. Being alive is what matters, not being capable of feeling pain." In one or two paragraphs declare what you think would be Singer's reply.

9. Do you think it is worse to kill an animal for its fur than to kill, cook, and eat an animal? Is it worse to kill an animal for sport than to kill it for medical experimentation? What is Singer's view? Explain your view, making use of Singer's if you wish, in an essay of 500 words.

10. Are there any arguments, in your opinion, that show the immorality of eating human flesh (cannibalism) but that do not show a similar objection to eating animal flesh? Write a 500-word essay in which you discuss the issue.

Jonathan Swift

Jonathan Swift (1667–1745) was born in Ireland of English stock. An Anglican clergyman, he became Dean of St. Patrick's in Dublin in 1723, but the post he really wanted, one of high office in England, was never given to him. A prolific pamphleteer on religious and political issues, Swift today is known not as a churchman but as a satirist. His best known works are Gulliver's Travels *(1726, a serious satire but now popularly thought of as a children's book) and "A Modest Proposal" (1729). In "A Modest Proposal," which was published anonymously, Swift addresses the great suffering that the Irish endured under the British.*

A Modest Proposal

For Preventing the Children of Poor People in Ireland from Being a Burden to Their Parents or Country, and for Making Them Beneficial to the Public

It is a melancholy object to those who walk through this great town or travel in the country, when they see the streets, the roads, and cabin doors, crowded with beggars of the female sex, followed by three, four, or six children, all in rags and importuning every passenger for an alms. These mothers, instead of being able to work for their honest livelihood, are forced to employ all their time in strolling to beg sustenance for their helpless infants: who as they grow up either turn thieves for want of work, or leave their dear native country to fight for the Pretender in Spain, or sell themselves to the Barbadoes.

I think it is agreed by all parties that this prodigious number of children in the arms, or on the backs, or at the heels of their mothers, and frequently of their fathers, is in the present deplorable state of the kingdom a very great additional grievance; and, therefore, whoever could find out a fair, cheap, and easy method of making these children sound, useful members of the commonwealth, would deserve so well of the public as to have his statue set up for a preserver of the nation.

But my intention is very far from being confined to provide only for the children of professed beggars; it is of a much greater extent, and shall take in the whole number of infants at a certain age who are born of parents in effect as little able to support them as those who demand our charity in the streets.

As to my own part, having turned my thoughts for many years upon this important subject, and maturely weighed the several schemes of our projectors,[1] I have always found them grossly mistaken in their computation. It is true, a child just dropped from its dam may be supported by her milk for a solar year, with little other nourishment; at most not above the value of 2s.,[2] which the mother may certainly get, or the value in scraps, by her lawful occupation of begging; and it is exactly at one year old that I propose to provide for them in such a manner as instead of being a charge upon their parents or the parish, or wanting food and raiment for the rest of their lives, they shall on the contrary contribute to the feeding, and partly to the clothing, of many thousands.

There is likewise another great advantage in my scheme, that it will prevent those voluntary abortions, and that horrid practice of women murdering their bastard children, alas! too frequent among us! sacrificing the poor innocent babes I doubt more to avoid the expense than the shame, which would move tears and pity in the most savage and inhuman breast.

The number of souls in this kingdom being usually reckoned one million and a half, of these I calculate there may be about 200,000 couple whose wives are breeders; from which number I subtract 30,000 couple who are able to maintain their own children (although I apprehend there cannot be so many, under the present distress of the kingdom); but this being granted, there will remain 170,000 breeders. I again subtract 50,000 for those women who miscarry, or whose children die

---

[1]**projectors** Persons who devise plans. [All notes are the editors'.]
[2]**2s.** Two shillings. In paragraph 7, "£" is an abbreviation for pounds sterling and "d" for pence.

by accident or disease within the year. There only remain 120,000 children of poor parents annually born. The question therefore is, how this number shall be reared and provided for? which, as I have already said, under the present situation of affairs, is utterly impossible by all the methods hitherto proposed. For we can neither employ them in handicraft or agriculture; we neither build houses (I mean in the country) nor cultivate land; they can very seldom pick up a livelihood by stealing, till they arrive at six years old, except where they are of towardly parts; although I confess they learn the rudiments much earlier; during which time they can, however, be properly looked upon only as probationers; as I have been informed by a principal gentleman in the county of Cavan, who protested to me that he never knew above one or two instances under the age of six, even in a part of the kingdom so renowned for the quickest proficiency in that art.

I am assured by our merchants, that a boy or a girl before twelve years old is no salable commodity; and even when they come to this age they will not yield above 3£. or 3£. 2s. 6d. at most on the exchange; which cannot turn to account either to the parents or kingdom, the charge of nutriment and rags having been at least four times that value.

I shall now therefore humbly propose my own thoughts, which I hope will not be liable to the least objection.

I have been assured by a very knowing American of my acquaintance in London, that a young healthy child well nursed is at a year old a most delicious, nourishing, and wholesome food, whether stewed, roasted, baked, or broiled; and I make no doubt that it will equally serve in a fricassee or a ragout.

I do therefore humbly offer it to public consideration that of the 10 120,000 children already computed, 20,000 may be reserved for breed, whereof only one-fourth part to be males; which is more than we allow to sheep, black cattle, or swine; and my reason is, that these children are seldom the fruits of marriage, a circumstance not much regarded by our savages; therefore one male will be sufficient to serve four females. That the remaining 100,000 may, at a year old, be offered in sale to the persons of quality and fortune through the kingdom; always advising the mother to let them suck plentifully in the last month, so as to render them plump and fat for a good table. A child will make two dishes at an entertainment for friends; and when the family dines alone, the fore or hind quarter will make a reasonable dish, and seasoned with a little pepper or salt will be very good boiled on the fourth day, especially in winter.

I have reckoned upon a medium that a child just born will weigh twelve pounds, and in a solar year, if tolerably nursed, will increase to twenty-eight pounds.

I grant this food will be somewhat dear, and therefore very proper for landlords, who, as they have already devoured most of the parents, seem to have the best title to the children.

Infant's flesh will be in season throughout the year, but more plentiful in March, and a little before and after: for we are told by a grave author, an eminent French physician, that fish being a prolific diet, there are more children born in Roman Catholic countries about nine months after Lent than at any other season; therefore, reckoning a year after Lent, the markets will be more glutted than usual, because the number of popish infants is at least three to one in this kingdom: and therefore it will have one other collateral advantage, by lessening the number of papists among us.

I have already computed the charge of nursing a beggar's child (in which list I reckon all cottagers, laborers, and four-fifths of the farmers) to be about 2s. per annum, rags included; and I believe no gentleman would repine to give 10s. for the carcass of a good fat child, which, as I have said, will make four dishes of excellent nutritive meat, when he has only some particular friend or his own family to dine with him. Thus the squire will learn to be a good landlord, and grow popular among the tenants; the mother will have 8s. net profit, and be fit for work till she produces another child.

Those who are more thrifty (as I must confess the times require) may flay the carcass; the skin of which artificially dressed will make admirable gloves for ladies, and summer boots for fine gentlemen.

As to our city of Dublin, shambles[3] may be appointed for this purpose in the most convenient parts of it, and butchers we may be assured will not be wanting: although I rather recommend buying the children alive, and dressing them hot from the knife as we do roasting pigs.

A very worthy person, a true lover of his country, and whose virtues I highly esteem, was lately pleased in discoursing on this matter to offer a refinement upon my scheme. He said that many gentlemen of this kingdom, having of late destroyed their deer, he conceived that the want of venison might be well supplied by the bodies of young lads and maidens, not exceeding fourteen years of age nor under twelve; so great a number of both sexes in every country being now ready to starve for want of work and service; and these to be disposed of by their parents, if alive, or otherwise by their nearest relations. But with due deference to so excellent a friend and so deserving a patriot, I cannot be altogether in his sentiments; for as to the males, my American acquaintance assured me from frequent experience that their flesh was generally tough and lean, like that of our schoolboys by continual exercise, and their taste disagreeable; and to fatten them would not answer the charge. Then as to the females, it would, I think, with humble submission be a loss to the public, because they soon would become breeders themselves: and besides, it is not improbable that some scrupulous people might be apt to censure such a practice (although indeed very unjustly), as a little bor-

___

[3] **shambles** Slaughterhouses.

dering upon cruelty; which, I confess, has always been with me the strongest objection against any project, how well soever intended.

But in order to justify my friend, he confessed that this expedient was put into his head by the famous Psalmanazar[4] a native of the island Formosa, who came from thence to London about twenty years ago: and in conversation told my friend, that in his country when any young person happened to be put to death, the executioner sold the carcass to persons of quality as a prime dainty; and that in his time the body of a plump girl of fifteen, who was crucified for an attempt to poison the emperor, was sold to his imperial majesty's prime minister of state, and other great mandarins of the court, in joints from the gibbet, at 400 crowns. Neither indeed can I deny, that if the same use were made of several plump young girls in this town, who without one single groat to their fortunes cannot stir abroad without a chair, and appear at the playhouse and assemblies in foreign fineries which they never will pay for, the kingdom would not be the worse.

Some persons of a depending spirit are in great concern about the vast number of poor people, who are aged, diseased, or maimed, and I have been desired to employ my thoughts what course may be taken to ease the nation of so grievous an encumbrance. But I am not in the least pain upon that matter, because it is very well known that they are every day dying and rotting by cold and famine, and filth and vermin, as fast as can be reasonably expected. And as to the young laborers, they are now in as hopeful a condition: They cannot get work, and consequently pine away for want of nourishment, to a degree that if at any time they are accidentally hired to common labor, they have not strength to perform it; and thus the country and themselves are happily delivered from the evils to come.

I have too long digressed, and therefore shall return to my subject. I 20 think the advantages by the proposal which I have made are obvious and many, as well as of the highest importance.

For first, as I have already observed, it would greatly lessen the number of papists, with whom we are yearly overrun, being the principal breeders of the nation as well as our most dangerous enemies; and who stay at home on purpose to deliver the kingdom to the Pretender, hoping to take their advantage by the absence of so many good Protestants, who have chosen rather to leave their country than stay at home and pay tithes against their conscience to an Episcopal curate.

Secondly, The poor tenants will have something valuable of their own, which by law may be made liable to distress and help to pay their landlord's rent, their corn and cattle being already seized, and money a thing unknown.

[4]**Psalmanazar** George Psalmanazar (c. 1679–1763), a Frenchman who claimed to be from Formosa (now Taiwan); he wrote *An Historical and Geographical Description of Formosa* (1704). The hoax was exposed soon after publication.

Thirdly, Whereas the maintenance of 100,000 children from two years old and upward, cannot be computed at less than 10s. a-piece per annum, the nation's stock will be thereby increased £50,000 per annum, beside the profit of a new dish introduced to the tables of all gentlemen of fortune in the kingdom who have any refinement in taste. And the money will circulate among ourselves, the goods being entirely of our own growth and manufacture.

Fourthly, The constant breeders beside the gain of 8s. sterling per annum by the sale of their children, will be rid of the charge of maintaining them after the first year.

Fifthly, This food would likewise bring great custom to taverns, where the vintners will certainly be so prudent as to procure the best receipts for dressing it to perfection, and consequently have their houses frequented by all the fine gentlemen, who justly value themselves upon their knowledge in good eating; and a skilful cook who understands how to oblige his guests, will contrive to make it as expensive as they please.

Sixthly, This would be a great inducement to marriage, which all wise nations have either encouraged by rewards or enforced by laws and penalties. It would increase the care and tenderness of mothers toward their children, when they were sure of a settlement for life to the poor babes, provided in some sort by the public, to their annual profit instead of expense. We should see an honest emulation among the married women, which of them would bring the fattest child to the market. Men would become as fond of their wives during the time of their pregnancy as they are now of their mares in foal, their cows in calf, their sows when they are ready to farrow; nor offer to beat or kick them (as is too frequent a practice) for fear of a miscarriage.

Many other advantages might be enumerated. For instance, the addition of some thousand carcasses in our exportation of barreled beef, the propagation of swine's flesh, and improvement in the art of making good bacon, so much wanted among us by the great destruction of pigs, too frequent at our table; which are no way comparable in taste or magnificence to a well-grown, fat, yearling child, which roasted whole will make a considerable figure at a lord mayor's feast or any other public entertainment. But this and many others I omit, being studious of brevity.

Supposing that 1,000 families in this city would be constant customers for infants' flesh, besides others who might have it at merry-meetings, particularly at weddings and christenings, I compute that Dublin would take off annually about 20,000 carcasses; and the rest of the kingdom (where probably they will be sold somewhat cheaper) the remaining 80,000.

I can think of no one objection that will possibly be raised against this proposal, unless it should be urged that the number of people will be thereby much lessened in the kingdom. This I freely own, and it was indeed one principal design in offering it to the world. I desire the reader will observe, that I calculate my remedy for this one individual kingdom of Ireland and for no other that ever was, is, or I think ever can be upon earth. Therefore let no man talk to me of other expedients: of taxing our absentees at 5s. a pound; of using neither clothes nor household furniture except what is of our own growth and manufacture; of utterly rejecting the materials and instruments that promote foreign luxury; of curing the expensiveness of pride, vanity, idleness, and gaming in our women; of introducing a vein of parsimony, prudence, and temperance; of learning to love our country, in the want of which we differ even from Laplanders and the inhabitants of Topinamboo; of quitting our animosities and factions, nor acting any longer like the Jews, who were murdering one another at the very moment their city was taken; of being a little cautious not to sell our country and conscience for nothing; of teaching landlords to have at least one degree of mercy toward their tenants; lastly, of putting a spirit of honesty, industry, and skill into our shopkeepers; who, if a resolution could now be taken to buy only our native goods, would immediately unite to cheat and exact upon us in the price the measure, and the goodness, nor could ever yet be brought to make one fair proposal of just dealing, though often and earnestly invited to it.

Therefore I repeat, let no man talk to me of these and the like expedients, till he has at least some glimpse of hope that there will be ever some hearty and sincere attempt to put them in practice.

But as to myself, having been wearied out for many years with offering vain, idle, visionary thoughts, and at length utterly despairing of success, I fortunately fell upon this proposal; which, as it is wholly new, so it has something solid and real, of no expense and little trouble, full in our own power, and whereby we can incur no danger in disobliging England. For this kind of commodity will not bear exportation, the flesh being of too tender a consistence to admit a long continuance in salt, although perhaps I could name a country which would be glad to eat up our whole nation without it.

After all, I am not so violently bent upon my own opinion as to reject any offer proposed by wise men, which shall be found equally innocent, cheap, easy, and effectual. But before something of that kind shall be advanced in contradiction to my scheme, and offering a better, I desire the author or authors will be pleased maturely to consider two points. First, as things now stand, how they will be able to find food and raiment for 100,000 useless mouths and backs. And secondly, there being a round million of creatures in human figure throughout this kingdom, whose subsistence put into a common stock would leave them in debt 2,000,000£. sterling, adding those who are beggars by profession to the bulk of farmers, cottagers, and laborers, with the wives and children who are beggars in effect; I desire those politicians who dislike my overture, and may perhaps be so bold as to attempt an answer, that they will first ask the parents of these mortals, whether they would not at this day think it a great happiness to have been sold for food at a year old in the manner I prescribe, and thereby have avoided such a perpetual scene of misfortunes as they have since gone through by the oppression of landlords, the impossibility of paying rent without money or trade, the want of common sustenance, with neither house nor clothes to cover them from the inclemencies of the weather, and the most inevitable prospect of entailing the like or greater miseries upon their breed for ever.

I profess, in the sincerity of my heart, that I have not the least personal interest in endeavoring to promote this necessary work, having no other motive than the public good of my country, by advancing our trade, providing for infants, relieving the poor, and giving some pleasure to the rich. I have no children by which I can propose to get a single penny; the youngest being nine years old, and my wife past childbearing.

Topics for Critical Thinking and Writing

1. In paragraph 4 the speaker of the essay mentions proposals set forth by "projectors," that is, by advocates of other proposals or projects. On the basis of the first two paragraphs of "A Modest Proposal," how would you characterize *this* projector, the speaker of the essay? Write your characterization in one paragraph. Then, in a second paragraph, characterize the projector as you understand him, having read the entire essay. In your second paragraph, indicate what *he thinks he is*, and also what the reader sees he really is.

2. The speaker or persona of "A Modest Proposal" is confident that selling children "for a good table" is a better idea than any of the then current methods of disposing of unwanted children, including abortion and infanticide. Can you think of any argument that might favor abortion or infanticide for parents in dire straits, rather than the projector's scheme?

3. In paragraph 29 the speaker considers, but dismisses out of hand, several other solutions to the wretched plight of the Irish poor. Write a 500-word essay in which you explain each of these ideas and their combined merits as an alternative solution to the one he favors.

4. What does the projector imply are the causes of the Irish poverty he deplores? Are there possible causes he has omitted? (If so, what are they?)

5. Imagine yourself as one of the poor parents to whom Swift refers, and write a 250-word essay explaining why you prefer not to sell your infant to the local butcher.

6. The modern version of the problem to which the proposal is addressed is called "population policy." How would you describe our nation's current population policy? Do we have a population policy, in fact? If not, what would you propose? If we do have one, would you propose any changes in it? Why, or why not?

7. It is sometimes suggested that just as persons need to get a license to drive a car, to hunt with a gun, or to marry, a husband and wife ought

to be required to get a license to have a child. Would you favor this idea, assuming that it applied to you as a possible parent? Would Swift? Explain your answers in an essay of 500 words.

8. Consider the six arguments advanced in paragraphs 21–26, and write a 1,000-word essay criticizing all of them. Or, if you find that one or more of the arguments is really unanswerable, explain why you find it so compelling.

5

Developing an Argument
of Your Own

PLANNING, DRAFTING, AND
REVISING AN ARGUMENT

First, hear the wisdom of Mark Twain: "When the Lord finished the world, He pronounced it good. That is what I said about my first work, too. But Time, I tell you, Time takes the confidence out of these incautious early opinions."

All of us, teachers and students, have our moments of confidence, but for the most part we know that we have trouble writing clear, thoughtful prose. In a conversation we can cover ourselves with such expressions as "Well, I don't know, but I sort of think . . . ," and we can always revise our position ("Oh, well, I didn't mean it that way"), but once we have handed in the final version of our writing we are helpless. We are (putting it strongly) naked to our enemies.

Getting Ideas

In Chapter 1 we quoted Robert Frost, "To learn to write is to learn to have ideas," and we offered suggestions about getting ideas, a process traditionally called **invention.** A moment ago we said that we often improve our ideas when we try to explain them to someone else. Partly, of course, we are responding to questions or objections raised by our companion in the conversation, but partly we are responding to ourselves; almost as soon as we hear what we have to say, we may find that it won't do, and, if we are lucky, we may find a better idea surfacing. One of the best ways of getting ideas is to talk things over.

The process of talking things over usually begins with the text that you are reading; your marginal notes, your summary, and your queries parenthetically incorporated within your summary are a kind of dialogue between you and the author you are reading. More obviously, when you talk with friends about your topic you are trying out and developing ideas. Finally, after reading, taking notes, and talking, you may feel that you now have clear ideas and you need only put them into writing. And so you take a sheet of blank paper, and perhaps a paralyzing thought suddenly strikes: "I have ideas but just can't put them into words."

Despite what many people believe, writing is not only a matter of putting one's ideas into words. Just as talking with others is a way of getting ideas, *writing is a way of getting and developing ideas*. Writing, in short, can be an important part of critical thinking. If fear of putting ourselves on record is one big reason we have trouble writing, another big reason is our fear that we have no ideas worth putting down. But by jotting down notes—or even free associations—and by writing a draft, however weak, we can help ourselves to think our way toward good ideas.

Freewriting   Writing for five or six minutes, nonstop, without censoring what you produce is one way of getting words down on paper that will help to lead to improved thoughts. Some people who write on a computer find it useful to dim the screen so they won't be tempted to look up and fiddle too soon with their words. Later they illuminate the screen, scroll back, and notice some key words or passages that can be used later in drafting a paper.

Listing   Jotting down items, just as you do when you make a shopping list, is another way of getting ideas. When you make a shopping list, you write *ketchup* and the act of writing it reminds you that you also need hamburger rolls—and *that* in turn reminds you (who knows how or why?) that you also need a can of tuna fish. Similarly, when you prepare a list of ideas for a paper, jotting down one item will generate another. Of course, when you look over the list you will probably drop some of these ideas—the dinner menu will change—but you are making progress.

Diagramming   Making some sort of visual representation of an essay is a kind of listing. Three methods of diagramming are especially common.

- *Clustering*. Write, in the middle of a sheet of paper, a word or phrase summarizing your topic (for instance, *health care*), circle it, and then write down and circle a related word (for example, *gov't-provided*). Perhaps this leads you to write *higher taxes,* and you then circle this phrase and connect it to *gov't-provided*. The next thing that occurs to you is *employer-provided*—and so you write this down and circle it. Obviously you will not connect this to *higher taxes,* but you will connect it to *health care* because it is a sort of parallel to *gov't-provided.* The next thing that occurs to you is *unemployed people.* Obviously this category does not connect easily with *employer-provided,* so you won't connect these two terms with a line, but you probably will connect *unemployed people* with *health care,* and maybe also with *gov't-provided.* Keep going, jotting down ideas, and making connections where possible, indicating relationships.

- *Branching.* Some writers find it useful to build a tree, moving from the central topic to the main branches (chief ideas) and then to the twigs (aspects of the chief ideas).

- *Comparing in columns.* Draw a line down the middle of the page, and then set up oppositions. For instance, if you are concerned with health care, you might head one column *gov't-provided* and the other *employer-provided,* and you might then, under the first column, write *covers unemployed* and under the second column, write *omits unemployed.* You might go on to write, under the first column, *higher taxes,* and under the second, *higher prices* — or whatever else relevant comes to mind.

All of these methods can of course be executed with pen and paper, but if you write on a computer you may also be able to use them, depending on the capabilities of your program.

Whether you are using a computer or a pen, you put down some words and almost immediately see that they need improvement, not simply a little polishing but a substantial overhaul. You write, "Truman was justified in dropping the atom bomb for two reasons," and as soon as you write these words, a third reason comes to mind. Or perhaps one of those "two reasons" no longer seems very good. As the little girl shrewdly replied when an adult told her to think before she spoke, "How do I know what I think before I hear what I say?" We have to see what we say, we have to get something down on paper, before we realize that we need to make it better.

Writing, then, is really **rewriting,** that is, **revising,** and a revision is a *re-vision,* a second look. The paper that you hand in should be clear and may even seem effortless to the reader, but in all likelihood the clarity and apparent ease are the result of a struggle with yourself, a struggle during which you greatly improved your first thoughts. You begin by putting down your ideas, such as they are, perhaps even in the random order in which they occurred, but sooner or later comes the job of looking at them critically, developing what is useful in them and chucking out what is not. If you follow this procedure you will be in the company of Picasso, who said that he "advanced by means of destruction."

Whether you advance bit by bit (writing a sentence, revising it, writing the next, and so on) or whether you write an entire first draft and then revise it and revise it again and again is chiefly a matter of temperament. Probably most people combine both approaches, backing up occasionally but trying to get to the end fairly soon so that they can see rather quickly what they know, or think they know, and can then start the real work of thinking, of converting their initial ideas into something substantial.

Getting Ideas by Asking Questions   Getting ideas, we said when we talked about **topics** and **invention** strategies in Chapter 1 (p. 5) is mostly a matter of asking (and then thinking about) questions. We append questions to the end of each argumentative essay in this book, not in order to torment you but in order to help you to think about the arguments, for instance to turn your attention to especially important matters. If your instructor asks you to write an answer to one of these questions, you are lucky: Examining the question will stimulate your mind to work in a definite direction. But if a topic is not assigned, and you are asked to write an argument, you will find that some ideas (possibly poor ones, at this stage, but that doesn't matter because you will soon revise) will come to mind if you ask yourself questions. Five basic questions by which you can begin finding where you stand on an issue (**stasis**) are:

1. What is X?
2. What is the value of X?
3. What are the causes (or the consequences) of X?
4. What should (or ought or must) we do about X?
5. What is the evidence for my claims?

Let's spend a moment looking at each of these questions.

1. **What is X?** We can hardly argue about the number of people sentenced to death in the United States in 1995—a glance at the appropriate government report will give the answer—but we can argue about whether or not capital punishment as administered in the United States is discriminatory. Does the evidence, we can ask, support the view that in the United States the death penalty is unfair? Similarly, we can ask whether a human fetus is a human being (in saying what something is, must we take account of its potentiality?), and, even if we agree that a fetus is a human being, we can further ask about whether it is a *person*. In *Roe v. Wade* the Supreme Court ruled that even the "viable" unborn human fetus is not a "person" as that term is used in the Fifth and Fourteenth Amendments. Here the question is this: Is the essential fact about the fetus that it is a person?

An argument of this sort makes a claim—that is, it takes a stand—but notice that it does not have to argue for an action. Thus, it may argue that the death penalty is administered unfairly—that's a big enough issue—but it need not therefore go on to argue that the death penalty should be abolished. After all, another possibility is that the death penalty should be administered fairly. The writer of the essay may be doing enough if he or she establishes the truth of the claim and leaves to others the possible courses of action.

2. **What is the value of** *X?* No one can argue with you if you say you prefer the plays of Tennessee Williams to those of Arthur Miller. But as soon as you say that Williams is a better playwright than Miller, you have based your preference on implicit standards, and it is incumbent on you to support your preference by giving evidence about the relative skill, insight, and accomplishments of Williams and Miller. Your argument is an evaluation. The question now at issue is the merits of the two authors and the standards appropriate for such an appraisal. (For a discussion of literary evaluations, see pp. 339–43.)

In short, an essay offering an evaluation normally has two purposes: (a) to set forth an assessment, and (b) to convince the reader that the assessment is reasonable. In writing an evaluation you will have to establish criteria, and these will vary depending on your topic. For instance, if you are comparing the artistic merit of the plays of Williams and Miller, you may want to talk about the quality of the characterization, the significance of the theme, and so on. But if the topic is, Which playwright is more suitable to be taught in high school?, other criteria may be appropriate, such as the difficulty of the language, the presence of obscenity, and so on.

3. **What are the causes (or the consequences) of** *X?* Why did the rate of auto theft increase during a specific period? If we abolish the death penalty, will that cause the rate of murder to increase? Notice, by the way, that such problems may be complex. The phenomena that people usually argue about—say, such things as inflation, war, suicide, crime—have many causes, and it is therefore often a mistake to speak of *the* cause of *X.* A writer in *Time* mentioned that the life expectancy of an average American male is about sixty-seven years, a figure that compares unfavorably with the life expectancy of males in Japan and Israel. The *Time* writer suggested that an important cause of the relatively short life span is "the pressure to perform well in business." Perhaps. But the life expectancy of plumbers is no greater than that of managers and executives. Nutrition authority Jean Mayer, in an article in *Life,* attributed the relatively poor longevity of American males to a diet that is "rich in fat and poor in nutrients." Doubtless other authorities propose other causes, and in all likelihood no one cause accounts for the phenomenon.

4. **What should (or ought or must) we do about** *X?* Must we always obey the law? Should the law allow eighteen-year-olds to drink alcohol? Should eighteen-year-olds be drafted to do one year of social service? Should pornography be censored? Should steroid use by athletes be banned? Ought there to be "Good Samaritan" laws, making it a legal duty to intervene to save a person from death or great bodily harm, when one might do so with little or no risk to oneself? These questions involve conduct and policy; how we answer them will reveal our values and principles.

An essay of this sort usually begins by explaining what the issue is—and why the reader should care about it—and then offers the proposal, paying attention to the counterarguments.

5. **What is the evidence for my claims?** Critical reading, writing, and thinking depend essentially on identifying and evaluating the evidence for and against the claims one makes and encounters in the writings of others. It is not enough to have an *opinion* or belief one way or the other; you need to be able to support your opinions—the bare fact of your sincere belief in what you say or write is not itself any *evidence* that what you believe is true.

So what are good reasons for opinions, adequate evidence for one's beliefs? The answer, of course, depends on what kind of belief or opinion, assertion or hypothesis, claim or principle, you want to assert. For example, there is good evidence that President John F. Kennedy was assassinated on November 22, 1963, because this is the date for his death reported in standard almanacs. You could further substantiate the date by checking the back issues of the *New York Times*. But a different kind of evidence is needed to support the proposition that the chemical composition of water is H_2O; and you will need still other kinds of evidence to support your beliefs about the likelihood of rain tomorrow, whether the Red Sox will win the pennant this year, the twelfth digit in the decimal expansion of pi, the average cumulative grades of the graduating seniors over the past three years in your college, whether *Hamlet* is greater than *Death of a Salesman*, and whether sexual harassment is morally wrong. None of these issues is merely a matter of opinion; yet on some of them, educated and informed people may disagree over the reasons and the evidence and what they show. Your job as a critical thinker is to be alert to the relevant reasons and evidence, and to make the most of them as you present your views.

Again, an argument may take in two or more of these five issues. Someone who argues that pornography should (or should not) be censored will have to mark out the territory of the discussion by defining pornography (our first issue: What is *X?*). The argument probably will also need to examine the consequences of adopting the preferred policy (our third issue), and may even have to argue about its value—our second issue. (Some people maintain that pornography produces crime, but others maintain that it provides a harmless outlet for impulses that otherwise might vent themselves in criminal behavior.) Further, someone arguing about the wisdom of censoring pornography might have to face the objection that censorship, however desirable on account of some of its consequences, may be unconstitutional, and that even if censorship were constitutional it would (or might) have undesirable side effects, such as repressing freedom of political opinion. And one will always have to keep asking oneself the fifth question, What is the evidence for my claims?

Thinking about one or more of these questions may get you going. For instance, thinking about the first question, What is *X?*, will require you to produce a definition, and as you work at producing a satisfactory definition, you may find new ideas arising. If a question seems relevant, start writing, even if you write only a fragmentary sentence. You'll probably find that one word leads to another and that ideas begin to appear. Even if these ideas seem weak as you write them, don't be discouraged; you have put something on paper, and returning to these words, perhaps in five minutes or perhaps the next day, you will probably find that some are not at all bad, and that others will stimulate you to better ones.

It may be useful to record your ideas in a special notebook reserved for the purpose. Such a **journal** can be a valuable resource when it comes time to write your paper. Many students find it easier to focus their thoughts on writing if during the period of gestation they have been jotting down relevant ideas on something more substantial than slips of paper or loose sheets. The very act of designating a notebook as your journal for a course can be the first step in focusing your attention on the eventual need to write a paper.

If what we have just said does not sound convincing, and you know from experience that you often have trouble getting started with your writing, don't despair; first aid is at hand in a sure-fire method that we will now explain.

The Thesis

Let's assume that you are writing an argumentative essay—perhaps an evaluation of an argument in this book—and you have what seems to be a pretty good draft, or at least a bunch of notes that are the result of hard thinking. You really do have ideas now, and you want to present them effectively. How will you organize your essay? No one formula works best for every essayist and for every essay, but it is usually advisable to formulate a basic **thesis,** a central point, a chief position, and to state it early. Every essay that is any good, even a book-length one, has a thesis, a main point, which can be stated briefly. Remember Coolidge's remark on the preacher's sermon on sin: "He was against it." Don't confuse the **topic** (here it is sin) with the thesis (opposition to sin). The thesis is the argumentative theme, the author's primary claim or contention, the proposition that the rest of the essay will explain and defend. Of course the thesis may sound commonplace, but the book or essay or sermon ought to develop it interestingly and convincingly.

Here are some sample theses:

Smoking should be prohibited in all enclosed public places.

Smoking should be limited to specific parts of enclosed public places and entirely prohibited in small spaces, such as elevators.

Proprietors of public places such as restaurants and sports arenas should be free to determine whether they wish to prohibit, limit, or impose no limitations on smokers.

Imagining an Audience

Of course the questions that you ask yourself, in order to stimulate your thoughts, will depend primarily on what you are writing about, but additional questions are always relevant:

- Who are my readers?
- What do they believe?
- How much common ground do we share?
- What do I want my readers to believe?
- What do they need to know?

These questions require a little comment. The literal answer to the first probably is "the teacher," but (unless you are given instructions to the contrary) you should not write specifically for the teacher; instead, you should write for an audience that is, generally speaking, like your classmates. In short, your imagined audience is literate, intelligent, and moderately well informed, but it does not know everything that you know, and it does not know your response to the problem that you are addressing.

The essays in this book are from many different sources, each with its own audience. An essay from the *New York Times* is addressed to the educated general reader; an essay from *Ms.* is addressed to readers sympathetic to the feminist movement. An essay from *Commonweal,* a Roman Catholic publication addressed to the nonspecialist, is likely to differ in point of view or tone from one in *Time,* even though both articles may advance approximately the same position. The writer of the article in *Commonweal* may, for example, effectively cite church fathers and distinguished Roman Catholic writers as authorities, whereas the writer of an article addressed largely to non-Catholic readers probably will cite few or even none of these figures because the audience might be unfamiliar with them or, even if familiar, might be unimpressed by their views.

The tone as well as the gist of the argument is in some degree shaped by the audience. For instance, popular journals, such as *The National Review* and *Ms.,* are more likely to use ridicule than are journals chiefly addressed to, say, an academic audience.

The Audience as Collaborator

If you imagine an audience, and keep asking yourself what this audience needs to be told and what it doesn't need to be told, you will find that material comes to mind, just as it comes to mind when a friend asks you what a film was about, and who was in it, and how you liked it. Your readers do not have to be told that Thomas Jefferson was an American statesman in the early years of this country's history, but they do have to be told that Thomas Huxley was a late-nineteenth-century

English advocate of Darwinism. You would identify Huxley because it's your hunch that your classmates never heard of him, or even if they may have heard the name, they can't quite identify it. But what if your class has been assigned an essay by Huxley? In that case your imagined reader knows Huxley's name and knows at least a little about him, so you don't have to identify Huxley as an Englishman of the nineteenth century. But you do still have to remind your reader about relevant aspects of his essay, and you do have to tell your reader about your responses to them.

After all, even if the instructor has assigned an essay by Huxley, you cannot assume that your classmates know the essay inside out. Obviously you can't say, "Huxley's third reason is also unconvincing," without reminding the reader, by means of a brief summary, of his third reason. Again, think of your classmates as your imagined readers; put yourself in their shoes, and be sure that your essay does not make unreasonable demands. If you ask yourself, "What do my readers need to know?" (and "What do I want them to believe?") you will find some answers arising, and you will start writing.

We have said that you should imagine your audience as your classmates. But this is not the whole truth. In a sense, your argument is addressed not simply to your classmates but to the world interested in ideas. Even if you can reasonably assume that your classmates have read only one work by Huxley, you will not begin your essay by writing "Huxley's essay is deceptively easy." You will have to name the work; it is possible that a reader has read some other work by Huxley. And by precisely identifying your subject you help to ease the reader into your essay.

Similarly, you won't begin by writing,

```
The majority opinion in Walker v. City of Birmingham
was that . . .
```

Rather, you'll write something like this:

```
In Walker v. City of Birmingham, the Supreme Court
ruled in 1966 that city authorities acted lawfully when
they jailed Martin Luther King, Jr., and other clergy-
men in 1963 for marching in Birmingham without a per-
mit. Justice Potter Stewart delivered the majority
opinion, which held that . . .
```

By the way, if you think you suffer from a writing block, the mere act of writing out such obvious truths will help you to get started. You will find that putting a few words down on paper, perhaps merely copying the essay's title or an interesting quotation from the essay, will stimulate you to jot down thoughts that you didn't know you had in you.

Here, again, are the questions about audience. If you write with a word processor, consider putting these questions into a file. For each assignment, copy (with the "copy" command) the questions into the file you are currently working on, and then, as a way of generating ideas, *enter your responses, indented, under each question.*

- Who are my readers?
- What do they believe?
- How much common ground do we share?
- What do I want my readers to believe?
- What do they need to know?

Thinking about your audience can help you to put some words on paper; even more important, it can help you to get ideas. Our second and third questions about the audience ("What do they believe?" and "How much common ground do we share?") will usually help you get ideas flowing. Presumably your imagined audience does not share your views, or at least does not fully share them. But why? How can these readers hold a position that to you seems unreasonable? If you try to put yourself into your readers' shoes, and if you think about what your audience knows or thinks it knows, you will find yourself getting ideas.

You do not believe (let's assume) that people should be allowed to smoke in enclosed public places, but you know that some people hold a different view. Why do they hold it? Try to state their view in a way that would be satisfactory to them. Having done so, you may come to perceive that your conclusions and theirs differ because they are based on different premises, perhaps different ideas about human rights. Examine the opposition's premises carefully, and explain, first to yourself and ultimately to your readers, why you find some premises unsound.

Possibly some facts are in dispute, such as whether nonsmokers may be harmed by exposure to tobacco. The thing to do, then, is to check the facts. If you find that harm to nonsmokers has not been proved, but you nevertheless believe that smoking should be prohibited in enclosed public places, of course you can't premise your argument on the wrongfulness of harming the innocent (in this case, the nonsmokers). You will have to develop arguments that take account of the facts, whatever they are.

Among the relevant facts there surely are some that your audience or your opponent will not dispute. The same is true of the values relevant to the discussion; the two of you are very likely to agree, if only you stop to think about it, that you share belief in some of the same values (such as the principle mentioned above, that it is wrong to harm the innocent). These areas of shared agreement are crucial to effective persuasion in argument. If you wish to persuade, you'll have to begin by finding *premises you can share with your audience.* Try to identify and isolate these areas of agreement. There are two good reasons for doing so.

1. There is no point in disputing facts or values on which you and your readers really agree.

2. It usually helps to establish goodwill between you and your opponent when you can point to beliefs, assumptions, facts, and values that the two of you share.

In a few moments we will return to the need to share some of the opposition's ideas.

Recall that in writing college papers it is usually best to write for a general audience, an audience rather like your classmates but without the specific knowledge that they all share as students enrolled in one course. If the topic is smoking in public places, the audience presumably consists of smokers and nonsmokers. Thinking about our fifth question on page 167 — What do the readers need to know? — may prompt you to give statistics about the harmful effects of smoking. Or, if you are arguing on behalf of smokers, it may prompt you to cite studies claiming that no evidence conclusively demonstrates that cigarette smoking is harmful to nonsmokers. If indeed you are writing for a general audience, and you are not advancing a highly unfamiliar view, our second question (What does the audience believe?) is less important here, but if the audience is specialized, such as an antismoking group, or a group of restaurant owners who fear that antismoking regulations will interfere with their business, or a group of civil libertarians, obviously an effective essay will have to address their special beliefs.

In addressing their beliefs (let's assume that you do not share them or do not share them fully), you must try to establish some common ground. If you advocate requiring restaurants to provide nonsmoking areas, you should at least recognize the possibility that this arrangement will result in inconvenience for the proprietor. But perhaps (the good news) it will regain some lost customers or will attract some new customers. This thought should prompt you to think of kinds of evidence, perhaps testimony or statistics.

When one formulates a thesis and asks questions about it, such as who the readers are, what do they believe, what do they know, and what do they need to know, one begins to get ideas about how to organize the material, or at least one begins to see that some sort of organization will have to be worked out. The thesis may be clear and simple, but the reasons (the argument) may take many pages. The thesis is the point; the argument sets forth the evidence that is offered to support the thesis.

The Title

It's not a bad idea to announce your thesis in your **title.** If you scan the table of contents of this book, you will notice that a fair number of essayists use the title to let the readers know, at least in a very general way, what position will be advocated. Here are a few examples:

Gay Marriages: Make Them Legal

Students Should Not Be above the Law

Why Handguns Must Be Outlawed

True, these titles are not especially engaging, but the reader welcomes them because they give some information about the writer's thesis.

Some titles do not announce the thesis but they at least announce the topic:

Is All Discrimination Unfair?

On Racist Speech

Why Make Divorce Easy?

Although not clever or witty, these titles are informative.

Some titles seek to attract attention or to stimulate the imagination:

A First Amendment Junkie

A Crime of Compassion

Addicted to Health

All of these are effective, but a word of caution is appropriate here. In your effort to engage your reader's attention, be careful not to sound like a wise guy. You want to engage your readers, not turn them off.

Finally, be prepared to rethink your title *after* you have finished the last draft of your paper. A title somewhat different from your working title may be an improvement because the emphasis of your finished paper may have turned out to be rather different from what you expected when you first thought of a title.

The Opening Paragraphs

A good introduction arouses the reader's interest and helps prepare the reader for the rest of the paper. How? Opening paragraphs usually do at least one (and often all) of the following:

- attract the reader's interest (often with a bold statement of the thesis, or with an interesting statistic, quotation, or anecdote);
- prepare the reader's mind by giving some idea of the topic, and often of the thesis;
- give the reader an idea of how the essay is organized;
- define a term.

You may not wish to announce your thesis in your title, but if you don't announce it there, you should set it forth very early in the argument, in your introductory paragraph or paragraphs. In her title "Human Rights and Foreign Policy," Jeanne J. Kirkpatrick merely announces her topic (subject) as opposed to her thesis (point), but she begins to hint at the thesis in her first paragraph, by deprecating President Jimmy Carter's policy:

> In this paper I deal with three broad subjects: first, the content and consequences of the Carter administration's human rights policy; second, the prerequisites of a more adequate theory of human rights; and third, some characteristics of a more successful human rights policy.

Or consider this opening paragraph from Peter Singer's "Animal Liberation":

> We are familiar with Black Liberation, Gay Liberation, and a variety of other movements. With Women's Liberation some thought we had come to the end of the road. Discrimination on the basis of sex, it has been said, is the last form of discrimination that is universally accepted and practiced without pretense, even in those liberal circles which have long prided themselves on their freedom from racial discrimination. But one should always be wary of talking of "the last remaining form of discrimination." If we have learned anything from the liberation movements, we should have learned how difficult it is to be aware of the ways in which we discriminate until they are forcefully pointed out to us. A liberation movement demands an expansion of our moral horizons, so that practices that were previously regarded as natural and inevitable are now seen as intolerable.

Although Singer's introductory paragraph nowhere mentions animal liberation, in conjunction with its title it gives us a good idea of what Singer is up to and where he is going. Singer knows that his audience will be skeptical, so he reminds them that many of us in previous years were skeptical of reforms that we now take for granted. He adopts a strategy used fairly often by writers who advance highly unconventional theses: Rather than beginning with a bold announcement of a thesis that may turn off some of his readers because it sounds offensive or absurd, Singer warms his audience up, gaining their interest by cautioning them politely that although they may at first be skeptical of animal liberation, if they stay with his essay they may come to feel that they have expanded their horizons.

Notice, too, that Singer begins by establishing common ground with his readers; he assumes, probably correctly, that they share his view that other forms of discrimination (now seen to be unjust) were once widely practiced and were assumed to be acceptable and natural. In this paragraph, then, Singer is not only showing himself to be fair-minded but is also letting us know that he will advance a daring idea. His opening wins our attention and our goodwill. A writer can hardly hope to do more. (In a few pages we will talk a little more about winning the audience.)

In your introductory paragraphs you may have to give some background informing or reminding your readers of material that they will have to be familiar with if they are to follow your essay. You may wish to define some terms, if the terms are unfamiliar or if you are using familiar terms in an unusual sense. In writing, or at least in revising these paragraphs, remember to keep in mind this question: What do my readers need to know? Remember, your aim throughout is to write *reader-friendly* prose, and keeping the needs and interests of your audience constantly in mind will help you achieve this goal.

After announcing the topic, giving the necessary background, and stating your position (and perhaps the opposition's) in as engaging a manner as possible, it is usually a good idea to give the reader an idea of how you will proceed. Look on the preceding page at Kirkpatrick's opening paragraph, for an obvious illustration. She tells us she will deal with three subjects, and she names them. Her approach in the paragraph is concise, obvious, and effective.

Similarly, you may, for instance, want to announce fairly early that there are four common objections to your thesis, and that you will take them up one by one, beginning with the weakest (or most widely held, or whatever) and moving to the strongest (or least familiar), after which you will advance your own view in greater detail. Of course not every argument begins with refuting the other side, though many arguments do. The point to remember is that you usually ought to tell your readers where you will be taking them and by what route.

Organizing and Revising the Body of the Essay

Most argumentative essays more or less follow this organization:

1. Statement of the problem
2. Statement of the structure of the essay
3. Statement of alternative solutions
4. Arguments in support of the proposed solution
5. Arguments answering possible objections
6. A summary, resolution, or conclusion

Let's look at each of these six steps.

1. **Statement of the problem.** Whether the problem is stated briefly or at length depends on the nature of the problem and the writer's audience. If you haven't already defined unfamiliar terms or terms you use in a special way, probably now is the time to do so. In any case, it is advisable here to state the problem objectively (thereby gaining the trust of the reader) and to indicate why the reader should care about the issue.

2. **Statement of the structure of the essay.** After stating the problem at the appropriate length, the writer often briefly indicates the structure of the rest of the essay. The commonest structure is suggested below, in points 3 and 4.

3. **Statement of alternative solutions.** In addition to stating the alternatives fairly, the writer probably conveys willingness to

recognize not only the integrity of the proposers but also the (partial) merit of at least some of the alternative solutions.

The point made in the previous sentence is important and worth amplifying. Because it is important to convey your goodwill—your sense of fairness—to the reader, it is advisable to let your reader see that you are familiar with the opposition, and that you recognize the integrity of those who hold that view. This you do by granting its merits as far as you can. (For more about this approach, see the essay by Carl Rogers on p. 301.)

The next stage, which constitutes most of the body of the essay, usually is this:

4. **Arguments in support of the proposed solution.** The evidence offered will, of course, depend on the nature of the problem. Relevant statistics, authorities, examples, or analogies may or may not come to mind or be available. This is usually the longest part of the essay.

5. **Arguments answering possible objections.** These arguments may suggest that

    a. the proposal won't work (perhaps it is alleged to be too expensive, or to make unrealistic demands on human nature, or to fail to get to the heart of the problem);

    b. the proposed solution will create problems greater than the difficulty to be resolved. (A good example of a proposal that produced dreadful unexpected results is the law mandating a prison term for anyone over eighteen in possession of an illegal drug. Heroin dealers then began to use children as runners, and cocaine importers followed the practice.)

6. **A summary, resolution, or conclusion.** Here the writer may seek to accommodate the views of the opposition as far as possible, but clearly suggests that the writer's own position makes good sense. A conclusion—the word comes from the Latin *claudere*, "to shut"—ought to provide a sense of closure, but it can be much more than a restatement of the writer's thesis. It can, for instance, make a quiet emotional appeal by suggesting that the issue is important and that the ball is now in the reader's court.

Of course not every essay will follow this six-part pattern, but let's assume that in the introductory paragraphs you have sketched the topic (and have shown or nicely said, or implied, that the reader doubtless is interested in it), and have fairly and courteously set forth the opposition's view, recognizing its merits and indicating the degree to which you can share part of that view. You now want to set forth your arguments explaining why you differ on some essentials.

In setting forth your own position, you can begin either with your strongest reasons or your weakest. Each method of organization has advantages and disadvantages. If you begin with your strongest, the essay may seem to peter out; if you begin with the weakest, you build to a climax but your readers may not still be with you because they may have felt at the start that the essay was frivolous. The solution to this last possibility is to make sure that even your weakest argument is an argument of some strength. You can, moreover, assure your readers that stronger points will soon be offered and you offer this point first only because you want to show that you are aware of it, and that, slight though it is, it deserves some attention. The body of the essay, then, is devoted to arguing a position, which means not only offering supporting reasons but also offering refutations of possible objections to these reasons.

Doubtless you will sometimes be uncertain, as you draft your essay, whether to present a given point before or after another point. When you write, and certainly when you revise, try to put yourself into your reader's shoes: Which point do you think the reader needs to know first? Which point *leads to* which further point? Your argument should not be a mere list of points, of course; rather, it should clearly integrate one point with another in order to develop an idea. But in all likelihood you won't have a strong sense of the best organization until you have written a draft and have reread it. You are likely to find that the organization needs some revising in order to make your argument clear to a reader.

Checking Paragraphs   When you revise your draft, watch out also for short paragraphs. Although a paragraph of only two or three sentences (like some in this chapter) may occasionally be helpful as a transition between complicated points, most short paragraphs are undeveloped paragraphs. (Newspaper editors favor very short paragraphs because they can be read rapidly when printed in the narrow columns typical of newspapers. Many of the essays reprinted in this book originally were published in newspapers, hence they're very short paragraphs. There is no reason for you to imitate this style in the argumentative essays you will be writing.)

In revising, when you find a paragraph of only a sentence or two or three, check first to see if it should be joined to the paragraph that precedes or follows. Second, if on rereading you are certain that a given paragraph should not be tied to what comes before or after, think about amplifying the paragraph with supporting detail (this is not the same as mere padding).

Checking Transitions   Make sure, too, in revising, that the reader can move easily from the beginning of a paragraph to the end, and from one paragraph to the next. Transitions help the reader to perceive the connections between the units of the argument. For example (that's a transition, of course), they may

> **illustrate:** *for example, for instance, consider this case;*
>
> **establish a sequence:** *a more important objection, a stronger example, the best reason;*
>
> **connect logically:** *thus, as a result, therefore, so, it follows;*
>
> **compare:** *similarly, in like manner, just as, analogously;*
>
> **contrast:** *on the other hand, in contrast, however, but;*
>
> **summarize:** *in short, briefly.*

Expressions such as these serve as guideposts that enable your reader to move easily through your essay.

When writers revise an early draft they chiefly

- unify the essay by eliminating irrelevancies;
- organize the essay by keeping in mind an imagined audience;
- clarify the essay by fleshing out thin paragraphs, by making certain that the transitions are adequate, and by making certain that generalizations are adequately supported by concrete details and examples.

We are not talking about polish or elegance; we are talking about fundamental matters. Be especially careful not to abuse the logical connectives (*thus, as a result,* and so on). If you write several sentences followed by *therefore* or a similar word or phrase, be sure that what you write after the *therefore* really *does follow* from what has gone before. Logical connectives are not mere transitional devices used to link disconnected bits of prose. They are supposed to mark a real movement of thought—the essence of an argument.

The Ending

What about concluding paragraphs, in which you try to summarize the main points and reaffirm your position? If you can look back over your essay and can add something that enriches it and at the same time wraps it up, fine, but don't feel compelled to say, "Thus, in conclusion, I have argued X, Y, and Z, and I have refuted Jones." After all, *conclusion* can have two meanings: (1) ending, or finish, as the ending of a joke or a novel; (2) judgment or decision reached after deliberation. Your essay should finish effectively (the first sense), but it need not announce a judgment (the second).

If the essay is fairly short, so that a reader can more or less keep the whole thing in mind, you may not need to restate your view. Just make sure that you have covered the ground, and that your last sentence is a good one. Notice that the essay printed later in this chapter (p. 187) does not end with a formal conclusion, though it ends conclusively, with a note of finality.

By a note of finality we do *not* mean a triumphant crowing. It's usually far better to end with the suggestion that you hope you have by now indicated why those who hold a different view may want to modify it and accept yours.

If you study the essays in this book, or, for that matter, the editorials and Op-Ed pieces in a newspaper, you will notice that writers often provide a sense of closure by using one of the following devices:

- a return to something in the introduction;
- a glance at the wider implications of the issue (for example, if smoking is restricted, other liberties are threatened);
- an anecdote that engagingly illustrates the thesis;
- a brief summary (but this sort of ending may seem unnecessary and even tedious, especially if the paper is short and if the summary merely repeats what has already been said).

The Uses of an Outline

Some writers find it useful to sketch an **outline** as soon as they think they know what they want to say, even before they write a first draft; others write an outline after a draft that has given them additional ideas. These procedures can be helpful in planning a tentative organization, but remember that in revising a draft new ideas will arise, and the outline may have to be modified. A preliminary outline is chiefly useful as a means of getting going, not as a guide to the final essay.

The Outline as a Way of Checking a Draft   Whether or not you use a preliminary outline, we suggest that after you have written what you hope is your last draft, you make an outline of it; there is no better way of finding out whether the essay is well organized.

Go through the draft and jot down the chief points, in the order in which you make them. That is, prepare a table of contents—perhaps a phrase for each paragraph. Next, examine your jottings to see what kind of sequence they reveal in your paper.

1. Is the sequence reasonable? Can it be improved?
2. Are any passages irrelevant?
3. Does something important seem to be missing?

If no structure or sequence clearly appears in the outline, then the full prose version of your argument probably doesn't have any, either. Therefore, produce another draft, moving things around, adding or subtracting paragraphs—cutting and pasting into a new sequence, with transitions as needed—and then make another outline to see if the sequence now is satisfactory.

You are probably familiar with the structure known as a **formal outline.** A major point is indicated by I, and points within this major point are indicated by A, B, C, and so on. Divisions within A, B, C, are indicated by 1, 2, 3, and so on, thus:

I. Arguments for opening all Olympic sports to professionals
  A. Fairness
    1. Some Olympic sports are already open to professionals
    2. Some athletes who really are not professionals are classified as professionals
  B. Quality (achievements would be higher)

You may want to outline your draft according to this principle, or it may be enough if you simply jot down a phrase for each paragraph and indent the subdivisions. But keep this point in mind: It is not enough for the parts to be ordered reasonably; the order must be made clear to the reader, probably by means of transitions such as *for instance, on the other hand, we can now turn to an opposing view,* and so on.

Tone and the Writer's Persona

Although this book is chiefly about argument in the sense of rational discourse—the presentation of reasons in support of a thesis or conclusion—the appeal to reason is only one form of persuasion. Another form is the appeal to emotion—to pity, for example. Aristotle saw, in addition to the appeal to reason and the appeal to emotion, a third form of persuasion, the appeal to the character of the speaker. He called it the **ethical appeal** (the Greek word for this kind of appeal is **ethos,** "character"). The idea is that effective speakers convey the suggestion that they are

- informed,
- intelligent,
- benevolent,
- honest.

Because they are perceived as trustworthy, their words inspire confidence in their listeners. It is, of course, a fact that when we read an argument we are often aware of the *person* or *voice* behind the words, and our assent to the argument depends partly on the extent to which we can share the speaker's assumptions, look at the matter from the speaker's point of view—in short, *identify* with this speaker.

How can a writer inspire the confidence that lets readers identify themselves with the writer? To begin with, the writer should possess the virtues Aristotle specified: intelligence or good sense, honesty, and benevolence or goodwill. As the Roman proverb puts it, "No one gives what he does not have." Still, possession of these qualities is not a guarantee that you will convey them in your writing. Like all other writers, you will have to revise your drafts so that these qualities become apparent, or, stated more moderately, you will have to revise so that nothing in the essay causes a reader to doubt your intelligence, honesty, and goodwill. A blunder in logic, a misleading quotation, a snide remark — all such slips can cause readers to withdraw their sympathy from the writer.

But of course all good argumentative essays do not sound exactly alike; they do not all reveal the same speaker. Each writer develops his or her own voice or (as literary critics and teachers call it) **persona.** In fact, one writer will have several voices or personae, depending on the topic and the audience. The president of the United States delivering an address on the State of the Union has one persona; chatting with a reporter at his summer home he has another. This change is not a matter of hypocrisy. Different circumstances call for different language. As a French writer put it, there is a time to speak of "Paris," and a time to speak of "the capital of the nation." When Lincoln spoke at Gettysburg, he didn't say "Eighty-seven years ago," but "Four score and seven years ago." We might say that just as some occasions required him to be the folksy Honest Abe, the occasion of the dedication of hallowed ground required him to be formal and solemn, and so the president of the United States appropriately used biblical language. The election campaigns called for one persona, and this occasion called for a different persona.

When we talk about a writer's persona, we mean the way in which the writer presents his or her attitudes:

the attitude toward *the self,*
toward *the audience,* and
toward *the subject.*

Thus, if a writer says,

I have thought long and hard about this subject, and I can say with assurance that . . .

we may feel that we are listening to a self-satisfied ass who probably is simply mouthing other people's opinions. Certainly he is mouthing other people's clichés: "long and hard," "say with assurance."

Let's look at a slightly subtler example of an utterance that reveals an attitude. When we read that

President Nixon was hounded out of office by journalists

we hear a respectful attitude toward Nixon ("President Nixon") and a hostile attitude toward the press (they are beasts, curs who "hounded" our elected leader). If the writer's attitudes were reversed, she might have said something like this:

The press turned the searchlight on Tricky Dick's criminal shenanigans.

"Tricky Dick" and "criminal" are obvious enough, but notice that "shenanigans" also implies the writer's contempt for Nixon, and of course "turned the searchlight" suggests that the press is a source of illumination, a source of truth. The original version and the opposite version both say that the press was responsible for Nixon's resignation, but the original version ("President Nixon was hounded") conveys indignation toward journalists, whereas the revision conveys contempt for Nixon.

These two versions suggest two speakers who differ not only in their view of Nixon but also in their manner, including the seriousness with which they take themselves. Although the passage is very short, it seems to us that the first speaker conveys righteous indignation ("hounded"), whereas the second conveys amused contempt ("shenanigans"). To our ears the tone, as well as the point, differs in the two versions.

We are talking about **loaded words,** words that convey the writer's attitude and that by their connotations are meant to win the reader to the writer's side. Compare "freedom fighter" with "terrorist," "pro-choice" with "pro-abortion," or "pro-life" with "anti-abortion." "Freedom fighter," "pro-choice," and "pro-life" sound like good things; speakers who use these words are seeking to establish themselves as virtuous people who are supporting worthy causes. The **connotations** (associations, overtones) of these pairs of words differ, even though the **denotations** (explicit meanings, dictionary definitions) are the same, just as the connotations of "mother" and "female parent" differ, although the denotations are the same. Similarly, although "four score and seven" and "eighty-seven" both denote "thirteen less than one hundred," they differ in connotation.

Tone is not only a matter of connotations ("hounded out of office," versus, let's say, "compelled to resign," or "pro-choice" versus "pro-abortion"); it is also a matter of such things as the selection and type of examples. A writer who offers many examples, especially ones drawn from ordinary life, conveys a persona different from that of a writer who offers no examples, or only an occasional invented instance. The first of these probably is, one might say, friendlier, more down-to-earth.

Last Words on Tone   On the whole, in writing an argument it is advisable to be courteous, respectful of your topic, of your audience, and of people who hold views you are arguing against. It is rarely good for one's own intellectual development to regard as villains or fools persons who hold views different from one's own, especially if some of them are in the audience. Keep in mind the story of the two strangers on a train who, striking up a conversation, found that both were clergymen, though of different faiths. Then one said to the other, "Well, why shouldn't we be friends? After all, we both serve God, you in your way and I in His."

Complacency is all right when telling jokes but not in arguments. Recognize opposing views, assume they are held in good faith, state them fairly (if you don't, you do a disservice not only to the opposition but to your own position, because the perceptive reader will not take you seriously), and be temperate in arguing your own position: "If I understand their view correctly . . ."; "It seems reasonable to conclude that . . ."; "Perhaps, then, we can agree that . . ."

"We," "One," or "I"?

The use of *we* in the last sentence brings us to another point: May the first-person pronouns *I* and *we* be used? In this book, because two of us are writing, we often use *we* to mean the two authors. And we sometimes use *we* to mean the authors and the readers, as in phrases like the one that ends the previous paragraph. This shifting use of one word can be troublesome, but we hope (clearly the *we* here refers only to the authors) that we have avoided any ambiguity. But can, or should, or must, an individual use *we* instead of *I*? The short answer is no.

If you are simply speaking for yourself, use *I*. Attempts to avoid the first person singular by saying things like "This writer thinks . . . ," and "It is thought that . . . ," and "One thinks that . . . ," are far more irritating (and wordy) than the use of *I*. The so-called editorial *we* is as odd sounding in a student's argument as is the royal *we*. Mark Twain said that the only ones who can appropriately say *we* are kings, editors, and people with a tapeworm. And because one *one* leads to another, making the sentence sound (James Thurber's words) "like a trombone solo," it's best to admit that you are the author, and to use *I*. But of course there is no need to preface every sentence with "I think." The reader knows that the essay is yours; just write it, using *I* when you must, but not needlessly.

Avoiding Sexist Language

Courtesy (as well as common sense) requires that you respect the feelings of your readers. Many people today find offensive the implicit sexism in the use of male pronouns to denote not only men but also women ("As the reader follows the argument, he will find . . ."). And sometimes the use of the male pronoun to denote all people is ridiculous: "An individual, no matter what his sex, . . ."

In most contexts there is no need to use gender-specific nouns or pronouns. One way to avoid using *he* when you mean any person is to use *he or she* (or *she or he*) instead of *he*, but the result is sometimes a bit cumbersome—although it is superior to the overly conspicuous *he/she* and to *s/he*.

A PEER REVIEW CHECKLIST FOR
A DRAFT OF AN ARGUMENT

Read the draft through, quickly. Then read it again, with the following questions in mind.

✓ Does the draft show promise of fulfilling the assignment?

✓ Looking at the essay as a whole, what thesis (main idea) is advanced?

✓ Are the needs of the audience kept in mind? For instance, do some words need to be defined? Is the evidence (for instance, the examples, and the testimony of authorities) clear and effective?

✓ Can you accept the assumptions? If not, why not?

✓ Is any obvious evidence (or counterevidence) overlooked?

If the writer is proposing a solution,

✓ Are other equally attractive solutions adequately examined?

✓ Has the writer overlooked some unattractive effects of the proposed solution?

Here are two simple ways to solve the problem:

1. *use the plural* ("As readers follow the argument, they will find . . ."), or
2. *recast the sentence* so that no pronoun is required ("Readers following the argument will find . . .").

Because *man* and *mankind* strike many readers as sexist when used in such expressions as "Man is a rational animal" and "Mankind has not yet solved this problem," consider using such words as *human being, person, people, humanity,* and *we.* (*Examples:* "Human beings are rational animals"; "We have not yet solved this problem.")

PEER REVIEW

Your instructor may suggest—or may even require—that you submit an early draft of your essay to a fellow student or small group of students for comment. Such a procedure benefits both author and readers: You get the responses of a reader, and the student-reader gets experience in thinking about the problems of developing an argument, especially in thinking about such matters as the degree of detail that a writer needs to offer to a reader, and the importance of keeping the organization evident to a reader.

Looking at each paragraph separately:
- ✓ What is the basic point?
- ✓ How does each paragraph relate to the essay's main idea or to the previous paragraph?
- ✓ Should some paragraphs be deleted? Be divided into two or more paragraphs? Be combined? Be put elsewhere? (If you outline the essay by jotting down the gist of each paragraph, you will get help in answering these questions.)
- ✓ Is each sentence clearly related to the sentence that precedes and to the sentence that follows?
- ✓ Is each paragraph adequately developed? Are there sufficient details, perhaps brief supporting quotations from the text?
- ✓ Are the introductory and concluding paragraphs effective?

✓ What are the paper's chief strengths?

✓ Make at least two specific suggestions that you think will assist the author to improve the paper.

A STUDENT'S ESSAY, FROM ROUGH NOTES TO FINAL VERSION

While we were revising this textbook we asked the students in one of our classes to write a short essay (500–750 words) on some ethical problem that concerned them. Because this assignment was the first writing assignment in the course, we explained that a good way to get ideas is to ask oneself some questions, jot down responses, question those responses, and write freely for ten minutes or so, not worrying about contradictions. We invited our students to hand in their initial jottings along with the finished essay, so that we could get a sense of how they proceeded as writers. Not all of them chose to hand in their jottings, but we were greatly encouraged by those who did. What was encouraging was the confirmation of an old belief, the belief—we call it a fact—that students will hand in a thoughtful essay if before they prepare a final version they nag themselves, ask themselves *why* they think this or that, jot down their responses, and are not afraid to change their minds as they proceed.

Here are the first jottings of a student, Emily Andrews, who elected to write about whether to give money to street beggars. She simply put down ideas, one after the other.

```
Help the poor? Why do I (sometimes) do it?

I feel guilty, and think I should help them: poor,
    cold, hungry (but also some of them are thirsty
```

for liquor, and will spend the money on liquor,
not on food).

I also feel annoyed by them--most of them:

Where does the expression "the deserving poor" come
    from?

And "poor but honest"? Actually, that sounds a bit odd.
    Wouldn't "rich but honest" make more sense?

Why don't they work? Fellow with red beard, always by
    bus stop in front of florist's shop, always wants
    a handout. He is a regular, there all day every
    day, so I guess he is in a way "reliable," so why
    doesn't he put the same time in on a job?

Or why don't they get help? Don't they know they need
    it? They must know they need it.

Maybe that guy with the beard is just a con artist.
    Maybe he makes more money by panhandling than he
    would by working, and it's a lot easier!

Kinds of poor--how to classify??
        drunks, druggies, etc.
        mentally ill (maybe drunks belong here too)
        decent people who have had terrible luck

Why private charity?

Doesn't it makes sense to say we (fortunate individu-
    als) should give something--an occasional handout--
    to people who have had terrible luck? (I suppose
    some people might say that there is no need for
    any of us to give anything--the government takes
    care of the truly needy--but I do believe in giv-
    ing charity. A month ago a friend of the family
    passed away, and the woman's children suggested
    that people might want to make a donation in her
    name, to a shelter for battered women. I know my
    parents made a donation.)

BUT how can I tell who is who, which are which? Which
    of these people asking for "spare change" really
    need (deserve???) help, and which are phonies? Im-
    possible to tell.

Possibilities:
        Give to no one
        Give to no one but make an annual donation, maybe
        to United Way
        Give a dollar to each person who asks. This would
        probably not cost me even a dollar a day

Occasionally do without something--maybe a CD--or
a meal in a restaurant--and give the money I save
to people who seem worthy.

WORTHY? What am I saying? How can I, or anyone, tell?
The neat-looking guy who says he just lost his job
may be a phony, and the dirty bum--probably a
drunk--may desperately need food. (OK, so what if
he spends the money on liquor instead of food? At
least he'll get a little pleasure in life. No!
It's not all right if he spends it on drink.)

Other possibilities:
Do some volunteer work?
To tell the truth, I don't want to put in the
time. I don't feel that guilty.

So what's the problem?

Is it, How I can help the very poor (handouts, or
through an organization)? or

How I can feel less guilty about being lucky enough to
be able to go to college, and to have a supportive
family?

I can't quite bring myself to believe I should help
every beggar who approaches, but I also can't
bring myself to believe that I should do nothing,
on the grounds that:

a. it's probably their fault

b. if they are deserving, they can get gov't help.
No, I just can't believe that. Maybe some are
too proud to look for government help, or don't
know that they are entitled to it.

What to do?

On balance, it seems best to
a. give to United Way
b. maybe also give to an occasional individual, if
I happen to be moved, without worrying about
whether he or she is "deserving" (since it's
probably impossible to know).

A day after making these notes Emily reviewed them, added a few
points, and then made a very brief selection from them, to serve as an
outline for her first draft.

Opening para.: "poor but honest"? Deserve "spare
change"?

```
Charity: private or through organizations?
         pros and cons
         guy at bus
         it wouldn't cost me much, but . . . better to
         give through organizations


Concluding para.: still feel guilty?
                  maybe mention guy at bus again?
```

After writing and revising a draft, Emily Andrews submitted her essay to a fellow student for peer review. She then revised her work in light of the suggestions she received, and in light of her own further thinking.

On the next page we give the final essay. If after reading the final version you reread the early jottings, you will notice that some of the jottings never made it into the final version. But without the jottings, the essay probably could not have been as interesting as it is. When the writer made the jottings, she was not so much putting down her ideas as *finding* ideas by the process of writing.

Andrews 1

Emily Andrews
Professor Barnet
English 102
January 13, 1998

Why I Don't Spare "Spare Change"

"Poor but honest." "The deserving poor." I
don't know the origin of these quotations, but
they always come to mind when I think of "the
poor." But I also think of people who, perhaps
through alcohol or drugs, have ruined not only
their own lives but also the lives of others in
order to indulge in their own pleasure. Perhaps
alcoholism and drug addiction really are "dis-
eases," as many people say, but my own feeling--
based, of course, not on any serious study--is
that most alcoholics and drug addicts can be
classified with the "underserving poor." And that
is largely why I don't distribute spare change
to panhandlers.

But surely among the street people there
are also some who can rightly be called "deserving." Deserving what? My spare change? Or simply
the government's assistance? It happens that I
have been brought up to believe that it is appropriate to make contributions to charity--
let's say a shelter for battered women--but if I
give some change to a panhandler, am I making a
contribution to charity and thereby helping
someone, or, on the contrary, am I perhaps simply encouraging someone not to get help? Or,
maybe even worse, am I supporting a con artist?

If one believes in the value of private
charity, one can either give to needy individu-

als or to charitable organizations. In giving
to a panhandler one may indeed be helping a
person who badly needs help, but one cannot be
certain that one is giving to a needy individual. In giving to an organization such as the
United Way, on the other hand, one can feel
that one's money is likely to be used wisely.
True, confronted by a beggar one may feel that
this particular unfortunate individual needs
help at this moment--a cup of coffee, or a
sandwich--and the need will not be met unless I
put my hand in my pocket right now. But I have
come to think that the beggars whom I encounter
can get along without my spare change, and indeed perhaps they are actually better off for
not having money to buy liquor or drugs.

It happens that in my neighborhood I encounter few panhandlers. There is one fellow
who is always by the bus stop where I catch the
bus to the college, and I never give him anything precisely because he is always there. He
is such a regular that, I think, he ought to be
able to hold a regular job. Putting him aside,
I probably don't encounter more than three or
four beggars in a week. (I'm not counting
street musicians. These people seem quite able
to work for a living. If they see their "work"
as playing or singing, let persons who enjoy
their performances pay them. I do not consider
myself among their audience.) The truth of the
matter is that, since I meet so few beggars, I
could give each one a dollar and hardly feel
the loss. At most, I might go without seeing a

Andrews 3

movie some week. But I know nothing about these
people, and it's my impression--admittedly
based on almost no evidence--that they simply
prefer begging to working. I am not generalizing about street people, and certainly I am not
talking about street people in the big urban
centers. I am talking only about the people
whom I actually encounter.

That's why I usually do not give "spare
change," and I don't think I will in the future.
These people will get along without me. Someone
else will come up with money for their coffee or
their liquor, or, at worst, they will just have
to do without. I will continue to contribute occasionally to a charitable organization, not
simply (I hope) to salve my conscience but because I believe that these organizations actually do good work. But I will not attempt to be
a mini-charitable organization, distributing
(probably to the unworthy) spare change.

Finally, here are a few comments about the essay:

The title is informative, alerting the reader to the topic and the author's
position. (By the way, the student told us that in her next-to-last
draft the title was "Is It Right to Spare 'Spare Change'?" This title,
like the revision, introduces the topic but not the author's position.
The revised version seems to us to be more striking.)

The opening paragraph holds a reader's interest, partly by alluding to the
familiar phrase, "the deserving poor," and partly by introducing the
*un*familiar phrase, "the *un*deserving poor." Notice, too, that this
opening paragraph ends by clearly asserting the author's thesis. Of
course writers need not always announce their thesis early, but it is

usually advisable to do so. Readers like to know where they are going.

The second paragraph begins by voicing what probably is the reader's somewhat uneasy—perhaps even negative—response to the first paragraph. That is, *the writer has a sense of her audience;* she knows how her reader feels, and she takes account of the feeling.

The third paragraph clearly sets forth the alternatives. A reader may disagree with the writer's attitude, but the alternatives seem to be stated fairly.

The last two paragraphs are more personal than the earlier paragraphs. The writer, more or less having stated what she takes to be the facts, now is entitled to offer a highly personal response to them.

The final paragraph nicely wraps things up by means of the words *spare change,* which go back to the title and to the end of the first paragraph. The reader thus experiences a sensation of completeness. The essayist of course has not solved the problem for all of us for all time, but she presents a thoughtful argument and she ends the essay effectively.

Exercise

In an essay of 500 words state a claim and support it with evidence. Choose an issue in which you are genuinely interested and about which you already know something. You may want to interview a few experts and do some reading, but don't try to write a highly researched paper. Sample topics:

1. Students in laboratory courses should not be required to participate in the dissection of animals.
2. Washington, D.C., should be granted statehood.
3. Puerto Rico should be granted statehood.
4. Women should, in wartime, be exempted from serving in combat.
5. The annual Miss America contest is an insult to women.
6. The government should not offer financial support to the arts.
7. The chief fault of the curriculum in high school was . . .
8. Grades should be abolished in college and university courses.
9. No specific courses should be required in colleges or universities.

6

Using Sources

WHY USE SOURCES?

We have pointed out that one gets ideas by writing; in the exercise of writing a draft, ideas begin to form, and these ideas stimulate further ideas, especially when one questions—when one *thinks* about—what one has written. But of course in writing about complex, serious questions, nobody is expected to invent all the answers. On the contrary, a writer is expected to be familiar with the chief answers already produced by others, and to make use of them through selective incorporation and criticism. In short, writers are not expected to reinvent the wheel; rather, they are expected to make good use of it, and perhaps round it off a bit or replace a defective spoke. In order to think out your own views in writing, you are expected to do some preliminary research into the views of others.

We use the word *research* broadly. It need not require taking copious notes on everything written on your topic; rather, it can involve no more than familiarizing yourself with at least some of the chief responses to your topic. In one way or another, almost everyone does some research. If we are going to buy a car, we may read an issue or two of a magazine or visit a Web site that rates cars, or we may talk to a few people who own models that we are thinking of buying, and then we visit a couple of dealers to find out who is offering the best price.

Research, in short, is not an activity conducted only by college professors or by students who visit the library in order to write research papers. It is an activity that all of us engage in to some degree. In writing a research paper, you will engage in it to a great degree. But doing research is not the whole of a research paper. The reader expects the writer to have *thought* about the research, and to develop an argument based on the findings. Many businesses today devote an entire section to research and development. That's what is needed in writing, too. The reader wants not only a lot of facts but also a developed idea, a point to which the facts lead. Don't let your reader say of your paper what Gertrude Stein said of Oakland, California: "When you get there, there isn't any there there."

Consider arguments about whether athletes should be permitted to take anabolic steroids, drugs that supposedly build up muscle, restore energy, and enhance aggressiveness. A thoughtful argument on this subject will have to take account of information that the writer can gather only by doing some research. Do steroids really have the effects commonly attributed to them? And are they dangerous? If they are dangerous, how dangerous are they? (After all, competitive sports are inherently dangerous, some of them highly so. Many boxers, jockeys, and football players have suffered severe injury, even death, from competing. Does anyone believe that anabolic steroids are more dangerous than the contests themselves?) Obviously, again, a respectable argument about steroids will have to show awareness of what is known about them.

Or take this question: Why did President Truman order that atomic bombs be dropped on Hiroshima and Nagasaki? The most obvious answer is, to end the war, but some historians believe he had a very different purpose. In their view, Japan's defeat was ensured before the bombs were dropped, and the Japanese were ready to surrender; the bombs were dropped not to save American (or Japanese) lives, but to show Russia that we were not to be pushed around. Scholars who hold this view, such as Gar Alperovitz in *Atomic Diplomacy*, argue that Japanese civilians in Hiroshima and Nagasaki were incinerated not to save the lives of American soldiers who otherwise would have died in an invasion of Japan, but to teach Stalin a lesson. Dropping the bombs, it is argued, marked not the end of the Pacific War but the beginning of the cold war.

One must ask: What evidence supports this argument or claim or thesis, which assumes that Truman could not have thought the bomb was needed to defeat the Japanese because the Japanese knew they were defeated and would soon surrender without a hard-fought defense that would cost hundreds of thousands of lives? What about the momentum that had built up to use the bomb? After all, years of effort and $2 billion had been expended to produce a weapon with the intention of using it to end the war against Germany. But Germany had been defeated without the use of the bomb. Meanwhile, the war in the Pacific continued unabated. If the argument we are considering is correct, all this background counted for little or nothing in Truman's decision, a decision purely diplomatic and coolly indifferent to human life. The task for the writer is to evaluate the evidence available, and then to argue for or against the view that Truman's purpose in dropping the bomb was to impress the Soviet government.

A student writing on the topic will certainly want to read the chief books on the subject (Alperovitz's, cited above, Martin Sherwin's *A World Destroyed*, and John Toland's *The Rising Sun*), and perhaps reviews of them, especially the reviews in journals devoted to political science. (Reading a searching review of a serious scholarly book is a good way to identify quickly some of the book's main contributions and controversial claims.) Truman's letters and statements, and books and articles about Truman, are also clearly relevant, and doubtless important articles are to be found in recent issues of scholarly journals. In fact, even an essay on such a topic as whether Truman was morally justified in using the atomic bomb for *any* purpose will be a stronger essay if it is well informed about such matters as the estimated loss of life that an invasion would have cost, the international rules governing weapons, and Truman's own statements about the issue.

How does one go about finding the material needed to write a well-informed argument? We will provide help, but first we want to offer a few words about choosing a topic.

CHOOSING A TOPIC

We will be brief. If a topic is not assigned, choose one that

1. interests you, and that
2. can be researched with reasonable thoroughness in the allotted time.

Topics such as censorship, the environment, and sexual harassment obviously impinge on our lives, and it may well be that one such topic is of especial interest to you. But of course the scope of these topics makes researching them potentially overwhelming. Type the word *censorship* into an **Internet** search engine and you might be referred to thousands of information sources.

This brings us to our second point—a compassable topic. Any of the topics above would need to be narrowed substantially before you could begin searching in earnest. Similarly, a topic such as the causes of World War II can hardly be mastered in a few weeks or argued in a ten-page paper. It is simply too big.

You can, however, write a solid paper analyzing, evaluating, and arguing for or against General Eisenhower's views on atomic warfare. What were they, and when did he hold them? (In his books of 1948 and 1963 Eisenhower says that he opposed the use of the bomb before Hiroshima, and that he argued with Secretary of War Henry Stimson against dropping it, but what evidence supports these claims? Was

Eisenhower attempting to rewrite history in his books?) Eisenhower's own writings, and books on Eisenhower, will of course be the major sources for a paper on this topic, but you will also want to look at books and articles about Stimson, and at publications that contain information about the views of other generals, so that, for instance, you can compare Eisenhower's view with Marshall's or MacArthur's.

Your instructor understands that you are not going to spend a year writing a 200-page book, but you should understand that you must do more than consult the article on Eisenhower in one encyclopedia and the article on atomic energy in another encyclopedia.

FINDING MATERIAL

Your sources will of course depend on your topic. Some topics will require no more than a trip to the library or an afternoon spent at your personal computer, but others may require interviews. If you are writing about some aspect of AIDS, for instance, you probably will find it useful to consult your college or community health center.

For facts, you ought to try to consult experts—for instance, members of the faculty or other local authorities on art, business, law, and so forth; for opinions and attitudes, you will usually consult interested laypersons. Remember, however, that experts have their biases, and that "ordinary" people may have knowledge that experts lack. When interviewing experts, keep in mind Picasso's comment: "You musn't always believe what I say. Questions tempt you to tell lies, particularly when there is no answer."

INTERVIEWING PEERS AND LOCAL AUTHORITIES

If you are interviewing your peers, you will probably want to make an effort to get a representative sample. Of course, even within a group not all members share a single view—many African Americans favor affirmative action but not all do, and many gays favor legalizing gay marriage but, again, some don't. Make an effort to talk to a range of people who might be expected to offer varied opinions. You may learn some unexpected things.

Here we will concentrate, however, on interviews with experts.

1. **Finding subjects for interviews.** If you are looking for expert opinions, you may want to start with a faculty member on your campus. You may already know the instructor, or you may have to scan the catalog to see who teaches courses relevant to your topic. Department secretaries are good sources of information about the special interests of the faculty, and also about lecturers who will be visiting the campus.

2. **Doing preliminary homework.** (1) Know something about the person whom you will be interviewing. Biographical reference works such as *Who's Who in America, Who's Who Among Black Americans, Who's Who of American Women,* and *Directory of American Scholars* may include your interviewee, or, again, a departmental secretary may be able to provide a vita for a faculty member. (2) In requesting the interview, make evident your interest in the topic and in the person. (If you know something about the person, you will be able to indicate why you are asking him or her.) (3) Request the interview, preferably in writing, a week in advance, and ask for ample time—probably half an hour to an hour. Indicate whether or not the material will be confidential, and (if you want to use a recorder) ask if you may record the interview. (4) If the person accepts the invitation, ask if he or she recommends any preliminary reading, and establish a time and a suitable place, preferably not the cafeteria during lunchtime.

3. **Preparing thoroughly.** (1) If your interviewee recommended any reading, or has written on the topic, read the material. (2) Tentatively formulate some questions, keeping in mind that (unless you are simply gathering material for a survey of opinions) you want more than "yes" or "no" answers. Questions beginning with "Why" and "How" will usually require the interviewee to go beyond "yes" and "no."

Even if your subject has consented to let you bring a recorder, be prepared to take notes on points that strike you as especially significant; without written notes, you will have nothing if the recorder has malfunctioned. Further, by taking occasional notes you will give the interviewee some time to think, and perhaps to rephrase or to amplify a remark.

4. **Conducting the interview.** (1) Begin by engaging in brief conversation, without taking notes. If the interviewee has agreed to let you use a recorder, settle on the place where you will put the recorder. (2) Come prepared with an opening question or two, but as the interview proceeds don't hesitate to ask questions that you had not anticipated asking. (3) Near the end—you and your subject have probably agreed on the length of the interview—ask the subject if he or she wishes to add anything, perhaps by way of clarifying some earlier comment. (4) Conclude by thanking the interviewee, and by offering to provide a copy of the final version of your paper.

5. **Writing up the interview.** (1) As soon as possible—certainly within twenty-four hours after the interview—review your notes and clarify them. At this stage, you can still remember the meaning of your abbreviated notes and shorthand devices (maybe you have been using *n* to stand for *nurses* in clinics where abortions are performed), but if you wait even a whole day you may be puzzled by your own notes. If you have recorded the interview, you may want to transcribe all of it—the laboriousness of this task is one good reason why many interviewers do not use recorders—and you may then want to scan the whole and mark

the parts that now strike you as especially significant. If you have taken notes by hand, type them up, along with your own observations, for example, "Jones was very tentative on this matter, but she said she was inclined to believe that . . . ." (2) Be especially careful to indicate which words are direct quotations. If in doubt, check with the interviewee.

USING THE LIBRARY

Most topics, as we have said, will require research in the library. Notice that we have spoken of a topic, not of a thesis or even of a *hypothesis* (tentative thesis). Advanced students, because they are familiar with the rudiments of a subject (say, the origins of the cold war) usually have not only a topic but also a hypothesis or even a thesis in mind. Less experienced students are not always in this happy position: Before they can offer a hypothesis, they have to find a problem. Some instructors assign topics; others rely on students to find their own topics, based on readings in the course or in other courses.

When you have a *topic* ("Eisenhower and the atomic bomb"), and perhaps a *thesis* (an attitude toward the topic, a claim that you want to argue, such as "Eisenhower's disapproval of the bomb was the product of the gentleman-soldier code that he had learned at West Point"), it is often useful to scan a relevant book. You may already know of a relevant book, and it is likely in turn to cite others. If, however, you don't know of any book, you can find one by consulting the catalog in the library, which lists books not only by author and by title but also by subject. There are many computerized cataloguing systems; your librarian can teach you how to use the one in your college or university library.

If there are many books on the topic, how do you choose just one? Choose first a fairly thin one, of fairly recent date, published by a reputable publisher. You may even want to jot down two or three titles and then check reviews of these books before choosing one book to skim. Five indexes enable you easily to locate book reviews in newspapers and periodicals:

Book Review Digest (1905–)

Book Review Index (1965–)

Humanities Index (1974–)

Index to Book Reviews in the Humanities (1960–)

Social Sciences Index (1974–)

Book Review Digest includes brief extracts from the reviews, and so look there first, but its coverage is not as broad as the other indexes.

Skimming a recent academic book is a good way to get an overview of a topic, and it may help you to form a tentative thesis and focus your research further. But because the publication process takes a year or more, even a book with a publication date of this year may have been written at least a year earlier (and on some issues, for instance regulations concerning cloning or censorship of the Internet, some of the information in the source may be outdated). Articles in academic journals, too, usually are written many months before they are published, but magazines and newspapers can provide you with up-to-date information. Articles, whether in academic journals or in current magazines, have the further advantage of being short, so they are likely to be more focused than a book; they therefore may speak more directly to your tentative thesis.

To find articles in periodicals, begin with the computerized search tools that now are available in most college and university libraries. The two most popular search tools are *InfoTrac* and the *Readers' Guide to Periodical Literature*. Your library probably has at least one of these CD-ROM systems, each of which indexes several hundred popular and semi-popular magazines (like *Time* and *Scientific American*) and well-respected newspapers (like the *New York Times* and the *Washington Post*). If your topic is one in which there is wide public interest, these **databases** will point you toward many potential research sources. Using these systems is simply a matter of launching the appropriate software, typing in one or two key words related to your topic, and perhaps narrowing the search with additional words if the database turns up more than a few references to the terms you enter.

Even better than *InfoTrac* and the *Readers' Guide*, however, are the many specialized academic indexes now available on CD-ROM. These indexes, which list scholarly books and articles in specialized academic journals, are up-to-date and therefore are among the most valued tools. To find articles in journals, consult the *Humanities Index* and the *MLA International Bibliography* for topics in the humanities; for topics in psychology and other social sciences, consult *PsycLit* and the *Social Science Index*. Your college librarian can guide you to indexes for engineering and hard sciences, business and industry, education, the arts, or whatever field you are working in. Some of these indexes (such as the popular education index ERIC and the *Newspaper Abstracts*) not only provide bibliographic information but also include abstracts, or short summaries, of the articles they index. Which search tools you use will depend, obviously, both on your topic and on what is available in your library. All of the major systems are designed to be easy to use, but if you experience difficulty don't hesitate to ask the librarian for advice about which system to use and how to use it.

Annual print versions of many of these bibliographies and indexes also exist. If you prefer to use a print document or if your library doesn't have the CD-ROM database you need, ask your librarian for advice about using a more traditional search method.

FINDING INFORMATION ONLINE

If you have an Internet connection, you don't have to go any further than your personal computer to access a wealth of information for your research paper. This information may come from a number of online sources, including text archives, listservs (e-mail discussion groups), and Usenet newsgroups. But unless you already know of a particular source for your paper, the best place to begin an Internet search is with the hypertext and hypermedia portion of the Internet known as the **World Wide Web**. The Web is the largest and fastest-growing portion of the Net, as well as the easiest to use. In addition, a good Web site will often, along with providing information, point to other on- and offline sources of related interest.

All popular Internet browsers (the software, such as Netscape or Internet Explorer, through which you access the Web) have a "search" feature that hooks you up with a range of Internet search engines, programs to search the Net for relevant documents and provide you with hypertext links to those documents. These search engines are of two basic types. With most engines—some popular examples are Excite, Lycos, and Info-Seek—you type in a key word or words and the software scans the Net for documents containing those words. If your topic is highly focused and you have clear and specific search terms, a key word may work well, but if you enter a broad topic like "affirmative action" or "euthanasia" you will turn up thousands of "hits," leaving you overwhelmed with choices. The other sort of engine allows you to start with a very broad topic area, such as "government" or "entertainment," and narrow the topic through a series of menus until you reach a more specific topic, like "divorce law" or "television violence." The most popular engine of this type is called Yahoo!, and many researchers find it a good first choice.

We have two words of caution if you plan to use the Internet for serious research. First, the early stages of your research may take longer than planned. The Net is huge, fast-changing, and chaotic, and navigating it is not easy. Computer systems crash, Web pages move or disappear altogether, and the discourse surrounding a controversial topic like censorship or abortion can change overnight. Second, remember that the Net is highly democratic; anyone who can get online can express an opinion. The advantage is that knowledgeable people can offer information quickly, but the disadvantage is that careless scholars, blowhards, and liars can shed misinformation. It is always important for researchers to evaluate their sources, but evaluation is especially important when the source is online.

In the Appendix you will find reference to a few Web sites that provide reliable information on many of the topics in this book.

EVALUATING SOURCES

Finding a source of information related to your topic is not sufficient; you must be sure that the source is both valid and appropriate for your purposes. A quick evaluation of your sources before you begin carefully reading and taking notes on them may save you an enormous amount of time and frustration. Skim each source quickly, and keep the following in mind as you skim.

A recent book or article is usually preferable to an older one. Not only should your information be as up-to-date as possible, but recent works often effectively summarize previous research. (An exception to the rule "newer is better" would be if you have chosen an older work for a specific purpose, such as to compare it to more recent work to demonstrate changing attitudes.) In the case of Internet sources, sites will often indicate when they were last updated; if the one you use doesn't, you have no way of knowing reliably how fresh the information is.

A CHECKLIST FOR EVALUATING SOURCES

For Books (also useful for CD-ROMs and published databases):
- ✓ Is the book recent? If not, is the information you will be using from it unlikely to change over time?
- ✓ How credible is the author?
- ✓ Is the book published by a respectable press?
- ✓ Is the book broad enough in its focus, and written in a style you can understand?
- ✓ Does the book relate directly to your tentative thesis, or is it of only tangential interest?
- ✓ Do the arguments in the book seem sound, based on what you have learned about skillful critical reading and writing?

For Articles from Periodicals:
- ✓ Is the periodical recent?
- ✓ Is the author's name given? Does he or she seem a credible source?
- ✓ Is the periodical respectable and serious?
- ✓ How directly does the article speak to your topic and tentative thesis?
- ✓ If the article is from a scholarly journal, are you sure you understand it?

For Internet Sources:
- ✓ How up-to-date is the site?
- ✓ Is there an author listed for the site or document?
- ✓ Is the information associated with a reliable host site?
- ✓ Does the site rely on substance—or on flash alone?

As far as possible, try to determine the credibility of the author. The author's credentials are often briefly described on the book jacket or at the back of the book; these may reveal if the author is indeed an expert in the field, and even his or her possible biases about the topic. But what if the work is anonymous, as many newspaper articles and Internet sources are? Anonymous articles are not necessarily bad sources, but approach them with a bit of caution; why might an author not have put his or her name on a piece?

You will also want to determine the credibility of the publisher (especially in the case of anonymous works). Though publisher credibility may be difficult for you to judge, you can usually trust large, nationally recognized companies and presses associated with universities more than smaller, less well-known publishers. (If you have doubts, ask your instructor or librarian about a particular publisher.) Remember that academic journals tend to be more respectable than popular magazines, and that among magazines a hierarchy exists; an article from *Newsweek* usually is more credible than one from *People*. A similar hierarchy exists for newspapers: the *Washington Post* is powerfully credible, while tabloids such as the *Midnight Globe* are not. With online sources you often can tell, either from the document itself or from a close look at the Internet address, if a Web site, archive, or other source is associated with a reliable institution, such as a university, library, or government agency. While this does not guarantee accuracy, it does help to establish the credibility of the information. A final word about Internet sources: Don't let a flashy, expensive-looking Web site distract you from thinking critically about the site's content. While graphics, fancy fonts, audio and video clips, and the like can enhance a good site, a reliable source must offer more than a good show.

TAKING NOTES

When it comes to taking notes, all researchers have their own habits that they swear by, and they can't imagine any other way of working. Some people prefer to take notes by hand, others on a computer. Possibly you already are fixed in your habits, but if not, you may want to borrow ours. We use 4-by-6-inch index cards. Smaller cards don't have space for enough notes, and larger cards have space for too much. We recommend the following techniques.

1. Write in ink (pencil gets smudgy).
2. Put only one idea on each card (though an idea may include several facts).
3. Write on only one side of the card (notes on the back usually get lost).
4. Summarize, for the most part, rather than quote at length.

5. Quote only passages in which the writing is especially effective, or passages that are in some way crucial.

6. Make sure that all quotations are exact. Enclose quoted words within quotation marks, indicate omissions by ellipses (three spaced periods: . . .), and enclose within square brackets ([ ]) any insertions or other additions you make.

7. *Never* copy a passage, changing an occasional word. *Either* copy it word for word, with punctuation intact, and enclose it within quotation marks, *or* summarize it drastically. If you copy a passage but change a word here and there, you may later make the mistake of using your note verbatim in your essay, and you will be guilty of plagiarism.

8. Give the page number of your source, whether you summarize or quote. If a quotation you have copied runs in the original from the bottom of page 210 to the top of page 211, in your notes put a diagonal line (/) after the last word on page 210, so that later, if in your paper you quote only the material from page 210, you will know that you must cite 210 and not 210–11.

9. Indicate the source. The author's last name is enough if you have consulted only one work by the author; but if you consult more than one work by an author, you need further identification, such as the author's name and a short title.

10. Add your own comments about the substance of what you are recording. Such comments as "but contrast with Sherwin" or "seems illogical" or "evidence?" will ensure that you are thinking as well as writing, and will be of value when you come to transform your notes into a draft. Be sure, however, to enclose such notes within double diagonals (//), or to mark them in some other way, so that later you will know they are yours and not your source's.

11. Put a brief heading on the card, such as "Truman's last words on A-bomb."

12. Write a bibliographic card for each source. The information on this card will vary, depending on whether the source is a book, a periodical, an electronic document, and so forth. The kind of information (for example, author and title) needed for each type of source can be found in the sections on Works Cited or References (pp. 216, 227).

A WORD ABOUT PLAGIARISM

Plagiarism is the unacknowledged use of someone else's work. The word comes from a Latin word for "kidnapping," and plagiarism is indeed the stealing of something engendered by someone else. We won't deliver a sermon on the dishonesty (and folly) of plagiarism; we intend only to help you understand exactly what plagiarism is. The first thing to say is that plagiarism is not limited to the unacknowledged quotation of words.

A *paraphrase* is a sort of word-by-word or phrase-by-phrase translation of the author's language into your language. True, if you paraphrase you are using your own words, but you are also using someone else's ideas, and, equally important, you are using this other person's sequence of thoughts. Even if you change every third word in your source, and you do not give the author credit, you are plagiarizing. Here is an example of this sort of plagiarism, based on the previous sentence:

> Even if you alter every third or fourth word from your source, and you fail to give credit to the author, you will be guilty of plagiarism.

Even if the writer of this paraphrase had cited a source after it, the writer would still be guilty of plagiarism, because the passage borrows not only the idea but the shape of the presentation, the sentence structure. The writer of this passage hasn't really written anything; he or she has only adapted something. What the writer needs to do is to write something like this:

> Changing an occasional word does not free the writer from the obligation to cite a source.

And the source would still need to be cited, if the central idea were not a commonplace one.

You are plagiarizing if without giving credit you use someone else's ideas—even if you put these ideas entirely into your own words. When you use another's ideas, you must indicate your indebtedness by saying something like "Alperovitz points out that . . ." or "Secretary of War Stimson, as Martin Sherwin notes, never expressed himself on this point." Alperovitz and Sherwin pointed out something that you had not thought of, and so you must give them credit if you want to use their findings.

Again, even if after a paraphrase you cite your source, you are plagiarizing. How, you may wonder, can you be guilty of plagiarism if you cite a source? Easy. A reader assumes that the citation refers to information or an opinion, *not* to the presentation or development of the idea; and of course in a paraphrase you are not presenting or developing the material in your own way.

Now consider this question: *Why* paraphrase? Often there is no good answer. Since a paraphrase is as long as the original, you may as well quote the original, if you think that a passage of that length is worth quoting. Probably it is *not* worth quoting in full; probably you should *not* paraphrase but rather should drastically *summarize* most of it, and perhaps quote a particularly effective phrase or two.

Generally what you should do is to take the idea and put it entirely into your own words, perhaps reducing a paragraph of a hundred words to a sentence of ten words, but of course you must still give credit for the idea. If you believe that the original hundred words are so perfectly put that they cannot be transformed without great loss, you'll have to quote them, and cite your source. But clearly there is no point in paraphrasing the author's hundred words into a hundred of your own. Either quote or summarize, but cite the source.

Keep in mind, too, that almost all generalizations about human nature, no matter how common and familiar (for instance, "males are innately more aggressive than females") are not indisputable facts; they are at best hypotheses on which people differ and therefore should either not be asserted at all or should be supported by some cited source or authority. Similarly, because nearly all statistics (whether on the intelligence of criminals or the accuracy of lie detectors) are the result of some particular research and may well have been superseded or challenged by other investigators, it is advisable to cite a source for any statistics you use unless you are convinced they are indisputable, such as the number of registered voters in Memphis in 1988.

On the other hand, there is something called **common knowledge,** and the sources for such information need not be cited. The term does not, however, mean exactly what it seems to. It is common knowledge, of course, that Ronald Reagan was an American president (so you don't cite a source when you make that statement), and under the conventional interpretation of this doctrine, it is also common knowledge that he was born in 1911. In fact, of course, few people other than Reagan's wife and children know this date. Still, information that can be found in many places and that is indisputable belongs to all of us; therefore a writer need not cite her source when she says that Reagan was born in 1911. Probably she checked a dictionary or an encyclopedia for the date, but the source doesn't matter. Dozens of sources will give exactly the same information and, in fact, no reader wants to be bothered with a citation on such a point.

Some students have a little trouble developing a sense of what is and what is not common knowledge. Although, as we have just said, readers don't want to hear about the sources for information that is indisputable and can be documented in many places, if you are in doubt about whether to cite a source, cite it. Better risk boring the reader a bit than risk being accused of plagiarism.

COMPILING AN ANNOTATED BIBLIOGRAPHY

When several sources have been identified and gathered, many researchers prepare an annotated bibliography. This is a list providing all relevant bibliographic information (just as it will appear in your Works Cited or Reference list) as well as a brief descriptive and evaluative summary of each source—perhaps one to three sentences. Your instructor may ask you to provide an annotated bibliography for your research project.

An annotated bibliography serves three main purposes. First, constructing such a document helps you to master the material contained in any given source. To find the heart of the argument presented in an article or book, phrase it briefly, and comment on it, you must understand it fully. Second, creating an annotated bibliography helps you to think about how each portion of your research fits into the whole of your project, how you will use it, and how it relates to your topic and thesis. Finally, in constructing an annotated bibliography at this early stage, you will get some hands-on practice at bibliographic format, thereby easing the job of creating your final bibliography (the Works Cited or Reference list for your paper).

Below are two examples of entries for an annotated bibliography in MLA (Modern Language Association) format for a project on the effect of violence in the media. The first is for a book, the second for an article from a periodical. Notice that each

- begins with a bibliographic entry (author—last name first—title, and so forth), and then
- provides information about the content of the work under consideration, suggesting how each may be of use to the final research paper.

Clover, Carol J. <u>Men, Women, and Chain Saws: Gender in the Modern Horror Film</u>. Princeton: Princeton UP, 1992. The author focuses on Hollywood horror movies of the 1970s and 1980s. She studies representations of women and girls in these movies and the responses of male viewers to female characters, suggesting that this relationship is more complex and less exploitative than the common wisdom claims.

Winerip, Michael. "Looking for an 11 O'Clock Fix." <u>New York Times Magazine</u>. 11 Jan. 1998: 30-40. The article focuses on the rising levels of violence on local television news and highlights a station in Orlando, Florida, that tried to reduce its depictions of violence and lost viewers as a result. Winerip suggests that people only claim to be against media violence, while their actions prove otherwise.

WRITING THE PAPER

Organizing Your Notes

If you have read thoughtfully and taken careful (and, again, thoughtful) notes on your reading, and then (yet again) have thought about these notes, you are well on the way to writing a good paper. You have, in fact, already written some of it, in your notes. By now you should clearly have in mind the thesis you intend to argue. But of course you still have to organize the material, and, doubtless, even as you set about organizing it you will find points that will require you to do some additional research and much additional thinking.

Sort the index cards into packets, each packet devoted to one theme or point (for instance, one packet on the extent of use of steroids, another on evidence that steroids are harmful, yet another on arguments that even if harmful they should be permitted). Put aside all notes that — however interesting — you now see are irrelevant to your paper.

Next, arrange the packets into a tentative sequence. In effect, you are preparing a **working outline.** At its simplest, say, you will give three arguments on behalf of *X*, and then three counterarguments. (Or you might decide that it is better to alternate material from the two sets of three packets each, following each argument with an objection. At this stage, you can't be sure of the organization you will finally use, but make a tentative decision.)

The First Draft

Draft the essay, without worrying much about an elegant opening paragraph. Just write some sort of adequate opening that states the topic and your thesis. When you revise the whole later, you can put some effort into developing an effective opening. (Most experienced writers find that the opening paragraph in the final version is almost the last thing they write.)

If your notes are on cards, carefully copy into the draft all quotations that you plan to use. If your notes are in a computer, you may simply cut and paste them from one file to another. Do keep in mind, however, that rewriting or retyping quotations will make you think carefully about them, and may result in a more focused and thoughtful paper. (In the next section of this chapter we will talk briefly about leading into quotations, and about the form of quotations.) Be sure to include citations in your drafts, so that if you must check a reference later it will be easy to do so.

Later Drafts

Give the draft, and yourself, a rest, perhaps for a day or two, and then go back to it, read it over, make necessary revisions, and then

outline it. That is, on a sheet of paper chart the organization and development, perhaps by jotting down a sentence summarizing each paragraph or each group of closely related paragraphs. Your outline or map may now show you that the paper obviously suffers from poor organization. For instance, it may reveal that you neglected to respond to one argument, or that one point is needlessly treated in two places. It may also help you to see that if you gave three arguments and then three counterarguments, you probably should instead have followed each argument with its rebuttal. Or, on the other hand, if you alternated arguments and objections, it may now seem better to use two main groups, all the arguments and then all the criticisms.

No one formula is always right. Much will depend on the complexity of the material. If the arguments are highly complex, it is better to respond to them one by one than to expect a reader to hold three complex arguments in mind before you get around to responding. If, however, the arguments can be stated briefly and clearly, it is effective to state all three, and then to go on to the responses. If you write on a word processor you will find it easy, even fun, to move passages of text around. Even so, you will probably want to print out a hard copy from time to time to review the structure of your paper. Allow enough time to produce several drafts.

A few more words about organization: There is a difference between

a. a paper that *has* an organization and
b. a paper that *shows* what the organization is.

Write papers of the second sort, but (there is always a "but") take care not to belabor the obvious. Inexperienced writers sometimes either hide the organization so thoroughly that a reader cannot find it, or, on the other hand, they so ploddingly lay out the structure ("Eighth, I will show . . .") that the reader becomes impatient. Yet it is better to be overly explicit than to be obscure.

The ideal, of course, is the middle route. Make the overall strategy of your organization evident by occasional explicit signs at the beginning of a paragraph ("We have seen . . . ," "It is time to consider the objections . . . ," "By far the most important . . ."); elsewhere make certain that the implicit structure is evident to the reader. When you reread your draft, if you try to imagine that you are one of your classmates, you will probably be able to sense exactly where explicit signs are needed and where they are not needed. Better still, exchange drafts with a classmate in order to exchange (tactful) advice.

Choosing a Tentative Title

By now a couple of tentative titles for your essay should have crossed your mind. If possible, choose a title that is both interesting and informative. Consider these three titles:

```
Are Steroids Harmful?
The Fuss over Steroids
Steroids: A Dangerous Game
```

"Are Steroids Harmful?" is faintly interesting, and it lets the reader know the gist of the subject, but it gives no clue about the writer's thesis, the writer's contention or argument. "The Fuss over Steroids" is somewhat better, for it gives information about the writer's position. "Steroids: A Dangerous Game" is still better; it announces the subject ("steroids") and the thesis ("dangerous"), and it also displays a touch of wit, because "game" glances at the world of athletics.

Don't try too hard, however; better a simple, direct, informative title than a strained, puzzling, or overly cute one. And remember to make sure that everything in your essay is relevant to your title. In fact, your title should help you to organize the essay and to delete irrelevant material.

The Final Draft

When at last you have a draft that is for the most part satisfactory, check to make sure that **transitions** from sentence to sentence and from paragraph to paragraph are clear ("Further evidence," "On the other hand," "A weakness, however, is apparent"), and then worry about your opening and your closing paragraphs. Your **opening paragraph** should be clear, interesting, and focused; if neither the title nor the first paragraph announces your thesis, the second paragraph probably should do so.

The **final paragraph** need not say, "In conclusion, I have shown that . . . ." It should effectively end the essay, but it need not summarize your conclusions. We have already offered a few words about final paragraphs (p. 174), but the best way to learn how to write such paragraphs is to study the endings of some of the essays in this book, and to adopt the strategies that appeal to you.

Be sure that all indebtedness is properly acknowledged. We have talked about plagiarism; now we will turn to the business of introducing quotations effectively.

QUOTING FROM SOURCES

The Use and Abuse of Quotations

When is it necessary, or appropriate, to quote? Sometimes the reader must see the exact words of your source; the gist won't do. If you are arguing that Z's definition of *rights* is too inclusive, your readers have to know exactly how Z defined *rights*. Your brief summary of the definition may be unfair to Z; in fact, you want to convince your readers that you are being fair, and so you quote Z's definition, word for word. Moreover, if the passage is only a sentence or two long, or even if it runs to a paragraph, it may be so compactly stated that it defies summary. And to attempt to paraphrase it—substituting *natural* for *inalienable*, and so forth—saves no space and only introduces imprecision. There is nothing to do but to quote it, word for word.

Second, you may want to quote a passage that could be summarized but that is so effectively stated that you want your readers to have the pleasure of reading the original. Of course readers will not give you credit for writing these words, but they will give you credit for your taste, and for your effort to make especially pleasant the business of reading your paper.

In short, use (but don't overuse) quotations. Speaking roughly, quotations should occupy no more than 10 or 15 percent of your paper, and they may occupy much less. Most of your paper should set forth your ideas, not other people's ideas.

How to Quote

Long and Short Quotations   **Long quotations** (five or more lines of typed prose, or three or more lines of poetry) are set off from your text. To set off material, start on a new line, indent one inch from the left margin and type the quotation double-spaced. Do not enclose quotations within quotation marks if you are setting them off.

Short quotations are treated differently. They are embedded within the text; they are enclosed within quotation marks but otherwise they do not stand out.

All quotations, whether set off or embedded, must be exact. If you omit any words, you must indicate the ellipsis by substituting three spaced periods for the omission; if you insert any words or punctuation, you must indicate the addition by enclosing it within square brackets, not to be confused with parentheses.

Leading into a Quotation   Now for a less mechanical matter, the way in which a quotation is introduced. To say that it is "introduced" implies that one leads into it, though on rare occasions a quotation appears without an introduction, perhaps immediately after the title. Normally one leads into a quotation by giving the name of the author and (no less important) clues about the content of the quotation and the purpose it serves in the present essay. For example:

```
William James provides a clear answer to Huxley when he
says that ". . ."
```

The writer has been writing about Huxley, and now is signaling readers that they will be getting James's reply. The writer is also signaling (in "a clear answer") that the reply is satisfactory. If the writer believed that James's answer was not really acceptable, the lead-in might have run thus:

```
William James attempts to answer Huxley, but his re-
sponse does not really meet the difficulty Huxley calls
attention to. James writes, ". . . ."
```

Or:

```
William James provided what he took to be an answer to
Huxley when he said that ". . . ."
```

In this last example, clearly the words "what he took to be an answer" imply that the essayist will show, after the quotation from James, that the answer is in some degree inadequate. Or the essayist may wish to suggest the inadequacy even more strongly:

```
William James provided what he took to be an answer to
Huxley, but he used the word "religion" in a way that
Huxley would not have allowed. James argues that ". . . ."
```

If after reading something by Huxley the writer had merely given us "William James says . . . ," we wouldn't know whether we were getting confirmation, refutation, or something else. The essayist would have put a needless burden on the readers. Generally speaking, the more difficult the quotation, the more important is the introductory or explanatory lead-in, but even the simplest quotation profits from some sort of brief lead-in, such as "James reaffirms this point when he says . . ."

DOCUMENTATION

In the course of your essay, you will probably quote or summarize material derived from a source. You must give credit, and although there is no one form of documentation to which all scholarly fields subscribe, you will probably be asked to use one of two. One, established by the Modern Language Association (MLA), is used chiefly in the humanities; the other, established by the American Psychological Association (APA), is used chiefly in the social sciences.

We include two papers that use sources. "Why Trials Should Not Be Televised" (p. 232), uses the MLA format. (You may notice that various styles are illustrated in other selections we have included.)

A Note on Footnotes (and Endnotes)

Before discussing these two formats a few words about footnotes are in order. Before the MLA and the APA developed their rules of style, citations commonly were given in footnotes. Although today footnotes are not so frequently used to give citations, they still may be useful for another purpose. (The MLA suggests endnotes rather than footnotes, and of course endnotes are easier to type, unless you use a word processing program, but all readers know that in fact footnotes are preferable to endnotes. After all, who wants to keep shifting from a page of text to a page of notes at the rear?) If you want to include some material that may seem intrusive in the body of the paper, you may relegate it to a footnote. For example, in a footnote you might translate a quotation given in a foreign language, or you might demote from text to footnote a paragraph explaining why you are not taking account of such-and-such a point. By putting the matter in a footnote you are signaling the reader that it is dispensable; it is something relevant but not essential, something extra that you are, so to speak, tossing in. Don't make a habit of writing this sort of note, but there are times when it is appropriate.

MLA Format

This discussion is divided into two parts, a discussion of citations within the text of the essay, and a discussion of the list of references, called Works Cited, that is given at the end of the essay.

Citations within the Text   Brief citations within the body of the essay give credit, in a highly abbreviated way, to the sources for material you quote, summarize, or make use of in any other way. These *in-text citations* are made clear by a list of sources, titled Works Cited, appended to the essay. Thus, in your essay you may say something like this:

> Commenting on the relative costs of capital punishment
> and life imprisonment, Ernest van den Haag says that he
> doubts "that capital punishment really is more expen-
> sive" (33).

The **citation,** the number 33 in parentheses, means that the quoted words come from page 33 of a source (listed in Works Cited) written by van den Haag. Without Works Cited, a reader would have no way of knowing that you are quoting from page 33 of an article that appeared in the February 8, 1985, issue of *The National Review.*

Usually the parenthetic citation appears at the end of a sentence, as in the example just given, but it can appear elsewhere; its position will depend chiefly on your ear, your eye, and the context. You might, for example, write the sentence thus:

```
Ernest van den Haag doubts that "capital punishment
really is more expensive" than life imprisonment (33),
but other writers have presented figures that contra-
dict him.
```

Five points must be made about these examples:

1. **Quotation marks.** The closing quotation mark appears after the last word of the quotation, *not* after the parenthetic citation. Since the citation is not part of the quotation, the citation is not included within the quotation marks.

2. **Omission of words (ellipsis).** If you are quoting a complete sentence or only a phrase, as in the examples given, you do not need to indicate (by three spaced periods) that you are omitting material before or after the quotation. But if for some reason you want to omit an interior part of the quotation, you must indicate the omission by inserting an *ellipsis,* the three spaced dots. To take a simple example, if you omit the word "really" from van den Haag's phrase, you must alert the reader to the omission:

```
Ernest van den Haag doubts that "capital punishment
. . . is more expensive" than life imprisonment (33).
```

Suppose you are quoting a sentence but wish to omit material from the end of the sentence. Suppose, also, that the quotation forms the end of your sentence. Write a lead-in phrase, then quote as much from your source as you need, then type three spaced periods for the omission, close the quotation, give the parenthetic citation, and finally type a fourth period to indicate the end of your sentence.

Here's an example. Suppose you want to quote the first part of a sentence that runs, "We could insist that the cost of capital punishment be reduced so as to diminish the differences." Your sentence would incorporate the desired extract as follows:

```
Van den Haag says, "We could insist that the cost of
capital punishment be reduced . . ." (33).
```

3. **Punctuation with parenthetic citations.** In the preceding examples, the punctuation (a period or a comma in the examples) *follows* the citation. If, however, the quotation ends with a question mark, include the question mark *within* the quotation, since it is part of the quotation, and put a period *after* the citation.

```
Van den Haag asks, "Isn't it better--more just and
more useful--that criminals, if they do not have the
```

certainty of punishment, at least run the risk of suffering it?" (35).

But if the question mark is your own, and not in the source, put it after
the citation, thus:

What answer can be given to van den Haag's doubt that
"capital punishment really is more expensive" (33)?

4. **Two or more works by an author.** If your list of Works Cited
includes two or more works by an author, you cannot, in your essay,
simply cite a page number, because the reader will not know which of
the works you are referring to. You must give additional information.
You can give it in your lead-in, thus:

In "New Arguments against Capital Punishment," van den
Haag expresses doubt "that capital punishment really is
more expensive" than life imprisonment (33).

Or you can give the title, in a shortened form, within the citation:

Van den Haag expresses doubt that "capital punishment
really is more expensive" than life imprisonment ("New
Arguments" 33).

5. **Citing even when you do not quote.** Even if you don't quote a
source directly, but use its point in a paraphrase or a summary, you will
give a citation:

Van den Haag thinks that life imprisonment costs more
than capital punishment (33).

Note that in all of the previous examples, the author's name is given in
the text (rather than within the parenthetic citation). But there are several other ways of giving the citation, and we shall look at them now.
(We have already seen, in the example given under paragraph 4, that
the title and the page number can be given within the citation.)

AUTHOR AND PAGE NUMBER IN PARENTHESES

It has been argued that life imprisonment is more
costly than capital punishment (van den Haag 33).

AUTHOR, TITLE, AND PAGE NUMBER IN PARENTHESES

We have seen that if Works Cited includes two or more works by an
author, you will have to give the title of the work on which you are

drawing, either in your lead-in phrase or within the parenthetic citation. Similarly, if you are citing someone who is listed more than once in Works Cited, and for some reason you do not mention the name of the author or the work in your lead-in, you must add the information in your citation:

> Doubt has been expressed that capital punishment is as costly as life imprisonment (van den Haag, "New Arguments" 33).

A GOVERNMENT DOCUMENT OR A WORK
OF CORPORATE AUTHORSHIP

Treat the issuing body as the author. Thus, you will write something like this:

> The Commission on Food Control, in Food Resources Today, concludes that there is no danger (37–38).

A WORK BY TWO OR MORE AUTHORS

If a work is by *two or three authors,* give the names of all authors, either in the parenthetic citation (the first example below) or in a lead-in (the second example below):

> There is not a single example of the phenomenon (Smith, Dale, and Jones 182–83).

> Smith, Dale, and Jones insist there is not a single example of the phenomenon (182–83).

If there are *more than three authors,* give the last name of the first author, followed by "et al." (an abbreviation for *et alii,* Latin for "and others"), thus:

> Gittleman et al. argue (43) that . . .

Or:

> On average, the cost is even higher (Gittleman et al. 43).

PARENTHETIC CITATION OF AN INDIRECT SOURCE
(CITATION OF MATERIAL THAT ITSELF WAS QUOTED
OR SUMMARIZED IN YOUR SOURCE)

Suppose you are reading a book by Jones, in which she quotes Smith, and you wish to use Smith's material. Your citation must refer the reader to Jones—the source you are using—but of course you cannot attribute the words to Jones. You will have to make it clear that you are quoting Smith, and so, after a lead-in phrase like "Smith says," followed by the quotation, you will give a parenthetic citation along these lines:

```
(qtd. in Jones 324-25).
```

PARENTHETIC CITATION OF TWO OR MORE WORKS

```
The costs are simply too high (Smith 301; Jones 28).
```

Notice that a semicolon, followed by a space, separates the two sources.

A WORK IN MORE THAN ONE VOLUME

This is a bit tricky. If you have used only one volume, in Works Cited you will specify the volume, and so in the parenthetic in-text citation you will not need to specify the volume. All that you need to include in the citation is a page number, as illustrated by most of the examples that we have given.

If you have used more than one volume, your parenthetic citation will have to specify the volume as well as the page, thus:

```
Jackson points out that fewer than one hundred fifty
people fit this description (2: 351).
```

The reference is to page 351 in volume 2 of a work by Jackson.

If, however, you are citing not a page but an entire volume—let's say volume 2—your parenthetic citation will look like this:

```
Jackson exhaustively studies this problem (vol. 2).
```

Or:

```
Jackson (vol. 2) exhaustively studies this problem.
```

Notice the following points:

1. In citing a volume and page, the volume number, like the page number, is given in arabic (not roman) numerals, even if the original used roman numerals.
2. The volume number is followed by a colon, then a space, then the page number.
3. If you cite a volume number without a page number, as in the last example quoted, the abbreviation is "vol." Otherwise do *not* use such abbreviations as "vol." and "p." and "pg."

AN ANONYMOUS WORK

For an anonymous work, give the title in your lead-in, or give it in a shortened form in your parenthetic citation:

A Prisoner's View of Killing includes a poll taken of the inmates on death row (32).

Or:

A poll is available (Prisoner's View 32).

AN INTERVIEW

Probably you won't need a parenthetic citation, because you'll say something like

Vivian Berger, in an interview, said . . .

or

According to Vivian Berger, in an interview . . .

and when your reader turns to Works Cited, he or she will see that Berger is listed, along with the date of the interview. But if you do not mention the source's name in the lead-in, you will have to give it in the parentheses, thus:

Contrary to popular belief, the death penalty is not reserved for serial killers and depraved murderers (Berger).

AN ELECTRONIC SOURCE

Electronic sources, such as those found on CD-ROMs or the Internet, are generally not divided into pages. Therefore, the in-text citation for such sources cite the author's name (or, if a work is anonymous, the title) only:

According to the World Wide Web site for the American Civil Liberties Union . . .

If the source does use pages, or breaks down further into paragraphs or screens, insert the appropriate identifier or abbreviation (*p.* or *pp.* for page or pages; *par.* or *pars.* for paragraph or paragraphs; *screen* or *screens*) before the relevant number:

The growth of day care has been called "a crime against
posterity" by a spokesman for the Institute for the
American Family (Terwilliger, screens 1-2).

The List of Works Cited (MLA Format)

As the previous pages explain, parenthetic documentation consists of references that become clear when the reader consults the list titled Works Cited, given at the end of an essay.

The list of Works Cited continues the pagination of the essay; if the last page of text is 10, then Works Cited begins on its own page, in this case page 11. Type the page number in the upper right corner, a half inch from the top of the sheet and flush with the right margin. Next, type the heading: Works Cited (*not* enclosed within quotation marks), centered, one inch from the top, then double-space and type the first entry.

An Overview   Here are some general guidelines.

FORM ON THE PAGE

1. Begin each entry flush with the left margin, but if an entry runs to more than one line, indent five spaces, or a half inch, for each succeeding line of the entry.
2. Double-space each entry, and double-space between entries.
3. Underline titles of works published independently—for instance, books, pamphlets, and journals. Enclose within quotation marks a work not published independently—for instance, an article in a journal, or a short story.
4. If you are citing a book that includes the title of another book, underline the main title but do *not* underline the title mentioned. Example:

   A Study of Mill's On Liberty

5. In the sample entries below, pay attention to the use of commas, colons, and the space after punctuation.

ALPHABETIC ORDER

1. Arrange the list alphabetically by author, with the author's last name first.
2. For information about anonymous works, works with more than one author, and two or more works by one author, see below.

A Closer Look   Here is more detailed advice.

THE AUTHOR'S NAME

Notice that the last name is given first, but otherwise the name is given as on the title page. Do not substitute initials for names written out on the title page.

If your list includes two or more works by an author, do not repeat the author's name for the second title but represent it by three hyphens followed by a period. The sequence of the works is determined by the alphabetic order of the titles. Thus, Smith's book titled *Poverty* would be listed ahead of her book *Welfare*. See the example on page 218, listing two works by Roger Brown.

Anonymous works are listed under the first word of the title, or the second word if the first is *A, An,* or *The,* or a foreign equivalent. In a few moments we will discuss books by more than one author, government documents, and works of corporate authorship.

THE TITLE

After the period following the author's name, allow one space and then give the title. Take the title from the title page, not from the cover or the spine, but disregard any unusual typography such as the use of all capital letters or the use of the ampersand (&) for *and*. Underline the title and subtitle (separate them by a colon) with one continuous underline, to indicate italics, but do not underline the period that concludes this part of the entry.

Capitalize the first and the last word.

Capitalize all nouns, pronouns, verbs, adjectives, adverbs, and subordinating conjunctions (for example, *although, if, because*).

Do not capitalize (unless it's the first or last word of the title) articles (*a, an, the*), prepositions (for instance, *in, on, toward, under*), coordinating conjunctions (for instance, *and, but, or, for*), or the *to* in infinitives.

Examples:

<u>The Death Penalty: A New View</u>

<u>On the Death Penalty: Toward a New View</u>

<u>On the Penalty of Death in a Democracy</u>

PLACE OF PUBLICATION, PUBLISHER, AND DATE

For the place of publication, provide the name of the city; you can usually find it either on the title page or on the reverse of the title page. If a number of cities are listed, provide only the first. If the city is not likely to be known, or if it may be confused with another city of the same name (as is Oxford, Mississippi with Oxford, England), add the name of the state, abbreviated (use the newer two-letter postal code: IL, not Ill.).

The name of the publisher is abbreviated. Usually the first word is enough (Random House becomes Random), but if the first word is a first name, such as in Alfred A. Knopf, the surname (Knopf) is used instead. University presses are abbreviated thus: Yale UP, U of Chicago P, State U of New York P.

The date of publication of a book is given when known; if no date appears on the book, write n.d. to indicate "no date."

SAMPLE ENTRIES   Here are some examples, illustrating the points we have covered thus far:

Brown, Roger. Social Psychology. New York: Free, 1965.

---. Words and Things. Glencoe, IL: Free, 1958.

Douglas, Ann. The Feminization of American Culture. New
      York: Knopf, 1977.

Hartman, Chester. The Transformation of San Francisco.
      Totowa: Rowman, 1984.

Kellerman, Barbara. The Political Presidency: Practice
      of Leadership from Kennedy through Reagan. New
      York: Oxford UP, 1984.

Notice that a period follows the author's name, and another period follows the title. If a subtitle is given, as it is for Kellerman's book, it is separated from the title by a colon and a space. A colon follows the place of publication, a comma follows the publisher, and a period follows the date.

A BOOK BY MORE THAN ONE AUTHOR

The book is alphabetized under the last name of the first author named on the title page. If there are *two or three authors,* the names of these are given (after the first author's name) in the normal order, *first name first.*

Gilbert, Sandra M., and Susan Gubar. The Madwoman in
      the Attic: The Woman Writer and the Nineteenth-
      Century Literary Imagination. New Haven: Yale UP,
      1979.

Notice, again, that although the first author's name is given *last name first,* the second author's name is given in the normal order, first name

first. Notice, too, that a comma is put after the first name of the first author, separating the authors.

If there are *more than three authors,* give the name only of the first
and then add (but *not* enclosed within quotation marks) "et al." (Latin
for "and others").

> Altshuler, Alan, et al. The Future of the Automobile.
>   Cambridge: MIT P, 1984.

GOVERNMENT DOCUMENTS

If the writer is not known, treat the government and the agency as
the author. Most federal documents are issued by the Government Printing Office (abbreviated to GPO) in Washington, D.C.

> United States Congress. Office of Technology Assess-
>   ment. Computerized Manufacturing Automation:
>   Employment, Education, and the Workplace. Washing-
>   ton: GPO, 1984.

WORKS OF CORPORATE AUTHORSHIP

Begin the citation with the corporate author, even if the same body
is also the publisher, as in the first example:

> American Psychiatric Association. Psychiatric Glossary.
>   Washington: American Psychiatric Association,
>   1984.

> Carnegie Council on Policy Studies in Higher Education.
>   Giving Youth a Better Chance: Options for Educa-
>   tion, Work, and Service. San Francisco: Jossey,
>   1980.

A REPRINT, FOR INSTANCE A PAPERBACK VERSION
OF AN OLDER CLOTHBOUND BOOK

> Gray, Francine du Plessix. Divine Disobedience: Pro-
>   files in Catholic Radicalism. 1970. New York: Vin-
>   tage, 1971.

After the title, give the date of original publication (it can usually be
found on the reverse of the title page of the reprint you are using), then
a period, and then the place, publisher, and date of the edition you are
using. The example indicates that Gray's book was originally published
in 1970 and that the student is using the Vintage reprint of 1971.

A BOOK IN SEVERAL VOLUMES

If you have used more than one volume, in a citation within your essay you will (as explained on p. 214) indicate a reference to, say, page 250 of volume 3 thus: (3: 250).

If, however, you have used only one volume of the set—let's say volume 3—in your entry in Works Cited, specify which volume you used, as in the next example:

```
Friedel, Frank. Franklin D. Roosevelt. Vol. 3. Boston:
     Little, 1973. 4 vols.
```

With such an entry in Works Cited, the parenthetic citation within your essay would be to the page only, not to the volume and page, because a reader who consults Works Cited will understand that you used only volume 3. In Works Cited, you may specify volume 3 and not give the total number of volumes, or you may add the total number of volumes, as in the example above.

ONE BOOK WITH A SEPARATE TITLE
IN A SET OF VOLUMES

Sometimes a set with a title makes use also of a separate title for each book in the set. If you are listing such a book, use the following form:

```
Churchill, Winston. The Age of Revolution. New York:
     Dodd, 1957. Vol. 3 of History of the English-
     Speaking Peoples. 4 vols. 1956–58.
```

A BOOK WITH AN AUTHOR AND AN EDITOR

```
Churchill, Winston, and Franklin D. Roosevelt. The Com-
     plete Correspondence. Ed. Warren F. Kimball. 3
     vols. Princeton: Princeton UP, 1985.

Kant, Immanuel. The Philosophy of Kant: Immanuel Kant's
     Moral and Political Writings. Ed. Carl J.
     Friedrich. New York: Modern, 1949.
```

If the book has one editor, the abbreviation is "ed."; if two or more editors, "eds."

If you are making use of the editor's introduction or other editorial material rather than of the author's work, list the book under the name of the editor rather than of the author, as shown below under "An Introduction, Foreword, or Afterword."

A REVISED EDITION OF A BOOK

Arendt, Hannah. <u>Eichmann in Jerusalem</u>. Rev. and en-
　　larged ed. New York: Viking, 1965.

Honour, Hugh, and John Fleming. <u>The Visual Arts: A His-
　　tory</u>. 2nd ed. Englewood Cliffs: Prentice, 1986.

A TRANSLATED BOOK

Franqui, Carlos. <u>Family Portrait with Fidel: A Memoir</u>.
　　Trans. Alfred MacAdam. New York: Random, 1984.

AN INTRODUCTION, FOREWORD, OR AFTERWORD

Goldberg, Arthur J. Foreword. <u>An Eye for an Eye? The
　　Morality of Punishing by Death</u>. By Stephen
　　Nathanson. Totowa: Rowman, 1987. v-vi.

Usually a book with an introduction or some such comparable material
is listed under the name of the author of the book (here Nathanson)
rather than under the name of the writer of the foreword (here Goldberg), but if you are referring to the apparatus rather than to the book itself, use the form just given. The words *Introduction, Preface, Foreword,*
and *Afterword* are neither enclosed within quotation marks nor underlined.

A BOOK WITH AN EDITOR BUT NO AUTHOR

Let's assume that you have used a book of essays written by various
people but collected by an editor (or editors), whose name appears on
the collection.

LaValley, Albert J., ed. <u>Focus on Hitchcock</u>. Englewood
　　Cliffs: Prentice, 1972.

A WORK WITHIN A VOLUME OF WORKS BY ONE AUTHOR

The following entry indicates that a short work by Susan Sontag, an
essay called "The Aesthetics of Silence," appears in a book by Sontag
titled *Styles of Radical Will.* Notice that the inclusive page numbers of the
short work are cited, not merely page numbers that you may happen to
refer to but the page numbers of the entire piece.

Sontag, Susan. "The Aesthetics of Silence." In <u>Styles
　　of Radical Will</u>. New York: Farrar, 1969. 3-34.

A BOOK REVIEW

Here is an example, citing Gerstein's review of Walker's book. Gerstein's review was published in a journal called *Ethics*.

```
Gerstein, Robert S. Rev. of Punishment, Danger and
     Stigma: The Morality of Criminal Justice, by Nigel
     Walker. Ethics 93 (1983): 408-10.
```

If the review has a title, give the title between the period following the reviewer's name and "Rev."

If a review is anonymous, list it under the first word of the title, or under the second word if the first word is *A, An,* or *The.* If an anonymous review has no title, begin the entry with "Rev. of" and then give the title of the work reviewed; alphabetize the entry under the title of the work reviewed.

AN ARTICLE OR ESSAY—NOT A REPRINT— IN A COLLECTION

A book may consist of a collection (edited by one or more persons) of new essays by several authors. Here is a reference to one essay in such a book. (The essay by Balmforth occupies pages 19–35 in a collection edited by Bevan.)

```
Balmforth, Henry. "Science and Religion." Steps to
     Christian Understanding. Ed. R. J. W. Bevan. Lon-
     don: Oxford UP, 1958. 19-35.
```

AN ARTICLE OR ESSAY REPRINTED IN A COLLECTION

The previous example (Balmforth's essay in Bevan's collection) was for an essay written for a collection. But some collections reprint earlier material, such as essays from journals or chapters from books. The following example cites an essay that was originally printed in a book called *The Cinema of Alfred Hitchcock.* This essay has been reprinted in a later collection of essays on Hitchcock, edited by Arthur J. LaValley, and it was LaValley's collection that the student used.

```
Bogdanovich, Peter. "Interviews with Alfred Hitchcock."
     The Cinema of Alfred Hitchcock. New York: Museum
     of Modern Art, 1963. 15-18. Rpt. in Focus on
     Hitchcock. Ed. Albert J. LaValley. Englewood
     Cliffs: Prentice, 1972. 28-31.
```

The student has read Bogdanovich's essay or chapter, but not in Bogdanovich's book, where it occupied pages 15–18. The material was actually read on pages 28–31 in a collection of writings on Hitchcock, edited by LaValley. Details of the original publication—title, date, page numbers, and so forth—were found in LaValley's collection. Almost all editors will include this information, either on the copyright page or at the foot of the reprinted essay, but sometimes they do not give the original page numbers. In such a case, you need not include the original numbers in your entry.

Notice that the entry begins with the author and the title of the work you are citing (here, Bogdanovich's interviews), not with the name of the editor of the collection or the title of the collection.

AN ENCYCLOPEDIA OR OTHER ALPHABETICALLY ARRANGED REFERENCE WORK

The publisher, place of publication, volume number, and page number do *not* have to be given. For such works, list only the edition (if it is given) and the date.

For a *signed* article, begin with the author's last name. (If the article is signed with initials, check elsewhere in the volume for a list of abbreviations, which will inform you who the initials stand for, and use the following form.)

    Williams, Donald C. "Free Will and Determinism." Ency-
        clopedia Americana. 1987 ed.

For an *unsigned article,* begin with the title of the article:

    "Automation." The Business Reference Book. 1977 ed.

    "Tobacco." Encyclopaedia Britannica: Macropaedia. 1988
        ed.

A TELEVISION OR RADIO PROGRAM

    "Back to My Lai." Narr. Mike Wallace. 60 Minutes. CBS.
        29 Mar. 1998.

    "Juvenile Justice." Narr. Ray Suarez. Talk of the Na-
        tion. Natl. Public Radio. WBUR, Boston. 15 Apr.
        1998.

AN ARTICLE IN A SCHOLARLY JOURNAL The title of the article is enclosed within quotation marks, and the title of the journal is underlined to indicate italics.

Some journals are paginated consecutively; the pagination of the second issue begins where the first issue leaves off. Other journals begin each issue with page 1. The forms of the citations differ slightly.

A JOURNAL THAT IS PAGINATED CONSECUTIVELY

```
Vilas, Carlos M. "Popular Insurgency and Social Revolu-
       tion in Central America." Latin American Perspec-
       tives 15 (1988): 55-77.
```

Vilas's article occupies pages 55–77 in volume 15, which was published in 1988. (Notice that the volume number is followed by a space, and then by the year, in parentheses, and then by a colon, a space, and the page numbers of the entire article.) Because the journal is paginated consecutively, the issue number does *not* need to be specified.

A JOURNAL THAT BEGINS EACH ISSUE WITH PAGE 1

If the journal is, for instance, a quarterly, there will be four page 1's each year, so the issue number must be given. After the volume number, type a period and (without hitting the space bar) the issue number, as in the next example:

```
Greenberg, Jack. "Civil Rights Enforcement Activity of
       the Department of Justice." The Black Law Journal
       8.1 (1983): 60-67.
```

Greenberg's article appeared in the first issue of volume 8 of *The Black Law Journal.*

AN ARTICLE IN A WEEKLY, BIWEEKLY, OR MONTHLY PUBLICATION

```
Lamar, Jacob V. "The Immigration Mess." Time 27 Feb.
       1989: 14-15.
```

AN ARTICLE IN A NEWSPAPER

Because a newspaper usually consists of several sections, a section number or a capital letter may precede the page number. The example indicates that an article begins on page 1 of section 2 and is continued on a later page.

```
Chu, Harry. "Art Thief Defends Action." New York Times
       8 Feb. 1989, sec. 2: 1+.
```

AN UNSIGNED EDITORIAL

```
"The Religious Tyranny Amendment." Editorial. New York
       Times 15 Mar. 1998, sec. 4: 16.
```

A LETTER TO THE EDITOR

Lasken, Douglas. "Teachers Reject Bilingual Education."
     Letter. New York Times 15 Mar. 1998, sec. 4: 16.

AN INTERVIEW

Jevgrafovs, Alexandre L. Personal [or Telephone] inter-
     view. 14 Dec. 1997.

PERSONAL CORRESPONDENCE

Raso, Robert. Letter [or E-mail] to the author. 6 Jan.
     1998.

CD-ROM

CD-ROMs are cited very much like their printed counterparts. To the usual print citation information, add (1) the title of the database, underlined; (2) the medium ("CD-ROM"); (3) the vendor's name; and (4) the date of electronic publication.

Louisberg, Margaret. Charlie Brown Meets Godzilla: What
     Are Our Children Watching? Urbana: ERIC Clearing-
     house on Elementary and Early Childhood Educ.,
     1990. ERIC. CD-ROM. SilverPlatter. May 1997.

"Pornography." The Oxford English Dictionary. 2nd ed.
     CD-ROM. Oxford: Oxford UP, 1992.

THE INTERNET

Include as much of the following information as is available, in the order and format specified: (1) author's name, last name first; (2) title of section (subject lines for e-mails and newsgroup postings) in quotation marks; (3) title of the full document or site, underlined or in italics; (4) date of publication or most recent update; (5) protocol (World Wide Web, FTP, Usenet newsgroup, listserv, and so forth); (6) date of access; (7) electronic address (URL) or path, in angle brackets. Break the URL only after a slash (or, for a double slash, after the second slash).

Ricci, Paul. "Global Warming." Online posting. 10 June
     1996. Global Electronic Science Conference. 22
     Sept. 1997 <http://www.science.envir/earth>.

Trammell, George W. "Cirque du O. J." Court Technology
     Bulletin July/Aug. 1995. World Wide Web. 12 Sept.

```
1995 <http://www.ncsc.dni.us/ncsc/bulletin/
v07n04.htm>.
```

A DATABASE SOURCE

Treat material obtained from a computer service, such as Bibliographies Retrieval Service (BRS), like other printed material, but at the end of the entry add (if available) the title of the database (underlined), publication medium (*Online*), name of the computer service, and date of access.

```
Jackson, Morton. "A Look at Profits." Harvard Business
     Review 40 (1962): 106-13. Online. BRS. 23 Dec.
     1995.
```

Caution: Although we have covered the most usual kinds of sources, it is entirely possible that you will come across a source that does not fit any of the categories that we have discussed. For approximately two hundred pages of explanations of these matters, covering the proper way to cite all sorts of troublesome and unbelievable (but real) sources, see Joseph Gibaldi, *MLA Handbook for Writers of Research Papers,* Fourth Edition (New York: Modern Language Association of America, 1995).

APA Format

Your paper will conclude with a separate page headed "References," in which you list all of your sources. If the last page of your essay is numbered 10, number the first page of references 11.

Citations within the Text   The APA style emphasizes the date of publication; the date appears not only in the list of references at the end of the paper, but also in the paper itself, when you give a brief parenthetic citation of a source that you have quoted or summarized or in any other way used. Here is an example:

```
Statistics are readily available (Smith, 1989, p. 20).
```

The title of Smith's book or article will be given at the end of your paper, in the list titled "References." We will discuss the form of the material listed in References in a moment, but first we will look at some typical citations within the text of a student's essay.

A SUMMARY OF AN ENTIRE WORK

```
Smith (1988) holds the same view.
```

Or

```
Similar views are held widely (Smith, 1988; Jones &
Metz, 1990).
```

A REFERENCE TO A PAGE OR TO PAGES

```
Smith (1988) argues that "the death penalty is a lot-
tery, and blacks usually are the losers" (p. 17).
```

A REFERENCE TO AN AUTHOR WHO IN THE
LIST OF REFERENCES IS REPRESENTED BY
MORE THAN ONE WORK

If in References you list two or more works that an author published in the same year, the works are listed in alphabetic order, by the first letter of the title. The first work is labeled *a*, the second *b*, and so on. Here is a reference to the second work that Smith published in 1989:

```
Florida presents "a fair example" of how the death
penalty is administered (Smith, 1989b, p. 18).
```

References   Your brief parenthetic citations are made clear when the reader consults the list you give in References. Type this list on a separate page, continuing the pagination of your essay.

AN OVERVIEW   Here are some general guidelines.

FORM ON THE PAGE
1. Begin each entry flush with the left margin, but if an entry runs to more than one line, indent five spaces for each succeeding line of the entry.
2. Double-space each entry, and double-space between entries.

ALPHABETIC ORDER
1. Arrange the list alphabetically by author.
2. Give the author's last name first, then the initial of the first and of the middle name (if any).
3. If there is more than one author, name all of the authors, again inverting the name (last name first) and giving only initials for first and middle names. (But do not invert the editor's name when the entry begins with the name of an author who has written an article in an edited book.) When there are two or more authors, use an ampersand (&) before the name of the last author. Example (here, of an article in the tenth volume of a journal called *Developmental Psychology*):

Drabman, R. S., & Thomas, M. H. (1974). Does media violence increase children's tolerance of real-life aggression? <u>Developmental Psychology, 10</u>, 418–421.

4. If you list more than one work by an author, do so in the order of publication, the earliest first. If two works by an author were published in the same year, give them in alphabetic order by the first letter of the title, disregarding *A, An,* or *The,* and their foreign equivalent. Designate the first work as "a," the second as "b." Repeat the author's name at the start of each entry.

Donnerstein, E. (1980a). Aggressive erotica and violence against women. <u>Journal of Personality and Social Psychology, 39</u>, 269–277.

Donnerstein, E. (1980b). Pornography and violence against women. <u>Annals of the New York Academy of Sciences, 347</u>, 227–288.

Donnerstein, E. (1983). Erotica and human aggression. In R. Green and E. Donnerstein (Eds.), <u>Aggression: Theoretical and empirical reviews</u> (pp. 87–103). New York: Academic Press.

FORM OF TITLE

1. In references to books, capitalize only the first letter of the first word of the title (and of the subtitle, if any) and capitalize proper nouns. Underline the complete title (but not the period at the end).
2. In references to articles in periodicals or in edited books, capitalize only the first letter of the first word of the article's title (and subtitle, if any), and all proper nouns. Do not put the title within quotation marks. Type a period after the title of the article. For the title of the journal, and the volume and page numbers, see the next instruction.
3. In references to periodicals, give the volume number in arabic numerals, and underline it. Do *not* use *vol.* before the number, and do not use *p.* or *pg.* before the page numbers.

Sample References   Here are some samples to follow.

A BOOK BY ONE AUTHOR

Pavlov, I. P. (1927). <u>Conditioned reflexes</u> (G. V. Anrep, Trans.). London: Oxford University Press.

A BOOK BY MORE THAN ONE AUTHOR

Belenky, M. F., Clinchy, B. M., Goldberger, N. R., &
    Torule, J. M. (1986). Women's ways of knowing: The
    development of self, voice, and mind. New York:
    Basic Books.

A COLLECTION OF ESSAYS

Christ, C. P., & Plaskow, J. (Eds.). (1979). Woman-
    spirit rising: A feminist reader in religion. New
    York: Harper & Row.

A WORK IN A COLLECTION OF ESSAYS

Fiorenza, E. (1979). Women in the early Christian move-
    ment. In C. P. Christ & J. Plaskow (Eds.), Woman-
    spirit rising: A feminist reader in religion (pp.
    84–92). New York: Harper & Row.

GOVERNMENT DOCUMENTS

If the writer is not known, treat the government and the agency as
the author. Most federal documents are issued by the Government Printing Office in Washington, D.C. If a document number has been assigned,
insert that number in parentheses between the title and the following
period.

United States Congress. Office of Technology Assess-
    ment. (1984). Computerized manufacturing automa-
    tion: Employment, education, and the workplace.
    Washington, DC: U.S. Government Printing Office.

AN ARTICLE IN A JOURNAL WITH CONTINUOUS PAGINATION

Tversky, A., & Kahneman, D. (1981). The framing of de-
    cisions and the psychology of choice. Science,
    211, 453–458.

AN ARTICLE IN A JOURNAL THAT PAGINATES
EACH ISSUE SEPARATELY

Foot, R. J. (1988-89). Nuclear coercion and the ending
    of the Korean conflict. International Security,
    13(4), 92–112.

The reference informs us that the article appeared in issue number 4 of volume 13.

AN ARTICLE FROM A MONTHLY OR WEEKLY MAGAZINE

Greenwald, J. (1989, February 27). Gimme shelter. Time,
    133, 50-51.

Maran, S. P. (1988, April). In our backyard, a star ex-
    plodes. Smithsonian, 19, 46-57.

AN ARTICLE IN A NEWSPAPER

Connell, R. (1989, February 6). Career concerns at
    heart of 1980s' campus protests. Los Angeles
    Times, pp. 1, 3.

(*Note:* If no author is given, simply begin with the title followed by the date in parentheses.)

A BOOK REVIEW

Daniels, N. (1984). Understanding physician power [Re-
    view of the book, The social transformation of
    American medicine]. Philosophy and Public Affairs,
    13, 347-356.

Daniels is the reviewer, not the author of the book. The book under review is called *The Social Transformation of American Medicine,* but the review, published in volume 13 of *Philosophy and Public Affairs,* had its own title, "Understanding Physician Power."

If the review does not have a title, retain the square brackets and use the material within as the title. Proceed as in the example just given.

For a full account of the APA method of dealing with all sorts of unusual citations, see the fourth edition (1994) of the APA manual, *Publication Manual of the American Psychological Association.*

AN ANNOTATED
STUDENT RESEARCH PAPER

The following argument makes good use of sources. Early in the semester the students were asked to choose one topic from a list of ten, and to write a documented argument of 750 to 1,250 words (three to five pages of double-spaced typing). The completed paper was due two weeks after the topics were distributed. The assignment, a prelude to working on a research paper of 2,500 to 3,000 words, was in part designed to give students practice in finding and in using sources. Citations are given in the MLA form.

A CHECKLIST FOR PAPERS USING SOURCES

✓ All borrowed words and ideas credited?

✓ Quotations and summaries not too long?

✓ Quotations accurate?

✓ Quotations provided with helpful lead-ins?

✓ Documentation in proper form?

And of course you will also ask yourself the questions that you would ask of a paper that did not use sources, such as:

✓ Topic sufficiently narrowed?

✓ Thesis (to be advanced or refuted) stated early and clearly, perhaps even in title?

✓ Audience kept in mind? Opposing views stated fairly and as sympathetically as possible? Controversial terms defined?

✓ Assumptions likely to be shared by readers? If not, are they argued rather than merely asserted?

✓ Focus clear (for example, evaluation, or recommendation of policy)?

✓ Evidence (examples, testimony, statistics) adequate and sound?

✓ Inferences valid?

✓ Organization clear? (Effective opening, coherent sequence of arguments, unpretentious ending?)

✓ All worthy opposition faced?

✓ Tone appropriate?

✓ Has the paper been carefully proofread?

✓ Is the title effective?

✓ Is the opening paragraph effective?

✓ Is the structure reader-friendly?

✓ Is the closing paragraph effective?

The *MLA
Handbook* does not
insist on a title
page and outline,
but many
instructors prefer
them.

Title one-third
down page.

Why Trials Should Not Be Televised

By

Theresa Washington

All lines centered.

Professor Wilson

English 102

December 12, 1997

Washington i

Outline

Thesis: The televising of trials is a bad idea
because it has several negative effects
on the First Amendment: it gives viewers
a deceptive view of particular trials
and of the judicial system in general,
and it degrades the quality of media reporting outside the courtroom.

  I. Introduction
     A. Trend toward increasing trial coverage
     B. First Amendment versus Sixth Amendment
 II. Effect of televising trials on First
     Amendment
     A. Provides deceptive version of truth
        1. Confidence in verdicts misplaced
           a. Willie Smith trial
           b. Rodney King trial
        2. Nature of TV as a medium
           a. Distortion in sound bites
           b. Stereotyping trial participants
           c. Misleading camera angles
           d. Commentators and commercials
     B. Confuses viewers about judicial system
        1. Contradicts basic concept "innocent
           until proven guilty"
        2. Can't explain legal complexities
     C. Contributes to media circus outside of
        court
        1. Blurs truth and fiction
        2. Affects print media in negative ways
        3. Media makes itself the story
        4. Distracts viewers from other issues
III. Conclusion

Small roman
numerals for page
with outline.

Roman numerals
for chief units (I,
II, etc.); capital
letters for chief
units within these
largest units;
then, for smaller
and smaller units,
arabic numerals
and lowercase
letters.

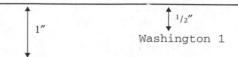

Washington 1

Title is focused
and announces
the thesis.

Double-space
between title and
first paragraph—
and throughout
the essay.

1" margin on each
side and at
bottom.

Summary of
opposing
positions.

Parenthetic
reference to an
anonymous
source and also to
a source with a
named author.

Superscript
numerals indicate
endnotes.

Why Trials Should Not Be Televised

Although trials have been televised on and off since the 1950s,[1] in the last few years the availability of trials for a national audience has increased dramatically.[2] Media critics, legal scholars, social scientists, and journalists continue to debate the merits of this trend.

Proponents of cameras in the courtroom argue, falsely, I believe, that confidence in the fairness of our institutions, including the judicial system, depends on a free press, guaranteed by the First Amendment. Keeping trials off television is a form of censorship, they say. It limits the public's ability to understand (1) what is happening in particular trials, and (2) how the judicial system operates, which is often confusing to laypeople. Opponents claim that televising trials threatens the defendant's Sixth-Amendment rights to a fair trial because it can alter the behavior of the trial participants, including the jury ("Tale"; Thaler).

Regardless of its impact on due process of law,[3] TV in court does not serve the First Amendment well. Consider the first claim, that particular trials are easier to understand when televised. But does watching trials on television really allow the viewer to "see it like it is," to get the full scope and breadth of a trial? Steven Brill, founder of Court TV, would like us to believe so. He points out that most high-profile defendants in televised trials

Washington 2

have been acquitted; he names William Kennedy
Smith, Jimmy Hoffa, John Connally, and John
Delorean as examples (Clark 821). "Imagine if
[Smith's trial] had not been shown and he got
off. Millions of people would have said the
Kennedys fixed the case" (Brill qtd. in "Tale"
29). Polls taken after the trial seem to confirm this claim, since they showed the public
by and large agreed with the jury's decision to
acquit (Quindlen).

　　However, Thaler points out that the public
can just as easily disagree with the verdict as
agree, and when this happens, the effects can
be catastrophic. One example is the Rodney King
case. Four white Los Angeles police officers
were charged in 1991 with severely beating
African American Rodney King, who, according to
the officers, had been resisting arrest. At
their first trial, all four officers were acquitted. This verdict outraged many African
Americans throughout the country; they felt the
evidence from watching the trial overwhelmingly
showed the defendants to be guilty. The black
community of south-central Los Angeles expressed its feelings by rioting for days
(Thaler 50-51).

　　Clearly the black community did not experience the trial the same way the white community and the white jury did. Why? Marty Rosen-
baum, an attorney with the New York State
Defenders Association, points out that viewers
cannot experience a trial the same way trial
participants do. "What you see at home 'is not

Parenthetic
reference to
author and page.

Parenthetic
reference to an
indirect source (a
borrowed quo-
tation).

what jurors see'" (qtd. in Thaler 70). The
trial process is slow, linear, and methodical,
as the defense and prosecution each build their
case, one piece of information at a time

Although no
words are quoted,
the idea is
borrowed and so
the source is cited.

(Thaler 11). The process is intended to be
thoughtful and reflective, with the jury weighing all the evidence in light of the whole
trial (Altheide 299-301). And it emphasizes
words--both spoken and written--rather than images (Thaler 11).

Clear transition
("In contrast").

In contrast, TV's general strength is in
handling visual images that entertain or that
provoke strong feelings. News editors and reporters choose footage for its assumed visual
and emotional impact on viewers. Words are made
to fit the images, not the other way around,
and they tend to be short catchy phrases, easy
to understand (Thaler 4, 7). As a result, the
15- to 30-second "sound bites" in nightly news-
casts often present trial events out of context, emphasizing moments of drama rather than

Parenthetic
citation of two
sources.

of legal importance (Thaler 7; Zoglin 62).

Furthermore, this emphasis on emotional
visuals leads to stereotyping the participants,
making larger-than-life symbols out of them,
especially regarding social issues (Thaler 9):
abused children (the Menendez brothers), the
battered wife (Hedda Nussbaum), the abusing
husband (Joel Steinberg, O. J. Simpson), the
jealous lover (Amy Fisher), the serial killer
(Jeffrey Dahmer), and date rapist (Willie
Smith). It becomes difficult for viewers to see
defendants as ordinary human beings.

Washington 4

One can argue, as Brill has done, that gavel-to-gavel coverage of trials counteracts the distortions in sound-bite journalism (Clark 821). Yet even here a number of editorial assumptions and decisions affect what viewers see. Camera angles and movements reinforce in the viewer differing degrees of intimacy with the trial participant; close-ups are often used for sympathetic witnesses, three-quarter shots for lawyers, and profile shots for defendants (Entner 73-75).[4]

On-air commentators also shape the viewers' experience. Several media critics have noted how much commentators' remarks often have the play-by-play tone of sportscasters informing viewers of what each side (the defense and the prosecution) needs in order to win (Cole 245; Thaler 71, 151). Continual interruptions for commercials add to the impression of watching a spectacle. "The CNN coverage [of the Smith trial] isn't so much gavel-to-gavel, actually, as gavel-to-commercial-to-gavel, with former CNN Gulf War correspondent Charles Jaco acting more as ringleader than reporter" (Bianculli 60). This encourages a sensationalistic tone to the proceedings that the jury does not experience. In addition, breaking for ads frequently occurs at important points in the trial (Thaler 48).

In-court proponents also believe that watching televised trials will help viewers understand the legal aspects of the judicial system. In June 1991, a month before Court TV went

Summary of an opposing view, then countered with a clear transition ("Yet").

Author lets reader hear the opposition by means of a

on the air, Vincent Blasi, a law professor at Columbia University, told *Time* magazine, "Today most of us learn about judicial proceedings from lawyers' sound bites and artists'

Omitted material indicated by three periods, with a fourth to mark the end of a sentence.

sketches. . . . Televised proceedings [such as Court TV] ought to dispel some of the myth and mystery that shroud our legal system" (qtd. in Zoglin 62).

But after several years of Court TV and CNN, we can now see this is not so. As a medium, TV is not good at educating the general public, either about concepts fundamental to our judicial system or about the complexities in particular cases.

For example, one basic concept--"innocent until proven guilty"--is contradicted in televised trials in numerous subtle ways: Commentators sometimes make remarks about (or omit comment on) actions of the defense or prosecution that show a bias against the defendant.

Media critic Lewis Cole, watching the trial of Lorena Bobbitt on Court TV in 1994, observed:

Quotation of more than four lines, indented 1″ from left margin (ten spaces), double-spaced, parenthetic reference set off from quotation.

> Court TV commentators rarely challenged the state's characterization of what it was doing, repeating without comment, for instance, the prosecution's claims about protecting the reputation of Lorena Bobbitt and concentrating on the prosecution decision to pursue both cases as a tactical matter, rather than inquiring how the prosecution's view of the incident as a "barroom brawl" had limited its approach to and understanding of the case. (245)

Washington 6

Camera angles play a role also: Watching
the defendant day after day in profile, which
makes him or her seem either vulnerable or remote, tends to reinforce his or her guilt
(Entner 158).

Thaler points out that these editorial effects arise because the goals of the media
(print as well as electronic) differ from the
goals of the judicial system. His argument runs
as follows: The court is interested in determining only whether the defendant broke the
law. The media (especially TV) focus on acts in
order to reinforce social values, whether
they're codified into law or not. This can lead
viewers to conclude that a defendant is guilty
because pretrial publicity or courtroom testimony reveals he or she has transgressed against
the community's moral code, even when the legal
system later acquits. This happened in the case
of Claus von Bulow, who between 1982 and 1985
was tried and acquitted twice for attempting to
murder his wife, and who clearly had behaved in
reprehensible ways in the eyes of the public
(35). It also happened in the case of Joel
Steinberg, who was charged with murdering his
daughter. Extended televised testimony by his
ex-partner, Hedda Nussbaum, helped paint a portrait of "a monster" in the eyes of the public
(140-42). Yet the jury chose to convict him on
the lesser charge of manslaughter. When many
viewers wrote to the prosecutor, Peter Caso-
laro, asking why the verdict was not first-
degree murder, he had to conclude that TV does

Argument
supported by
specific examples.

Washington 7

not effectively teach about due process of law
(176).

   In addition to being poor at handling
basic judicial concepts, television has difficulty conveying more complex and technical aspects of the law. Sometimes the legal nature of
the case makes for a poor translation to the
screen. Brill admitted that, despite attempts
at hourly summaries, Court TV was unable to
convey to its viewers any meaningful understanding of the case of Manuel Noriega (Thaler
61), the Panamanian leader who was convicted by
the United States in 1992 of drug trafficking
and money laundering ("Former"). In other
cases, like the Smith trial, the "civics lesson" gets swamped by its sensational aspects
(Thaler 45). In most cases print media are better at exploring and explaining legal issues
than is TV (Thaler 4).

   In addition to shaping the viewer's per-
ceptions of trial reality directly, in-court TV
also negatively affects the quality of trial
coverage outside of court, which in turn limits
the public's "right to know." Brill likes to
claim that Court TV helps to counteract the
sensationalism of such tabloid TV shows as A
Current Affair and Hard Copy, which pay trial
participants to tell their stories and publish
leaks from the prosecution and defense. "I
think cameras in the courtroom is [sic] the
best antidote to that garbage" (Brill qtd. in
Clark 821). However, as founder and editor of
Court TV, he obviously has a vested interest in

Transition (briefly summarizes, then moves to a new point).

Author uses "[sic]" (Latin for "thus") to indicate that the oddity is in the source and is not by the author of the paper.

Washington 8

affirming his network's social and legal worth.
There are several ways that in-court TV, rather
than supplying a sobering contrast, helps to
feed the media circus surrounding high-profile
trials (Thaler 43).

One way is by helping to blur the line between reality and fiction. This is an increasing trend among all media, but is especially
true of TV, whose footage can be combined and
recombined in so many ways. An excellent example of this is the trial of Amy Fisher, who
pleaded guilty in September 1992 to shooting
her lover's wife, and whose sentencing was
televised by Court TV (Thaler 83). Three TV
movies about this love triangle appeared on
network TV in the same week, just one month
after she had been sentenced to five to fifteen
years of jail (Thaler 82). Then Geraldo Rivera,
the syndicated TV talk-show host, held a mock
grand jury trial of her lover, Joey Buttafuoco;
even though Buttafuoco had not at that point
been charged with a crime, Geraldo felt many
viewers thought he ought to have been (Thaler
83). Then A Current Affair had a series that
"tried" Fisher for events and behaviors that
never got resolved in the actual trial. The an-
nouncer on the program said, "When Ms. Fisher
copped a plea and went to jail she robbed the
public of a trial, leaving behind many unan-
swered questions. Tonight we will try to . . .
complete the unwritten chapter" ("Trial").
Buttafuoco's lawyer from the trial served as a
consultant on this program (Thaler 84). This is

also a good example of how tabloid TV rein-

Useful analysis of
effect of TV.

forces people's beliefs and plays on people's
feelings. Had her trial not been televised, the
excitement surrounding her case would not have
been so high. Tabloid TV played off the audience's expectation for what a televised trial
should and could reveal. Thus in-court television becomes one more ingredient in the mix of
docudramas, mock trials, talk shows, and
tabloid journalism. This limits the public's
"right to know" by making it difficult to keep

Square brackets to
indicate author
has altered text
from capital to
lowercase letter.

fact separate from storytelling.

In-court TV also affects the quality of
print journalism. Proponents like to claim that
"[f]rom the standpoint of the public's right to
know, there is no good reason why TV journalists should be barred from trials while print
reporters are not" (Zoglin 62). But when TV is
present, there is no level playing field among
the media. Because it provides images, sound,
and movement and a greater sense of speed and
immediacy, TV can easily out-compete other
media for audience attention and thus for advertising dollars. In attempts to keep pace,
newspapers and magazines offer more and more of
the kinds of stories that once were beneath
their standards, such as elaborate focus both
on sensational aspects of the case and on "per-
sonalities, analysis, and prediction" rather
than news (Thaler 45). While these attributes
have always been part of TV and the tabloid
print press, this trend is increasingly apparent in supposedly reputable papers like the New

Washington 10

York Times. During the Smith trial, for example, the Times violated previously accepted boundaries of propriety by not only identifying the rape victim but also giving lots of intimate details about her past (Thaler 45).

Because the media are, for the most part, commercial, slow periods--and all trials have them--must always be filled with some "story." One such story is increasingly the media self-consciously watching and analyzing itself, to see how it is handling (or mishandling) coverage of the trial (Thaler 43). At the Smith trial, for example, one group of reporters was covering the trial while another group covered the other reporters (Thaler 44).[5] As bizarre as this "media watching" is, there would be no "story" if the trial itself had not been televised.

Last but not least, televising trials distracts viewers from other important issues. Some of these are abstract and thus hard to understand (like the savings-and-loan scandal in the mid-1980s or the causes of lingering unemployment in the 1990s), while others are painful to contemplate (like overseas wars and famines). Yet we have to stay aware of these issues if we are to function as active citizens in a democracy.

Altogether, televising trials is a bad idea. Not only does it provide deceptive impressions about what's happening in particular trials; it also doesn't reveal much about our judicial system. In addition, televising trials

No citation needed for a point that can be considered common knowledge, but notice that point in the second sentence *is* documented.

Useful summary of main points.

Washington 11

helps to lower the quality of trial coverage
outside of court, thus increasingly depriving
the public of neutral, fact-based reporting. A
healthy free press depends on balance and knowing when to accept limits. Saturating viewers
with extended media coverage of sensational
trials oversteps those limits. In this case,
more is not better.

　　　Yet it is unlikely that TV coverage will
be legally removed from the courtroom, now that
it is here. Only one state (New York) has ever
legislated a return to nontelevised trials (in
1991), and even it changed its mind in 1992
(Thaler 78). Perhaps the best we can do is to
educate ourselves about the pitfalls of televising the judicial system, as we struggle to
do so with the televised electoral process.

Realistic appraisal
of the current
situation and a
suggestion of what
the reader can do.

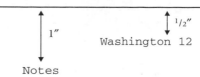

Washington 12

Notes

Double-space between heading and notes, and throughout notes.

¹ Useful discussions of this history can be found in Clark (829-32) and Thaler (19-31).

² Cable networks have been showing trial footage to national audiences since at least 1982, when Cable News Network (CNN) covered the trial of Claus von Bulow (Thaler 33). It continues to show trials. In the first week of February 1995, four to five million homes accounted for the top fifteen most-watched shows on cable TV; all were CNN segments of the O. J. Simpson trial ("Cable TV"). In July 1991, Steven Brill founded the Courtroom Television Network, or "Court TV" (Clark 821). Like CNN, it broadcasts around the clock, showing gavel-to-gavel coverage. It now claims over fourteen million cable subscribers (Clark 821) and, as of January 1994, had televised over 280 trials ("In Camera" 27).

Superscript number followed by one space.

³ Thaler's study The Watchful Eye is a thoughtful examination of the subtle ways in which TV in court can affect trial participants, inhibiting witnesses from coming forward, provoking grandstanding in attorneys and judges, and pressuring juries to come up with verdicts acceptable to a national audience.

Each note begins with ½″ indent (five typewriter spaces), but subsequent notes of each line are flush left.

⁴ Sometimes legal restrictions determine camera angles. For example, in the Steinberg trial (1988), the audience and the jury were not allowed to be televised by New York state law. This required placing the camera so that the judge and witnesses were seen in "full frontal view" (generally a more neutral or pos-

itive stance). The lawyers could only be seen
from the rear when questioning witnesses, and
the defendant was shot in profile (Thaler
110-11). These camera angles, though not chosen
for dramatic effect, still resulted in emotionally laden viewpoints not experienced by the
jury. George W. Trammell, a Los Angeles Superior Court Judge, has written on how technology
can interfere with the fairness of the trial
system. He claims that "Technology, well managed, can be a great benefit. Technology poorly
managed benefits no one."

5 At the Smith trial a journalist from one
German newspaper inadvertently filmed another
German reporter from a competing newspaper
watching the Smith trial in the pressroom outside the courtroom (Thaler 44).

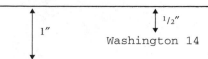

Washington 14

Works Cited

Altheide, David. "TV News and the Social Con-
    struction of Justice." Justice and the
    Media: Issues and Research. Ed. Ray
    Surette. Springfield, IL: Thomas, 1984.
    292-304.

Bianculli, David. "Shame on You, CNN." New York
    Post 11 Dec. 1992: 60.

"Cable TV Squeezes High Numbers and Aces Com-
    petition." All Things Considered. Natl.
    Public Radio. 9 Feb. 1994. Unedited tran-
    script. Segment 12. NPR Audience Services.
    Washington.

Clark, Charles S. "Courts and the Media." CQ
    Researcher 23 Sept. 1994: 817-40.

Cole, Lewis. "Court TV." Nation 21 Feb. 1994:
    243-45.

Entner, Roberta. "Encoding the Image of the
    American Judiciary Institution: A Semiotic
    Analysis of Broadcast Trials to Ascertain
    Its Definition of the Court System." Diss.
    New York U, 1993.

"Former Panamanian Leader Noriega Sentenced."
    Facts on File 16 July 1992: 526. InfoTrac:
    Magazine Index Plus 1992-Feb. 1995. CD-
    ROM. Information Access. Feb. 1995.

"In Camera with Court TV." New Yorker 24 Jan.
    1994: 27-28.

Quindlen, Anna. "The Glass Eye." New York Times
    18 Dec. 1991: A29.

"A Tale of a Rug." Economist 15 Jan. 1994:
    28-29.

Alphabetical by author's last name.

Indent turnovers $1/2''$ (five typewriter spaces).

Transcript of radio program.

The title of an unpublished work is not italicized but enclosed within quotation marks.

CD-ROM source.

Anonymous source alphabetized under first word (or second if first is *A, An,* or *The*).

Washington 15

Thaler, Paul. <u>The Watchful Eye</u>: American Jus-
      tice in the Age of the Television Trial.
      Westport: Praeger, 1994.

"The Trial That Had to Happen: The People ver-
      sus Amy Fisher." <u>A Current Affair</u>. Fox.
      WFXT, Boston. 1–4 Feb. 1993.

Trammell, George W. "Cirque du O. J." <u>Court</u>
      <u>Technology Bulletin</u> July/Aug. 1995. World
      Wide Web. 12 Sept. 1995 <http://
      www.ncsc.dni.us/ncsc/bulletin/v07n04.htm>.

Zoglin, Richard. "Justice Faces a Screen Test."
      <u>Time</u> 17 June 1991: 62.

Television pro-
gram.

No page reference
for this in-text
Internet citation.

Part Three

FURTHER VIEWS
ON ARGUMENT

7

A Philosopher's View: The Toulmin Model

In Chapter 3, we explained the contrast between *deductive* and *inductive* arguments in order to focus on the two main ways in which we reason, either

> making explicit something concealed in what we already accept (**deduction**), or

> using what we have observed as a basis for asserting or proposing something new (**induction**).

Both types of reasoning share some structural features, as we also noticed. Thus, all reasoning is aimed at establishing some **thesis** (or conclusion) and does so by means of some **reasons**. These are two basic characteristics that any argument contains.

After a little scrutiny we can in fact point to several features shared by all arguments, deductive and inductive, good and bad alike. Using the vocabulary popularized by Stephen Toulmin in his book *An Introduction to Reasoning* (1979; second edition 1984), they are as follows:

THE CLAIM

Every argument has a purpose, goal, or aim, namely to establish a **claim** (*conclusion* or *thesis*). Suppose you were arguing in favor of equal rights for women. You might state your thesis or claim as follows:

    Men and women ought to have equal rights.

A more precise formulation of the claim might be

    Men and women ought to have equal legal rights.

A still more precise formulation might be

> Equal legal rights for men and women ought to be pro-
> tected by our Constitution.

The third version of this claim states what the controversy in the 1970s over the Equal Rights Amendment was all about.

Consequently, in reading or analyzing someone else's argument, your first question should naturally be: What is the argument intended to prove or establish? *What claim is it making?* Has this claim been clearly and precisely formulated, so that it unambiguously asserts what its advocate wants to assert?

GROUNDS

Once we have the argument's purpose or point clearly in mind and thus know what the arguer is claiming to establish, then we can ask for the evidence, reasons, support, in short, for the **grounds** on which that claim is based. In a deductive argument these grounds are the premises from which the claim is deduced; in an inductive argument the grounds are the evidence — a sample, observation, or experiment — that makes the claim plausible or probable.

Obviously not every kind of claim can be supported by every kind of ground, and conversely, not every kind of ground gives equally good support for every kind of claim. Suppose I claim that half the students in the classroom are women. I can ground this claim in any of several ways.

(1) I can count all the women and all the men. Suppose the total equals fifty. If the number of women is twenty-five, and the number of men is twenty-five, I have vindicated my claim.

(2) I can count a sample of, say, ten students, and find that in the sample, five of the students are women, and thus have inductive — plausible but not conclusive — grounds for my claim.

(3) I can point out that the students in the college divide equally into men and women, and claim that this class is a representative sample of the whole college.

Obviously ground (1) is stronger than ground (2), and (2) is far stronger than ground (3).

So far we have merely restated points about premises and conclusions covered in Chapter 3. But now we want to consider four additional features of arguments.

WARRANTS

Once we have the claim or the point of an argument fixed in mind, and the evidence or reasons offered in its support, the next question to ask is *why* these reasons support this conclusion. What is the **warrant**, or guarantee, that the reasons proffered do support the claim or lead to the conclusion? In simple deductive arguments, the warrant takes different forms, as we shall see. In the simplest cases, we can point to the way in which the *meanings* of the key terms are really equivalent. Thus, if John is taller than Bill, then Bill must be shorter than John because of the meaning in English of "is shorter than" and "is taller than." In this case, the warrant is something we can state quite literally and explicitly.

In other cases, we may need to be more resourceful. A reliable tactic is to think up a simple *parallel argument*, that is, an argument exactly parallel in form and structure to the argument we are trying to defend. We then point out that if we are ready to accept the simpler argument then we must accept the more complex argument because both arguments have exactly the same structure. For example, in her much-discussed essay of 1972 on the abortion controversy, "A Defense of Abortion," philosopher Judith Thomson argues that a pregnant woman has the right to an abortion to save her life, even if it involves the death of her unborn child. She anticipates that some readers may balk at her reasoning, and so she offers this parallel argument: Suppose you were locked in a tiny room with another human being, which through no fault of its own is growing uncontrollably, with the result that it is slowly crushing you to death. Of course it would be morally permissible to kill the other person to save your own life. With the reader's presumed agreement on that conclusion, the parallel argument concerning the abortion situation—so Thomson hopes—is obvious and convincing.

In simple inductive arguments, we are likely to point to the way in which observations or sets of data constitute a *representative sample* of a whole (unexamined) population. Here, the warrant is the representativeness of the sample. For instance, in projecting a line on a graph through a set of points, we defend one projection over alternatives on the ground that it makes the smoothest fit through most of the points. In this case, the warrant is *simplicity* and *inclusiveness*. Or in defending one explanation against competing explanations of a phenomenon, we appeal to the way in which the preferred explanation can be seen as a *special case* of generally accepted physical laws. Examples of such warrants for inductive reasoning will be offered in following pages (see Chapter 8, "A Logician's View," p. 260).

Establishing the warrants for our reasoning—that is, explaining why our grounds really support our claims—can quickly become a highly technical and exacting procedure that goes far beyond what we can hope to explain in this book. Only a solid course or two in formal deductive logic and statistical methods can do justice to our current state of knowledge about these warrants. Developing a "feel" for why reasons or grounds are or are not relevant to what they are alleged to support is the most we can hope to do here without recourse to more rigorous techniques.

Even without formal training, however, one can sense that something is wrong with many bad arguments. Here is an example. British professor C. E. M. Joad found himself standing on a station platform, annoyed because he had just missed his train, when another train, making an unscheduled stop, pulled up to the platform in front of him. He decided to jump aboard, only to hear the porter say "I'm afraid you'll have to get off, sir. This train doesn't stop here." "In that case," replied Joad, "don't worry. I'm not on it."

BACKING

The kinds of reasons appropriate to support an amendment to the Constitution are completely different from the kinds appropriate to settle the question of what caused the defeat of Napoleon's invasion of Russia. Arguments for the amendment might be rooted in an appeal to fairness, whereas arguments about the military defeat might be rooted in letters and other documents in the French and Russian archives. The canons of good argument in each case derive from the ways in which the scholarly communities in law and history, respectively, have developed over the years to support, defend, challenge, and undermine a given kind of argument. Thus, the support or **backing** appropriate for one kind of argument might be quite inappropriate for another kind of argument.

Another way of stating this point is to recognize that once you have given reasons for a claim, you are then likely to be challenged to explain why these reasons are good reasons—why, that is, one should believe these reasons rather than regard them skeptically. Why (a simple example) should we accept the testimony of Dr. X when Dr. Y, equally renowned, supports the opposite side? Or: Why is it safe to rest a prediction on a small though admittedly carefully selected sample? Or: Why is it legitimate to argue that (a) if I dream I am the King of France then I must exist, whereas it is illegitimate to argue that (b) if I dream I am the King of France, then the King of France must exist? To answer these kinds of challenges is to *back up* one's reasoning, and no argument is any better than its backing.

MODAL QUALIFIERS

As we have seen, all arguments are made up of assertions or propositions, which can be sorted into four categories:

the **claim** (conclusion, thesis to be established),

the **grounds** (explicit reasons advanced),

the **warrant** (the principle that connects the ground to the claim), and

the **backing** (implicit assumptions).

All these kinds of propositions have an explicit or tacit **modality,** in which they are asserted, indicating the scope and character with which they are believed to hold true. Is the claim, for instance, believed to be *necessary*—or only *probable*? Is the claim believed to be *plausible*—or only *possible*? Of two reasons for a claim, both may be *good*, but one may be *better* than the other. Indicating the modality with which an assertion is advanced is crucial to any argument for or against it.

Empirical generalizations are typically *contingent* on various factors, and it is important to indicate such contingencies to protect the generalization against obvious counterexamples. Thus, consider this empirical generalization:

Students do best on final examinations if they study hard for them.

Are we really to believe that students who study regularly throughout the whole course and so do not need to cram for the final will do less well than students who neglect regular work in favor of several all-nighters at the last minute? Probably not; what is really meant is that *all other things being equal* (in Latin, *caeteris paribus*), concentrated study just before an exam will yield good results. Alluding to the contingencies in this way shows that the writer is aware of possible exceptions and that they are conceded right from the start.

Assertions also have varying **scope,** and indicating their scope is equally crucial to the role that an assertion plays in argument. Thus, suppose you are arguing against smoking, and the ground for your claim is this:

Heavy smokers cut short their life span.

Such an assertion will be clearer, as well as more likely to be true, if it is explicitly **quantified**. Here, there are three obvious alternative quantifications to choose among: *all* smokers cut short their life span, or *most* do, or only *some* do. Until the assertion is quantified in one of these ways, we really do not know what is being asserted—and so we do not know what degree and kind of evidence and counterevidence is relevant.

In sum, sensitivity to the quantifiers and qualifiers appropriate for each of our assertions, whatever their role in an argument, will help prevent you from asserting exaggerations and other misguided generalizations.

REBUTTALS

Very few arguments of any interest are beyond dispute, conclusively knockdown affairs, in which the claim of the argument is so rigidly tied to its grounds, warrants, and backing, and its quantifiers and qualifiers so precisely orchestrated that it really proves its conclusion beyond any possibility of doubt. On the contrary, most arguments have many counterarguments, and sometimes it is one of these counterarguments that is the more convincing.

Suppose one has taken a sample that appears to be random—an interviewer on your campus accosts the first ten students whom she sees, and seven of them happen to be fraternity or sorority members. She is now ready to argue: Seven-tenths of the student body belong to Greek organizations.

You believe, however, that the Greeks are in the minority and point out that she happens to have conducted her interview around the corner from the Panhellenic Society's office just off Sorority Row. Her random sample is anything but. The ball is now back in her court as you await her response to your rebuttal.

As this example illustrates, it is safe to say that we do not understand our own arguments very well until we have tried to get a grip on the places in which they are vulnerable to criticism, counterattack, or refutation. Edmund Burke (quoted in Chapter 3 but worth repeating) said, "He that wrestles with us strengthens our nerves, and sharpens our skill. Our antagonist is our helper." Therefore, cultivating alertness to such weak spots, girding one's loins to defend at these places, always helps strengthen one's position.

A MODEL ANALYSIS USING
THE TOULMIN METHOD

In order to see how the Toulmin method can be used, let's apply it to an argument in this book, Susan Jacoby's "A First Amendment Junkie," on page 29.

The Claim   Jacoby's central thesis or claim is this: Any form of *censorship*—including feminist censorship of pornography in particular— *is wrong.*

Grounds   Jacoby offers six main reasons or grounds for her claim, roughly in this sequence (but arguably not in this order of importance).

First, feminists exaggerate the harm caused by pornography because they confuse expression of offensive ideas with harmful conduct.

Second, letting the government censor the expression of ideas and attitudes is the wrong response to the failure of parents to control the printed materials that get into the hands of their children.

Third, there is no unanimity even among feminists over what is pornography and what isn't.

Fourth, permitting censorship of pornography, in order to please feminists, could well lead to censorship on many issues of concern to feminists ("rape, abortion, menstruation, contraception, lesbianism").

Fifth, censorship under law shows a lack of confidence in the democratic process.

Finally, censorship of words and pictures is suppression of self-expression, and that violates the First Amendment.

Warrants   The grounds Jacoby has offered provide support for her central claim in three ways, although Jacoby (like most writers) is not so didactic as to make these warrants explicit.

First, since the First Amendment protects speech in the broadest sense, the censorship that the feminist attack on pornography advocates is *inconsistent* with the First Amendment.

Second, if feminists want to be consistent, then they must advocate censorship of *all* offensive self-expression; but such a radical interference with free speech (amounting virtually to repeal of the First Amendment) is indefensible.

Third, feminists ought to see that *they risk losing more than they can hope to gain* if they succeed in censoring pornography, because antifeminists will have equal right to censor the things they find offensive but that many feminists seek to publish.

Backing   Why should the reader agree with Jacoby's grounds? She does not appeal to expert authority, the results of experimental tests or other statistical data, or the support of popular opinion. Instead, she relies principally on two things—but without saying so explicitly.

First, she assumes that the reader accepts the propositions that *freedom of self-expression is valuable* and that *censoring self-expression requires the strongest of reasons*. If there is no fundamental agreement on these propositions, several of her reasons cease to support her claim.

Second, she relies on the reader's open-mindedness and willingness to evaluate commonsense (untechnical, ordinary, familiar) considerations at each step of the way. She relies also on the reader having had some personal experience with erotica, pornography, and art. Without that open-mindedness and experience, a reader is not likely to be persuaded by her rejection of the feminist demand for censorship.

Modal Qualifiers   Jacoby defends what she calls an "absolute interpretation" of the First Amendment, that is, the view that *all* censorship of words, pictures, ideas is not only inconsistent with the First Amendment, it is also politically unwise and morally objectionable. She allows that *some* pornography is highly offensive (it offends her, she insists); she allows that *some* pornography ("kiddie porn") may even be harmful to *some* viewers. But she also insists that *more* harm than good would result from the censorship of pornography. She points out that *some* paintings of nude women are art, not pornography; she implies that it is *impossible* to draw a sharp line between permissible erotic pornography and impermissible offensive pornography. She clearly believes that *all* Americans ought to understand and defend the First Amendment under the "absolute interpretation" she favors.

Rebuttals   Jacoby mentions several objections to her views, and perhaps the most effective aspect of her entire argument is her skill in identifying possible objections and meeting them effectively. (Notice the diversity of the objections and the various ways in which she replies.)

Objection: Some of her women friends tell her she is wrong.

Rebuttal: She admits she's a "First Amendment junkie" and she doesn't apologize for it.

Objection: "Kiddie porn" is harmful and deserves censorship.

Rebuttal: Such material is *not* protected by the First Amendment, because it is an "abuse of power" of adults over children.

Objection: Pornography is a form of violence against women, and therefore it is especially harmful.

Rebuttal: (a) No, it really isn't harmful, but it is disgusting and offensive. (b) In any case, it's surely not as harmful as allowing American neo-Nazis to parade in Jewish neighborhoods. (Jacoby is referring to the march in Skokie, Illinois, in 1977, upheld by the courts as permissible political expression under the First Amendment despite its offensiveness to survivors of the Nazi concentration camps.)

Objection: Censoring pornography advances public respect for women.

Rebuttal: Censoring *Ms.* magazine, which antifeminists have already done, undermines women's freedom and self-expression.

Objection: Reasonable people can tell pornography when they see it, so censoring it poses no problems.

Rebuttal: Yes, there are clear cases of gross pornography; but there are lots of borderline cases, as women themselves prove when they disagree over whether a photo in *Penthouse* is offensively erotic or "lovely" and "sensuous."

A CHECKLIST FOR
USING THE TOULMIN METHOD

✓ What claim does the argument make?

✓ What grounds are offered for the claim?

✓ What warrants the inferences from the grounds to the claim?

✓ What backing supports the claims?

✓ With what modalities are the claim and grounds asserted?

✓ To what rebuttals are the claims, grounds, and backing vulnerable?

8

A Logician's View: Deduction, Induction, Fallacies

In Chapter 3 we introduced these terms. Now we will discuss them in greater detail.

DEDUCTION

The basic aim of deductive reasoning is to start with some assumption or premise, and extract from it consequences that are concealed but implicit in it. Thus, taking the simplest case, if I assert

1. The cat is on the mat,

it is a matter of simple deduction to infer that

2. The mat is under the cat.

Everyone would grant that (2) is entailed by, or follows from (1)—or, that (2) can be validly deduced from (1)—because of the meaning of the key connective concepts in each proposition. Anyone who understands English knows that, whatever A and B are, if A is *on* B, then B must be *under* A. Thus, in this and all other cases of valid deductive reasoning, we can say not only that we are entitled to *infer* the conclusion from the premise—in this case, infer (2) from (1)—but that the premise *implies* or entails the conclusion. Remember, too, the inference of (2) from (1) does not depend on the truth of (1). (2) follows from (1) whether or not (1) is true; consequently, if (1) is true then so is (2); but if (1) is false then (2) is false, also.

Let's take another example—more interesting, but comparably simple:

3. President Truman was underrated by his critics.

Given (3), a claim amply verified by events of the 1950s, one is entitled to infer

4. The critics underrated President Truman.

On what basis can we argue that (3) implies (4)? The two propositions are equivalent because a rule of English grammar assures us that we can convert the position of subject and predicate phrases in a sentence by shifting from the passive to the active voice (or vice versa) without any change in the conditions that make the proposition true (or false).

Both pairs of examples illustrate that in deductive reasoning, our aim is to transform, reformulate, or restate in our conclusion some (or, as in the two examples above, all) of the information contained in our premises.

Remember, even though a proposition or statement follows from a previous proposition or statement, the statements need not be true. We can see why if we consider another example. Suppose someone asserts or claims that

5. The Hudson River is longer than the Mississippi.

As every student of American geography knows, (5) is false. But, false or not, we can validly deduce from it:

6. The Mississippi is shorter than the Hudson.

This inference is valid (even though the conclusion is untrue) because the conclusion follows logically (more precisely, deductively) from (5): In English, as we know, the meaning of "A is shorter than B," which appears in (6), is simply the converse of "B is longer than A," which appears in (5).

The deductive relation between (5) and (6) reminds us again that the idea of *validity*, which is so crucial to deduction, is not the same as the idea of *truth*. False propositions have implications—logical consequences—too, every bit as precisely as do true propositions.

In the three pairs of examples so far, what can we point to as the *warrant* for our claims? Well, look at the reasoning in each case; the arguments rely on rules of ordinary English. In the first and third pairs of examples, it is a rule of English semantics; in the second pair it is a rule of English syntax. Change those rules and the inferences will no longer be valid; fail to comply with those rules and one will not trust the inferences.

In many cases, of course, the deductive inference or pattern of reasoning is much more complex than that which we have seen in the examples so far. When we introduced the idea of deduction in Chapter 3, we gave as our primary example the *syllogism*. Here is another example:

7. Texas is larger than California; California is larger than Arizona; therefore, Texas is larger than Arizona.

The conclusion in this syllogism is derivable from the two premises; that is, anyone who asserts the two premises is committed to accepting the conclusion as well, whether or not one thinks of it.

Notice again that the *truth* of the conclusion is not established merely by validity of the inference. The conclusion in this syllogism happens to be true. And the premises of this syllogism imply the conclusion. But the argument *proves* the conclusion only because both of the premises on which the conclusion depends are true. Even a Californian admits that Texas is larger than California, which in turn is larger than Arizona. In other words, argument (7) is a *sound* argument, because (as we explained in Chapter 3) it is valid and all its premises are true. All — and only — arguments that *prove* their conclusions have these two traits.

How might we present the warrant for the argument in (7)? Short of a crash course in formal logic, either of two strategies might suffice. One is to argue from the fact that the validity of the inference depends on the meaning of a key concept, *being larger than,* which has the property of *transitivity,* a property that many concepts share (for example, *is equal to, is to the right of, is smarter than* — all are transitive concepts). Consequently, whatever A, B, and C are, if A is larger than B, and B is larger than C, then A will be larger than C. The final step is to substitute "Texas," "California," and "Arizona" for A, B, and C, respectively.

A second strategy is to think of representing Texas, California, and Arizona by concentric circles, with the largest for Texas, a smaller circle inside it for California, and a smaller one inside California for Arizona. (This is an adaptation of the technique used in elementary formal logic known as Venn diagrams.) In this manner one can give graphic display to the important fact that the conclusion follows from the premises, because one can literally *see* the conclusion represented by nothing more than a representation of the premises.

Both of these strategies bring out the fact that validity of deductive inference is a purely *formal* property of argument. Each strategy abstracts the form from the content of the propositions involved to show how the concepts in the premises are related to the concepts in the conclusion.

Not all deductive reasoning occurs in syllogisms, however, or at least not in syllogisms like the one in (7). (The term *syllogism* is sometimes used to refer to any deductive argument of whatever form, provided only that it has two premises.) In fact, syllogisms such as (7) are not the commonest form of our deductive reasoning at all. Nor are they the simplest (and of course not the most complex). For an argument that is even simpler, consider this:

8. If the horses are loose, then the barn door was left unlocked. The horses are loose. Therefore, the barn door was left unlocked.

Here the pattern of reasoning is called **modus ponens,** which means positing or laying down the minor premise ("the horses are loose"). It is also called **hypothetical syllogism,** because its major premise ("if the horses are loose, then the barn door was left unlocked") is a hypothetical or conditional proposition. The argument has the form: If A then B; A; therefore, B. Notice that the content of the assertions represented by A and B do not matter; any set of expressions having the same form or structure will do equally well, including assertions built out of meaningless terms, as in this example:

> 9. If the slithy toves, then the gyres gimble. The slithy toves. Therefore, the gyres gimble.

Argument (9) has exactly the same form as argument (8), and as a piece of deductive inference it is every bit as good. Unlike (8), however, (9) is of no interest to us because none of its assertions make any sense (unless you are a reader of Lewis Carroll's "Jabberwocky," and even then the sense of (9) is doubtful). You cannot, in short, use a valid deductive argument to prove anything unless the premises and the conclusion are *true,* but they can't be true unless they *mean* something in the first place.

This parallel between arguments (8) and (9) shows once again that deductive validity in an argument rests on the *form* or structure of the argument, and not on its content or meaning. If all one can say about an argument is that it is valid—that is, its conclusion follows from the premises—one has not given a sufficient reason for accepting the argument's conclusion. It has been said that the Devil can quote Scripture; similarly, an argument can be deductively valid and of no further interest or value whatever, because valid (but false) conclusions can be drawn from false or even meaningless assumptions. Nevertheless, although validity by itself is not enough, it is a necessary condition of any deductive argument that purports to *prove* its conclusion.

Now let us consider another argument with the same form as (8) and (9), only more interesting.

> 10. If President Truman knew the Japanese were about to surrender, then it was immoral of him to order that atom bombs be dropped on Hiroshima and Nagasaki. Truman knew the Japanese were about to surrender. Therefore, it was immoral of him to order dropping those bombs.

As in the two previous examples, anyone who assents to the premises in argument (10) must assent to the conclusion; the form of arguments (8), (9), and (10) is identical. But do the premises of argument (10) *prove* the conclusion? That depends on whether both premises are true. Well, are they? This turns on a number of considerations, and it is worthwhile pausing to examine this argument closely to illustrate the kinds of things that are involved in answering this question.

Let us begin by examining the second (minor) premise. Its truth is controversial even to this day. Autobiography, memoranda, other documentary evidence—all are needed to assemble the evidence to back up the grounds for the thesis or claim made in the conclusion of this valid argument. Evaluating this material effectively will probably involve not only further deductions, but inductive reasoning as well.

Now consider the first (major) premise in argument (10). Its truth doesn't depend on what history shows, but on the moral principles one accepts. The major premise has the form of a hypothetical proposition ("if . . . then . . ."), and asserts a connection between two very different kinds of things. The antecedent of the hypothetical (the clause following "if") mentions facts about Truman's *knowledge,* and the consequent of the hypothetical (the clause following "then") mentions facts about the *morality* of his conduct in light of such knowledge. The major premise as a whole can thus be seen as expressing a principle of *moral responsibility.*

Such principles can, of course, be controversial. In this case, for instance, is the principle peculiarly relevant to the knowledge and conduct of a president of the United States? Probably not; it is far more likely that this principle is merely a special case of a more general proposition about anyone's moral responsibility. (After all, we know a great deal more about the conditions of our own moral responsibility than we do about those of high government officials.) We might express this more general principle in this way: If we have knowledge that would make our violent conduct unnecessary, then we are immoral if we deliberately act violently anyway. Thus, accepting this general principle can serve as a basis for defending the major premise of argument (10).

We have examined this argument in some detail because it illustrates the kinds of considerations needed to test whether a given argument is not only valid but whether its premises are true—that is, whether its premises really prove the conclusion.

The great value of the form of argument known as hypothetical syllogism, exemplified by arguments (8), (9), and (10), is that the structure of the argument is so simple and so universally applicable in reasoning that it is often both easy and worthwhile to formulate one's claims so that they can be grounded by an argument of this sort.

Before leaving the subject of deductive inference, consider three other forms of argument, each of which can be found in actual use elsewhere in the readings in this volume. The simplest of these is **disjunctive syllogism,** so called because, again, it has two premises, and its major premise is a **disjunction.** That is, a disjunctive syllogism is a complex assertion built from two or more alternatives joined by the conjunction "or"; each of these alternatives is called a **disjunct.** For example,

11. Either censorship of television shows is overdue, or our society is indifferent to the education of its youth. Our society is not indif-

ferent to the education of its youth. Therefore, censorship of television is overdue.

Notice, by the way, that the validity of an argument, as in this case, does not turn on pedantic repetition of every word or phrase as the argument moves along; nonessential elements can be dropped, or equivalent expressions substituted for variety without adverse effect on the reasoning. Thus, in conversation, or in writing, the argument in (11) might actually be presented like this:

12. Either censorship of television is overdue, or our society is indifferent to the education of its youth. But, of course, we aren't indifferent; it's censorship that's overdue.

The key feature of disjunctive syllogism, as example (12) suggests, is that the conclusion is whichever of the disjuncts is left over after the others have been negated in the minor premise. Thus, we could easily have a very complex disjunctive syllogism, with a dozen disjuncts in the major premise, and seven of them denied in the minor premise, leaving a conclusion of the remaining five. Usually, however, a disjunctive argument is formulated in this manner: Assert a disjunction with two or more disjuncts in the major premise; then *deny all but one* in the minor premise; and infer validly the remaining disjunct as the conclusion. That was the form of argument (12).

Another type of argument, especially favored by orators and rhetoricians, is the **dilemma.** Ordinarily we use the term *dilemma* in the sense of an awkward predicament, as when we say, "His dilemma was that he didn't have enough money to pay the waiter." But when logicians refer to a dilemma, they mean a forced choice between two or more equally unattractive alternatives. For example, the predicament of the U.S. government during the mid-1980s as it faced the crisis brought on by terrorist attacks on American civilian targets, which were believed, during that time, to be inspired and supported by the Libyan government, can be formulated in a dilemma:

13. If the United States bombs targets in Libya, innocent people will be killed and the Arab world will be angered. If the United States doesn't bomb Libyan targets, then terrorists will go unpunished and the United States will lose respect among other governments. Either the United States bombs Libyan targets or it doesn't. Therefore, in either case unattractive consequences will follow: The innocent will be killed or terrorists will go unpunished.

Notice first the structure of the argument: two conditional propositions asserted as premises, followed by another premise that states a **necessary truth.** (The premise, "Either we bomb the Libyans or we don't," is a disjunction of two exhaustive alternatives, and so one of the two alternatives must be true. Such a statement is often called analytically true, or a *tautology*.) No doubt the conclusion of this dilemma follows from its premises.

But does the argument prove, as it purports to do, that whatever the U.S. government does, it will suffer undesirable consequences? If the two conditional premises failed to exhaust the possibilities, then one can escape from the dilemma by going "between the horns"; that is, by finding a third alternative. If (as in this case) that is not possible, one can still ask whether both of the main premises are true. (In this argument, it should be clear that neither of these main premises spells out all or even most of the consequences that could be foreseen.) Even so, in cases where both these conditional premises are true, it may be that the consequences of one alternative are nowhere nearly so bad as those of the other. If that is true, but our reasoning stops before evaluating that fact, we may be guilty of failing to distinguish between the greater and the lesser of two admitted evils. The logic of the dilemma itself cannot decide this choice for us. Instead, we must bring to bear empirical inquiry and imagination to the evaluation of the grounds of the dilemma itself.

Writers commonly use the term *dilemma* without explicitly formulating the dilemma to which they refer, leaving it for the readers to do. And sometimes, what is called a dilemma really isn't one. (Remember the dog's tail? Calling it a leg doesn't make it one.) As an example, consider Elizabeth Whelan's reference in her essay on teenage drinking (p. 84) to her "daughter's dilemma." Like most writers, Whelan does not trouble to formulate the dilemma with any precision. With a little effort, one can see that it must read more or less as follows:

> Either the law ought to treat teenagers as adults, or it ought not. If they are going to be treated as adults, then they ought to be allowed to purchase alcoholic beverages as other adults are. If they are not to be treated as adults, then there is no good reason for permitting them to vote, make contracts, and so on. Either way, the current laws affecting teenage behavior need to be reformed.

What this formulation shows is that, strictly speaking, Whelan's daughter does *not* face a dilemma at all. Why? She doesn't face a dilemma because we cannot formulate a conclusion to Whelan's argument consisting of two alternatives, both of which are repellant. What Whelan has done, under the term *dilemma*, is to point to the *inconsistency* in current law, under which teenagers are sometimes treated as full adults and at other times not treated as adults. This behavior may be a problem, but not every problem is a dilemma.

Finally, one of the most powerful and dramatic forms of argument is **reductio ad absurdum** (from the Latin, meaning "reduction to absurdity"). The idea of a reductio argument is to establish a conclusion by refuting its opposite, and it is an especially attractive tactic when you can use it to refute your opponent's position in order to prove your own. For example, in Plato's *Republic,* Socrates asks an old gentleman, Cephalus, to define what right conduct is. Cephalus says that it is paying your debts and keeping your word. Socrates rejects this answer by showing that it leads to a contradiction. He argues that Cephalus cannot have given the correct answer because if we assume that he did, we will be quickly led into contradictions; in some cases when you keep your word you will nonetheless be doing the wrong thing. For suppose, says Socrates, that you borrowed a weapon from a man, promising to return it when he asks for it. One day he comes to your door, demanding his weapon and swearing angrily that he intends to murder a neighbor. Keeping your word under those circumstances is absurd, Socrates implies; and the reader of the dialogue is left to infer that Cephalus's definition, which led to this result, is refuted.

Let's take a closer look at another example. Suppose you are opposed to any form of gun control, whereas I am in favor of gun control. I might try to refute your position by attacking it with a reductio argument. To do that, I start out by assuming the very opposite of what I believe or favor, and try to establish a contradiction that results from following out the consequences of this initial assumption. My argument might look like this:

14. Let's assume your position, namely, that there ought to be no legal restrictions whatever on the sale and ownership of guns. That means that you'd permit having every neighborhood hardware store sell pistols and rifles to whoever walks in the door. But that's not all. You apparently also would permit selling machine guns to children, antitank weapons to lunatics, small-bore cannons to the near-sighted, as well as guns and the ammunition to go with them to anyone with a criminal record. But this is utterly preposterous. No one could favor such a dangerous policy. So the only question worth debating is what *kind* of gun control is necessary.

Now in this example, my reductio of your position on gun control is not based on claiming to show that you have strictly contradicted yourself, for there is no purely logical contradiction in opposing all forms of gun control. Instead, what I have tried to do (just as Socrates did) is to show that there is a contradiction between what you profess—no gun controls whatever—and what you probably really believe, if only you will stop to think about it—no lunatic should be allowed to buy a loaded machine gun.

My refutation of your position rests on whether I succeed in establishing an inconsistency among your own beliefs. If it turns out that you really believe lunatics should be free to purchase guns and ammunition, then my attempted refutation fails.

In explaining reductio ad absurdum, we have had to rely on another idea fundamental to logic, that of **contradiction,** or inconsistency. (We used this idea, remember, to define validity in Chapter 3. A deductive argument is valid if and only if affirming the premises and denying the conclusion results in a contradiction.) The opposite of contradiction is **consistency,** a notion of hardly less importance to good reasoning than validity. These concepts deserve a few words of further explanation and illustration. Consider this pair of assertions:

15. Abortion is homicide.
16. Racism is unfair.

No one would plausibly claim that we can infer or deduce (16) from (15), or, for that matter, (15) from (16). This almost goes without saying, because there is no evident connection between (15) and (16). They are unrelated assertions; logically speaking, they are *independent* of each other. In such cases the two assertions are mutually consistent; that is, both could be true—or both could be false. But now consider another proposition:

17. Euthanasia is not murder.

Could a person assert (15) *abortion is homicide* and also assert (17), and be consistent? This question is equivalent to asking whether one could assert the **conjunction** of these two propositions, namely,

18. Abortion is homicide and euthanasia is not murder.

It is not so easy to say whether (18) is consistent or inconsistent. The kinds of moral scruples that might lead a person to assert one of these conjuncts (that is, one of the two initial propositions, *Abortion is homicide* and *Euthanasia is not murder*) might lead to the belief that the other one must be false, and thus to the conclusion that (18) is inconsistent. (Notice that if [15] were the assertion that *Abortion is murder,* instead of *Abortion is homicide,* the problem of asserting consistently both [15] and [17] would be more acute.) Yet, if we think again, we might imagine someone being convinced that there is no inconsistency in asserting that *Abortion is homicide,* say, and that *Euthanasia is not murder,* or even the reverse. (For instance, suppose you believed that the unborn deserve a chance to live, and that putting elderly persons to death in a painless manner and with their consent confers a benefit on them.)

Let us generalize: We can say of any set of propositions that they are *consistent* if and only if *all could be true together.* (Notice that it follows from this definition that propositions that mutually imply each other, as do *The cat is on the mat* and *The mat is under the cat,* are consistent.) Remember that, once again, the truth of the assertions in question does not matter. Propositions can be consistent or not, quite apart from whether they are true. Not so their falsehood: It follows from our definition of consistency that an *inconsistent* proposition must be *false.* (We have relied on this idea in explaining how a reductio ad absurdum works.)

Assertions or claims that are not consistent can take either of two forms. Suppose you assert proposition (15), that abortion is homicide, early in an essay you are writing, but after you say

19. Abortion is harmless.

You have now asserted a position on abortion that is strictly **contrary** to the one with which you began; contrary in the sense that both assertions (15) and (19) cannot be true. It is simply not true that if an abortion involves killing a human being (which is what *homicide* strictly means) then it causes no one any harm (killing a person always causes harm— even if it is excusable, or justifiable, or not wrong, or the best thing to do in the circumstances, and so on). Notice that although (15) and (19) cannot both be true, they can both be false. In fact, many people who are perplexed about the morality of abortion believe precisely this. They concede that abortion does harm the fetus, so (19) must be false; but they also believe that abortion doesn't kill a person, so (15) must also be false.

Or consider another, simpler case. If you describe the glass as half empty and I describe it as half full, both of us can be right; the two assertions are consistent, even though they sound vaguely incompatible. (This is the reason that disputing over whether the glass is half full or half empty has become the popular paradigm of a futile, purely *verbal disagreement*.) But if I describe the glass as half empty whereas you insist that it is two-thirds empty, then we have a real disagreement; your description and mine are strictly contrary, in that both cannot be true—although both can be false. (Both are false if the glass is only one-quarter full.)

This, by the way, enables us to define the difference between a pair of contradictory propositions and a pair of contrary propositions. Two propositions are contrary if and only if both cannot be true (though both can be false); two propositions are contradictory if and only if they are such that if one is true the other must be false, and vice versa. Thus, if Jack says that Alice Walker's *The Color Purple* is a better novel than Mark Twain's *Huckleberry Finn*, and Jill says, "No, *Huckleberry Finn* is better than *The Color Purple*," she is contradicting Jack. If what either one of them says is true, then what the other says must be false. A more subtle case of contradiction arises when two or more of one's own beliefs implicitly contradict each other. We may find ourselves saying "Travel is broadening," and saying an hour later, "People don't really change." Just beneath the surface of these two beliefs lies a self-contradiction: How can travel broaden us unless it influences—and changes—our beliefs, values, and outlook? But if we can't really change ourselves, then traveling to new places won't change us, either. (Indeed, there is a Roman saying to the effect that travelers change the skies above them, not their hearts.) "Travel is broadening" and "People don't change" collide with each other; something has to give.

Our point, of course, is not that you must never say today something that contradicts something you said yesterday. Far from it; if you think you were mistaken yesterday, of course you will take a different position today. But what you want to avoid is what George Orwell called *doublethink* in his novel *1984*: "*Doublethink* means the power of holding two contradictory beliefs in one's mind simultaneously, and accepting them both."

Genuine contradiction, and not merely contrary assertion, is the situation we should expect to find in some disputes. Someone advances a thesis—such as the assertion in (15), *Abortion is homicide*—and someone else flatly contradicts it by the simple expedient of negating it, thus:

20. Abortion is not homicide.

If we can trust public opinion polls, many of us are not sure whether to agree with (15) or with (20). But we should agree that whichever is true, *both* cannot be true, and *both* cannot be false. The two assertions, between them, exclude all other possibilities; they pose a forced choice for our belief. (Again, we have met this idea, too, in a reductio ad absurdum.)

Now it is one thing for Jack and Jill in a dispute or argument to contradict each other. It is quite another matter for Jack to contradict himself. One wants (or should want) to avoid self-contradiction because of the embarrassing position in which one then finds oneself. Once I have contradicted myself, what are others to believe I really believe? What, indeed, *do* I believe, for that matter?

It may be, as Emerson observed, that a "foolish consistency is the hobgoblin of little minds"—that is, it may be shortsighted to purchase a consistency in one's beliefs at the expense of flying in the face of common sense. But making an effort to avoid a foolish inconsistency is the hallmark of serious thinking.

While we are speaking of inconsistency, we should spend a moment on **paradox.** The word refers to two different things: (1) an assertion that is essentially self-contradictory and therefore cannot be true, and (2) a seemingly contradictory assertion that nevertheless may be true. An example of the first might be, "Evaluations concerning quality in literature are all a matter of personal judgment, but Shakespeare is the world's greatest writer." It is hard to make any sense out of this assertion. Contrast it with a paradox of the second sort, a *seeming* contradiction that may make sense, such as "The longest way round is the shortest way home," or "Work is more fun than fun," or "The best way to find happiness is not to look for it." Here we have assertions that are striking because as soon as we hear them we realize that although they seem inconsistent and self-defeating, they contain (or may contain) profound truths. Paradoxes of this second sort are especially common in religious texts, where they may imply a mysterious reality concealed by a world of contradictory appearances. Examples are "Some who are last shall be first, and some who are first shall be last" (Jesus, quoted in Luke 13.30), and "Death, thou shalt die" (the poet John Donne, alluding to the idea that the person who has faith in Jesus dies to this world but lives eternally). If you use the word *paradox* in your own writing—for instance, to characterize an argument that you are reading—be sure that your reader will understand in which sense you are using the word. (And, of course, you will not want to write paradoxes of the first, self-contradictory sort.)

INDUCTION

Deduction involves logical thinking that applies to any assertion or claim whatever—because every possible statement, true or false, has its deductive logical consequences. Induction is relevant to one kind of assertion only; namely, to **empirical** or *factual* claims. Other kinds of assertions (such as definitions, mathematical equations, and moral or legal norms) simply are not the product of inductive reasoning and cannot serve as a basis for further inductive thinking.

And so, in studying the methods of induction, we are exploring tactics and strategies useful in gathering and then using **evidence**—empirical, observational, experimental—in support of a belief as its ground. Modern scientific knowledge is the product of these methods, and they differ somewhat from one science to another because they depend on the theories and technology appropriate to each of the sciences. Here, all we can do is discuss generally the more abstract features common to inductive inquiry generally. For fuller details, you must eventually consult your local physicist, chemist, geologist, or their colleagues and counterparts in other scientific fields.

Observation and Inference

Let us begin with a simple example. Suppose we have evidence (actually we don't, but that will not matter for our purposes) in support of the claim that

1. Two hundred and thirty persons observed in a sample of 500 smokers have cardiovascular disease.

The basis for asserting (1)—the evidence or ground—would be, presumably, straightforward physical examination of the 500 persons in the sample, one by one.

With this claim in hand, we can think of the purpose and methods of induction as being pointed in both of two opposite directions: toward establishing the basis or ground of the very empirical proposition with which we start, in this example the observation stated in (1); or toward understanding what that observation indicates or suggests as a more general, inclusive, or fundamental fact of nature.

In each case, we start from something we *do* know (or take for granted and treat as a sound starting point)—some fact of nature, perhaps a striking or commonplace event that we have observed and recorded—and then go on to something we do *not* fully know and perhaps cannot directly observe. In example (1), only the second of these two orientations is of any interest, and so let us concentrate exclusively on it. Let us also generously treat as a *method* of induction any regular pattern or style of nondeductive reasoning that we could use to support a claim such as that in (1).

Anyone truly interested in the observed fact that (1) *230 of 500 smokers have cardiovascular disease* is likely to start speculating about, and thus be interested in finding out, whether any or all of several other propositions are also true. For example, one might wonder whether

2. *All* smokers have cardiovascular disease or will develop it during their lifetimes.

This claim is a straightforward generalization of the original observation as reported in claim (1). When we think inductively about the linkage between (1) and (2), we are reasoning from an observed sample (some smokers, that is, 230 of the 500 *observed*) to the entire membership of a more inclusive class (*all* smokers, whether observed or not). The fundamental question raised by reasoning from the narrower claim (1) to the broader claim (2) is whether we have any ground for believing that what is true of *some* members of a class is true of them *all*. So the difference between (1) and (2) is that of *quantity* or scope.

We can also think inductively about the *relation* between the factors mentioned in (1). Having observed data as reported in (1), we may be tempted to assert a different and profounder kind of claim:

3. Smoking *causes* cardiovascular disease.

Here our interest is not merely in generalizing from a sample to a whole class; it is the far more important one of *explaining* the observation with which we began in claim (1). Certainly the preferred, even if not the only, mode of explanation for a natural phenomenon is a *causal* explanation. In proposition (3), we propose to explain the presence of one phenomenon (cardiovascular disease) by the prior occurrence of an independent phenomenon (smoking). The observation reported in (1) is now being used as evidence or support for this new conjecture stated in (3).

Our original claim in (1) asserted no causal relation between anything and anything else; whatever the cause of cardiovascular disease may be, that cause is not observed, mentioned, or assumed in assertion (1). Similarly, the observation asserted in claim (1) is consistent with many explanations. For example, the explanation of (1) might not be (3), but some other, undetected, carcinogenic factor unrelated to smoking, for instance, exposure to high levels of radon. The question one now faces is what can be added to (1), or teased out of it, in order to produce an adequate ground for claiming (3). (We shall return to this example for closer scrutiny.)

But there is a third way to go beyond (1). Instead of a straightforward generalization, as we had in (2), or a pronouncement on the cause of a phenomenon, as in (3), we might have a somewhat more complex and cautious further claim in mind, such as this:

4. Smoking is a factor in the causation of cardiovascular disease in some persons.

This proposition, like (3), advances a claim about causation. But (4) is obviously a weaker claim than (3). That is, other observations, theories, or evidence that would require us to reject (3) might be consistent with (4); evidence that would support (4) could easily fail to be enough to support (3). Consequently, it is even possible that (4) is true although (3) is false, because (4) allows for other (unmentioned) factors in the causation of cardiovascular disease (genetic or dietary factors, for example) which may not be found in all smokers.

Propositions (2), (3), and (4) differ from proposition (1) in an important respect. We began by assuming that (1) states an empirical fact based on direct observation, whereas these others do not. Instead, they state empirical *hypotheses* or conjectures—tentative generalizations not fully confirmed—each of which goes beyond the observed facts asserted in (1). Each of (2), (3), and (4) can be regarded as an *inductive inference* from (1). We can also say that (2), (3), and (4) are hypotheses relative to (1), even if relative to some other starting point (such as all the information that scientists today really have about smoking and cardiovascular disease) they are not.

Probability

Another way of formulating the last point is to say that whereas proposition (1), a statement of observed fact, has a **probability** of 1.0— that is, it is absolutely certain—the probability of each of the hypotheses stated in (2), (3), and (4), *relative* to (1) is smaller than 1.0. (We need not worry here about how much smaller than 1.0 the probabilities are, nor about how to calculate these probabilities precisely.) Relative to some starting point other than (1), however, the probability of these same three hypotheses might be quite different. Of course, it still would not be 1.0, absolute certainty. But it takes only a moment's reflection to realize that, whatever may be the probability of (2) or (3) or (4) relative to (1), those probabilities in each case will be quite different relative to different information, such as this:

5. Ten persons observed in a sample of 500 smokers have cardiovascular disease.

The idea that a given proposition can have different probabilities relative to different bases is fundamental to all inductive reasoning. It can be convincingly illustrated by the following example. Suppose we want to consider the probability of this proposition being true:

6. Susanne Smith will live to be eighty.

Taken as an abstract question of fact, we cannot even guess what the probability is with any assurance. But we can do better than guess; we can in fact even calculate the answer, if we are given some further information. Thus, suppose we are told that

7. Susanne Smith is seventy-nine.

Our original question then becomes one of determining the probability that (6) is true given (7); that is, relative to the evidence contained in proposition (7). No doubt, if Susanne Smith really is seventy-nine, then the probability that she will live to be eighty is greater than if we know only that

8. Susanne Smith is more than nine years old.

Obviously, a lot can happen to Susanne in the seventy years between nine and seventy-nine that is not very likely to happen to her in the one year between seventy-nine and eighty. And so, proposition (6) is more probable relative to proposition (7) than it is relative to proposition (8).

Let us disregard (7) and instead further suppose for the sake of the argument that the following is true:

9. Ninety percent of the women alive at seventy-nine live to be eighty.

Given this additional information, we now have a basis for answering our original question about proposition (6) with some precision. But suppose, in addition to (8), we are also told that

10. Susanne Smith is suffering from inoperable cancer.

and also that

11. The survival rate for women suffering from inoperable cancer is 0.6 years (that is, the average life span for women after a diagnosis of inoperable cancer is about seven months).

With this new information, the probability that (6) will be true has dropped significantly, all because we can now estimate the probability in relation to a new body of evidence.

The probability of an event, thus, is not a fixed number, but one that varies, because it is always relative to some evidence—and given different evidence, one and the same event can have different probabilities. In other words, the probability of any event is always relative to how much is known (assumed, believed), and because different persons may know different things about a given event, or the same person may know different things at different times, one and the same event can have two or more probabilities. This conclusion is not a paradox but a logical consequence of the concept of what it is for an event to have (that is, to be assigned) a probability.

If we shift to the *calculation* of probabilities, we find that generally we have two ways to calculate them. One way to proceed is by the method of **a priori** or **equal probabilities,** that is, by reference to the relevant possibilities taken abstractly and apart from any other information. Thus, in an election contest with only two candidates, A and B, each of the candidates has a fifty-fifty chance of winning (whereas in a three-candidate race, each candidate would have one chance in three of winning). Therefore the probability that candidate A will win is 0.5, and the probability that candidate B will win is also 0.5. (The sum of the probabilities of all possible independent outcomes must always equal 1.0, which is obvious enough if you think about it.)

But in politics the probabilities are not reasonably calculated so abstractly. We know that many empirical factors affect the outcome of an election, and that a calculation of probabilities in ignorance of those factors is likely to be drastically misleading. In our example of the two-candidate election, suppose candidate A has strong party support and is the incumbent, whereas candidate B represents a party long out of power and is further handicapped by being relatively unknown. No one who knows anything about electoral politics would give B the same chance of winning as A. The two events are not equiprobable in relation to all the information available.

Not only that, a given event can have more than one probability. This happens whenever we calculate a probability by relying on different bodies of data that report how often the event in question has been observed to happen. Probabilities calculated in this way are **relative frequencies.** Our earlier hypothetical example of Susanne Smith provides an illustration. If she is a smoker and we have observed that 100 out of a random set of 500 smokers are observed to have cardiovascular disease, we have a basis for claiming that she has a probability of 100 in 500, or 0.2 (one-fifth), of having this disease. However, if we had other data showing that 250 out of 500 women smokers aged eighty or older have cardiovascular disease, we have a basis for believing that there is a probability of 250 in 500, or 0.5 (one-half), that she has this disease. Notice, of course, that in both calculations we assume that Susanne Smith is not among the persons we have examined. In both cases we infer the probability with which she has this disease from observing its frequency in populations that exclude her.

Both methods of calculating probabilities are legitimate; in each case the calculation is relative to observed circumstances. But, as the examples show, it is most reasonable to have recourse to the method of equiprobabilities only when few or no other factors affecting possible outcomes are known.

Mill's Methods

Let us return to our earlier discussion of smoking and cardiovascular disease, and consider in greater detail the question of a causal connection between the two phenomena. We began thus:

1. Two hundred and thirty persons observed in a sample of 500 smokers have cardiovascular disease.

We regarded (1) as an observed fact, though in truth, of course, it is mere supposition. Our question now is, how might we augment this information so as to strengthen our confidence that

3. Smoking causes cardiovascular disease,

or at least

4. Smoking is a factor in the causation of cardiovascular disease in some persons.

Suppose further examination showed that

12. In the sample of 230 smokers with cardiovascular disease, no other suspected factor (such as genetic predisposition, lack of physical exercise, age over fifty) was also observed.

Such an observation would encourage us to believe (3) or (4) is true. Why? We are encouraged to believe it because we are inclined to believe also that whatever the cause of a phenomenon is, it must *always* be present when its effect is present. Thus, the inference from (1) to (3) or (4) is supported by (12), using **Mill's Method of Agreement,** named after the British philosopher, John Stuart Mill (1806–1873), who first formulated it. It is called a method of agreement because of the way in which the inference relies on *agreement* among the observed phenomena where a presumed cause is thought to be *present.*

Let us now suppose that in our search for evidence to support (3) or (4) we conduct additional research, and discover:

13. In a sample of 500 nonsmokers, selected to be representative of both sexes, different ages, dietary habits, exercise patterns, and so on, none is observed to have cardiovascular disease.

This observation would further encourage us to believe that we had obtained significant additional confirmation of (3) or (4). Why? Because we now know that factors present (such as male sex, lack of exercise, family history of cardiovascular disease) in cases where the effect is absent (no cardiovascular disease observed) cannot be the cause. This is an example of **Mill's Method of Difference,** so called because the cause or causal factor of an effect must be *different* from whatever the factors are that are present when the effect is *absent.*

Suppose now that, increasingly confident we have found the cause of cardiovascular disease, we study our first sample of 230 smokers ill with the disease, and discover this:

14. Those who smoke two or more packs of cigarettes daily for ten or more years have cardiovascular disease either much younger or much more severely than those who smoke less.

This is an application of **Mill's Method of Concomitant Variation,** perhaps the most convincing of the three methods. Here we deal not merely with the presence of the conjectured cause (smoking) or the absence of the effect we are studying (cardiovascular disease), as we were previously, but with the more interesting and subtler matter of the *degree and regularity of the correlation* of the supposed cause and effect. According to the observations reported in (14), it strongly appears that the more we have of the "cause" (smoking) the sooner or the more intense the onset of the "effect" (cardiovascular disease).

Notice, however, what happens to our confirmation of (3) and (4) if, instead of the observation reported in (14), we had observed:

15. In a representative sample of 500 nonsmokers, cardiovascular disease was observed in 34 cases.

(Let us not pause here to explain what makes a sample more or less representative of a population, although the representativeness of samples is vital to all statistical reasoning.) Such an observation would lead us almost immediately to suspect some other or additional causal factor: Smoking might indeed be *a* factor in causing cardiovascular disease, but it can hardly be *the* cause, because (using Mill's Method of Difference) we cannot have the effect, as we do in the observed sample reported in (15), unless we also have the cause.

An observation such as the one in (15), however, is likely to lead us to think our hypothesis that *smoking causes cardiovascular disease* has been disconfirmed. But we have a fall-back position ready; we can still defend a weaker hypothesis, namely (4), *Smoking is a factor in the causation of cardiovascular disease in some persons.* Even if (3) stumbles over the evidence in (15), (4) does not. It is still quite possible that smoking is a factor in causing this disease, even if it is not the *only* factor—and if it is, then (4) is true.

Confirmation, Mechanism, and Theory

Notice that in the discussion so far, we have spoken of the *confirmation* of a hypothesis, such as our causal claim in (4), but not of its *verification.* (Similarly, we have imagined very different evidence, such as that stated in [15], leading us to speak of the *dis*confirmation of [3], though not of its *falsi*fication.) Confirmation (getting some evidence for) is weaker than verification (getting sufficient evidence to regard as true);

and our (imaginary) evidence so far in favor of (4) falls well short of conclusive support. Further research—the study of more representative or much larger samples, for example—might yield very different observations. It might lead us to conclude that although initial research had confirmed our hypothesis about smoking as the cause of cardiovascular disease, the additional information obtained subsequently disconfirmed the hypothesis. For most interesting hypotheses, both in detective stories and in modern science, there is both confirming and disconfirming evidence simultaneously. The challenge is to evaluate the hypothesis by considering such conflicting evidence.

As long as we confine our observations to *correlations* of the sort reported in our several (imaginary) observations, such as proposition (1), *230 smokers in a group of 500 have cardiovascular disease*, or (12), *230 smokers with the disease share no other suspected factors*, such as lack of exercise, any defense of a *causal* hypothesis such as claim (3), *Smoking causes cardiovascular disease*, or claim (4), *Smoking is a factor in causing the disease*, is not likely to convince the skeptic or lead those with beliefs alternative to (3) and (4) to abandon them and agree with us. Why is that? It is because a causal hypothesis without any account of the *underlying mechanism* by means of which the (alleged) cause produces the effect will seem superficial. Only when we can specify in detail *how* the (alleged) cause produces the effect will the causal hypothesis be convincing.

In other cases, in which no mechanism can be found, we seek instead to embed the causal hypothesis in a larger *theory,* one that rules out as incompatible any causal hypothesis except the favored one. (That is, we appeal to the test of consistency and thereby bring deductive reasoning to bear on our problem.) Thus, perhaps we cannot specify any mechanism—any underlying structure that generates a regular sequence of events, one of which is the effect we are studying—to explain why, for example, the gravitational mass of a body causes it to attract other bodies. But we can embed this claim in a larger body of physical theory that rules out as inconsistent any alternative causal explanation. To do that convincingly in regard to any given causal hypothesis, as this example suggests, requires detailed knowledge of the current state of the relevant body of scientific theory, something far beyond our aim or need to consider in further detail here.

FALLACIES

The straight road on which sound reasoning proceeds gives little latitude for cruising about. Irrationality, carelessness, passionate attachment to one's unexamined beliefs, and the sheer complexity of some issues, not to mention Original Sin, occasionally spoil the reasoning of even the best of us. Although in this book we reprint many varied voices and arguments, we hope we have reprinted no readings that exhibit the most flagrant errors or commit the graver abuses against the canons of good reasoning. Nevertheless, an inventory of those abuses and their close examination can be an instructive (as well as an amusing) exercise. Instructive, because the diagnosis and repair of error helps to fix more clearly the principles of sound reasoning on which such remedial labors depend. Amusing, because we are so constituted that our perception of the nonsense of others can stimulate our mind, warm our heart, and give us comforting feelings of superiority.

The discussion that follows, then, is a quick tour through the twisting lanes, mudflats, forests, and quicksands of the faults that one sometimes encounters in reading arguments that stray from the highway of clear thinking.

We can and do apply the term *fallacy* to many types of errors, mistakes, and confusions in oral and written discourse, in which our reasoning has gone awry. For convenience, we can group the fallacies by referring to the six aspects of reasoning identified in the Toulmin Method, described earlier (p. 251). Let us take up first those fallacies that spoil our *claims* or our *grounds* for them. These are errors in the meaning, clarity, or sense of a sentence, or of some word or phrase in a sentence, being used in the role of a claim or ground. They are thus not so much errors of *reasoning* as they are errors in *reasons* or in the *claims* that our reasons are intended to support or criticize.

Many Questions

The old saw, "Have you stopped beating your wife?" illustrates the **fallacy of many questions.** This question, as one can readily see, is unanswerable unless both of its implicit presuppositions are true. The questioner presupposes that (a) the addressee has or had a wife, and that (b) he used to beat her. If either of these presuppositions is false, then the question is pointless; it cannot be answered strictly and simply either with a yes or a no.

Ambiguity

Near the center of the town of Concord, Massachusetts, is an empty field with a sign reading "Old Calf Pasture." Hmm. A pasture in former times in which calves grazed? A pasture now in use for old calves? An erstwhile pasture for old calves? These alternative readings arise because of **ambiguity;** brevity in the sign has produced a group of words that give rise to more than one possible interpretation, confusing the reader and (presumably) frustrating the sign-writer's intentions.

Consider a more complex example. Suppose someone asserts *People have equal rights* and also *Everyone has a right to property.* Many people believe both these claims, but their combination involves an ambiguity. On one interpretation, the two claims entail that everyone has an *equal right* to property. (That is, you and I each have an equal right to whatever property we have.) But the two claims can also be interpreted to mean that everyone has a *right to equal property*. (That is, whatever property you have a right to, I have a right to the same, or at least equivalent, property.) The latter interpretation is radically revolutionary, whereas the former is not. Arguments over equal rights often involve this ambiguity.

Death by a Thousand Qualifications

In a letter of recommendation, sent in support of an applicant for a job on your newspaper, you find this sentence: "Young Smith was the best student I've ever taught in an English course." Pretty strong endorsement, you think, except that you do not know, because you have not been told, the letter writer is a very junior faculty member, has been teaching for only two years, is an instructor in the history department, and taught a section of freshman English as a courtesy for a sick colleague, and only eight students were enrolled in the course. Thanks to these implicit qualifications, the letter writer did not lie or exaggerate in his praise; but the effect of his sentence on you, the unwitting reader, is quite misleading. The explicit claim in the letter, and its impact on you, is quite different from the tacitly qualified claim in the mind of the writer.

Death by a thousand qualifications gets its name from the ancient torture of death by a thousand small cuts. Thus, a bold assertion can be virtually killed, its true content reduced to nothing, bit by bit, as all the appropriate or necessary qualifications are added to it. Consider another example. Suppose you hear a politician describing another country (let's call it Ruritania so as not to offend anyone) as a "democracy"—except it turns out that Ruritania doesn't have regular elections, lacks a written constitution, has no independent judiciary, prohibits religious worship except of the state-designated deity, and so forth. So what is left of the original claim that Ruritania is a democracy is little or nothing. The qualifications have taken all the content out of the original description.

Oversimplification

"Poverty causes crime," "Taxation is unfair," "Truth is stranger than fiction"—these are examples of generalizations that exaggerate and therefore oversimplify the truth. Poverty as such can't be the sole cause of crime, because many poor people do not break the law. Some taxes may be unfairly high, others unfairly low—but there is no reason to believe that *every* tax is unfair to all those who have to pay it. Some true stories do amaze us as much or more than some fictional stories, but the reverse is true, too. (In the language of the Toulmin Method, **oversimplification** is the result of a failure to use suitable modal qualifiers in formulating one's claims or grounds or backing.)

False Dichotomy

Sometimes oversimplification takes a more complex form, in which contrary possibilities are wrongly presented as though they were exhaustive and exclusive. "Either we get tough with drug users or we must surrender and legalize all drugs." Really? What about doing neither, and instead offering education and counseling, detoxification programs and incentives to "Say No"? A favorite of debaters, the either/or assertion always runs the risk of ignoring a third (or fourth) possibility. Some disjunctions are indeed exhaustive: "Either we get tough with drug users or we do not." This proposition, though vague (what does "get tough" really mean?), is a tautology; it cannot be false, and there is no third alternative. But most disjunctions do not express a pair of *contradictory* alternatives—they offer only a pair of *contrary* alternatives, and mere contraries do not exhaust the possibilities (recall our discussion of contraries versus contradictories, on pp. 269–70).

An example of **false dichotomy** can be found in the essay by Jeff Jacoby on flogging (p. 119). His entire discussion is built on the relative superiority of whipping over imprisonment, as though there was no alternative punishment worth considering. But of course there is, notably community service (especially for white-collar offenders, juveniles, and many first offenders).

Equivocation

In a delightful passage in Lewis Carroll's *Through the Looking Glass,* the king asks his messenger, "Who did you pass on the road?" and the messenger replies, "Nobody." This prompts the king to observe, "Of course, nobody walks slower than you," provoking the messenger's sullen response: "I do my best. I'm sure nobody walks much faster than I do." At this the king remarks with surprise, "He can't do that or else he'd have been here first!" (This, by the way, is the classic predecessor of the famous comic dialogue "Who's on First?" between the comedians Bud Abbott and Lou Costello.) The king and the messenger are equivocating on the term *nobody.* The messenger uses it in the normal way as an indefinite pronoun equivalent to "not anyone." But the king uses the word as though it were a proper noun, *Nobody,* the rather odd name of some person. No wonder the king and the messenger talk right past each other.

Equivocation (from the Latin for "equal voice," that is, giving utterance to two meanings at the same time in one word or phrase) can ruin otherwise good reasoning, as in this example: *Euthanasia is a good death; one dies a good death when one dies peacefully in old age; therefore euthanasia is dying peacefully in old age.* The etymology of *euthanasia* is literally "a good death," and so the first premise is true. And the second premise is certainly plausible. But the conclusion of this syllogism is false. Euthanasia cannot be defined as a peaceful death in one's old age, for two reasons. First, euthanasia requires the intervention of another person who kills someone (or lets the person die); second, even a very young person can be given euthanasia. The problem arises because "a good death" is used in the second premise in a manner that does not apply to euthanasia. Both meanings of "a good death" are legitimate, but when used together they constitute an equivocation that spoils the argument.

The fallacy of equivocation takes us from the discussion of confusions in individual claims or grounds to the more troublesome fallacies that infect the linkages between the claims we make and the grounds (or reasons) for them. These are the fallacies that occur in statements that, following the vocabulary of the Toulmin Method, are called the *warrant* of reasoning. Each fallacy is an example of reasoning that involves a **non sequitur** (Latin for "It does not follow"). That is, the *claim* (the conclusion) does not follow from the *grounds* (the premises).

For a start, here is an obvious *non sequitur:* "He went to the movies on three consecutive nights, so he must love movies." Why doesn't the claim ("he must love movies") follow from the grounds ("He went to the movies on three consecutive nights")? Perhaps the person was just fulfilling an assignment in a film course (maybe he even hated movies so much that he had postponed three assignments to see films, and now had to see them all in quick succession), or maybe he went with a girlfriend who was a movie buff, or maybe . . . , well, one can think of any number of other possible reasons.

Composition

Could an all-star team of professional basketball players beat the Boston Celtics in their heyday, say the team of 1985–1986? Perhaps in one game or two, but probably not in seven out of a dozen games in a row. As students of the game know, teamwork is an indispensable part of outstanding performance, and the 1985–1986 Celtics were famous for their self-sacrificing style of play.

The **fallacy of composition** can be convincingly illustrated, therefore, in this argument: *A team of five NBA all-stars is the best team in basketball if each of the five players is the best at his position.* The fallacy is called composition because the reasoning commits the error of arguing from the true premise that each member of a group has a certain property to the false conclusion that the group (the composition) itself has the property. (That is, because A is the best player at forward, B is the best center, and so on, therefore the team of A, B . . . is the best team.)

Division

In the Bible, we are told that the apostles of Jesus were twelve and that Matthew was an apostle. Does it follow that Matthew was twelve? No. To argue in this way from a property of a group to a property of a member of that group is to commit the **fallacy of division.** The example of the apostles may not be a very tempting instance of this error; here is a classic version that is a bit more interesting. If it is true that the average American family has 1.8 children, does it follow that your brother and sister-in-law are likely to have 1.8 children? If you think it does, you have committed the fallacy of division.

Poisoning the Well

During the 1970s some critics of the Equal Rights Amendment (ERA) argued against it by pointing out that Marx and Engels, in their *Communist Manifesto,* favored equality of women and men—and therefore the ERA is immoral, or undesirable, and perhaps even a communist plot. This kind of reasoning is an attempt to **poison the well;** that is, an attempt to shift attention from the merits of the argument—the validity of the reasoning, the truth of the claims—to the source or origin of the argument. Such criticism nicely deflects attention from the real issue; namely, whether the view in question is true and what the quality of evidence is in its support. The mere fact that Marx (or Hitler, for that matter) believed something does not show that the belief is false or immoral; just because some scoundrel believes the world is round, that is no reason for you to believe it is flat.

Ad Hominem

Closely allied to poisoning the well is another fallacy, **ad hominem** argument (from the Latin for "against the person"). Since arguments and theories are not natural occurrences but are the creative products of particular persons, a critic can easily yield to the temptation to attack an argument or theory by trying to impeach or undercut the credentials of its advocates.

The Genetic Fallacy

Another member of the family of related fallacies that includes poisoning the well and ad hominem is the **genetic fallacy.** Here the error takes the form of arguing against some claim by pointing out that its origin (genesis) is tainted or that it was invented by someone deserving our contempt. Thus, one might attack the ideas of the Declaration of Independence by pointing out that its principal author, Thomas Jefferson, was a slaveholder. Assuming that it is not anachronistic and inappropriate to criticize a public figure of two centuries ago for practicing slavery,

and conceding that slavery is morally outrageous, it is nonetheless fallacious to attack the ideas or even the sincerity of the Declaration by attempting to impeach the credentials of its author. Jefferson's moral faults
do not by themselves falsify, make improbable, or constitute counterevidence to the truth or other merits of the claims made in his writings. At
most, one's faults cast doubt on one's integrity or sincerity if one makes
claims at odds with one's practice.

The genetic fallacy can take other forms less closely allied to ad
hominem argument. For example, an opponent of the death penalty
might argue:

> Capital punishment arose in barbarous times; but we claim to be civi-
> lized; therefore we should discard this relic of the past.

Such reasoning shouldn't be persuasive, because the question of the
death penalty for our society must be decided by the degree to which it
serves our purposes—justice and defense against crime, presumably—
to which its historic origins are irrelevant. The practices of beer- and
wine-making are as old as human civilization, but their origin in antiq-
uity is no reason to outlaw them in our time. The curious circumstances
in which something originates usually play no role whatever in its validity. Anyone who would argue that nothing good could possibly come
from molds and fungi is refuted by Sir Alexander Fleming's discovery of
penicillin in 1928.

Appeal to Authority

The example of Jefferson can be turned around to illustrate another
fallacy. One might easily imagine someone from the South in 1860 defending the slavocracy of that day by appealing to the fact that no less a
person than Jefferson—a brilliant public figure, thinker, and leader by
any measure—owned slaves. Or, today, one might defend capital punishment on the ground that Abraham Lincoln, surely one of the nation's
greatest presidents, signed many death warrants during the Civil War,
authorizing the execution of Union soldiers. No doubt the esteem in
which such figures as Jefferson and Lincoln are deservedly held amounts
to impressive endorsement for whatever acts and practices, policies and
institutions, they supported. But the **authority** of these figures in itself
is not *evidence* for the truth of their views, and so their authority cannot
be a reason for anyone to agree with them. Obviously, Jefferson and
Lincoln themselves could not support their beliefs by pointing to the fact
that they held them. Because their own authority is no reason for them
to believe what they believe, it is no reason for anyone else, either.

Sometimes the appeal to authority is fallacious because the authoritative person is not an expert on the issue in dispute. The fact that a
high-energy physicist has won the Nobel Prize is no reason for attaching
any special weight to her views on the causes of cancer, the reduction of

traffic accidents, or the legalization of marijuana. On the other hand, one would be well advised to attend to her views on the advisability of ballistic missile-defense systems. For there may be a connection between the kind of research for which she received the prize and the defense research projects.

All of us depend heavily on the knowledge of various experts and authorities, and so it ill-behooves us to ignore their views. Conversely, we should resist the temptation to accord their views on diverse subjects the same respect that we grant them in the area of their expertise.

The Slippery Slope

One of the most familiar arguments against any type of government regulation is that if it is allowed, then it will be just the first step down the path that leads to ruinous interference, overregulation, and totalitarian control. Fairly often we encounter this mode of argument in the public debates over handgun control, the censorship of pornography, and physician-assisted suicide. The argument is called the **slippery slope argument** (or the **wedge argument,** from the way we use the thin end of a wedge to split solid things apart; it is also called, rather colorfully, "letting the camel's nose under the tent"). The fallacy here is in implying that the first step necessarily leads to the second, and so on down the slope to disaster, when in fact there is no necessary slide from the first step to the second at all. (Would handgun registration lead to a police state? Well, it hasn't in Switzerland.) Sometimes the argument takes the form of claiming that a seemingly innocent or even attractive principle that is being applied in a given case (censorship of pornography, to avoid promoting sexual violence) requires one for the sake of consistency to apply the same principle in other cases, only with absurd and catastrophic results (censorship of everything in print, to avoid hurting anyone's feelings).

Here's an extreme example of this fallacy in action:

> Automobiles cause more deaths than handguns do. If you oppose handguns on the ground that doing so would save lives of the innocent, you'll soon find yourself wanting to outlaw the automobile.

Does opposition to handguns have this consequence? Not necessarily. Most people accept without dispute the right of society to regulate the operation of motor vehicles by requiring drivers to have a license, a greater restriction than many states impose on gun ownership. Besides, a gun is a lethal weapon designed to kill whereas an automobile or truck is a vehicle designed for transportation. Private ownership and use in both cases entail risks of death to the innocent. But there is no inconsistency in a society's refusal to tolerate this risk in the case of guns and its willingness to do so in the case of automobiles.

Closely related to the slippery slope is what lawyers call a **parade of horrors,** an array of examples of terrible consequences that will or might follow if we travel down a certain path. A good example appears in Justice William Brennan's opinion for the Supreme Court in *Texas v. Johnson* (p. 316), concerned with a Texas law against burning the American flag in political protest. If this law is allowed to stand, Brennan suggests, we may next find laws against burning the presidential seal, state flags, and the Constitution.

Appeal to Ignorance

In the controversy over the death penalty, the issues of deterrence and executing the innocent are bound to be raised. Because no one knows how many innocent persons have been convicted for murder and wrongfully executed, it is tempting for abolitionists to argue that the death penalty is too risky. It is equally tempting for the proponent of the death penalty to argue that since no one knows how many people have been deterred from murder by the threat of execution, we abolish it at our peril.

Each of these arguments suffers from the same flaw: the **fallacy of appeal to ignorance.** Each argument invites the audience to draw an inference from a premise that is unquestionably true—but what is that premise? It asserts that there is something "we don't know." But what we *don't* know cannot be *evidence* for (or against) anything. Our ignorance is no reason for believing anything, except perhaps that we ought to try to undertake an appropriate investigation in order to reduce our ignorance and replace it with reliable information.

Begging the Question

The argument we have just considered also illustrates another fallacy. From the fact that you were not murdered yesterday, we cannot infer that the death penalty was a deterrent. Yet it is tempting to make this inference, perhaps because—all unawares—we are relying on the **fallacy of begging the question.** If someone tacitly assumes from the start that the death penalty is an effective deterrent, then the fact that you weren't murdered yesterday certainly looks like evidence for the truth of that assumption. But it isn't, so long as there are competing but unexamined alternative explanations, as in this case. (The fallacy is called "begging the question," *petitio principii* in Latin, because the conclusion of the argument is hidden among its assumptions—and so the conclusion, not surprisingly, follows from the premises.)

Of course, the fact that you weren't murdered is *consistent* with the claim that the death penalty is an effective deterrent, just as someone else's being murdered is also consistent with that claim (for an effective deterrent need not be a *perfect* deterrent). In general, from the fact that two propositions are consistent with each other, we cannot infer that either is evidence for the other.

False Analogy

Argument by analogy, as we have pointed out in Chapter 3, and as many of the selections in this book show, is a familiar and even indispensable mode of argument. But it can be treacherous, because it runs the risk of the **fallacy of false analogy.** Unfortunately, we have no simple or foolproof way of distinguishing between the useful and legitimate analogies, and the others. The key question to ask yourself is this: Do the two things put into analogy differ in any essential and relevant respect, or are they different only in unimportant and irrelevant aspects?

In a famous example from his discussion in support of suicide, philosopher David Hume rhetorically asked: "It would be no crime in me to divert the Nile or Danube from its course, were I able to effect such purposes. Where then is the crime of turning a few ounces of blood from their natural channel?" This is a striking analogy, except that it rests on a false assumption. No one has the right to divert the Nile or the Danube or any other major international watercourse; it would be a catastrophic crime to do so without the full consent of people living in the region, their government, and so forth. Therefore, arguing by analogy, one might well say that no one has the right to take his or her own life, either. Thus, Hume's own analogy can be used to argue against his thesis that suicide is no crime. But let us ignore the way in which his example can be turned against him. The analogy is a terrible one in any case. Isn't it obvious that the Nile, whatever its exact course, would continue to nourish Egypt and the Sudan, whereas the blood flowing out of someone's veins will soon leave that person dead? The fact that the blood is the same blood, whether in one's body or in a pool on the floor (just as the water of the Nile is the same body of water whatever path it follows to the sea) is, of course, irrelevant to the question of whether one has the right to commit suicide.

Let us look at a more complex example. During the 1960s, when the nation was convulsed over the purpose and scope of our military involvement in Southeast Asia, advocates of more vigorous United States military participation appealed to the so-called domino effect, supposedly inspired by a passing remark from President Eisenhower in the 1950s. The analogy refers to the way in which a row of standing dominoes will collapse, one after the other, if the first one is pushed. If Vietnam turns communist, according to this analogy, so too will its neighbors, Laos and Cambodia, followed by Thailand and then Burma, until the whole region is as communist as China to the north. The domino analogy (or metaphor) provided, no doubt, a vivid illustration, and effectively portrayed the worry of many anticommunists. But did it really shed any light on the likely pattern of political and military developments in the region? The history of events there during the 1970s and 1980s did not bear out the domino analogy.

Post Hoc Ergo Propter Hoc

One of the most tempting errors in reasoning is to ground a claim about causation on an observed temporal sequence; that is, to argue "after this therefore because of this" (which is what the phrase **post hoc ergo propter hoc** means in Latin). About thirty-five years ago, when the medical community first announced that smoking tobacco caused lung cancer, advocates for the tobacco industry replied that the doctors were guilty of this fallacy.

These industry advocates argued the medical researchers had merely noticed that in some people, lung cancer developed *after* considerable smoking, indeed, years after; but (they insisted) this correlation was not at all the same as a causal relation between smoking and lung cancer. True enough. The claim that A *causes* B is not the same as the claim that B comes after A. After all, it was possible that smokers as a group had some other common trait and that this factor was the true cause of their cancer.

As the long controversy over the truth about the causation of lung cancer shows, to avoid the appearance of fallacious *post hoc* reasoning one needs to find some way to link the observed phenomena (the correlation of smoking and the onset of lung cancer). This step requires some further theory, and preferably some experimental evidence for the exact sequence or physical mechanism, in full detail, of how ingestion of tobacco smoke is a crucial factor—and is not merely an accidental or happenstance prior event—in the subsequent development of the cancer.

Protecting the Hypothesis

In Chapter 3, we contrast *reasoning* and *rationalization* (or the finding of bad reasons for what one intends to believe anyway). Rationalization can take subtle forms, as the following example indicates. Suppose you're standing with a friend on the shore or on a pier, and you watch as a ship heads out to sea. As it reaches the horizon, it slowly disappears—first the hull, then the upper decks, and finally the tip of the mast. Because the ship (you both assume) isn't sinking, it occurs to you that you have in this sequence of observations convincing evidence that the earth's surface is curved. Nonsense, says your companion. Light waves sag, or bend down, over distances of a few miles, and so a flat surface (such as the ocean) can intercept them. Hence the ship, which appears to be going "over" the horizon, really isn't—it's just moving steadily farther and farther away in a straight line. Your friend, you discover to your amazement, is a card-carrying member of the Flat Earth Society (yes, there really is such an organization). Now most of us would regard the idea that light rays bend down in the manner required by the Flat Earther's argument as a rationalization whose sole purpose is to protect the flat-earth doctrine against counterevidence. We would be convinced it was a rationalization, and not a very good one at that, if the Flat Earther held to it despite a patient and thorough explanation from a physicist that showed modern optical theory to be quite incompatible with the view that light waves sag.

This example illustrates two important points about the *backing* of arguments. First, it is always possible to protect a hypothesis by abandoning adjacent or connected hypotheses; this is the tactic our Flat Earth friend has used. This maneuver is possible, however, only because—and this is the second point—whenever we test a hypothesis, we do so by taking for granted (usually quite unconsciously) many other hypotheses as well. So the evidence for the hypothesis we think we are confirming is impossible to separate entirely from the adequacy of the connected hypotheses. As long as we have no reason to doubt that light rays travel in straight lines (at least over distances of a few miles), our Flat Earth friend's argument is unconvincing. But once that hypothesis is itself put in doubt, the idea that looked at first to be a pathetic rationalization takes on an even more troublesome character.

There are, then, not one but two fallacies exposed by this example. The first and perhaps graver is in rigging your hypothesis so that *no matter what* observations are brought against it, you will count nothing as falsifying it. The second and subtler is in thinking that as you test one hypothesis, all of your other background beliefs are left safely to one side, immaculate and uninvolved. On the contrary, our beliefs form a corporate structure, intertwined and connected to each other with great complexity, and no one of them can ever be singled out for unique and isolated application, confirmation, or disconfirmation, to the world around us.

A CHECKLIST FOR EVALUATING AN ARGUMENT FROM A LOGICAL POINT OF VIEW

✓ Is the argument purely deductive, purely inductive, or a mixture of the two?

✓ If it is deductive, is it valid?

✓ If it is valid, are all its premises and assumptions true?

✓ If it is not valid, what fallacy does it commit?

✓ If it is not valid, are the claims at least consistent with each other?

✓ If it is not valid, can you think of additional assumptions that would make it valid?

✓ If the argument is inductive, on what observations is it based?

✓ If the argument is inductive, how probable are its premises and its conclusion?

✓ In any case, can you think of evidence that would further confirm the conclusion? Disconfirm the conclusion?

Max Shulman

Having read about proper and improper arguments, you are now well equipped to read a short story on the topic.

Max Shulman (1919–1988) began his career as a writer when he was a journalism student at the University of Minnesota. Later he wrote humorous novels, stories, and plays. One of his novels, Barefoot Boy with Cheek *(1943), was made into a musical and another,* Rally Round the Flag, Boys! *(1957), was made into a film starring Paul Newman and Joanne Woodward. The* Tender Trap *(1954), a play he wrote with Robert Paul Smith, still retains its popularity with theater groups.*

"Love Is a Fallacy" was first published in 1951, when demeaning stereotypes about women and minorities were widely accepted in the marketplace as well as the home. Thus, jokes about domineering mothers-in-law or about dumb blondes routinely met with no objection.

Love Is a Fallacy

Cool was I and logical. Keen, calculating, perspicacious, acute, and astute—I was all of these. My brain was as powerful as a dynamo, as precise as a chemist's scales, as penetrating as a scalpel. And—think of it!—I was only eighteen.

It is not often that one so young has such a giant intellect. Take, for example, Petey Bellows, my roommate at the university. Same age, same background, but dumb as an ox. A nice enough fellow, you understand, but nothing upstairs. Emotional type. Unstable. Impressionable. Worst of all, a faddist. Fads, I submit, are the very negation of reason. To be swept up in every new craze that comes along, to surrender yourself to idiocy just because everybody else is doing it—this, to me, is the acme of mindlessness. Not, however, to Petey.

One afternoon I found Petey lying on his bed with an expression of such distress on his face that I immediately diagnosed appendicitis. "Don't move," I said. "Don't take a laxative. I'll call a doctor."

"Raccoon," he mumbled thickly.

"Raccoon?" I said, pausing in my flight.   5

"I want a raccoon coat," he wailed.

I perceived that his trouble was not physical, but mental. "Why do you want a raccoon coat?"

"I should have known it," he cried, pounding his temples. "I should have known they'd come back when the Charleston came back. Like a fool I spent all my money for textbooks, and now I can't get a raccoon coat."

"Can you mean," I said incredulously, "that people are actually wearing raccoon coats again?"

"All the Big Men on Campus are wearing them. Where've you   10 been?"

"In the library," I said, naming a place not frequented by Big Men on Campus.

He leaped from the bed and paced the room. "I've got to have a raccoon coat," he said passionately. "I've got to!"

"Petey, why? Look at it rationally. Raccoon coats are unsanitary. They shed. They smell bad. They weigh too much. They're unsightly. They——"

"You don't understand," he interrupted impatiently. "It's the thing to do. Don't you want to be in the swim?"

"No," I said truthfully.   15

"Well, I do," he declared. "I'd give anything for a raccoon coat. Anything!"

My brain, that precision instrument, slipped into high gear. "Anything?" I asked, looking at him narrowly.

"Anything," he affirmed in ringing tones.

I stroked my chin thoughtfully. It so happened that I knew where to get my hands on a raccoon coat. My father had had one in his undergraduate days; it lay now in a trunk in the attic back home. It also happened that Petey had something I wanted. He didn't *have* it exactly, but at least he had first rights on it. I refer to his girl, Polly Espy.

I had long coveted Polly Espy. Let me emphasize that my desire for   20
this young woman was not emotional in nature. She was, to be sure, a girl who excited the emotions, but I was not one to let my heart rule my head. I wanted Polly for a shrewdly calculated, entirely cerebral reason.

I was a freshman in law school. In a few years I would be out in practice. I was well aware of the importance of the right kind of wife in furthering a lawyer's career. The successful lawyers I had observed were, almost without exception, married to beautiful, gracious, intelligent women. With one omission, Polly fitted these specifications perfectly.

Beautiful she was. She was not yet of pin-up proportions, but I felt sure that time would supply the lack. She already had the makings.

Gracious she was. By gracious I mean full of graces. She had an erectness of carriage, an ease of bearing, a poise that clearly indicated the best of breeding. At table her manners were exquisite. I had seen her at the Kozy Kampus Korner eating the specialty of the house—a sandwich that contained scraps of pot roast, gravy, chopped nuts, and a dipper of sauerkraut—without even getting her fingers moist.

Intelligent she was not. In fact, she veered in the opposite direction. But I believed that under my guidance she would smarten up. At any rate, it was worth a try. It is, after all, easier to make a beautiful dumb girl smart than to make an ugly smart girl beautiful.

"Petey," I said, "are you in love with Polly Espy?"   25

"I think she's a keen kid," he replied, "but I don't know if you'd call it love. Why?"

"Do you," I asked, "have any kind of formal arrangement with her? I mean are you going steady or anything like that?"

"No. We see each other quite a bit, but we both have other dates. Why?"

"Is there," I asked, "any other man for whom she has a particular fondness?"

"Not that I know of. Why?"   30

I nodded with satisfaction. "In other words, if you were out of the picture, the field would be open. Is that right?"

"I guess so. What are you getting at?"

"Nothing, nothing," I said innocently, and took my suitcase out of the closet.

"Where you going?" asked Petey.

"Home for the week end." I threw a few things into the bag.   35

"Listen," he said, clutching my arm eagerly, "while you're home, you couldn't get some money from your old man, could you, and lend it to me so I can buy a raccoon coat?"

"I may do better than that," I said with a mysterious wink and closed my bag and left.

"Look," I said to Petey when I got back Monday morning. I threw open the suitcase and revealed the huge, hairy, gamy object that my father had worn in his Stutz Bearcat in 1925.

"Holy Toledo!" said Petey reverently. He plunged his hands into the raccoon coat and then his face. "Holy Toledo!" he repeated fifteen or twenty times.

"Would you like it?" I asked.   40

"Oh yes!" he cried, clutching the greasy pelt to him. Then a canny look came into his eyes. "What do you want for it?"

"Your girl," I said, mincing no words.

"Polly?" he said in a horrified whisper. "You want Polly?"

"That's right."

He flung the coat from him. "Never," he said stoutly.   45

I shrugged. "Okay. If you don't want to be in the swim, I guess it's your business."

I sat down in a chair and pretended to read a book, but out of the corner of my eye I kept watching Petey. He was a torn man. First he looked at the coat with the expression of a waif at a bakery window. Then he turned away and set his jaw resolutely. Then he looked back at the coat, with even more longing in his face. Then he turned away, but with not so much resolution this time. Back and forth his head swiveled, desire waxing, resolution waning. Finally he didn't turn away at all; he just stood and stared with mad lust at the coat.

"It isn't as though I was in love with Polly," he said thickly. "Or going steady or anything like that."

"That's right," I murmured.

"What's Polly to me, or me to Polly?"   50

"Not a thing," said I.

"It's just been a casual kick—just a few laughs, that's all."

"Try on the coat," said I.

He complied. The coat bunched high over his ears and dropped all the way down to his shoe tops. He looked like a mound of dead raccoons. "Fits fine," he said happily.

I rose from my chair. "Is it a deal?" I asked, extending my hand.   55

He swallowed. "It's a deal," he said and shook my hand.

I had my first date with Polly the following evening. This was in the nature of a survey; I wanted to find out just how much work I had to do to get her mind up to the standard I required. I took her first to dinner. "Gee, that was a delish dinner," she said as we left the restaurant. Then I took her to a movie. "Gee, that was a marvy movie," she said as we left the theater. And then I took her home. "Gee, I had a sensaysh time," she said as she bade me good night.

I went back to my room with a heavy heart. I had gravely underestimated the size of my task. This girl's lack of information was terrifying. Nor would it be enough merely to supply her with information. First she had to be taught to *think*. This loomed as a project of no small dimensions, and at first I was tempted to give her back to Petey. But then I got to thinking about her abundant physical charms and about the way she entered a room and the way she handled a knife and fork, and I decided to make an effort.

I went about it, as in all things, systematically. I gave her a course in logic. It happened that I, as a law student, was taking a course in logic myself, so I had all the facts at my fingertips. "Polly," I said to her when I picked her up on our next date, "tonight we are going over to the Knoll and talk."

"Oo, terrif," she replied. One thing I will say for this girl: You would   60
go far to find another so agreeable.

We went to the Knoll, the campus trysting place, and we sat down under an old oak, and she looked at me expectantly: "What are we going to talk about?" she asked.

"Logic."

She thought this over for a minute and decided she liked it. "Magnif," she said.

"Logic," I said, clearing my throat, "is the science of thinking. Before we can think correctly, we must first learn to recognize the common fallacies of logic. These we will take up tonight."

"Wow-dow!" she cried, clapping her hands delightedly.   65

I winced, but went bravely on. "First let us examine the fallacy called Dicto Simpliciter."

"By all means," she urged, batting her lashes eagerly.

"Dicto Simpliciter means an argument based on an unqualified generalization. For example: Exercise is good. Therefore everybody should exercise."

"I agree," said Polly earnestly. "I mean exercise is wonderful. I mean it builds the body and everything."

"Polly," I said gently, "the argument is a fallacy. *Exercise is good* is an 70
unqualified generalization. For instance, if you have heart disease, exercise is bad, not good. Many people are ordered by their doctors *not* to
exercise. You must *qualify* the generalization. You must say exercise is
usually good, or exercise is good *for most people*. Otherwise you have committed a Dicto Simpliciter. Do you see?"

"No," she confessed. "But this is marvy. Do more! Do more!"

"It will be better if you stop tugging at my sleeve," I told her, and
when she desisted, I continued. "Next we take up a fallacy called Hasty
Generalization. Listen carefully: You can't speak French. I can't speak
French. Petey Bellows can't speak French. I must therefore conclude
that nobody at the University of Minnesota can speak French."

"Really?" said Polly, amazed. "*Nobody?*"

I hid my exasperation. "Polly, it's a fallacy. The generalization is
reached too hastily. There are too few instances to support such a conclusion."

"Know any more fallacies?" she asked breathlessly. "This is more fun 75
than dancing even."

I fought off a wave of despair. I was getting nowhere with this girl,
absolutely nowhere. Still, I am nothing if not persistent. I continued.
"Next comes Post Hoc. Listen to this: Let's not take Bill on our picnic.
Every time we take him out with us, it rains."

"I know somebody just like that," she exclaimed. "A girl back
home—Eula Becker, her name is. It never fails. Every single time we
take her on a picnic——"

"Polly," I said sharply, "it's a fallacy. Eula Becker doesn't *cause* the
rain. She has no connection with the rain. You are guilty of Post Hoc if
you blame Eula Becker."

"I'll never do it again," she promised contritely. "Are you mad
at me?"

I sighed. "No, Polly, I'm not mad."   80

"Then tell me some more fallacies."

"All right. Let's try Contradictory Premises."

"Yes, let's," she chirped, blinking her eyes happily.

I frowned, but plunged ahead. "Here's an example of Contradictory
Premises: If God can do anything, can He make a stone so heavy that He
won't be able to lift it?"

"Of course," she replied promptly.   85

"But if He can do anything, He can lift the stone," I pointed out.

"Yeah," she said thoughtfully. "Well, then I guess He can't make the
stone."

"But He can do anything," I reminded her.

She scratched her pretty, empty head. "I'm all confused," she admitted.

"Of course you are. Because when the premises of an argument con- 90
tradict each other, there can be no argument. If there is an irresistible

force, there can be no immovable object. If there is an immovable object, there can be no irresistible force. Get it?"

"Tell me some more of this keen stuff," she said eagerly.

I consulted my watch. "I think we'd better call it a night. I'll take you home now, and you go over all the things you've learned. We'll have another session tomorrow night."

I deposited her at the girl's dormitory, where she assured me that she had had a perfectly terrif evening, and I went glumly home to my room. Petey lay snoring in his bed, the raccoon coat huddled like a great hairy beast at his feet. For a moment I considered waking him and telling him that he could have his girl back. It seemed clear that my project was doomed to failure. The girl simply had a logic-proof head.

But then I reconsidered. I had wasted one evening; I might as well waste another. Who knew? Maybe somewhere in the extinct crater of her mind a few embers still smoldered. Maybe somehow I could fan them into flame. Admittedly it was not a prospect fraught with hope, but I decided to give it one more try.

Seated under the oak the next evening I said, "Our first fallacy 95 tonight is called Ad Misericordiam."

She quivered with delight.

"Listen closely," I said. "A man applies for a job. When the boss asks him what his qualifications are, he replies that he has a wife and six children at home, the wife is a helpless cripple, the children have nothing to eat, no clothes to wear, no shoes on their feet, there are no beds in the house, no coal in the cellar, and winter is coming."

A tear rolled down each of Polly's pink cheeks. "Oh, this is awful, awful," she sobbed.

"Yes, it's awful," I agreed, "but it's no argument. The man never answered the boss's question about his qualifications. Instead he appealed to the boss's sympathy. He committed the fallacy of Ad Misericordiam. Do you understand?"

"Have you got a handkerchief?" she blubbered.   100

I handed her a handkerchief and tried to keep from screaming while she wiped her eyes. "Next," I said in a carefully controlled tone, "we will discuss False Analogy. Here is an example: Students should be allowed to look at their textbooks during examinations. After all, surgeons have X rays to guide them during an operation, lawyers have briefs to guide them during a trial, carpenters have blueprints to guide them when they are building a house. Why, then, shouldn't students be allowed to look at their textbooks during an examination?"

"There now," she said enthusiastically, "is the most marvy idea I've heard in years."

"Polly," I said testily, "the argument is all wrong. Doctors, lawyers, and carpenters aren't taking a test to see how much they have learned, but students are. The situations are altogether different, and you can't make an analogy between them."

"I still think it's a good idea," said Polly.

"Nuts," I muttered. Doggedly I pressed on. "Next we'll try Hypothe- 105 sis Contrary to Fact."

"Sounds yummy," was Polly's reaction.

"Listen: If Madame Curie had not happened to leave a photographic plate in a drawer with a chunk of pitchblende, the world today would not know about radium."

"True, true," said Polly, nodding her head. "Did you see the movie? Oh, it just knocked me out. That Walter Pidgeon is so dreamy. I mean he fractures me."

"If you can forget Mr. Pidgeon for a moment," I said coldly, "I would like to point out that the statement is a fallacy. Maybe Madame Curie would have discovered radium at some later date. Maybe somebody else would have discovered it. Maybe any number of things would have happened. You can't start with a hypothesis that is not true and then draw any supportable conclusions from it."

"They ought to put Walter Pidgeon in more pictures," said Polly. "I 110 hardly ever see him any more."

One more chance, I decided. But just one more. There is a limit to what flesh and blood can bear. "The next fallacy is called Poisoning the Well."

"How cute!" she gurgled.

"Two men are having a debate. The first one gets up and says, 'My opponent is a notorious liar. You can't believe a word that he is going to say.' . . . Now, Polly, think. Think hard. What's wrong?"

I watched her closely as she knit her creamy brow in concentration. Suddenly a glimmer of intelligence—the first I had seen—came into her eyes. "It's not fair," she said with indignation. "It's not a bit fair. What chance has the second man got if the first man calls him a liar before he even begins talking?"

"Right!" I cried exultantly. "One hundred percent right. It's not fair. 115 The first man has *poisoned the well* before anybody could drink from it. He has hamstrung his opponent before he could even start. . . . Polly, I'm proud of you."

"Pshaw," she murmured, blushing with pleasure.

"You see, my dear, these things aren't so hard. All you have to do is concentrate. Think—examine—evaluate. Come now, let's review everything we have learned."

"Fire away," she said with an airy wave of her hand.

Heartened by the knowledge that Polly was not altogether a cretin, I began a long, patient review of all I had told her. Over and over and over again I cited instances, pointed out flaws, kept hammering away without letup. It was like digging a tunnel. At first everything was work, sweat, and darkness. I had no idea when I would reach the light, or even *if* I would. But I persisted. I pounded and clawed and scraped, and finally I was rewarded. I saw a chink of light. And then the chink got bigger and the sun came pouring in and all was bright.

Five grueling nights this took, but it was worth it. I had made a logi- 120 cian out of Polly; I had taught her to think. My job was done. She was worthy of me at last. She was a fit wife for me, a proper hostess for my many mansions, a suitable mother for my well-heeled children.

It must not be thought that I was without love for this girl. Quite the contrary. Just as Pygmalion loved the perfect woman he had fashioned, so I loved mine. I decided to acquaint her with my feelings at our very next meeting. The time had come to change our relationship from academic to romantic.

"Polly," I said when next we sat beneath our oak, "tonight we will not discuss fallacies."

"Aw, gee," she said, disappointed.

"My dear," I said, favoring her with a smile, "we have now spent five evenings together. We have gotten along splendidly. It is clear that we are well matched."

"Hasty Generalization," said Polly brightly. 125

"I beg your pardon," said I.

"Hasty Generalization," she repeated. "How can you say that we are well matched on the basis of only five dates?"

I chuckled with amusement. The dear child had learned her lessons well. "My dear," I said, patting her hand in a tolerant manner, "five dates is plenty. After all, you don't have to eat a whole cake to know that it's good."

"False Analogy," said Polly promptly. "I'm not a cake. I'm a girl."

I chuckled with somewhat less amusement. The dear child had 130 learned her lesson perhaps too well. I decided to change tactics. Obviously the best approach was a simple, strong, direct declaration of love. I paused for a moment while my massive brain chose the proper words. Then I began:

"Polly, I love you. You are the whole world to me, and the moon and the stars and the constellations of outer space. Please, my darling, say that you will go steady with me, for if you will not, life will be meaningless. I will languish. I will refuse my meals. I will wander the face of the earth, a shambling, hollow-eyed hulk."

There, I thought, folding my arms, that ought to do it.

"Ad Misericordiam," said Polly.

I ground my teeth. I was not Pygmalion; I was Frankenstein, and my monster had me by the throat. Frantically I fought back the tide of panic surging through me. At all costs I had to keep cool.

"Well, Polly," I said, forcing a smile, "you certainly have learned 135 your fallacies."

"You're darn right," she said with a vigorous nod.

"And who taught them to you, Polly?"

"You did."

"That's right. So you do owe me something, don't you, my dear? If I hadn't come along you never would have learned about fallacies."

"Hypothesis Contrary to Fact," she said instantly.   140

I dashed perspiration from my brow. "Polly," I croaked, "You mustn't take all these things so literally. I mean this is just classroom stuff. You know that the things you learn in school don't have anything to do with life."

"Dicto Simpliciter," she said, wagging her finger at me playfully.

That did it. I leaped to my feet, bellowing like a bull. "Will you or will you not go steady with me?"

"I will not," she replied.

"Why not?" I demanded.   145

"Because this afternoon I promised Petey Bellows that I would go steady with him."

I reeled back, overcome with the infamy of it. After he promised, after he made a deal, after he shook my hand! "That rat!" I shrieked, kicking up great chunks of turf. "You can't go with him, Polly. He's a liar. He's a cheat. He's a rat."

"Poisoning the Well," said Polly, "and stop shouting. I think shouting must be a fallacy too."

With an immense effort of will, I modulated my voice. "All right," I said. "You're a logician. Let's look at this thing logically. How could you choose Petey Bellows over me? Look at me—a brilliant student, a tremendous intellectual, a man with an assured future. Look at Petey—a knothead, a jitterbug, a guy who'll never know where his next meal is coming from. Can you give me one logical reason why you should go steady with Petey Bellows?"

"I certainly can," declared Polly. "He's got a raccoon coat."   150

Topic for Critical Thinking and Writing

After you have finished reading "Love Is a Fallacy," you may want to write an argumentative essay of 500–750 words on one of the following topics: (1) the story, rightly understood, is not antiwoman; (2) if the story is antiwoman, it is equally antiman; (3) the story is antiwoman but nevertheless belongs in this book; or (4) the story is antiwoman and does not belong in the book.

9

A Psychologist's View:
Rogerian Argument

Carl R. Rogers (1902–1987), perhaps best known for his book entitled *On Becoming a Person* (1961), was a psychotherapist, not a teacher of writing. This short essay by Rogers has, however, exerted much influence on instructors who teach argument. Written in the 1950s, this essay reflects the political climate of the cold war between the United States and the USSR, which dominated headlines for more than forty years (1947–1989). Several of Rogers's examples of bias and frustrated communication allude to the tensions of that era.

On the surface, many arguments seem to show A arguing with B, presumably seeking to change B's mind; but A's argument is really directed not to B but to C. This attempt to persuade a nonparticipant is evident in the courtroom, where neither the prosecutor (A) nor the defense lawyer (B) is really trying to convince the opponent. Rather, both are trying to convince a third party, the jury (C). Prosecutors do not care whether they convince defense lawyers; they don't even mind infuriating defense lawyers, because their only real goal is to convince the jury. Similarly, the writer of a letter to a newspaper, taking issue with an editorial, does not expect to change the paper's policy. Rather, the writer hopes to convince a third party, the reader of the newspaper.

But suppose A really does want to bring B around to A's point of view. Suppose Mary really wants to persuade the teacher to allow her little lamb to stay in the classroom. Rogers points out that when we engage in an argument, if we feel our integrity or our identity is threatened, we will stiffen our position. (The teacher may feel that his or her dignity is compromised by the presence of the lamb, and will scarcely attend to Mary's argument.) The sense of threat may be so great that we are unable to consider the alternative views being offered, and we therefore remain unpersuaded. Threatened, we may defend ourselves rather than our argument, and little communication takes place. Of course a third party might say that we or our opponent presented the more convincing case, but we, and perhaps the opponent, have scarcely listened to each other, and so the two of us remain apart.

Rogers suggests, therefore, that a writer who wishes to communicate with someone (as opposed to convincing a third party) needs to reduce the threat. In a sense, the participants in the argument need to become partners rather than adversaries. Rogers writes, "Mutual communication tends to be pointed toward solving a problem rather than toward attacking a person or group." Thus, an essay on whether schools should test students for use of drugs, need not—and probably should not—see the issue as black or white, *either/or*. Such an essay might indicate that testing is undesirable because it may have bad effects, *but in some circumstances* it may be acceptable. This qualification does not mean that one must compromise. Thus, the essayist might argue that the potential danger to liberty is so great that no circumstances justify testing students for drugs. But even such an essayist should recognize the merit (however limited) of the opposition, and should grant that the position being advanced itself entails great difficulties and dangers.

A writer who wishes to reduce the psychological threat to the opposition, and thus facilitate the partnership in the study of some issue, can do several things: One can show sympathetic understanding of the opposing argument; one can recognize what is valid in it; and one can recognize and demonstrate that those who take the other side are nonetheless persons of goodwill.

Thus a writer who takes Rogers seriously will, usually, in the first part of an argumentative essay

1. state the problem,
2. give the opponent's position, and
3. grant whatever validity the writer finds in that position—for instance, will recognize the circumstances in which the position would indeed be acceptable.

Next, the writer will, if possible,

4. attempt to show how the opposing position will be improved if the writer's own position is accepted.

Sometimes, of course, the differing positions may be so far apart that no reconciliation can be proposed, in which case the writer will probably seek to show how the problem can best be solved by adopting the writer's own position. We have discussed these matters in Chapter 5, but not from the point of view of a psychotherapist, and so we reprint Rogers's essay here.

Carl R. Rogers

Communication:
Its Blocking and Its Facilitation

It may seem curious that a person whose whole professional effort is devoted to psychotherapy should be interested in problems of communication. What relationship is there between providing therapeutic help to individuals with emotional maladjustments and the concern of this conference with obstacles to communication? Actually the relationship is very close indeed. The whole task of psychotherapy is the task of dealing with a failure in communication. The emotionally maladjusted person, the "neurotic," is in difficulty first because communication within himself has broken down, and second because as a result of this his communication with others has been damaged. If this sounds somewhat strange, then let me put it in other terms. In the "neurotic" individual, parts of himself which have been termed unconscious, or repressed, or denied to awareness, become blocked off so that they no longer communicate themselves to the conscious or managing part of himself. As long as this is true, there are distortions in the way he communicates himself to others, and so he suffers both within himself, and in his interpersonal relations. The task of psychotherapy is to help the person achieve, through a special relationship with a therapist, good communication within himself. Once this is achieved he can communicate more freely and more effectively with others. We may say then that psychotherapy is good communication, within and between men. We may also turn that statement around and it will still be true. Good communication, free communication, within or between men, is always therapeutic.

It is, then, from a background of experience with communication in counseling and psychotherapy that I want to present here two ideas. I wish to state what I believe is one of the major factors in blocking or impeding communication, and then I wish to present what in our experience has proven to be a very important way to improving or facilitating communication.

I would like to propose, as an hypothesis for consideration, that the major barrier to mutual interpersonal communication is our very natural tendency to judge, to evaluate, to approve or disapprove, the statement of the person, or the other group. Let me illustrate my meaning with some very simple examples. As you leave the meeting tonight, one of the statements you are likely to hear is, "I didn't like that man's talk." Now what do you respond? Almost invariably your reply will be either approval or disapproval of the attitude expressed. Either you respond, "I didn't either. I thought it was terrible," or else you tend to reply, "Oh, I thought it was really good." In other words, your primary reaction is to evaluate what has just been said to you, to evaluate it from *your* point of view, your own frame of reference.

Or take another example. Suppose I say with some feeling, "I think the Republicans are behaving in ways that show a lot of good sound sense these days," what is the response that arises in your mind as you listen? The overwhelming likelihood is that it will be evaluative. You will find yourself agreeing, or disagreeing, or making some judgment about me such as "He must be a conservative," or "He seems solid in his thinking." Or let us take an illustration from the international scene. Russia says vehemently, "The treaty with Japan is a war plot on the part of the United States." We rise as one person to say "That's a lie!"

This last illustration brings in another element connected with my   5 hypothesis. Although the tendency to make evaluations is common in almost all interchange of language, it is very much heightened in those situations where feelings and emotions are deeply involved. So the stronger our feelings, the more likely it is that there will be no mutual element in the communication. There will be just two ideas, two feelings, two judgments, missing each other in psychological space. I'm sure you recognize this from your own experience. When you have not been emotionally involved yourself, and have listened to a heated discussion, you often go away thinking, "Well, they actually weren't talking about the same thing." And they were not. Each was making a judgment, an evaluation, from his own frame of reference. There was really nothing which could be called communication in any genuine sense. This tendency to react to any emotionally meaningful statement by forming an evaluation of it from our own point of view, is, I repeat, the major barrier to interpersonal communication.

But is there any way of solving this problem, of avoiding this barrier? I feel that we are making exciting progress toward this goal and I would like to present it as simply as I can. Real communication occurs, and this evaluative tendency is avoided, when we listen with understanding. What does that mean? It means *to see the expressed idea and attitude from the other person's point of view, to sense how it feels to him, to achieve his frame of reference in regard to the thing he is talking about.*

Stated so briefly, this may sound absurdly simple, but it is not. It is an approach which we have found extremely potent in the field of psychotherapy. It is the most effective agent we know for altering the basic personality structure of an individual, and improving his relationships and his communications with others. If I can listen to what he can tell me, if I can understand how it seems to him, if I can see its personal meaning for him, if I can sense the emotional flavor which it has for him, then I will be releasing potent forces of change in him. If I can really understand how he hates his father, or hates the university, or hates communists—if I can catch the flavor of his fear of insanity, or his fear of atom bombs, or of Russia—it will be of the greatest help to him in altering those very hatreds and fears, and in establishing realistic and harmonious relationships with the very people and situations toward which he has felt hatred and fear. We know from our research that such empathic understanding—understanding *with* a person, not *about* him—is such an effective approach that it can bring about major changes in personality.

Some of you may be feeling that you listen well to people, and that you have never seen such results. The chances are very great indeed that your listening has not been of the type I have described. Fortunately I can suggest a little laboratory experiment which you can try to test the quality of your understanding. The next time you get into an argument with your wife, or your friend, or with a small group of friends, just stop the discussion for a moment and for an experiment, institute this rule. "Each person can speak up for himself only *after* he has first restated the ideas and feelings of the previous speaker accurately, and to that speaker's satisfaction." You see what this would mean. It would simply mean that before presenting your own point of view, it would be necessary for you to really achieve the other speaker's frame of reference—to understand his thoughts and feelings so well that you could summarize them for him. Sounds simple, doesn't it? But if you try it you will discover it one of the most difficult things you have ever tried to do. However, once you have been able to see the other's point of view, your own comments will have to be drastically revised. You will also find the emotion going out of the discussion, the differences being reduced, and those differences which remain being of a rational and understandable sort.

Can you imagine what this kind of an approach would mean if it were projected into larger areas? What would happen to a labor-management dispute if it was conducted in such a way that labor, without necessarily agreeing, could accurately state management's point of view in a way that management could accept; and management, without approving labor's stand, could state labor's case in a way that labor agreed was accurate? It would mean that real communication was established, and one could practically guarantee that some reasonable solution would be reached.

If then this way of approach is an effective avenue to good communication and good relationships, as I am quite sure you will agree if you try the experiment I have mentioned, why is it not more widely tried and used? I will try to list the difficulties which keep it from being utilized.

In the first place it takes courage, a quality which is not too widespread. I am indebted to Dr. S. I. Hayakawa, the semanticist, for pointing out that to carry on psychotherapy in this fashion is to take a very real risk, and that courage is required. If you really understand another person in this way, if you are willing to enter his private world and see the way life appears to him, without any attempt to make evaluative judgments, you run the risk of being changed yourself. You might see it his way, you might find yourself influenced in your attitudes or your personality. This risk of being changed is one of the most frightening prospects most of us can face. If I enter, as fully as I am able, into the private world of a neurotic or psychotic individual, isn't there a risk that I might become lost in that world? Most of us are afraid to take that risk. Or if we had a Russian communist speaker here tonight, or Senator Joe McCarthy, how many of us would dare to try to see the world from each of these points of view? The great majority of us could not *listen;* we would find ourselves compelled to *evaluate,* because listening would seem too dangerous. So the first requirement is courage, and we do not always have it.

But there is a second obstacle. It is just when emotions are strongest that it is most difficult to achieve the frame of reference of the other person or group. Yet it is the time the attitude is most needed, if communication is to be established. We have not found this to be an insuperable obstacle in our experience in psychotherapy. A third party, who is able to lay aside his own feelings and evaluations, can assist greatly by listening with understanding to each person or group and clarifying the views and attitudes each holds. We have found this very effective in small groups in which contradictory or antagonistic attitudes exist. When the parties to a dispute realize that they are being understood, that someone sees how the situation seems to them, the statements grow less exaggerated and less defensive, and it is no longer necessary to maintain the attitude, "I am 100 percent right and you are 100 percent wrong." The influence of such an understanding catalyst in the group permits the members to come closer and closer to the objective truth involved in the relationship. In this way mutual communication is established and some type of agreement becomes much more possible. So we may say that though heightened emotions make it much more difficult to understand *with* an opponent, our experience makes it clear that a neutral, understanding, catalyst type of leader or therapist can overcome this obstacle in a small group.

This last phrase, however, suggests another obstacle to utilizing the approach I have described. Thus far all our experience has been with small face-to-face groups—groups exhibiting industrial tensions, religious tensions, racial tensions, and therapy groups in which many personal tensions are present. In these small groups our experience, confirmed by a limited amount of research, shows that this basic approach leads to improved communication, to greater acceptance of others and by others, and to attitudes which are more positive and more problem-solving in nature. There is a decrease in defensiveness, in exaggerated statements, in evaluative and critical behavior. But these findings are from small groups. What about trying to achieve understanding between larger groups that are geographically remote? Or between face-to-face groups who are not speaking for themselves, but simply as representatives of others, like the delegates at Kaesong?[1] Frankly we do not know the answers to these questions. I believe the situation might be put this way. As social scientists we have a tentative test-tube solution of the problem of breakdown in communication. But to confirm the validity of this test-tube solution, and to adapt it to the enormous problems of communication breakdown between classes, groups, and nations, would involve additional funds, much more research, and creative thinking of a high order.

Even with our present limited knowledge we can see some steps which might be taken, even in large groups, to increase the amount of listening *with,* and to decrease the amount of evaluation *about.* To be imaginative for a moment, let us suppose that a therapeutically oriented international group went to the Russian leaders and said, "We want to achieve a genuine understanding of your views and even more important, of your attitudes and feelings, toward the United States. We will summarize and resummarize the views and feelings if necessary, until you agree that our description represents the situation as it seems to you." Then suppose they did the same thing with the leaders in our own country. If they then gave the widest possible distribution to these two views, with the feelings clearly described but not expressed in name-calling, might not the effect be very great? It would not guarantee the type of understanding I have been describing, but it would make it much more possible. We can understand the feelings of a person who hates us much more readily when his attitudes are accurately described to us by a neutral third party, than we can when he is shaking his fist at us.

But even to describe such a first step is to suggest another obstacle to this approach of understanding. Our civilization does not yet have enough faith in the social sciences to utilize their findings. The opposite is true of the physical sciences. During the war[2] when a test-tube solution was found to the problem of synthetic rubber, millions of dollars and an army of talent was turned loose on the problem of using that finding. If synthetic rubber could be made in milligrams, it could and would be made in the thousands of tons. And it was. But in the social science realm, if a way is found of facilitating communication and mutual understanding in small groups, there is no guarantee that the finding will be utilized. It may be a generation or more before the money and the brains will be turned loose to exploit that finding.

In closing, I would like to summarize this small-scale solution to the problem of barriers in communication, and to point out certain of its characteristics.

15

---

[1] **the delegates at Kaesong** Representatives of North and South Korea met at the border town of Kaesong to arrange terms for an armistice to hostilities during the Korean War (1950–1953). [All notes are the editors'.]

[2] **the war** World War II.

I have said that our research and experience to date would make it appear that breakdowns in communication, and the evaluative tendency which is the major barrier to communication, can be avoided. The solution is provided by creating a situation in which each of the different parties come to understand the other from the *other's* point of view. This has been achieved, in practice, even when feelings run high, by the influence of a person who is willing to understand each point of view empathically, and who thus acts as a catalyst to precipitate further understanding.

This procedure has important characteristics. It can be initiated by one party, without waiting for the other to be ready. It can even be initiated by a neutral third person, providing he can gain a minimum of cooperation from one of the parties.

This procedure can deal with the insincerities, the defensive exaggerations, the lies, the "false fronts" which characterize almost every failure in communication. These defensive distortions drop away with astonishing speed as people find that the only intent is to understand, not judge.

This approach leads steadily and rapidly toward the discovery of the 20 truth, toward a realistic appraisal of the objective barriers to communication. The dropping of some defensiveness by one party leads to further dropping of defensiveness by the other party, and truth is thus approached.

This procedure gradually achieves mutual communication. Mutual communication tends to be pointed toward solving a problem rather than toward attacking a person or group. It leads to a situation in which I see how the problem appears to you, as well as to me, and you see how it appears to me, as well as to you. Thus accurately and realistically defined, the problem is almost certain to yield to intelligent attack, or if it is in part insoluble, it will be comfortably accepted as such.

This then appears to be a test-tube solution to the breakdown of communication as it occurs in small groups. Can we take this small-scale answer, investigate it further, refine it; develop it and apply it to the tragic and well-nigh fatal failures of communication which threaten the very existence of our modern world? It seems to me that this is a possibility and a challenge which we should explore.

A CHECKLIST FOR ANALYZING ROGERIAN ARGUMENT

✓ Have I stated the problem and indicated that a dialogue is possible?

✓ Have I stated at least one other point of view in a way that would satisfy its proponents?

✓ Have I been courteous to those who hold views other than mine?

✓ Have I enlarged my own understanding, to the extent that I can grant validity, at least in some circumstances, to at least some aspects of other positions?

✓ Have I stated my position and indicated the contexts in which I believe it is valid?

✓ Have I pointed out the ground that we share?

✓ Have I shown how other positions will be strengthened by accepting some aspects of my position?

10

A Lawyer's View: Steps toward Civic Literacy

When John Adams in 1774 said that ours is "a government of law, and not of men," he meant that much of public conduct is regulated, rightly, by principles of law that by general agreement ought to be enforced and that can be altered only by our duly elected representatives, whose power is derived from our consent. In a democracy it is laws, not individuals (for instance, kings or tyrants), that govern. Adams and other early Americans rejected the view attributed to Louis XIV, "I am the state" (*L'état c'est moi*).

But what exactly the law in a given situation is often causes hot debate (as we know from watching the TV news). Whether we are ever personally called on to decide the law—as are legislators, judges, jurors, or lawyers—all of us find our daily lives constantly affected by the law. It is fitting, therefore, even necessary that we develop **civic literacy,** the ability to understand the principles by which our government and its courts operate so that we can act appropriately. (In today's global community, our civic literacy must also include a knowledge of the ways our and others' governments function.)

From the time of Plato's *Apology*, reporting Socrates' trial before the Athenian assembly in 399 B.C. on charges of corrupting the young and preaching false gods, courtroom argument has been a staple of dramatic verbal cut-and-thrust. (Think of popular television shows such as *The Practice* and *Law and Order*.) Probably no profession prides itself more on the ability of its members to argue than does the legal profession. The uninitiated are easily intimidated by the skill with which a lawyer can marshal relevant considerations to support a client's interests. But legal argument is, after all, *argument,* and so its main features are those already discussed in Chapter 3 (such as defin-

ition, assumption, premise, deduction, conclusion, evidence, validity). What is distinctive about legal reasoning is fairly straightforward in all but the most unusual cases.

CIVIL AND CRIMINAL CASES

Legal cases are divided into civil and criminal. In a *civil* case one party (the plaintiff) brings suit against another party (the defendant), claiming that he or she has suffered some wrong at the hands of the defendant and deserves some remedy (for instance, due to a dispute over a property boundary or over fault in a multicar accident). The judge or jury decides for or against the plaintiff based on the evidence and the relevant law. All crimes are wrongs, but not all wrongs are crimes. For instance, an automobile accident that involves negligence on the part of one of the drivers and results in harm to another is surely a wrong, but the driver responsible for the accident, even if found guilty, does not face a prison sentence (that could happen only if the accident were in fact the result of driving with gross recklessness, or driving while intoxicated, or were no "accident" at all). Why? Because the harm inflicted was not criminal; that is, it was not intentional, deliberate, malicious, or premeditated.

Criminal cases involve someone (the defendant) charged either with a *felony* (a serious crime like assault or battery) or with a *misdemeanor* (a less serious crime, as in *Texas v. Johnson*, p. 316). In criminal cases the state, through its prosecutor, seeks to convict the defendant as charged; the defendant, through his or her attorney, seeks an acquittal or, at worst, a conviction on a lesser charge (manslaughter instead of murder) and a milder punishment. The decision to convict or acquit on the basis of the facts submitted in evidence and the relevant law is the duty of the jury (or the judge, if there is no jury). The prosecutor and defense lawyer present what they believe are the relevant facts. Defining the relevant law is the responsibility of the trial judge. Public interest in criminal cases is often high, especially when the crime is particularly heinous. (Think of the 1995 trial of O. J. Simpson, charged with the murder of his wife and one of her friends, and the 1997 trial of Timothy McVeigh for the Oklahoma City federal building bombing.)

As you begin reading a legal case, therefore, you will want to be sure you can answer this question:

- Is the court trying to decide whether someone accused of a crime is guilty as charged, or is the court trying to resolve some non-criminal (civil) dispute?

TRIAL AND APPEAL

Most cases (civil or criminal) never go to *trial* at all. Most civil cases are settled out of court, and most criminal cases are settled with a plea bargain in which the prosecutor and the defense attorney persuade the judge to accept the defendant's guilty plea in exchange for a less severe sentence. Of the cases that are settled by trial, the losing party usually does not try to reopen, or *appeal*, the case. If, however, the losing party believes that he or she should have won, the case may be appealed for review by a higher appellate court (provided, of course, the loser can finance the appeal). The party bringing the appeal (the appellant) typically argues that because the relevant law was misstated or misapplied during the trial, the decision must be reversed and a new trial ordered. On rare occasion the issue in dispute is appealed all the way to the highest court in the nation—the U.S. Supreme Court—for a final decision. (The cases we reprint for discussion in this book are all cases decided by the Supreme Court.)

A pair of useful questions to answer as you work your way through a reported case are these:

- What are the events that give rise to the legal controversy in this case?

- What are the intermediate steps the case went through before reaching the final court of appeal?

DECISION AND OPINION

With rare exceptions, only cases decided by the appellate courts are *reported*, that is, written up and published. A reported case consists of two very different elements: (1) the court's decision, or *holding* and (2) the court's *opinion* in support of its decision. Typically, a court's decision can be stated in a sentence; it amounts to the conclusion of the court's argument. The opinion, however, is more complex and lengthy; as with most arguments, the premises of judicial reasoning and their linkages with each other involve several steps.

To illustrate, in *Texas v. Johnson* (p. 316), the Supreme Court considered a Texas statute that made it a crime to burn the American flag in political protest. The Court decided that the statute was an unconstitutional interference with freedom of speech. (The decision, as you see, can be stated concisely.)

The Court's opinion, however, runs to several pages. The gist is this: The purpose of the First Amendment (reprinted on p. 316) prohibiting abridgment of speech by the government is to protect personal expression, especially where there is a political intention or significance to the speech. Previous decisions of the Court interpreting the amendment have established that the protection of "speech" applies also to nonverbal acts; flag burning in political protest is such an act. Under certain conditions the state may regulate "speech," but in no case may the state prohibit "speech" because of its content or meaning. The Texas statute did not merely regulate the circumstances of "speech"; rather, it regulated the content or meaning of the "speech." Therefore, the statute is unconstitutional.

Thus, in reading the report of a decided case, you will want to be able to answer these two questions:

- What did the court decide?
- What reasons did the court offer to justify its decision?

MAJORITY, CONCURRING, AND DISSENTING OPINIONS

Not all appellate court decisions are unanimous ones. A court's *majority opinion* contains the ruling and reasoning of a majority of its judges. In *Texas v. Johnson*, for example, Justice William Brennan wrote the majority opinion in which four of his colleagues joined. Occasionally one or more of the judges in the majority files a *concurring opinion*; in such cases the judge agrees with the majority's decision but disagrees with its reasoning. Justice John Paul Stevens wrote a concurring opinion in *Johnson*.

In any appellate court decision, at least one judge is likely to dissent from the majority opinion and file a *dissenting opinion* explaining why. (Throughout this book we make the point that intelligent, honorable people may differ on issues of importance.) In the *Johnson* case, four judges dissented but joined in one dissenting opinion. Minority opinions have much to offer for reflection, and in many instances today's dissenting opinion becomes tomorrow's law. The most famous example is Justice John Marshall Harlan's solitary dissent in *Plessy v. Ferguson* (1896), the case that upheld "separate but equal" racial segregation; Harlan's dissent was eventually vindicated by a unanimous vote of the Supreme Court in *Brown v. Board of Education* (1954).

Thus, where there are majority, concurring, and minority opinions, you will want to think about these questions:

- On what issues do the majority and concurring opinions agree?
- On what issues do they disagree?
- Where does the minority in its dissenting opinion(s) disagree with the majority?
- Which opinion is more convincing, the majority or the minority?

FACTS AND LAW

Every court's decision is based on the relevant facts and the relevant law. What the relevant facts are is often in dispute at the trial but not on appeal; appellate court judges rarely reexamine the facts as decided by the trial court. The appellate court, however, usually restates the relevant facts in the opening paragraphs of its opinion. An old joke told among lawyers is appropriate here: "Argue the facts if the facts are on your side, argue the law if the law is on your side; if neither the law nor the facts are on your side, pound the table!"

Unfortunately, a sharp distinction between facts and law cannot always be maintained. For example, if we describe the defendant's conduct as "careless," is that a matter of fact? Or is it in part a matter of law, because "careless" conduct may also be judged "negligent" conduct, and the law defines what counts as negligence?

As you read through the reported case, keep in mind these two questions:

- What are the relevant facts in the case, insofar as they can be determined by what the appellate court reported?
- Are there issues of fact omitted or ignored by the appellate court that, had they been addressed, might have shed light on the decision?

For instance, consider a case in which a cattle rancher finds one of her cows dead after it collided with a railroad train. She decides to sue for negligence, wins, and the defendant (the railroad company) appeals. Why did she sue the railroad in the first place, rather than the engineer of the train that killed her cow? Suppose the appellate court's opinion fails to mention whether there was a fence at the edge of the field to keep her cattle off the tracks; wouldn't that be relevant to deciding whether she was partly at fault for the accident? (Ought the railroad to have erected a fence on its property parallel to the track?) Information about such facts could well shed light on the strength and correctness of the court's opinion and decision.

Appellate court judges are almost entirely preoccupied with what they believe is the relevant law to deciding the case at hand. The law can come in any of several different forms: common law principles ("No one may enlist the courts to assist him in profiting from his own wrong"), statutes enacted by a legislature ("As of January 1, 1998, income taxes shall be levied according to the following formula . . ."), ordinances enacted by a town council ("Dogs must be leashed in public places"), a precedent found in a prior case decided by some appellate court ("The decision in the case before us is governed by the Supreme Court's earlier holding in . . ."), executive orders ("All persons of Japanese extraction currently resident in California shall be removed inland to a relocation center"), administrative regulations ("Milk shipped interstate must have a butterfat content not less than . . ."), as well as constitutional interpretations ("Statements critical of a public official but not malicious or uttered by one who knows they are false are not libelous and are permitted under the First Amendment"). Not all laws are of equal weight; as *Texas v. Johnson* shows, a state statute inconsistent with the federal Bill of Rights will be nullified, not the other way around.

Appellate court judges devote much of their attention to **interpretation,** trying to decide exactly what the relevant statute, regulation, or prior decision really means and whether it applies to the case before the court. For example, does a local ordinance prohibiting "four-wheeled vehicles" in the park apply to a nanny pushing a baby carriage? The answer often turns on what was the *purpose* of the law or the *intention* of the lawmaker.

It is not easy to decide what the lawmakers' **intention** was; lawmakers are rarely available to state for the courts what their intention was. Can we confidently infer what a legislature's intention was from the legislative history left behind in the form of debates or hearings? From what the relevant committee chairperson says it was? What if (as is typically true) the legislature never declared its intentions when it enacted a law? When a legislature creates a statute, do all those who vote for it act with the same intention? If not, which of the many intentions involved should dominate? How do we find out what those intentions were? What counts as relevant evidence for ascribing this rather than that as someone's intention?

Accordingly, as you read a reported legal case, your study of the court's opinion should lead you to ask such questions as this:

- Exactly what law or laws is the court trying to interpret?
- What evidence does the court cite in favor of its interpretation?

BALANCING INTERESTS

In Supreme Court cases, the decision often turns on how competing interests are to be *balanced* or weighed. This pattern of reasoning is especially relevant when one of the conflicting interests is apparently protected by the Constitution. The majority opinion in *New Jersey v. T.L.O.* (1985) (p. 332) is a good example of such balancing; there, the privacy interests of high school students are weighed (metaphorically speaking, of course—no one can literally "weigh" or "balance" anyone's interests) against the competing interest of school officials responsible for maintaining an orderly environment for teaching. The Court decided that the latter ought to prevail and concluded that "reasonable" searches are not forbidden under the Fourth Amendment's prohibition of "unreasonable searches and seizures."

This leads directly to several other questions you will want to try to answer in the legal cases you study:

- In a constitutional case, what are the conflicting interests?
- How does the Supreme Court propose to balance them?
- Why does it strike the balance one way rather than the other?

A WORD OF CAUTION

Lawyers are both officers of the court and champions for their clients' causes. In the first role they share with judges and other officials the duty to seek justice by honorable means. But in the second role lawyers often see their job as one in which they ought to bend every rule as far as they can in pursuit of their clients' interests (after all, it is the client who pays the bills). This attitude is nicely conveyed in the title of a recent book, *How to Argue and Win Every Time* (1995), by Gerry Spence, one of the nation's leading trial lawyers. And it is reinforced by a comment from defense attorney Alan Dershowitz: "All sides in a trial want to hide at least some of the truth."

Yet it would be wrong to see lawyers as motivated only by a ruthless desire to win at any cost. Lawyers have a civic duty to present their clients' cases in the most favorable light and to challenge whatever evidence and testimony is offered in court against them. (If you were hiring a lawyer to defend you, would you settle for anything less?) In a society such as ours—a society of law rather than of powerful individuals—it is right that accused persons be found guilty as charged only after the strongest defenses have been mounted.

To be sure, everyone concerned to argue on behalf of any claim, whether in or out of court, whether as a lawyer or in some other capacity, ought to take the challenge seriously. But it is too much to hope to "win every time"—and in fact winning is not the only, much less the highest, goal. Sometimes the other side does have the better argument, and in such cases we should be willing, indeed eager, to see the merits and to enlarge our minds.

In any case, in this book we think of argument not as a weapon for use in mortal combat but as a device for exploring the controversy or dispute under discussion, a tool for isolating the issues in contention and for helping in the evaluation of different possible outcomes. We expect you will use argument to persuade your audience to accept your views, just as a lawyer typically does; but we hope you will use argument sometimes—even often—to clarify your ideas *for yourself;* when you develop arguments for effective presentation to your colleagues and associates, you will probably improve the quality of your ideas.

A CHECKLIST FOR ANALYZING LEGAL ARGUMENTS

✓ Is the court trying to decide whether someone accused of a crime is guilty as charged, or is the court trying to resolve some noncriminal (civil) dispute?

✓ What events gave rise to the legal controversy in this case?

✓ What intermediate steps did the case go through before reaching the final court of appeal?

✓ What did the court decide?

✓ What reasons did the court offer to justify its decision?

✓ On what issues do the majority and concurring opinions agree?

✓ On what issues do they disagree?

✓ Where does the minority in its dissenting opinion(s) disagree with the majority?

✓ Which opinion is more convincing, the majority or the minority?

✓ What are the relevant facts in the case, insofar as they can be determined by what the appellate court reported?

✓ Are there issues of fact omitted or ignored by the appellate court that, had they been addressed, might have shed light on the decision?

✓ Exactly what law or laws is the court trying to interpret?

✓ What evidence does the court cite in favor of its interpretation?

✓ In constitutional cases, what are the conflicting interests?

✓ How does the Supreme Court propose to balance them?

✓ Why does it strike the balance one way rather than the other?

A CASEBOOK ON
THE LAW AND SOCIETY:
What Rights Do the
First and Fourth
Amendments Protect?

William J. Brennan, Jr. and
William H. Rehnquist

William J. Brennan, Jr. (1906–1990), appointed to the Supreme Court in 1956 by President Dwight D. Eisenhower, established himself as a strong supporter of individual liberties. William H. Rehnquist (b. 1924), appointed in 1971 by President Richard M. Nixon because of his emphasis on law and order, came to be regarded as the most conservative member of the Court.

Texas v. Johnson (1989) concerns the right to burn the American flag in political protest. (Recall that the First Amendment to the Constitution holds that "Congress shall make no law respecting an establishment of religion, or prohibiting the free exercise thereof; or abridging the freedom of speech, or of the press; or the right of the people peaceably to assemble, and to petition the government for a redress of grievances.") The case was decided by a vote of 5 to 4. Immediately after the Court's decision was announced, a resolution was drafted and filed in Congress to condemn the Court's decision. Also filed was the Flag Protection Act of 1989, making it a criminal offense to "knowingly mutilate, deface, burn, or trample upon" the flag. Another bill was designed to amend the Constitution so that criminal penalties for desecration of the flag would not violate the First Amendment. As of the spring of 1998, none of these bills has left the congressional committees charged with examining them. In the excerpt that follows, legal citations have been deleted and portions of the text omitted.

Texas v. Johnson

Associate Justice Brennan delivered the opinion of the Court.

After publicly burning an American flag as a means of political protest, Gregory Lee Johnson was convicted of desecrating a flag in violation of Texas law. This case presents the question whether his conviction is consistent with the First Amendment. We hold that it is not.

I

While the Republican National Convention was taking place in Dallas in 1984, respondent Johnson participated in a political demonstration dubbed the "Republican War Chest Tour." As explained in literature distributed by the demonstrators and in speeches made by them, the purpose of this event was to protest the policies of the Reagan administration and of certain Dallas-based corporations. The demonstrators marched through the Dallas streets, chanting political slogans and stopping at several corporate locations to stage "die-ins" intended to dramatize the consequences of nuclear war. On several occasions they spraypainted the walls of buildings and overturned potted plants, but Johnson himself took no part in such activities. He did, however, accept an American flag handed to him by a fellow protestor who had taken it from a flag pole outside one of the targeted buildings.

The demonstration ended in front of Dallas City Hall, where Johnson unfurled the American flag, doused it with kerosene, and set it on fire. While the flag burned, the protestors chanted, "America, the red, white, and blue, we spit on you." After the demonstrators dispersed, a witness to the flag burning collected the flag's remains and buried them in his backyard. No one was physically injured or threatened with injury, though several witnesses testified that they had been seriously offended by the flag burning.

Of the approximately 100 demonstrators, Johnson alone was charged with a crime. The only criminal offense with which he was charged was the desecration of a venerated object in violation of Tex. Penal Code Ann.[1] After a trial, he was convicted, sentenced to one year in prison, and fined $2,000. The Court of Appeals for the Fifth District of Texas at Dallas affirmed Johnson's conviction, but the Texas Court of Criminal Appeals reversed, holding that the state could not, consistent with the First Amendment, punish Johnson for burning the flag in these circumstances. . . .

II

. . . The First Amendment literally forbids the abridgement only of   5 "speech," but we have long recognized that its protection does not end at the spoken or written word. While we have rejected "the view that an apparently limitless variety of conduct can be labeled 'speech' whenever the person engaging in the conduct intends thereby to express an idea," we have acknowledged that conduct may be "sufficiently imbued with the elements of communication to fall within the scope of the First and Fourteenth Amendments." . . .

---

[1]Tex. Penal Code Ann. §42.09 (1989) ["Desecration of a Venerated Object"] provides in full:

"(a) A person commits an offense if he intentionally or knowingly desecrates: (1) a public monument; (2) a place of worship or burial; or (3) a state or national flag.

"(b) For purposes of this section, 'desecrate' means deface, damage, or otherwise physically mistreat in a way that the actor knows will seriously offend one or more persons likely to observe or discover his action.

"(c) An offense under this section is a Class A misdemeanor." [Court's note.]

IV

It remains to consider whether the state's interest in preserving the flag as a symbol of nationhood and national unity justifies Johnson's conviction.

As in *Spence* [*v. Washington*], "we are confronted with a case of prosecution for the expression of an idea through activity," and "accordingly, we must examine with particular care the interests advanced by [petitioner] to support its prosecution." Johnson was not, we add, prosecuted for the expression of just any idea; he was prosecuted for his expression of dissatisfaction with the policies of this country, expression situated at the core of our First Amendment values.

Moreover, Johnson was prosecuted because he knew that his politically charged expression would cause "serious offense." If he had burned the flag as a means of disposing of it because it was dirty or torn, he would not have been convicted of flag desecration under this Texas law: Federal law designates burning as the preferred means of disposing of a flag "when it is in such condition that it is no longer a fitting emblem for display," and Texas has no quarrel with this means of disposal. The Texas law is thus not aimed at protecting the physical integrity of the flag in all circumstances, but is designed instead to protect it only against impairments that would cause serious offense to others. Texas concedes as much: "Section 42.09(b) reaches only those severe acts of physical abuse of the flag carried out in a way likely to be offensive. The statute mandates intentional or knowing abuse, that is, the kind of mistreatment that is not innocent, but rather is intentionally designed to seriously offend other individuals."

Whether Johnson's treatment of the flag violated Texas law thus depended on the likely communicative impact of his expressive conduct. Our decision in *Boos v. Barry* tells us that this restriction on Johnson's expression is content based. In *Boos,* we considered the constitutionality of a law prohibiting "the display of any sign within 500 feet of a foreign embassy if that sign tends to bring that foreign government into 'public odium' or 'public disrepute.'" Rejecting the argument that the law was content neutral because it was justified by "our international law obligation to shield diplomats from speech that offends their dignity," we held that "the emotive impact of speech on its audience is not a 'secondary effect'" unrelated to the content of the expression itself. . . .

Texas argues that its interest in preserving the flag as a symbol of nationhood and national unity survives this close analysis. Quoting extensively from the writings of this Court chronicling the flag's historic and symbolic role in our society, the state emphasizes the "'special place'" reserved for the flag in our nation. The state's argument is not that it has an interest simply in maintaining the flag as a symbol of something, no matter what it symbolizes; indeed, if that were the state's position, it   10 would be difficult to see how that interest is endangered by highly symbolic conduct such as Johnson's. Rather, the state's claim is that it has an interest in preserving the flag as a symbol of *nationhood* and *national unity*, a symbol with a determinate range of meanings. According to Texas, if one physically treats the flag in a way that would tend to cast doubt on either the idea that nationhood and national unity are the flag's referents or that national unity actually exists, the message conveyed thereby is a harmful one and therefore may be prohibited.

If there is a bedrock principle underlying the First Amendment, it is that the government may not prohibit the expression of an idea simply because society finds the idea itself offensive or disagreeable.

We have not recognized an exception to this principle even where our flag has been involved. In *Street v. New York,* we held that a state may not criminally punish a person for uttering words critical of the flag. Rejecting the argument that the conviction could be sustained on the ground that Street had "failed to show the respect for our national symbol which may properly be demanded of every citizen," we concluded that "the constitutionally guaranteed 'freedom to be intellectually . . . diverse or even contrary,' and the 'right to differ as to things that touch the heart of the existing order,' encompass the freedom to express publicly one's opinions about our flag, including those opinions which are defiant or contemptuous." Nor may the government, we have held, compel conduct that would evince respect for the flag. "To sustain the compulsory flag salute we are required to say that a Bill of Rights which guards the individual's right to speak his own mind, left it open to public authorities to compel him to utter what is not in his mind." . . .

Texas's focus on the precise nature of Johnson's expression, moreover, misses the point of our prior decisions: their enduring lesson, that the government may not prohibit expression simply because it disagrees with its message, is not dependent on the particular mode in which one chooses to express an idea. If we were to hold that a state may forbid flag burning wherever it is likely to endanger the flag's symbolic role, but allow it wherever burning a flag promotes that role—as where, for example, a person ceremoniously burns a dirty flag—we would be saying that when it comes to impairing the flag's physical integrity, the flag itself may be used as a symbol—as a substitute for the written or spoken word or a "short cut from mind to mind"—only in one direction. We would be permitting a state to "prescribe what shall be orthodox" by saying that one may burn the flag to convey one's attitude toward it and its referents only if one does not endanger the flag's representation of nationhood and national unity.

We never before have held that the government may ensure that a symbol be used to express only one view of that symbol or its referents. Indeed, in *Schacht v. United States*, we invalidated a federal statute permitting an actor portraying a member of one of our armed forces to "'wear the uniform of that armed force if the portrayal does not tend to discredit that armed force.'" This proviso, we held, "which leaves Americans free to praise the war in Vietnam but can send persons like Schacht to prison for opposing it, cannot survive in a country which has the First Amendment."

We perceive no basis on which to hold that the principle underlying 15 our decision in *Schacht* does not apply to this case. To conclude that the government may permit designated symbols to be used to communicate only a limited set of messages would be to enter territory having no discernible or defensible boundaries. Could the government, on this theory, prohibit the burning of state flags? Of copies of the presidential seal? Of the Constitution? In evaluating these choices under the First Amendment, how would we decide which symbols were sufficiently special to warrant this unique status? To do so, we would be forced to consult our own political preferences, and impose them on the citizenry, in the very way that the First Amendment forbids us to do.

There is, moreover, no indication—either in the text of the Constitution or in our cases interpreting it—that a separate juridical category exists for the American flag alone. Indeed, we would not be surprised to learn that the persons who framed our Constitution and wrote the Amendment that we now construe were not known for their reverence for the Union Jack. The First Amendment does not guarantee that other concepts virtually sacred to our nation as a whole—such as the principle that discrimination on the basis of race is odious and destructive—will go unquestioned in the marketplace of ideas. We decline, therefore, to create for the flag an exception to the joust of principles protected by the First Amendment.

It is not the state's ends, but its means, to which we object. It cannot be gainsaid that there is a special place reserved for the flag in this nation, and thus we do not doubt that the government has a legitimate interest in making efforts to "preserve the national flag as an unalloyed symbol of our country." We reject the suggestion, urged at oral argument by counsel for Johnson, that the government lacks "any state interest whatsoever" in regulating the manner in which the flag may be displayed. Congress has, for example, enacted precatory regulations describing the proper treatment of the flag, and we cast no doubt on the legitimacy of its interest in making such recommendations. To say that the government has an interest in encouraging proper treatment of the flag, however, is not to say that it may criminally punish a person for burning a flag as a means of political protest. "National unity as an end which officials may foster by persuasion and example is not in question. The problem is whether under our Constitution compulsion as here employed is a permissible means for its achievement." . . .

We are tempted to say, in fact, that the flag's deservedly cherished place in our community will be strengthened, not weakened, by our holding today. Our decision is a reaffirmation of the principles of freedom and inclusiveness that the flag best reflects, and of the conviction that our toleration of criticism such as Johnson's is a sign and source of our strength. Indeed, one of the proudest images of our flag, the one immortalized in our own national anthem, is of the bombardment it survived at Fort McHenry. It is the nation's resilience, not its rigidity, that Texas sees reflected in the flag—and it is that resilience that we reassert today.

The way to preserve the flag's special role is not to punish those who feel differently about these matters. It is to persuade them that they are wrong. "To courageous, self-reliant men, with confidence in the power of free and fearless reasoning applied through the processes of popular government, no danger flowing from speech can be deemed clear and present, unless the incidence of the evil apprehended is so imminent that it may befall before there is opportunity for full discussion. If there be time to expose through discussion the falsehood and fallacies, to avert the evil by the processes of education, the remedy to be applied is more speech, not enforced silence." And, precisely because it is our flag that is involved, one's response to the flag burner may exploit the uniquely persuasive power of the flag itself. We can imagine no more appropriate response to burning a flag than waving one's own, no better way to counter a flag burner's message than by saluting the flag that burns, no surer means of preserving the dignity even of the flag that burned than by—as one witness here did—according its remains a respectful burial. We do not consecrate the flag by punishing its desecration, for in doing so we dilute the freedom that this cherished emblem represents. . . .

Chief Justice Rehnquist dissented.

. . . Both Congress and the states have enacted numerous laws regu-   20
lating misuse of the American flag. Until 1967, Congress left the regulation of misuse of the flag up to the states. Now, however, Title 18 U.S.C. §700(a) provides that:

> Whoever knowingly casts contempt upon any flag of the United States by publicly mutilating, defacing, defiling, burning, or trampling upon it shall be fined not more than $1,000 or imprisoned for not more than one year, or both.

Congress has also prescribed, inter alia, detailed rules for the design of the flag, the time and occasion of flag's display, the position and manner of its display, respect for the flag, and conduct during hoisting, lowering, and passing of the flag. With the exception of Alaska and Wyoming, all of the states now have statutes prohibiting the burning of the flag. Most of the state statutes are patterned after the Uniform Flag Act of 1917, which in §3 provides: "No person shall publicly mutilate, deface, defile, defy, trample upon, or by word or act cast contempt upon any such flag, standard, color, ensign or shield." Most were passed by the states at about the time of World War I. . . .

The American flag, then, throughout more than two hundred years of our history, has come to be the visible symbol embodying our nation. It does not represent the views of any particular political party, and it does not represent any particular political philosophy. The flag is not simply another "idea" or "point of view" competing for recognition in the marketplace of ideas. Millions and millions of Americans regard it with an almost mystical reverence regardless of what sort of social, political, or philosophical beliefs they may have. I cannot agree that the First Amendment invalidates the act of Congress, and the laws of forty-eight of the fifty states, which make criminal the public burning of the flag.

More than eighty years ago in *Halter v. Nebraska*, this Court upheld the constitutionality of a Nebraska statute that forbade the use of representations of the American flag for advertising purposes upon articles of merchandise. The Court there said:

> For that flag every true American has not simply an appreciation but a deep affection. . . . Hence, it has often occurred that insults to a flag have been the cause of war, and indignities put upon it, in the presence of those who revere it, have often been resented and sometimes punished on the spot. . . .

But the Court insists that the Texas statute prohibiting the public burning of the American flag infringes on respondent Johnson's freedom of expression. Such freedom, of course, is not absolute. In *Chaplinsky v. New Hampshire*, a unanimous Court said:

> Allowing the broadest scope to the language and purpose of the Fourteenth Amendment, it is well understood that the right of free speech is not absolute at all times and under all circumstances. There are certain well-defined and narrowly limited classes of speech, the prevention and punishment of which have never been thought to raise any Constitutional problem. These include the lewd and obscene, the profane, the libelous, and the insulting or 'fighting' words—those which by their very utterance inflict injury or tend to incite an immediate breach of the peace. It has been well observed that such utterances are no essential part of any exposition of ideas, and are of such slight social value as a step to truth that any benefit that may be derived from them is clearly outweighed by the social interest in order and morality. . . .

The result of the Texas statute is obviously to deny one in Johnson's frame of mind one of many means of "symbolic speech." Far from being a case of "one picture being worth a thousand words," flag burning is the equivalent of an inarticulate grunt or roar that, it seems fair to say, is most likely to be indulged in not to express any particular idea, but to antagonize others. . . . The Texas statute deprived Johnson of only one rather inarticulate symbolic form of protest—a form of protest that was profoundly offensive to many—and left him with a full panoply of other symbols and every conceivable form of verbal expression to express his deep disapproval of national policy. Thus, in no way can it be said that Texas is punishing him because his hearers—or any other group of people—were profoundly opposed to the message that he sought to convey. Such opposition is no proper basis for restricting speech or expression under the First Amendment. It was Johnson's use of this particular symbol, and not the idea that he sought to convey by it or by his many other expressions, for which he was punished.

Our prior cases dealing with flag desecration statutes have left open 25 the question that the Court resolves today. In *Street v. New York*, the defendant burned a flag in the street, shouting "We don't need no damned flag" and, "if they let that happen to Meredith we don't need an American flag." The Court ruled that since the defendant might have been convicted solely on the basis of his words, the conviction could not stand, but it expressly reserved the question whether a defendant could constitutionally be convicted for burning the flag. . . .

In *Spence v. Washington*, the Court reversed the conviction of a college student who displayed the flag with a peace symbol affixed to it by means of removable black tape from the window of his apartment. Unlike the instant case, there was no risk of a breach of the peace, no one other than the arresting officers saw the flag, and the defendant owned the flag in question. The Court concluded that the student's conduct was protected under the First Amendment, because "no interest the state may have in preserving the physical integrity of a privately owned flag was significantly impaired on these facts." The Court was careful to note, however, that the defendant "was not charged under the desecration statute, nor did he permanently disfigure the flag or destroy it."

In another related case, *Smith v. Goguen*, the appellee, who wore a small flag on the seat of his trousers, was convicted under a Massachusetts flag-misuse statute that subjected to criminal liability anyone who "publicly . . . treats contemptuously the flag of the United States." The Court affirmed the lower court's reversal of appellee's conviction, because the phrase "treats contemptuously" was unconstitutionally broad and vague. The Court was again careful to point out that "certainly nothing prevents a legislature from defining with substantial specificity what constitutes forbidden treatment of United States flags." ("The flag is a national property, and the Nation may regulate those who would make, imitate, sell, possess, or use it. I would not question those statutes which proscribe mutilation, defacement, or burning of the flag or which otherwise protect its physical integrity, without regard to whether such conduct might provoke violence. . . . There would seem to be little question about the power of Congress to forbid the mutilation of the Lincoln Memorial. . . . The flag is itself a monument, subject to similar protection"); ("Goguen's punishment was constitutionally permissible for harming the physical integrity of the flag by wearing it affixed to the seat of his pants").

But the Court today will have none of this. The uniquely deep awe and respect for our flag felt by virtually all of us are bundled off under the rubric of "designated symbols" that the First Amendment prohibits the government from "establishing." But the government has not "established" this feeling; two hundred years of history have done that. The government is simply recognizing as a fact the profound regard for the American flag created by that history when it enacts statutes prohibiting the disrespectful public burning of the flag.

The Court concludes its opinion with a regrettably patronizing civics lecture, presumably addressed to the members of both houses of Congress, the members of the forty-eight state legislatures that enacted prohibitions against flag burning, and the troops fighting under that flag in Vietnam who objected to its being burned: "The way to preserve the flag's special role is not to punish those who feel differently about these matters. It is to persuade them that they are wrong." The Court's role as the final expositor of the Constitution is well established, but its role as a platonic guardian admonishing those responsible to public opinion as if they were truant school children has no similar place in our system of government. The cry of "no taxation without representation" animated those who revolted against the English Crown to found our nation — the idea that those who submitted to government should have some say as to what kind of laws would be passed. Surely one of the high purposes of a democratic society is to legislate against conduct that is regarded as evil and profoundly offensive to the majority of people — whether it be murder, embezzlement, pollution, or flag burning.

Our Constitution wisely places limits on powers of legislative majori- 30 ties to act, but the declaration of such limits by this Court "is, at all times, a question of much delicacy, which ought seldom, if ever, to be decided in the affirmative, in a doubtful case." Uncritical extension of constitutional protection to the burning of the flag risks the frustration of the very purpose for which organized governments are instituted. The Court decides that the American flag is just another symbol, about which not only must opinions pro and con be tolerated, but for which the most minimal public respect may not be enjoined. The government may conscript men into the armed forces where they must fight and perhaps die for the flag, but the government may not prohibit the public burning of the banner under which they fight. I would uphold the Texas statute as applied in this case.

Topics for Critical Thinking and Writing

1. State the facts of this case describing Johnson's illegal conduct and the events in court, beginning with his arrest and culminating in the decision of the Supreme Court.

2. What does Justice Brennan state are the interests in conflict?

3. Why does Brennan (para. 10) describe Johnson's conduct as "highly symbolic"? What would count as less symbolic, or nonsymbolic, conduct having the same purpose as flag burning?

4. Chief Justice Rehnquist suggests (para. 24) that Johnson's flag burning is "equivalent" to "an inarticulate grunt or roar," with the intention "not to express any particular idea, but to antagonize others." Explain why you agree or disagree with these judgments.

5. Brennan cites the prior cases of *Street v. New York* and *Schacht v. United States* in his favor; Rehnquist cites several cases supporting his dissenting opinion. Which of these precedents (if any) do you find most relevant to the proper outcome of this case, and why?

6. Would it be a desecration of the flag to print the Stars and Stripes on paper towels to be sold for Fourth of July picnics? On toilet paper? Write a 250-word essay on the topic: "Desecration of the Flag: What It Is and What It Isn't."

7. In paragraph 15, Brennan uses a version of the slippery slope argument (see p. 285) in support of striking down the Texas statute. Explain whether you think this argument is effective and relevant.

8. In First Amendment cases, it is often said that the government may not restrict "speech" because of its "content," but it may be restricted in the "time, place, and manner" of expression. What might be plausible restrictions of these sorts on flag burning for political purposes?

John Marshall Harlan
and Harry A. Blackmun

During the 1960s, draft-age men often protested against the Selective Service System on grounds that it was administered unfairly and that it was being used to provide troops to fight an unjust war in Vietnam. Protest took varied forms, including civil disobedience and violent resistance. Peaceful objections were far more frequent, but in some cases it was hard to tell whether the protest was lawful or not. The conduct of Paul Robert Cohen is one of these borderline cases. Cohen was convicted in 1968 in Los Angeles of a misdemeanor for behaving in a manner that violated a California statute forbidding "tumultuous or offensive conduct." Cohen argued that his conduct was protected by the U.S. Constitution as an act of "free speech," but the California Court of Appeals disagreed and upheld his conviction. He appealed to the U.S. Supreme Court and won by a vote of 6 to 3. Excerpted here is the majority opinion, written by Associate Justice John Marshall Harlan (1899–1971), one of the most respected jurists to sit on the Court during the past generation. The facts of the case are briefly set out by Harlan in his opening paragraphs. We also reprint the main argument of the brief dissenting opinion, written by Associate Justice Harry A. Blackmun (b. 1908). Legal citations have been omitted.

Cohen v. California

Justice Harlan delivered the opinion of the Court.

This case may seem at first blush too inconsequential to find its way into our books, but the issue it presents is of no small constitutional significance.

Appellant Paul Robert Cohen was convicted in the Los Angeles Municipal Court of violating that part of California Penal Code §415 which prohibits "maliciously and willfully disturb[ing] the peace or quiet of any neighborhood or person, . . . by . . . offensive conduct. . . ." He was given thirty days' imprisonment. The facts upon which his conviction rests are detailed in the opinion of the Court of Appeal of California, Second Appellate District, as follows:

> On April 26, 1968 the defendant was observed in the Los Angeles County Courthouse in the corridor outside of Division 20 of the Municipal Court wearing a jacket bearing the words "Fuck the Draft" which were plainly visible. There were women and children present in the corridor. The defendant was arrested. The defendant testified that he wore the jacket as a means of informing the public of the depth of his feelings against the Vietnam War and the draft.
>
> The defendant did not engage in, nor threaten to engage in, nor did anyone as the result of his conduct in fact commit or threaten to commit any act of violence. The defendant did not make any loud or unusual noise, nor was there any evidence that he uttered any sound prior to his arrest.

In affirming the conviction the Court of Appeal held that "offensive conduct" means "behavior which has a tendency to provoke *others* to acts of violence or to in turn disturb the peace," and that the state had proved this element because, on the facts of this case, "[i]t was certainly reasonably foreseeable that such conduct might cause others to rise up to commit a violent act against the person of the defendant or attempt to forcibly remove his jacket." The California Supreme Court declined review by a divided vote. We brought the case here, postponing the consideration of the question of our jurisdiction over this appeal to a hearing of the case on the merits. We now reverse.

The question of our jurisdiction need not detain us long. Throughout the proceedings below, Cohen consistently claimed that, as construed to apply to the facts of this case, the statute infringed his rights to freedom of expression guaranteed by the First and Fourteenth Amendments of the federal Constitution. That contention has been rejected by the highest California state court in which review could be had. Accordingly, we are fully satisfied that Cohen has properly invoked our jurisdiction by this appeal.

I

In order to lay hands on the precise issue which this case involves, it is useful first to canvass various matters which this record does *not* present.

The conviction quite clearly rests upon the asserted offensiveness of the *words* Cohen used to convey his message to the public. The only "conduct" which the state sought to punish is the fact of communication. Thus, we deal here with a conviction resting solely upon "speech," not upon any separately identifiable conduct which allegedly was intended by Cohen to be perceived by others as expressive of particular views but which, on its face, does not necessarily convey any message and hence arguably could be regulated without effectively repressing Cohen's ability to express himself. Further, the state certainly lacks power to punish Cohen for the underlying content of the message the inscription conveyed. At least so long as there is no showing of an intent to incite disobedience to or disruption of the draft. Cohen could not, consistently with the First and Fourteenth Amendments, be punished for asserting the evident position on the inutility or immorality of the draft his jacket reflected.

Appellant's conviction, then, rests squarely upon his exercise of the "freedom of speech" protected from arbitrary governmental interference by the Constitution and can be justified, if at all, only as a valid regulation of the manner in which he exercised that freedom, not as a permissible prohibition on the substantive message it conveys. This does not end the inquiry, of course, for the First and Fourteenth Amendments have never been thought to give absolute protection to every individual to speak whenever or wherever he pleases, or to use any form of address in any circumstance that he chooses. In this vein, too, however, we think it important to note that several issues typically associated with such problems are not presented here.

In the first place, Cohen was tried under a statute applicable throughout the entire state. Any attempt to support this conviction on the ground that the statute seeks to preserve an appropriately decorous atmosphere in the courthouse where Cohen was arrested must fail in the absence of any language in the statute that would have put appellant on notice that certain kinds of otherwise permissible speech or conduct would nevertheless, under California law, not be tolerated in certain places. No fair reading of the phrase "offensive conduct" can be said sufficiently to inform the ordinary person that distinctions between certain locations are thereby created.[1]

In the second place, as it comes to us, this case cannot be said to fall 10 within those relatively few categories of instances where prior decisions

---

[1]It is illuminating to note what transpired when Cohen entered a courtroom in the building. He removed his jacket and stood with it folded over his arm. Meanwhile, a policeman sent the presiding judge a note suggesting that Cohen be held in contempt of court. The judge declined to do so and Cohen was arrested by the officer only after he emerged from the courtroom. [All notes are the Court's.]

have established the power of government to deal more comprehen-
sively with certain forms of individual expression simply upon a showing
that such a form was employed. This is not, for example, an obscenity
case. Whatever else may be necessary to give rise to the states' broader
power to prohibit obscene expression, such expression must be, in some
significant way, erotic. It cannot plausibly be maintained that this vulgar
allusion to the Selective Service System would conjure up such psychic
stimulation in anyone likely to be confronted with Cohen's crudely de-
faced jacket.

This Court has also held that the states are free to ban the simple
use, without a demonstration of additional justifying circumstances,
of so-called "fighting words," those personally abusive epithets which,
when addressed to the ordinary citizen, are, as a matter of common
knowledge, inherently likely to provoke violent reaction. While the
four-letter word displayed by Cohen in relation to the draft is not un-
commonly employed in a personally provocative fashion, in this instance
it was clearly not "directed to the person of the hearer." No individual
actually or likely to be present could reasonably have regarded the words
on appellant's jacket as a direct personal insult. Nor do we have here an
instance of the exercise of the state's police power to prevent a speaker
from intentionally provoking a given group to hostile reaction. There is,
as noted above, no showing that anyone who saw Cohen was in fact violently aroused or that appellant intended such a result.

Finally, in arguments before this Court much has been made of the
claim that Cohen's distasteful mode of expression was thrust upon unwilling or unsuspecting viewers, and that the state might therefore legitimately act as it did in order to protect the sensitive from otherwise unavoidable exposure to appellant's crude form of protest. Of course, the
mere presumed presence of unwitting listeners or viewers does not serve
automatically to justify curtailing all speech capable of giving offense.
While this Court has recognized that government may properly act in
many situations to prohibit intrusion into the privacy of the home of un-
welcome views and ideas which cannot be totally banned from the public dialogue, we have at the same time consistently stressed that "we are
often 'captives' outside the sanctuary of the home and subject to objectionable speech." The ability of government, consonant with the Constitution, to shut off discourse solely to protect others from hearing it is, in
other words, dependent upon a showing that substantial privacy interests are being invaded in an essentially intolerable manner. Any broader
view of this authority would effectively empower a majority to silence
dissidents simply as a matter of personal predilections.

In this regard, persons confronted with Cohen's jacket were in a
quite different posture than, say, those subjected to the raucous emis-
sions of sound trucks blaring outside their residences. Those in the Los
Angeles courthouse could effectively avoid further bombardment of
their sensibilities simply by averting their eyes. And, while it may be that

one has a more substantial claim to a recognizable privacy interest when walking through a courthouse corridor than, for example, strolling through Central Park, surely it is nothing like the interest in being free from unwanted expression in the confines of one's own home. Given the subtlety and complexity of the factors involved, if Cohen's "speech" was otherwise entitled to constitutional protection, we do not think the fact that some unwilling "listeners" in a public building may have been briefly exposed to it can serve to justify this breach of the peace conviction where, as here, there was no evidence that persons powerless to avoid appellant's conduct did in fact object to it, and where that portion of the statute upon which Cohen's conviction rests evinces no concern, either on its face or as construed by the California courts, with the special plight of the captive auditor, but, instead, indiscriminately sweeps within its prohibitions all "offensive conduct" that disturbs "any neighborhood or person."[2]

II

Against this background, the issue flushed by this case stands out in bold relief. It is whether California can excise, as "offensive conduct," one particular scurrilous epithet from the public discourse, either upon the theory of the court below that its use is inherently likely to cause violent reaction or upon a more general assertion that the states, acting as guardians of public morality, may properly remove this offensive word from the public vocabulary.

The rationale of the California court is plainly untenable. At most it reflects an "undifferentiated fear or apprehension of disturbance [which] is not enough to overcome the right to freedom of expression." We have been shown no evidence that substantial numbers of citizens are standing ready to strike out physically at whoever may assault their sensibilities with execrations like that uttered by Cohen. There may be some persons about with such lawless and violent proclivities, but that is an insufficient base upon which to erect, consistently with constitutional values, a governmental power to force persons who wish to ventilate their dissident views into avoiding particular forms of expression. The argument amounts to little more than the self-defeating proposition that to avoid physical censorship of one who has not sought to provoke such

[2]In fact, other portions of the same statute do make some such distinctions. For example, the statute also prohibits disturbing "the peace or quiet . . . by loud or unusual noise" and using "vulgar, profane or indecent language within the presence or hearing of women or children, in a loud and boisterous manner." . . . This second quoted provision in particular serves to put the actor on much fairer notice as to what is prohibited. It also buttresses our view that the "offensive conduct" portion, as construed and applied in this case, cannot legitimately be justified in this Court as designed or intended to make fine distinctions between differently situated recipients.

a response by a hypothetical coterie of the violent and lawless, the states may more appropriately effectuate that censorship themselves.

Admittedly, it is not so obvious that the First and Fourteenth Amendments must be taken to disable the states from punishing public utterance of this unseemly expletive in order to maintain what they regard as a suitable level of discourse within the body politic. We think, however, that examination and reflection will reveal the shortcoming of a contrary viewpoint.

At the outset, we cannot overemphasize that, in our judgment, most situations where the state has a justifiable interest in regulating speech will fall within one or more of the various established exceptions, discussed above but not applicable here, to the usual rule that governmental bodies may not prescribe the form or content of individual expression. Equally important to our conclusion is the constitutional backdrop against which our decision must be made. The constitutional right of free expression is powerful medicine in a society as diverse and populous as ours. It is designed and intended to remove governmental restraints from the arena of public discussion, putting the decision as to what views shall be voiced largely into the hands of each of us, in the hope that use of such freedom will ultimately produce a more capable citizenry and more perfect polity and in the belief that no other approach would comport with the premise of individual dignity and choice upon which our political system rests.

To many, the immediate consequence of this freedom may often appear to be only verbal tumult, discord, and even offensive utterance. These are, however, within established limits, in truth necessary side effects of the broader enduring values which the process of open debate permits us to achieve. That the air may at times seem filled with verbal cacophony is, in this sense, not a sign of weakness but of strength. We cannot lose sight of the fact that, in what otherwise might seem a trifling and annoying instance of individual distasteful abuse of a privilege, these fundamental societal values are truly implicated. That is why "[w]holly neutral futilities . . . come under the protection of free speech as fully as do Keats's poems or Donne's sermons," and why "so long as the means are peaceful, the communication need not meet standards of acceptability."

Against this perception of the constitutional policies involved, we discern certain more particularized considerations that peculiarly call for reversal of this conviction. First, the principle contended for by the state seems inherently boundless. How is one to distinguish this from any other offensive word? Surely the state has no right to cleanse public debate to the point where it is grammatically palatable to the most squeamish among us. Yet no readily ascertainable general principle exists for stopping short of that result were we to affirm the judgment below. For, while the particular four-letter word being litigated here is perhaps more distasteful than most others of its genre, it is nevertheless often true that one man's vulgarity is another's lyric. Indeed, we think it is largely because governmental officials cannot make principled distinctions in this area that the Constitution leaves matters of taste and style so largely to the individual.

Additionally, we cannot overlook the fact, because it is well illus- 20 trated by the episode involved here, that much linguistic expression serves a dual communicative function: It conveys not only ideas capable of relatively precise, detached explication, but otherwise inexpressible emotions as well. In fact, words are often chosen as much for their emotive as their cognitive force. We cannot sanction the view that the Constitution, while solicitous of the cognitive content of individual speech, has little or no regard for that emotive function which, practically speaking, may often be the more important element of the overall message sought to be communicated. Indeed, as Mr. Justice Frankfurter has said, "One of the prerogatives of American citizenship is the right to criticize public men and measures—and that means not only informed and responsible criticism but the freedom to speak foolishly and without moderation."

Finally, and in the same vein, we cannot indulge the facile assumption that one can forbid particular words without also running a substantial risk of suppressing ideas in the process. Indeed, governments might soon seize upon the censorship of particular words as a convenient guise for banning the expression of unpopular views. We have been able, as noted above, to discern little social benefit that might result from running the risk of opening the door to such grave results.

It is, in sum, our judgment that, absent a more particularized and compelling reason for its actions, the state may not, consistently with the First and Fourteenth Amendments, make the simple public display here involved of this single four-letter expletive a criminal offense. Because that is the only arguably sustainable rationale for the conviction here at issue, the judgment below must be reversed.

Justice Blackmun, with whom the Chief Justice and Justice Black join.

I dissent:

Cohen's absurd and immature antic, in my view, was mainly con- 25 duct and little speech. The California Court of Appeal appears so to have described it, and I cannot characterize it otherwise. . . .

Topics for Critical Thinking and Writing

1. After reading the facts of the case, do you agree with the dissenting opinion that what Cohen did was "mainly conduct and little speech"? Does it matter if this evaluation is correct?

2. State briefly and in your own words the several kinds of issues that, in the majority's opinion, the Cohen case does *not* involve. If the case doesn't involve them, why does the majority discuss them?

3. In Part II of the majority opinion, the Court gives its reasons for reversing Cohen's conviction. State those reasons in your own words, perhaps in three or four sentences.

4. Suppose Cohen's behavior and arrest had occurred in a neighborhood office of the Selective Service System (a local draft board), rather than in the county courthouse. Do you think this circumstance might have affected the Court's judgment? Explain in an essay of 250 words.

5. Suppose, contrary to fact, there had been evidence that Cohen's conduct actually had provoked others to acts of violence or to disturb the peace (para. 4). In an essay of 250 to 500 words, explain whether you think this evidence should have led the majority to uphold his conviction, and why.

Byron R. White
and John Paul Stevens

In January 1985, a majority of the U.S. Supreme Court, in a case called New Jersey v. T.L.O. (a student's initials), ruled 6 to 3 that a school official's search of a student who was suspected of disobeying a school regulation does not violate the Fourth Amendment's protection against unreasonable searches and seizures.

The case originated thus: An assistant principal in a New Jersey high school opened the purse of a fourteen-year-old girl who had been caught violating school rules by smoking in the lavatory. The girl denied that she ever smoked, and the assistant principal thought that the contents of her purse would show whether or not she was lying. The purse was found to contain cigarettes, marijuana, and some notes that seemed to indicate that she sold marijuana to other students. The school then called the police.

The case went through three lower courts; almost five years after the event occurred, the case reached the Supreme Court. Associate Justice Byron R. White wrote the majority opinion, joined by Chief Justice Warren E. Burger and by Associate Justices Lewis F. Powell, Jr., William H. Rehnquist, and Sandra Day O'Connor. Associate Justice Harry A. Blackmun concurred in a separate opinion. Associate Justices William J. Brennan, Jr., John Paul Stevens, and Thurgood Marshall dissented in part. In the excerpt that follows, legal citations have been omitted.

New Jersey v. T.L.O.

Justice White delivered the opinion of the Court.

In determining whether the search at issue in this case violated the Fourth Amendment, we are faced initially with the question whether that amendment's prohibition on unreasonable searches and seizures applies to searches conducted by public school officials. We hold that it does.

It is now beyond dispute that "the Federal Constitution, by virtue of the Fourteenth Amendment, prohibits unreasonable searches and seizures by state officers." Equally indisputable is the proposition that the Fourteenth Amendment protects the rights of students against encroachment by public school officials.

On reargument, however, the State of New Jersey has argued that the history of the Fourth Amendment indicates that the amendment was intended to regulate only searches and seizures carried out by law enforcement officers; accordingly, although public school officials are concededly state agents for purposes of the Fourteenth Amendment, the Fourth Amendment creates no rights enforceable against them.

But this Court has never limited the amendment's prohibition on unreasonable searches and seizures to operations conducted by the police. Rather, the Court has long spoken of the Fourth Amendment's strictures as restraints imposed upon "governmental action"—that is, "upon the activities of sovereign authority." Accordingly, we have held the Fourth Amendment applicable to the activities of civil as well as criminal authorities: building inspectors, OSHA inspectors, and even firemen entering privately owned premises to battle a fire, are all subject to the restraints imposed by the Fourth Amendment.

Notwithstanding the general applicability of the Fourth Amendment 5 to the activities of civil authorities, a few courts have concluded that school officials are exempt from the dictates of the Fourth Amendment by virtue of the special nature of their authority over schoolchildren. Teachers and school administrators, it is said, act *in loco parentis* [that is, in place of a parent] in their dealings with students: Their authority is that of the parent, not the state, and is therefore not subject to the limits of the Fourth Amendment.

Such reasoning is in tension with contemporary reality and the teachings of this Court. We have held school officials subject to the commands of the First Amendment, and the Due Process Clause of the Fourteenth Amendment. If school authorities are state actors for purposes of the constitutional guarantees of freedom of expression and due process, it is difficult to understand why they should be deemed to be exercising parental rather than public authority when conducting searches of their students.

In carrying out searches and other disciplinary functions pursuant to such policies, school officials act as representatives of the state, not merely as surrogates for the parents, and they cannot claim the parents' immunity from the strictures of the Fourth Amendment.

To hold that the Fourth Amendment applies to searches conducted by school authorities is only to begin the inquiry into the standards governing such searches. Although the underlying command of the Fourth Amendment is always that searches and seizures be reasonable, what is reasonable depends on the context within which a search takes place.

[STANDARD OF REASONABLENESS]

The determination of the standard of reasonableness governing any specific class of searches requires balancing the need to search against the invasion which the search entails. On one side of the balance are arrayed the individual's legitimate expectations of privacy and personal security; on the other, the government's need for effective methods to deal with breaches of public order.

We have recognized that even a limited search of the person is a 10 substantial invasion of privacy. A search of a child's person or of a closed purse or other bag carried on her person, no less than a similar search carried out on an adult, is undoubtedly a severe violation of subjective expectations of privacy.

Of course, the Fourth Amendment does not protect subjective expectations of privacy that are unreasonable or otherwise "illegitimate." The State of New Jersey has argued that because of the pervasive supervision to which children in the schools are necessarily subject, a child has virtually no legitimate expectation of privacy in articles of personal property "unnecessarily" carried into a school. This argument has two factual premises: (1) the fundamental incompatibility of expectations of privacy with the maintenance of a sound educational environment; and (2) the minimal interest of the child in bringing any items of personal property into the school. Both premises are severely flawed.

Although this Court may take notice of the difficulty of maintaining discipline in the public schools today, the situation is not so dire that students in the schools may claim no legitimate expectations of privacy.

[PRIVACY AND DISCIPLINE]

Against the child's interest in privacy must be set the substantial interest of teachers and administrators in maintaining discipline in the classroom and on school grounds. Maintaining order in the classroom has never been easy, but in recent years, school disorder has often taken particularly ugly forms; drug use and violent crime in the schools have become major social problems. Accordingly, we have recognized that maintaining security and order in the schools requires a certain degree of flexibility in school disciplinary procedures, and we have respected the value of preserving the informality of the student-teacher relationship.

How, then, should we strike the balance between the schoolchild's legitimate expectations of privacy and the school's equally legitimate need to maintain an environment in which learning can take place? It is evident that the school setting requires some easing of the restrictions to which searches by public authorities are ordinarily subject. The warrant requirement, in particular, is unsuited to the school environment; requiring a teacher to obtain a warrant before searching a child suspected of an infraction of school rules (or of the criminal law) would unduly interfere with the maintenance of the swift and informal disciplinary procedures needed in the schools. We hold today that school officials need not obtain a warrant before searching a student who is under their authority.

The school setting also requires some modification of the level 15 of suspicion of illicit activity needed to justify a search. Ordinarily, a search—even one that may permissibly be carried out without a warrant—must be based upon "probable cause" to believe that a violation of the law has occurred. However, "probable cause" is not an irreducible requirement of a valid search.

[BALANCING OF INTERESTS]

The fundamental command of the Fourth Amendment is that searches and seizures be reasonable, and although "both the concept of probable cause and the requirement of a warrant bear on the reasonableness of a search, . . . in certain limited circumstances neither is required." Thus, we have in a number of cases recognized the legality of searches and seizures based on suspicions that, although "reasonable," do not rise to the level of probable cause. Where a careful balancing of governmental and private interests suggests that the public interest is best served by a Fourth Amendment standard of reasonableness that stops short of probable cause, we have not hesitated to adopt such a standard.

We join the majority of courts that have examined this issue in concluding that the accommodation of the privacy interests of schoolchildren with the substantial need of teachers and administrators for freedom to maintain order in the schools does not require strict adherence to the requirement that searches be based on probable cause to believe that the subject of the search has violated or is violating the law.

Rather, the legality of a search of a student should depend simply on the reasonableness, under all the circumstances, of the search. Determining the reasonableness of any search involves a twofold inquiry; first, one must consider "whether the . . . action was justified at its inception," second, one must determine whether the search as actually conducted "was reasonably related in scope to the circumstances which justified the interference in the first place."

Under ordinary circumstances, a search of a student by a teacher or other school official will be "justified at its inception" when there are reasonable grounds for suspecting that the search will turn up evidence that the student has violated or is violating either the law or the rules of the school. Such a search will be permissible in its scope when the measures adopted are reasonably related to the objectives of the search and not excessively intrusive in light of the age and sex of the student and the nature of the infraction.

This standard will, we trust, neither unduly burden the efforts of 20 school authorities to maintain order in their schools nor authorize unrestrained intrusions upon the privacy of schoolchildren. By focusing attention on the question of reasonableness, the standard will spare teachers and school administrators the necessity of schooling themselves in the niceties of probable cause and permit them to regulate their conduct according to the dictates of reason and common sense. At the same time, the reasonableness standard should insure that the interests of students will be invaded no more than is necessary to achieve the legitimate end of preserving order in the schools.

There remains the question of the legality of the search in this case. We recognize that the "reasonable grounds" standard applied by the New Jersey Supreme Court in its consideration of this question is not substantially different from the standard that we have adopted today. Nonetheless, we believe that the New Jersey court's application of that standard to strike down the search of T.L.O.'s purse reflects a somewhat crabbed notion of reasonableness. Our review of the facts surrounding the search leads us to conclude that the search was in no sense unreasonable for Fourth Amendment purposes.

Justice Stevens, dissenting.

The majority holds that "a search of a student by a teacher or other school official will be 'justified at its inception' when there are reasonable grounds for suspecting that the search will turn up evidence *that the student has violated or is violating either the law or the rules of the school.*"

This standard will permit teachers and school administrators to search students when they suspect that the search will reveal evidence of [violation of] even the most trivial school regulation or precatory guideline for students' behavior. For the Court, a search for curlers and sunglasses in order to enforce the school dress code is apparently just as important as a search for evidence of heroin addiction or violent gang activity.

A standard better attuned to this concern would permit teachers and school administrators to search a student when they have reason to believe that the search will uncover *evidence that the student is violating the law or engaging in conduct that is seriously disruptive of school order, or the educational process.*

A standard that varies the extent of the permissible intrusion with 25 the gravity of the suspected offense is also more consistent with common-law experience and this Court's precedent. Criminal law has traditionally recognized a distinction between essentially regulatory offenses and serious violations of the peace, and graduated the response of the criminal justice system depending on the character of the violation.

Topics for Critical Thinking and Writing

1. In the majority opinion Justice White says (para. 14) that it is "evident that the school setting requires some easing of the restrictions to which searches by public authorities are ordinarily subject." Does White offer evidence supporting what he says is "evident"? List any evidence that White gives or any that you can think of.

2. What argument does White give to show that the Fourth Amendment prohibition against "unreasonable searches and seizures" applies to the behavior of school officials? Do you think his argument is reasonable, or not? Explain.

3. On what ground does White argue (para. 14) that school students have "legitimate expectations of privacy" and so New Jersey is wrong in arguing the contrary?

4. What are the conflicting interests involved in the case, according to White? How does the Supreme Court resolve this conflict?

5. Why does White argue (para. 15) that school authorities may search students without first obtaining a search warrant? (By the way, who issues a search warrant? Who seeks one?) What does he mean when he says that the requirement of "probable cause" is "not an irreducible requirement of a valid search" (para. 15)?

6. Could a search undertaken on the principle enunciated by the Court's majority mean that whenever authorities perceive what they choose to call "disorder" — perhaps in the activity of an assembly of protesters in the streets of a big city — they may justify otherwise unlawful searches and seizures?

7. Some forty years before this case, Justice Robert H. Jackson argued that the schools have a special responsibility for adhering to the Constitution: "That they are educating the young for citizenship is reason for scrupulous protection of constitutional freedoms of the individual, if we are not to strangle the free mind at its source and teach youth to discount important principles of our government as mere platitudes." Similarly, in 1967 in an analogous case involving another female pupil, Justice Brennan argued that "schools cannot expect their students to learn the lessons of good citizenship when the school authorities themselves disregard the fundamental principles underpinning our constitutional freedoms." Do you find these arguments compelling? Why, or why not?

8. Let's admit that maintaining order in schools may be extremely difficult. In your opinion, does the difficulty justify diminishing the rights

of citizens? Smoking is not an illegal activity, yet in this instance a student suspected of smoking—that is, merely of violating a school rule—was searched. In an essay of 250 words, consider whether the maintenance of school discipline in such a matter justifies a search.

9. White relies on a standard of "reasonableness." Do you think this criterion is too subjective to be a proper standard to distinguish between permissible and impermissible searches? Write a 500-word essay on the standard of reasonable searches and seizures, giving a hypothetical but plausible example of a reasonable search and seizure and then of an unreasonable search and seizure.

11

A Literary Critic's View:
Arguing about Literature

You might think that literature—fiction, poetry (including songs), drama—is meant only to be enjoyed, not to be argued about. Yet literature is constantly the subject of argumentative writing—not all of it by teachers of English. For instance, if you glance at the current issue of *Time* or *Newsweek* you probably will find a review of a play, suggesting that the play is worth seeing or is not worth seeing. Or, in the same magazine, you may find an article reporting that a senator or member of Congress argued that the National Endowment for the Humanities wasted its grant money by funding research on such-and-such an author, or that the National Endowment for the Arts insulted taxpayers by making an award to a writer who defamed the American family.

Probably most writing about literature, whether done by college students, their professors, journalists, members of Congress, or whomever, is devoted to interpreting, judging (evaluating), and theorizing. Let's look at each of these, drawing our examples chiefly from Shakespeare's *Macbeth*.

INTERPRETING

Interpreting is a matter of setting forth the *meaning* or the meanings of a work. For some readers, a work has *a* meaning, the one intended by the writer, which we may or may not perceive. For most critics today, however, a work has *many* meanings, for instance the meaning it had for the writer, the meanings it has accumulated over time, and the meanings it has for each of today's readers. Take *Macbeth*, a play about a Scottish king, written soon after a Scot—James VI of Scotland—had been installed as James I, King of England. The play must have meant something special to the king—we know that it was presented at court—and something a little different to the ordinary English citizen. And surely it means something different to us. For instance, few if any people today believe in the divine right of kings, although James I certainly did; and few if any people today believe in malignant witches, although witches play an important role in the tragedy. What *we* see in the play must be rather different from what Shakespeare's audience saw in it.

Many interpretations of *Macbeth* have been offered. Let's take two fairly simple and clearly opposed views.

1. Macbeth is a villain who, by murdering his lawful king, offends God's rule, so he is overthrown by God's earthly instruments, Malcolm and Macduff. Macbeth is justly punished; the reader or spectator rejoices in his defeat.

One can offer a good deal of evidence—and if one is taking this position in an essay of course one must *argue* it—by giving supporting reasons rather than merely assert the position. Here is a second view.

2. Macbeth is a hero-villain, a man who commits terrible crimes, but who never completely loses the reader's sympathy; although he is justly punished, the reader believes that with the death of Macbeth the world has become a smaller place.

Again, one *must* offer evidence in an essay that presents this thesis, or indeed presents any interpretation. For instance, one might offer as evidence the fact that the survivors, especially Macduff and Malcolm, have not interested us nearly as much as Macbeth has. One might argue, too, that although Macbeth's villainy is undeniable, his conscience never deserts him—here one would point to specific passages, and would offer some brief quotations. Macbeth's pained awareness of what he has done, it can be argued, enables the reader to sympathize with him continually.

Or consider an interpretation of Lady Macbeth. Is she simply evil through and through, or are there mitigating reasons for her actions? Might one argue, perhaps in a feminist interpretation, that despite her intelligence and courage she had no outlet for expression except through her husband? In order to make this argument, the writer might want to go beyond the text of the play, offering as evidence Elizabethan comments about the proper role of women.

JUDGING (OR EVALUATING)

Literary criticism is also concerned with such questions as these: Is *Macbeth* a great tragedy? Is *Macbeth* a greater tragedy than *Romeo and Juliet*? The writer offers an opinion about the worth of the literary work, but the opinion must be supported by an argument, expressed in sentences that offer supporting evidence.

Let's pause for a moment to think about evaluation in general. When we say "This is a great play," are we in effect saying only "I like this play"? That is, are we merely *expressing* our taste rather than *asserting* anything about something out there—something independent of our tastes and feelings? (The next few paragraphs will not answer this question, but they may start you thinking about your own answer.) Consider these three sentences.

1. It's raining outside.
2. I like vanilla.
3. This is a really good book.

If you are indoors and you say that it is raining outside, a hearer may ask for verification. Why do you say what you say? "Because," you reply, "I'm looking out the window." Or "Because Jane just came in, and she is drenched." Or "Because I just heard a weather report." If, on the other hand, you say that you like vanilla, it's almost unthinkable that anyone would ask you why. No one expects you to justify—to support, to give a reason for—an expression of taste.

Now consider the third statement, "This is a really good book." It is entirely reasonable, we think, for someone to ask you why you say that. And you reply, "Well, the characters are realistic, and the plot held my interest," or "It really gave me an insight into what life among the rich [or the poor] must be like," or some such thing. That is, statement 3 at least seems to be stating a fact, and it seems to be something we can discuss, even argue about, in a way that we cannot argue about a personal preference for vanilla. Almost everyone would agree that when we offer an aesthetic judgment we ought to be able to give reasons for it. At the very least, we might say, we hope to show *why* we evaluate the work as we do, and to suggest that if our readers try to see it from our point of view they may then accept our evaluation.

Evaluations are always based on assumptions, although these assumptions may be unstated, and in fact the writer may even be unaware of them. Some of these assumptions play the role of criteria; they control the sort of evidence the writer believes is relevant to the evaluation. What sorts of assumptions may underlie value judgments? We will mention a few, merely as examples. Other assumptions are possible, and all of these assumptions can themselves become topics of dispute:

1. A good work of art, although fictional, says something about real life.
2. A good work of art is complex yet unified.
3. A good work of art sets forth a wholesome view of life.
4. A good work of art is original.
5. A good work of art deals with an important subject.

Let's look briefly at these views, one by one.

1. *A good work of art, although fictional, says something about real life.* If you hold this view, that literature is connected to life, and you believe that human beings behave in fairly consistent ways, that is, that each of us has an enduring "character," you probably will judge as inferior a work in which the figures behave inconsistently or seem not to be adequately motivated. (The point must be made, however, that different literary forms or genres are governed by different rules. For instance, consistency of character is usually expected in tragedy but not in melodrama or in comedy, where last-minute reformations may be welcome and greeted with applause. The novelist Henry James said, "You will not write a good novel unless you possess the sense of reality." He is probably right—but does his view hold for the writer of farces?) In the case of *Macbeth* you might well find that the characters are consistent: Although the play begins by showing Macbeth as a loyal defender of King Duncan, Macbeth's later treachery is understandable, given the temptation and the pressure. Similarly, Lady Macbeth's descent into madness, although it may come as a surprise, may strike you as entirely plausible: At the beginning of the play she is confident that she can become an accomplice to a murder, but she has overestimated herself (or, we might say, she has underestimated her own humanity, the power of her guilty conscience, which drives her to insanity).

2. *A good work of art is complex yet unified.* If Macbeth is only a "tyrant" (Macduff's word) or a "butcher" (Malcolm's word), he is a unified character but he may be too simple and too uninteresting a character to be the subject of a great play. But, one argument holds, Macbeth in fact is a complex character, not simply a villain but a hero-villain, and the play as a whole is complex. *Macbeth* is a good work of art, one might argue, partly because it shows us so many aspects of life (courage, fear, loyalty, treachery, for a start) through a richly varied language (the diction ranges from a grand passage in which Macbeth says that his bloody hands will "incarnadine," or make red, "the multitudinous seas" to colloquial passages such as the drunken porter's "Knock, knock"). The play shows us the heroic Macbeth tragically destroying his own life, and it shows us the comic porter making coarse jokes about deceit and damnation, jokes that (although the porter doesn't know it) connect with Macbeth's crimes.

3. *A good work of art sets forth a wholesome view of life.* The idea that a work should be judged partly or largely on the moral view that it contains is widely held by the general public. (It has also been held by esteemed philosophers, notably Plato.) Thus, a story that demeans women—perhaps one that takes a casual view of rape—would be given a low rating and so would a play that treats a mass murderer as a hero.

Implicit in this approach is what is called an *instrumentalist* view— the idea that a work of art is an instrument, a means, to some higher value. Thus, many people hold that reading great works of literature makes us better—or at least does not make us worse. In this view, a work that is pornographic or in some other way thought to be immoral will be given a low value. At the time we are writing this chapter, a law requires the National Endowment for the Arts to take into account standards of decency when making awards.

Moral judgments, it should be noted, do not come only from the conservative right, the liberal left has been quick to detect political incorrectness. In fact, except for those people who subscribe to the now unfashionable view that a work of art is an independent aesthetic object with little or no connection to the real world—something like a pretty floral arrangement, or a wordless melody—most people judge works of literature largely by their content, by what the works seem to say about life. Marxist critics, for instance, have customarily held that literature should make the reader aware of the political realities of life; feminist critics are likely to hold that literature should make us aware of gender relationships—for example, aware of patriarchal power and of female accomplishments. Later in this chapter you will be asked to think about whether the militaristic passages in "The Star-Spangled Banner" perhaps stir the wrong sorts of sentiments in us.

4. *A good work of art is original.* This assumption puts special value on new techniques and new subject matter. Thus, the *first* playwright who introduces a new subject (say, AIDS) gets extra credit, so to speak. Or, to return to Shakespeare, one sign of his genius, it is held, is that he was so highly varied; none of his tragedies seems merely to duplicate another, each is a world of its own, a new kind of achievement. Compare, for instance, *Romeo and Juliet*, with its two youthful and innocent heroes, with *Macbeth*, with its deeply guilty hero. Both plays are tragedies, but we can hardly imagine two more different plays—even if a reader perversely argues that the young lovers are guilty of impetuosity and of disobeying appropriate authorities.

5. *A good work of art deals with an important subject.* Here we are concerned with theme: Great works, in this view, must deal with great themes. Love, death, patriotism, and God, say, are great themes; a work that deals with these may achieve a height, an excellence, that, say, a work describing a dog scratching for fleas may not. (Of course if the reader feels that the dog is a symbol of humanity plagued by invisible enemies, then the poem about the dog may reach the heights, but then, too, it is *not* a poem about a dog and fleas—it is really a poem about humanity and the invisible.)

The point: In writing an evaluation you must let your reader know *why* you value the work as you do. Obviously it is not enough just to keep saying that *this* work is great whereas *that* work is not so great; the reader wants to know *why* you offer the judgments that you do, which means that you will have to set forth your criteria and then offer evidence that is in accord with them.

THEORIZING

Some literary criticism is concerned with such theoretical questions as these:

> What is tragedy? Can the hero be a villain? How does tragedy differ from melodrama?
>
> Why do tragedies—works showing good or at least interesting people destroyed—give us pleasure?
>
> Does a work of art—a play or a novel, say, a made-up world with imagined characters—offer anything that can be called "truth"? Does an experience of a work of art affect our character?
>
> Does a work of art have meaning in itself, or is the meaning simply whatever anyone wishes to say it is? Does *Macbeth* tell us anything about life, or is it just an invented story?

And, yet again, one hopes that anyone asserting a thesis concerned with any of these topics will offer evidence, will, indeed, *argue* rather than merely assert.

A CHECKLIST FOR AN ARGUMENT ABOUT LITERATURE

✓ Is your imagined reader like a typical classmate of yours, someone who is not a specialist in literature but who is open-minded and interested in hearing your point of view about a work?

✓ Is the essay supported with evidence, usually from the text itself, but conceivably from other sources (such as a statement by the author, or a statement by a person regarded as an authority, or perhaps the evidence of comparable works)?

✓ Is the essay inclusive? Does it take into account all relevant details (which is not to say that it includes everything the writer knows about the work—for instance, that it was made into a film or that the author died poor)?

✓ Is the essay focused? Does the thesis stay steadily before the reader?

✓ Does the essay use quotations, but as evidence, not as padding? Whenever possible, does it abridge or summarize long quotations?

✓ Are all sources fully acknowledged? (For the form of documentation, see pp. 210–26.)

EXAMPLES:
Two Students Interpret
Robert Frost's "Mending Wall"

Let's consider two competing interpretations of a poem, Robert Frost's "Mending Wall." We say "competing" because these interpretations clash head-on. Differing interpretations need not be incompatible, of course. For instance, a historical interpretation of *Macbeth*, arguing that an understanding of the context of English-Scottish politics around 1605 helps us to appreciate the play, need not be incompatible with a psychoanalytic interpretation that tells us that Macbeth's murder of King Duncan is rooted in an Oedipus complex, the king being a father figure. Different approaches thus can illuminate different aspects of the work, just as they can emphasize or subordinate different elements in the plot or characters portrayed. But, again, in the next few pages we will deal with mutually incompatible interpretations of the meaning of Frost's poem—of what Frost's poem is about.

After reading the poem and the two interpretations written by students, spend a few minutes thinking about the questions that we raise after the second interpretation.

Robert Frost

Robert Frost (1874–1963) studied for part of one term at Dartmouth College in New Hampshire, then did odd jobs (including teaching), and from 1897 to 1899 was enrolled as a special student at Harvard. He then farmed in New Hampshire, published a few poems in newspapers, did some more teaching, and in 1912 left for England, where he hoped to achieve success as a writer. By 1915 he was known in England, and he returned to the United States. By the time of his death he was the nation's unofficial poet laureate. "Mending Wall" was first published in 1914.

Mending Wall

Something there is that doesn't love a wall,
That sends the frozen-ground-swell under it,
And spills the upper boulders in the sun;
And makes gaps even two can pass abreast.
The work of hunters is another thing: 5
I have come after them and made repair
Where they have left not one stone on a stone,
But they would have the rabbit out of hiding,
To please the yelping dogs. The gaps I mean,

No one has seen them made or heard them made,   10
But at spring mending-time we find them there.
I let my neighbor know beyond the hill;
And on a day we meet to walk the line
And set the wall between us once again.
We keep the wall between us as we go.   15
To each the boulders that have fallen to each.
And some are loaves and some so nearly balls
We have to use a spell to make them balance:
"Stay where you are until our backs are turned!"
We wear our fingers rough with handling them.   20
Oh, just another kind of outdoor game,
One on a side. It comes to little more:
There where it is we do not need the wall:
He is all pine and I am apple orchard.
My apple trees will never get across   25
And eat the cones under his pines, I tell him.
He only says, "Good fences make good neighbors."
Spring is the mischief in me, and I wonder
If I could put a notion in his head:
"*Why* do they make good neighbors? Isn't it   30
Where there are cows? But here there are no cows.
Before I built a wall I'd ask to know
What I was walling in or walling out,
And to whom I was like to give offense.
Something there is that doesn't love a wall,   35
That wants it down." I could say "Elves" to him,
But it's not elves exactly, and I'd rather
He said it for himself. I see him there
Bringing a stone grasped firmly by the top
In each hand, like an old-stone savage armed.   40
He moves in darkness as it seems to me,
Not of woods only and the shade of trees.
He will not go behind his father's saying,
And he likes having thought of it so well
He says again, "Good fences make good neighbors."   45

Jonathan Deutsch

Professor Walton

English 102

March 3, 1998

    The Deluded Speaker in Frost's "Mending Wall"

    Our discussions of "Mending Wall" in high
school showed that most people think Frost is
saying that walls between people are a bad
thing, and that we should not try to separate
ourselves from each other unnecessarily. Perhaps
the wall, in this view, is a symbol for race
prejudice or religious differences, and Frost is
suggesting that these differences are minor and
that they should not keep us apart. In this common view, the neighbor's words, "Good fences
make good neighbors" (lines 27 and 45) show that
the neighbor is shortsighted. I disagree with
this view, but first I want to present the evidence that might be offered for it, so that we
can then see whether it really is substantial.

    First of all, someone might claim that in
lines 23 to 26 Frost offers a good argument
against walls:

      There where it is we do not need the wall:
      He is all pine and I am apple orchard.
      My apple trees will never get across
      And eat the cones under his pines, I tell
        him.

The neighbor does not offer a valid reply to
this argument; in fact, he doesn't offer any
argument at all but simply says, "Good fences
make good neighbors."

Another piece of evidence supposedly showing that the neighbor is wrong, it is said, is
found in Frost's description of him as "an old-
stone savage," and someone who "moves in darkness" (40, 41). And a third piece of evidence
is said to be that the neighbor "will not go
behind his father's saying" (43), but he merely
repeats the saying.

There is, however, another way of looking
at the poem. As I see it, the speaker is a very
snide and condescending person. He is confident
that he knows it all and that his neighbor is
an ignorant savage; he is even willing to tease
his supposedly ignorant neighbor. For instance,
the speaker admits to "the mischief in me"
(28), and he is confident that he could tell
the truth to the neighbor but he arrogantly
thinks that it would be a more effective form
of teaching if the neighbor "said it for himself" (38).

The speaker is not only unpleasantly mis-
chievous and condescending toward his neighbor,
but he is also shallow, for he does not see the
great wisdom that there is in proverbs. The
American Heritage Dictionary of the English
Language, third edition, defines a proverb as
"A short, pithy saying in frequent and widespread use that expresses a basic truth."
Frost, or at least the man who speaks this
poem, does not seem to realize that proverbs
express truths. He just dismisses them, and
he thinks the neighbor is wrong not to "go behind his father's saying" (43). But there is

Deutsch 3

a great deal of wisdom in the sayings of our
fathers. For instance, in the Bible (in the Old
Testament) there is a whole book of proverbs,
filled with wise sayings such as "Reprove
not a scorner, lest he hate thee: rebuke a
wise man, and he will love thee" (9:8); "He
that trusteth in his riches shall fall"
(11:28); "The way of a fool is right in his
own eyes" (12:15; this might be said of the
speaker of "Mending Wall"); "A soft answer
turneth away wrath" (15:1); and (to cut
short what could be a list many pages long),
"Whoso diggeth a pit shall fall therein"
(26:27).

The speaker is confident that walls are unnecessary and probably bad, but he doesn't realize that even where there are no cattle, walls
serve the valuable purpose of clearly marking
out our territory. They help us to preserve our
independence and our individuality. Walls--man-
made structures--are a sign of civilization. A
wall more or less says, "This is mine, but I respect that as yours." Frost's speaker is so confident of his shallow view that he makes fun of
his neighbor for repeating that "Good fences
make good neighbors" (27, 45). But he himself
repeats his own saying, "Something there is that
doesn't love a wall" (1, 35). And at least the
neighbor has age-old tradition on his side,
since the proverb is the saying of his father.
On the other hand, the speaker has only his own
opinion, and he can't even say what the "something" is.

Deutsch 4

It may be that Frost meant for us to laugh at
the neighbor, and to take the side of the
speaker, but I think it is much more likely
that he meant for us to see that the speaker is
mean-spirited (or at least given to unpleasant
teasing), too self-confident, foolishly dismissing the wisdom of the old times, and entirely unaware that he has these unpleasant
characteristics.

Felicia Alonso

Professor Walton

English 102

March 3, 1998

The Debate in Robert Frost's "Mending Wall"

I think the first thing to say about Frost's "Mending Wall" is this: The poem is not about a debate over whether good fences do or do not make good neighbors. It is about two debaters: One of the debaters is on the side of vitality, and the other is on the side of an unchanging, fixed--dead, we might say--tradition.

How can we characterize the speaker? For one thing, he is neighborly. Interestingly, it is he, and not the neighbor, who initiates the repairing of the wall: "I let my neighbor know beyond the hill" (line 12). This seems strange, since the speaker doesn't see any point in this wall, whereas the neighbor is all in favor of walls. Can we explain this apparent contradiction? Yes; the speaker is a good neighbor, willing to do his share of the work, and willing (perhaps in order not to upset his neighbor) to maintain an old tradition even though he doesn't see its importance. It may not be important, he thinks, but it is really rather pleasant, "another kind of outdoor game" (21). In fact, sometimes he even repairs fences on his own, after hunters have destroyed them.

Second, we can say that the speaker is on the side of nature. "Something there is that doesn't love a wall," he says (1, 35), and of

course the "something" is nature itself. Nature
"sends the frozen-ground-swell" under the wall
and "spills the upper boulders in the sun; /
And makes gaps even two can pass abreast"(2-4).
Notice that nature itself makes the gaps, and
that "two can pass abreast," that is, people
can walk together in a companionable way. It is
hard to imagine the neighbor walking side by
side with anyone.

    Third, we can say that the speaker has a
sense of humor. When he thinks of trying to get
his neighbor interested in the issue, he admits
that "the mischief" is in him (28), and he
amusingly attributes his playfulness to a natural force, the spring. He playfully toys with
the obviously preposterous idea of suggesting
to his neighbor that elves caused the stones to
fall, but he stops short of making this amusing
suggestion to his very serious neighbor. Still,
the mere thought assures us that he has a playful, genial nature, and the idea also again implies that not only the speaker but also some
sort of mysterious natural force dislikes
walls.

    Finally, though of course he thinks he is
right and that his neighbor is mistaken, he at
least is cautious in his view. He does <u>not</u> call
his neighbor "an old-stone savage"; rather, he
uses a simile ("like") and he then adds that
this is only his opinion, so the opinion is
softened quite a bit. Here is the description
of the neighbor, with underlining added in
order to clarify my point. The neighbor is

. . . <u>like</u> an old-stone savage armed.
He moves in darkness <u>as it seems to me</u> . . .
    (40-41)

Of course the only things we know about
the neighbor are those things that the speaker
chooses to tell us, so it is not surprising
that the speaker comes out ahead. He comes out
ahead not because he is right about walls (real
or symbolic) and his neighbor is wrong--that's
an issue that is not settled in the poem. He
comes out ahead because he is a more interesting figure, someone who is neighborly, thoughtful, playful. Yes, maybe he seems to us to feel
superior to his neighbor, but we can be certain
that he doesn't cause his neighbor any embarrassment. Take the very end of the poem. The
speaker tells us that the neighbor

      . . . will not go behind his father's say-
          ing,
    And he likes having thought of it so well
    He says again, "Good fences make good
          neighbors."

The speaker is telling <u>us</u> that the neighbor
is utterly unoriginal and that the neighbor confuses <u>remembering</u> something with <u>thinking</u>. But
the speaker doesn't get into an argument; he
doesn't rudely challenge his neighbor and demand
reasons, which might force the neighbor to see
that he can't think for himself. And in fact we
probably like the neighbor just as he is, and we
don't want him to change his mind. The words

Alonso 4

that ring in our ears are not the speaker's but the neighbor's: "Good fences make good neighbors." The speaker of the poem is a good neighbor. After all, one can hardly be more neighborly than to let the neighbor have the last word.

Topics for Critical Thinking and Writing

1. State the thesis of each essay. Do you believe the theses are sufficiently clear and appear sufficiently early in the essays?

2. Consider the evidence that each essay offers by way of supporting its thesis. Do you find some of the evidence unconvincing? Explain.

3. Putting aside the question of which interpretation you prefer, comment on the organization of each essay. Is the organization clear? Do you want to propose some other pattern that you think might be more effective?

4. Consult the Checklist for Peer Review on pages 182–83, and offer comments on one of the two essays. Or: If you were the instructor in the course in which these two essays were submitted, what might be your final comments on each of them? Or: Write an analysis (250–500 words) of the strengths and weaknesses of either essay.

EXERCISES: Reading a Poem and Reading Two Stories

Andrew Marvell

Andrew Marvell (1621–1678), born in Hull, England, and educated at Trinity College, Cambridge, was traveling in Europe when the civil war between the royalists and the puritans broke out in England in 1642. The pu-

ritans were victorious and established the Commonwealth (the monarchy was restored later, in 1660), and Marvell became a tutor to the daughter of the victorious Lord-General. In 1657 he became an assistant to the blind poet John Milton, who held the title of Latin Secretary (Latin was the language of international diplomacy). In 1659 Marvell was elected to represent Hull in Parliament. As a man of letters, during his lifetime he was known chiefly for some satiric prose and poetry; most of the writings for which he is now esteemed were published posthumously. The following poem was first published in 1681.

To His Coy Mistress°

Had we but world enough, and time,
This coyness,° Lady, were no crime.
We would sit down, and think which way
To walk, and pass our long love's day.
Thou by the Indian Ganges' side   5
Shouldst rubies find; I by the tide
Of Humber° would complain. I would
Love you ten years before the Flood,
And you should, if you please, refuse
Till the Conversion of the Jews.°   10
My vegetable° love should grow
Vaster than empires and more slow;
An hundred years should go to praise
Thine eyes, and on thy forehead gaze;
Two hundred to adore each breast,   15
But thirty thousand to the rest;
An age at least to every part,
And the last age should show your heart.
For, Lady, you deserve this state,°
Nor would I love at lower rate.   20
    But at my back I always hear
Time's wingèd chariot hurrying near;
And yonder all before us lie
Deserts of vast eternity.
Thy beauty shall no more be found,   25
Nor, in thy marble vault, shall sound

---

1 Mistress Beloved woman.   **3 coyness** Reluctance.   **7 Humber** An estuary at Hull, Marvell's birthplace.   **10 the Conversion of the Jews** Something that would take place in the remote future, at the end of history.   **11 vegetable** Vegetative or growing.   **19 state** Ceremonious treatment.

My echoing song; then worms shall try°
That long-preserved virginity,
And your quaint° honour turn to dust,
And into ashes all my lust: 30
The grave's a fine and private place,
But none, I think, do there embrace.
   Now therefore, while the youthful hue
Sits on thy skin like morning dew,
And while thy willing soul transpires   35
At every pore with instant fires,
Now let us sport us while we may,
And now, like amorous birds of prey,
Rather at once our time devour
Than languish in his slow-chapt° power.   40
Let us roll all our strength and all
Our sweetness up into one ball,
And tear our pleasures with rough strife
Thorough° the iron gates of life:
Thus, though we cannot make our sun   45
Stand still, yet we will make him run.°

Topics for Critical Thinking and Writing

1. The motif that life is short and that we should seize the day (Latin: *carpe diem*) is old. Marvell's poem, in fact, probably has its ultimate source in a classical text called *The Greek Anthology*, a collection of about six thousand short Greek poems composed between the first century B.C. and the tenth century A.D. One poem goes thus, in a fairly literal translation:

   > You spare your maidenhead, and to what profit? For when you come to Hades you will not find your lover, girl. Among the living are the delights of Venus, but, maiden, we shall lie in the underworld mere bones and dust.

   If you find Marvell's poem more impressive, offer reasons for your belief.

2. A student, working from the translation just given, produced this rhyming version:

   > You keep your virginity, but to what end?
   > Below, in Hades, you won't find your friend.

---

27 try Test.   **29 quaint** Fastidious or finicky, with a pun on a coarse word defined in an Elizabethan dictionary as "a woman's privities."   **40 slow-chapt** Slow-jawed. **44 Thorough** Through.   **45–46 we cannot . . . still** An allusion to Joshua, the ancient Hebrew who, according to the Book of Joshua (10.12–13), made the sun stand still.

> On earth we enjoy Venus' sighs and moans;
> Buried below, we are senseless bones.

What do you think of this version? Why? Prepare your own version—
your instructor may divide the class into groups of four, and each group
can come up with a collaborative version—and then compare it with
other versions, giving reasons for your preferences.

3. Marvell's poem takes the form of a syllogism (see pp. 58–62). It can be
divided into three parts:

   1. "Had we" (line 1), a supposition, or suppositional premise;
   2. "But at my back" (line 21), a refutation;
   3. "Now, therefore" (line 33), a deduction.

Look closely at the poem and develop the argument using these three
parts, devoting a few sentences to each part.

4. A student wrote of this poem:

   > As a Christian I can't accept the lover's statement that "yonder all before
   > us lie / Deserts of vast eternity" (lines 23–24). The poem may contain
   > beautiful lines, and it may offer clever reasoning, but the reasoning is
   > based on what my religion tells me is wrong. I not only cannot accept the
   > idea of the poem, but I also cannot enjoy the poem, since it presents a
   > false view of reality.

What assumptions is this student making about a reader's response to a
work of literature? Do you agree or disagree? Why?

5. Here are three additional comments by students. For each, list the
writer's assumptions, and then evaluate each comment. You may agree
or disagree, in whole or in part, with any comment, but give your
reasons.

   > A. The poem is definitely clever, and that is part of what is wrong with it.
   > It is a blatant attempt at seduction. The man seems to think he is smarter
   > than the woman he is speaking to, and he "proves" that she should go to
   > bed with him. Since we don't hear her side of the argument, Marvell im-
   > plies that she has nothing to say and that his argument is sound. What
   > the poet doesn't seem to understand is that there is such a thing as
   > virtue, and a woman need not sacrifice virtue just because death is
   > inevitable.

   > B. On the surface, "To His Coy Mistress" is an attempt to persuade a
   > woman to go to bed with the speaker, but the poem is really less about
   > sex than it is about the terrifying shortness of life.

   > C. This is not a love poem. The speaker admits that his impulse is "lust"
   > (line 30), and he makes fun of the girl's conception of honor and virgin-
   > ity. If we enjoy this poem at all, our enjoyment must be in the hope that
   > this would-be date-rapist is unsuccessful.

6. Read the poem several times slowly, perhaps even aloud. Do certain
lines seem especially moving, especially memorable? If so, which ones?
Give reasons for your belief.

7. In *On Deconstruction* (1982), a study of contemporary literary theory,
Jonathan Culler remarks that feminist criticism has often stressed "read-

ing as a woman." This concept, Culler says, affirms the "continuity be-tween women's experience of social and familial structures and their experiences of readers." Do you agree with his suggestion that men and women often interpret literary works differently? Consider Marvell's poem in particular: Identify and discuss phrases and images in it to which men and women readers might (or might not) respond very differently.

8. A small point, but perhaps one of some interest. In the original text, line 34 ends with *glew*, not with *dew*. Most editors assume that the printer made an error, and—looking for a word to rhyme with *hue*—they re-place *glew* with *dew*. Another possible emendation is *lew*, an archaic word meaning "warmth." But the original reading has been defended, as a variant of the word *glow*. Your preference? Your reasons?

Jean Rhys

Jean Rhys (1890–1979) was the pseudonym used by Ella Gwendolen Rees Williams. She was born in the West Indies, in Dominica (at that time a British colony) and educated there and in England. In 1927, in England, she began to publish stories and novels (we reprint a story of 1931), but she did not achieve wide recognition until 1966 with the publication of Wide Sargasso Sea, *a retelling of Charlotte Bronte's* Jane Eyre *from the point of view of Rochester's first wife, the madwoman confined to the attic. In addi-tion to stories and five novels, she wrote an autobiography,* Smile Please: An Unfinished Autobiography *(1979).*

I Used to Live Here Once

She was standing by the river looking at the stepping stones and re-membering each one. There was the round unsteady stone, the pointed one, the flat one in the middle—the safe stone where you could stand and look round. The next wasn't so safe for when the river was full the water flowed over it and even when it showed dry it was slippery. But after that it was easy and soon she was standing on the other side.

The road was much wider than it used to be but the work had been done carelessly. The felled trees had not been cleared away and the bushes looked trampled. Yet it was the same road and she walked along feeling extraordinarily happy.

It was a fine day, a blue day. The only thing was that the sky had a glassy look that she didn't remember. That was the only word she could think of. Glassy. She turned the corner, saw that what had been the old pavé[1] had

---

[1]**pavé** Paved road. [Editors' note.]

been taken up, and there too the road was much wider, but it had the same unfinished look.

She came to the worn stone steps that led up to the house and her heart began to beat. The screw pine was gone, so was the mock summer house called the ajoupa, but the clove tree was still there and at the top of the steps the rough lawn stretched away, just as she remembered it. She stopped and looked towards the house that had been added to and painted white. It was strange to see a car standing in front of it.

There were two children under the big mango tree, a boy and a little   5
girl, and she waved to them and called "Hello" but they didn't answer her or turn their heads. Very fair children, as Europeans born in the West Indies so often are: as if the white blood is asserting itself against all odds.

The grass was yellow in the hot sunlight as she walked towards them. When she was quite close she called again, shyly: "Hello." Then, "I used to live here once," she said.

Still they didn't answer. When she said for the third time "Hello" she was quite near them. Her arms went out instinctively with the longing to touch them.

It was the boy who turned. His gray eyes looked straight into hers. His expression didn't change. He said: "Hasn't it gone cold all of a sudden. D'you notice? Let's go in." "Yes, let's," said the girl.

Her arms fell to her sides as she watched them running across the grass to the house. That was the first time she knew.

Topics for Critical Thinking and Writing

1. What do you make of the following details? (1) The sky (para. 3) has an unfamiliar "glassy" look. (2) The children don't reply. (3) The narrator speaks of "hot sunlight" (para. 6), but the boy comments (para. 8) on a sudden chilliness.

2. It is commonplace for adults to revisit the neighborhoods of their youth and to wistfully declare, "You can't go back again." Is this a plausible thesis to ascribe to Rhys's story? Why, or why not?

3. Rhys ends the story with the narrator saying, "That was the first time she knew." What is it that the speaker now knows for the first time? Make clear your answer by rewriting the final sentence as follows: "That was the first time that she knew that . . ."

4. Do you think the title is effective? If not, suggest a better title.

5. Write a short essay *evaluating* the story. Do you think the story is very good, pretty good, fair, or poor? Support your evaluation with reasons. You may want to devote a paragraph to each reason, in between an opening and a concluding paragraph. Thus, if you think the story is

good for two reasons (for instance, because it is brief and because the setting is sharply depicted) but is weak for one reason (for instance, because not much happens), you may find that five paragraphs are a convenient way of setting forth your views.

Kate Chopin

Kate Chopin (1851–1904) was born in St. Louis and named Katherine O'Flaherty. At the age of nineteen she married a cotton broker in New Orleans, Oscar Chopin (the name is pronounced something like "show pan"), who was descended from the early French settlers in Louisiana. After her husband's death in 1883, Kate Chopin turned to writing fiction. The following story was first published in 1894.

The Story of an Hour

Knowing that Mrs. Mallard was afflicted with a heart trouble, great care was taken to break to her as gently as possible the news of her husband's death.

It was her sister Josephine who told her, in broken sentences, veiled hints that revealed in half concealing. Her husband's friend Richards was there, too, near her. It was he who had been in the newspaper office when intelligence of the railroad disaster was received, with Brently Mallard's name leading the list of "killed." He had only taken the time to assure himself of its truth by a second telegram, and had hastened to forestall any less careful, less tender friend in bearing the sad message.

She did not hear the story as many women have heard the same, with a paralyzed inability to accept its significance. She wept at once, with sudden, wild abandonment, in her sister's arms. When the storm of grief had spent itself she went away to her room alone. She would have no one follow her.

There stood, facing the open window, a comfortable, roomy armchair. Into this she sank, pressed down by a physical exhaustion that haunted her body and seemed to reach into her soul.

She could see in the open square before her house the tops of trees 5 that were all aquiver with the new spring life. The delicious breath of rain was in the air. In the street below a peddler was crying his wares. The notes of a distant song which some one was singing reached her faintly, and countless sparrows were twittering in the eaves.

There were patches of blue sky showing here and there through the clouds that had met and piled one above the other in the west facing her window.

She sat with her head thrown back upon the cushion of the chair, quite motionless, except when a sob came up into her throat and shook her, as a child who has cried itself to sleep continues to sob in its dreams.

She was young, with a fair, calm face, whose lines bespoke repression and even a certain strength. But now there was a dull stare in her eyes, whose gaze was fixed away off yonder on one of those patches of blue sky. It was not a glance of reflection, but rather indicated a suspension of intelligent thought.

There was something coming to her and she was waiting for it, fearfully. What was it? She did not know; it was too subtle and elusive to name. But she felt it, creeping out of the sky, reaching toward her through the sounds, the scents, the color that filled the air.

Now her bosom rose and fell tumultuously. She was beginning to 10 recognize this thing that was approaching to possess her, and she was striving to beat it back with her will—as powerless as her two white slender hands would have been.

When she abandoned herself a little whispered word escaped her slightly parted lips. She said it over and over under her breath: "Free, free, free!" The vacant stare and the look of terror that had followed it went from her eyes. They stayed keen and bright. Her pulses beat fast, and the coursing blood warmed and relaxed every inch of her body.

She did not stop to ask if it were not a monstrous joy that held her. A clear and exalted perception enabled her to dismiss the suggestion as trivial.

She knew that she would weep again when she saw the kind, tender hands folded in death; the face that had never looked save with love upon her, fixed and gray and dead. But she saw beyond that bitter moment a long procession of years to come that would belong to her absolutely. And she opened and spread her arms out to them in welcome.

There would be no one to live for her during those coming years; she would live for herself. There would be no powerful will bending her in that blind persistence with which men and women believe they have a right to impose a private will upon a fellow creature. A kind intention or a cruel intention made the act seem no less a crime as she looked upon it in that brief moment of illumination.

And yet she had loved him—sometimes. Often she had not. What 15 did it matter! What could love, the unsolved mystery, count for in face of this possession of self-assertion which she suddenly recognized as the strongest impulse of her being.

"Free! Body and soul free!" she kept whispering.

Josephine was kneeling before the closed door with her lips to the keyhole, imploring for admission. "Louise, open the door! I beg; open the door—you will make yourself ill. What are you doing, Louise? For heaven's sake open the door."

"Go away. I am not making myself ill." No; she was drinking in a very elixir of life through that open window.

Her fancy was running riot along those days ahead of her. Spring days, and summer days, and all sorts of days that would be her own. She breathed a quick prayer that life might be long. It was only yesterday she had thought with a shudder that life might be long.

She arose at length and opened the door to her sister's importuni- 20 ties. There was a feverish triumph in her eyes, and she carried herself unwittingly like a goddess of Victory. She clasped her sister's waist, and together they descended the stairs. Richards stood waiting for them at the bottom.

Some one was opening the front door with a latchkey. It was Brently Mallard who entered, a little travel-stained, composedly carrying his gripsack and umbrella. He had been far from the scene of accident, and did not even know there had been one. He stood amazed at Josephine's piercing cry; at Richards' quick motion to screen him from the view of his wife.

But Richards was too late.

When the doctors came they said she had died of heart disease—of joy that kills.

Topic for Critical Thinking and Writing

Read the following assertions, and consider whether you agree or disagree, and why. For each assertion, draft a paragraph with your arguments.

1. The railroad accident is a symbol of the destructiveness of the industrial revolution.
2. The story claims that women rejoice in the deaths of their husbands.
3. Mrs. Mallard's death at the end is a just punishment for the joy she takes in her husband's death.
4. The story is rich in irony. Some examples: (1) The other characters think she is grieving, but she is rejoicing; (2) she prays for a long life, but she dies almost immediately; (3) the doctors say she died of "the joy that kills," but they think her joy was seeing her husband alive.
5. The story is excellent because it has a surprise ending.

THINKING ABOUT
THE EFFECTS OF LITERATURE

Works of art are artifacts—things constructed, made up, fashioned, just like houses and automobiles. In analyzing works of literature it is therefore customary to keep one's eye on the complex, constructed object, and not simply tell the reader how one feels about it. Instead of reporting their feelings, critics usually analyze the relationships between the parts and the relationship of the parts to the whole.

For instance, in talking about literature we can examine the relationship of plot to character, or of one character to another, or the relationship of one stanza in a poem to the next. Still, although we may try to engage in this sort of analysis as dispassionately as possible, we all know that inevitably we are not only examining something out there, but are also examining our own responses. Why? Because literature has an effect on us. Indeed, it probably has several kinds of effects, ranging from short-range emotional responses ("I really enjoyed this," "I burst out laughing," "It revolted me") to long-range effects ("I have always tried to live up to a line in *Hamlet*, 'This above all, to thine own self be true'"). Let's talk first, very briefly, about immediate emotional responses.

Analysis usually begins with a response: "This is marvelous," or "What a bore," and we then go on to try to account for our response. A friend mentions a book or a film to us, and we say, "I couldn't stay with it for five minutes." The friend expresses surprise, and we then go on to explain, giving reasons (to the friend and also to ourselves) why we couldn't stay with it. Perhaps the book seemed too remote from life, or perhaps, on the other hand, it seemed to be nothing more than a transcript of the boring talk that we can overhear on a bus or in an elevator.

In such discussions, when we draw on our responses, as we must, the work may disappear; we find ourselves talking about ourselves. Let's take two extreme examples: "I can't abide *Huckleberry Finn*. How am I expected to enjoy a so-called masterpiece that has a character in it called 'Nigger Jim.'" Or: "T. S. Eliot's anti-Semitism is too much for me to take. Don't talk to me about Eliot's skill with meter, when he has such lines as 'Rachel, *née* Rabinovitch / Tears at the grapes with murderous paws.'"

Although everyone agrees that literature can evoke this sort of strong emotional response, not everyone agrees on how much value we should put on our personal experience. Several of the Topics for Critical Thinking and Writing on page 364 invite you to reflect on this issue.

What about the *consequences of the effects* of literature? Does literature shape our character and therefore influence our behavior? It is fairly widely believed that literature does have an effect. One hears, for example, that literature (like travel) is broadening, which is to say that it makes us aware of, and tolerant of, kinds of behavior that differ from our own and from what we see around us. One of the chief arguments against pornography, for instance, is that it desensitizes us, makes us too tolerant of abusive relationships, relationships in which people (usually men) use other people (usually women) as mere things or instruments for pleasure. (A contrary view should be mentioned: Some people argue that pornography provides a relatively harmless outlet for fantasies that otherwise might be given release in the real world. In this view, pornography acts as a sort of safety valve.) Discussions of the effects of literature that get into the popular press almost always involve pornography, but other topics are also the subjects of controversy. For instance, in recent decades parents and educators have been much concerned with fairy tales. Does the violence in some fairy tales ("Little Red Riding Hood," "The Three Little Pigs") have a bad effect on children? Do some of the stories teach the wrong lessons, implying that women should be passive, men active ("Sleeping Beauty," for instance, in which the sleeping woman is brought to life by the action of the handsome prince)? The Greek philosopher Plato (427–347 B.C.) strongly believed that the literature we hear or read shapes our later behavior, and since most of the ancient Greek traditional stories (notably Homer's *Odyssey* and *Iliad*) celebrate acts of love and war rather than of justice, he prohibited the reading of such material in his ideal society. (We reprint a relevant passage from Plato on p. 365.)

Topics for Critical Thinking and Writing

1. If you have responded strongly (favorably or unfavorably) to some aspect of the social content of a literary work, for instance its depiction of women or of a particular minority group, in an essay of 250 to 500 words analyze the response, and try to determine whether you are talking chiefly about yourself or the work. (Two works widely regarded as literary masterpieces but nonetheless often banned from classrooms are Shakespeare's *The Merchant of Venice* and Mark Twain's *Huckleberry Finn*. If you have read either of these, you may want to write about it and your response.) Can we really see literary value—*really* see it—in a work that deeply offends us?

2. Most people believe that literature influences life—that in some perhaps mysterious way it helps to shape character. Certainly anyone who believes that some works should be censored, or at least should be made unavailable to minors, assumes that they can have a bad influence, so why not assume that other works can have a good influence?

   Read the following brief claims about literature, then choose one and write a 250-word essay offering support or taking issue with it.

   The pen is mightier than the sword.—ANONYMOUS

   The writer isn't made in a vacuum. Writers are witnesses. The reason we need writers is because we need witnesses to this terrifying century.—E. L. DOCTOROW

   When we read of human beings behaving in certain ways, with the approval of the author, who gives his benedictions to this behavior by his attitude towards the result of the behavior arranged by himself, we can be influenced towards behaving in the same way.—T. S. ELIOT

   Poetry makes nothing happen.—W. H. AUDEN

   Literature is *without proofs*. By which it must be understood that it cannot prove, not only *what* it says, but even that it is worth the trouble of saying it.—ROLAND BARTHES

> Of course the illusion of art is to make one believe that great literature is very close to life, but exactly the opposite is true. Life is amorphous, literature is formal. — FRANÇOISE SAGAN

3. At least since the time of Plato (see the piece directly following) some thoughtful people have wanted to ban certain works of literature because they allegedly stimulate the wrong sorts of pleasure or cause us to take pleasure in the wrong sorts of things. Consider, by way of comparison, bullfighting and cockfighting. Of course they cause pain to the animals, but branding animals also causes pain and it is not banned. Bullfighting and cockfighting probably are banned in the United States largely because most of us believe that people should not take pleasure in these activities. Now to return to literature: Should some kinds of writing be prohibited because they offer the wrong sorts of pleasure?

Plato

Plato (427–347 B.C.), an Athenian aristocrat by birth, was the student of one great philosopher (Socrates) and the teacher of another (Aristotle). His legacy of more than two dozen dialogues — imaginary discussions between Socrates and one or more other speakers, usually young Athenians — has been of such influence that the whole of Western philosophy can be characterized, A. N. Whitehead wrote, as "a series of footnotes to Plato." Plato's interests encompassed the full range of topics in philosophy: ethics, politics, logic, metaphysics, epistemology, aesthetics, psychology, and education.

This selection from Plato's Republic, *one of his best-known and longest dialogues, is about the education suitable for the rulers of an ideal society.* Republic *begins, typically, with an investigation into the nature of justice. Socrates (who speaks for Plato) convincingly explains to Glaucon that we cannot reasonably expect to achieve a just society unless we devote careful attention to the moral education of the young men who are scheduled in later life to become the rulers. (Here as elsewhere, Plato's elitism and aristocratic bias shows itself; as readers of* Republic *soon learn, Plato is no admirer of democracy or of a classless society.) Plato cares as much about what the educational curriculum should exclude as what it should include. His special target was the common practice in his day of using for pedagogy the Homeric tales and other stories about the gods. He readily embraces the principle of censorship, as the excerpt explains, because he thinks it is a necessary means to achieve the ideal society.*

"The Greater Part of the Stories Current Today We Shall Have to Reject"

"What kind of education shall we give them then? We shall find it difficult to improve on the time-honored distinction between the physical training we give to the body and the education we give to the mind and character."

"True."

"And we shall begin by educating mind and character, shall we not?"

"Of course."

"In this education you would include stories, would you not?"   5

"Yes."

"These are of two kinds, true stories and fiction.[1] Our education must use both, and start with fiction."

"I don't know what you mean."

"But you know that we begin by telling children stories. These are, in general, fiction, though they contain some truth. And we tell children stories before we start them on physical training."

"That is so."   10

"That is what I meant by saying that we must start to educate the mind before training the body."

"You are right," he said.

"And the first step, as you know, is always what matters most, particularly when we are dealing with those who are young and tender. That is the time when they are easily molded and when any impression we choose to make leaves a permanent mark."

"That is certainly true."

"Shall we therefore readily allow our children to listen to any   15 stories made up by anyone, and to form opinions that are for the most part the opposite of those we think they should have when they grow up?"

"We certainly shall not."

"Then it seems that our first business is to supervise the production of stories, and choose only those we think suitable, and reject the rest. We shall persuade mothers and nurses to tell our chosen stories to their children, and by means of them to mold their minds and characters which are more important than their bodies. The greater part of the stories current today we shall have to reject."

"Which are you thinking of?"

"We can take some of the major legends as typical. For all, whether major or minor, should be cast in the same mold and have the same effect. Do you agree?"

"Yes: but I'm not sure which you refer to as major."   20

"The stories in Homer and Hesiod and the poets. For it is the poets who have always made up fictions and stories to tell to men."

---

[1]The Greek word *pseudos* and its corresponding verb meant not only "fiction"—stories, tales—but also "what is not true" and so, in suitable contexts, "lies": and this ambiguity should be borne in mind. [Editors' note: All footnotes are by the translator, but some have been omitted.]

"What sort of stories do you mean and what fault do you find in them?"

"The worst fault possible," I replied, "especially if the fiction is an ugly one."

"And what is that?"

"Misrepresenting the nature of gods and heroes, like a portrait [25] painter whose portraits bear no resemblance to their originals."

"That is a fault which certainly deserves censure. But give me more details."

"Well, on the most important of subjects, there is first and foremost the foul story about Ouranos[2] and the things Hesiod says he did, and the revenge Cronos took on him. While the story of what Cronos did, and what he suffered at the hands of his son, is not fit as it is to be lightly repeated to the young and foolish, even if it were true; it would be best to say nothing about it, or if it must be told, tell it to a select few under oath of secrecy, at a rite which required, to restrict it still further, the sacrifice not of a mere pig but of something large and difficult to get."

"These certainly are awkward stories."

"And they shall not be repeated in our state, Adeimantus," I said. "Nor shall any young audience be told that anyone who commits horrible crimes, or punishes his father unmercifully, is doing nothing out of the ordinary but merely what the first and greatest of the gods have done before."

"I entirely agree," said Adeimantus, "that these stories are un- [30] suitable."

"Nor can we permit stories of wars and plots and battles among the gods; they are quite untrue, and if we want our prospective guardians to believe that quarrelsomeness is one of the worst of evils, we must certainly not let them be told the story of the Battle of the Giants or embroider it on robes, or tell them other tales about many and various quarrels between gods and heroes and their friends and relations. On the contrary, if we are to persuade them that no citizen has ever quarreled with any other, because it is sinful, our old men and women must tell children stories with this end in view from the first, and we must compel our poets to tell them similar stories when they grow up. But we can admit to our state no stories about Hera being tied up by her son, or Hephaestus being flung out of Heaven by his father for trying to help his mother when she was getting a beating, nor any of Homer's Battles of the Gods, whether their intention is allegorical or not. Children

---

[2]**Ouranos** (the sky), the original supreme god, was castrated by his son Cronos to separate him from Gaia (mother earth). Cronos was in turn deposed by Zeus in a struggle in which Zeus was helped by the Titans.

cannot distinguish between what is allegory and what isn't, and opinions formed at that age are usually difficult to eradicate or change; we should therefore surely regard it as of the utmost importance that the first stories they hear shall aim at encouraging the highest excellence of character."

"Your case is a good one," he agreed, "but if someone wanted details, and asked what stories we were thinking of, what should we say?"

To which I replied, "My dear Adeimantus, you and I are not engaged on writing stories but on founding a state. And the founders of a state, though they must know the type of story the poet must produce, and reject any that do not conform to that type, need not write them themselves."

"True: but what are the lines on which our poets must work when they deal with the gods?"

"Roughly as follows," I said. "God must surely always be represented 35 as he really is, whether the poet is writing epic, lyric, or tragedy."

"He must."

"And in reality of course god is good, and he must be so described."

"Certainly."

"But nothing good is harmful, is it?"[3]

"I think not." 40

"Then can anything that is not harmful do harm?"

"No."

"And can what does no harm do evil?"

"No again."

"And can what does no evil be the cause of any evil?" 45

"How could it?"

"Well then; is the good beneficial?"

"Yes."

"So it must be the cause of well-being."

"Yes." 50

"So the good is not the cause of everything, but only of states of well-being and not of evil."

"Most certainly," he agreed.

"Then god, being good, cannot be responsible for everything, as is commonly said, but only for a small part of human life, for the greater part of which he has no responsibility. For we have a far smaller share of good than of evil, and while god must be held to be the sole cause of good, we must look for some factors other than god as cause of the evil."

"I think that's very true," he said.

---

[3]The reader of the following passage should bear the following ambiguities in mind: (1) the Greek word for good (*agathos*) can mean (a) morally good, (b) beneficial or advantageous; (2) the Greek word for evil (*kakos*) can also mean harm or injury; (3) the adverb of *agathos* (*eu*—the well) can imply either morally right or prosperous. The word translated "cause of" could equally well be rendered "responsible for."

"So we cannot allow Homer or any other poet to make such a stupid 55
mistake about the gods, as when he says that

> Zeus has two jars standing on the floor of his palace, full of fates, good
> in one and evil in the other

and that the man to whom Zeus allots a mixture of both has 'varying
fortunes sometimes good and sometimes bad,' while the man to whom
he allots unmixed evil is 'chased by ravening despair over the face of the
earth.'[4] Nor can we allow references to Zeus as 'dispenser of good and
evil.' And we cannot approve if it is said that Athene and Zeus prompted
the breach of solemn treaty and oath by Pandarus, or that the strife and
contentions of the gods were due to Themis and Zeus. Nor again can we
let our children hear from Aeschylus that

> God implants a fault in man, when he wishes to destroy a house utterly.

No: We must forbid anyone who writes a play about the sufferings of
Niobe (the subject of the play from which these last lines are quoted), or
the house of Pelops, or the Trojan war, or any similar topic, to say they
are acts of god; or if he does he must produce the sort of interpretation
we are now demanding, and say that god's acts were good and just, and
that the sufferers were benefited by being punished. What the poet must
not be allowed to say is that those who were punished were made
wretched through god's action. He may refer to the wicked as wretched
because they needed punishment, provided he makes it clear that in
punishing them god did them good. But if a state is to be run on the
right lines, every possible step must be taken to prevent anyone, young
or old, either saying or being told, whether in poetry or prose, that god,
being good, can cause harm or evil to any man. To say so would be sinful, inexpedient, and inconsistent."

"I should approve of a law for this purpose and you have my vote for
it," he said.

"Then of our laws laying down the principles which those who write
or speak about the gods must follow, one would be this: *God is the cause,
not of all things, but only of good.*"

"I am quite content with that," he said.

Topics for Critical Thinking and Writing

1. In the beginning of the dialogue Plato says that adults recite fictions to
   very young children, and that these fictions help to mold character.

---

[4]Quotations from Homer are generally taken from the translations by Dr. Rieu in the Penguin series. At times (as here) the version quoted by Plato differs slightly from the accepted
text.

Think of some stories that you heard or read when young, such as "Snow White and the Seven Dwarfs" or "Ali Baba and the Forty Thieves." Try to think of a story that, in the final analysis, is not in accord with what you consider to be proper morality, such as a story in which a person triumphs through trickery, or a story in which evil actions—perhaps murders—are set forth without unfavorable comment. (Was it naughty of Jack to kill the giant?) Upon reflection, do you think children should not be told such stories? Why, or why not? Or think of the early film westerns, in which, on the whole, the Indians (except for an occasional Uncle Tonto) are depicted as bad guys and the whites (except for an occasional coward or rustler) are depicted as good guys. Many people who now have gray hair enjoyed such films in their childhood. Are you prepared to say that such films are not damaging? Or, on the other hand, are you prepared to say they are damaging and should be prohibited?

2. It is often objected that censorship of reading matter and of television programs available to children underrates their ability to think for themselves and to discount the dangerous, obscene, and tawdry. Do you agree with this objection? Does Plato?

3. Plato says that allowing poets to say what they please about the gods in his ideal state would be "inconsistent." Explain what he means by this criticism, and then explain why you agree or disagree with it.

4. Do you believe that parents should censor the "fiction" their children encounter (literature, films, pictures, music), but that the community should not censor the "fiction" of adults? Write an essay of 500 words on one of these topics: "Censorship and Rock Lyrics"; "X-rated Films"; "Ethnic Jokes." (These topics are broadly worded; you can narrow one, and offer whatever thesis you wish.)

5. Were you taught that any of the founding fathers ever acted disreputably, or that any American hero had any serious moral flaw? Or that America ever acted immorally in its dealings with other nations? Do you think it appropriate for children to hear such things?

THINKING ABOUT
GOVERNMENT FUNDING FOR THE ARTS

Our government supports the arts, including writers, by giving grants to numerous institutions. On the other hand, the amount that the government contributes is extremely small when compared to the amounts given to the arts by most European governments. Consider the following questions.

1. Should taxpayers' dollars be used to support the arts? Why, or why not?

2. What possible public benefit can come from supporting the arts? Can one argue that we should support the arts for the same reasons that we support the public schools, that is, to have a civilized society?

3. If dollars are given to the arts, should the political content of the works be taken into account, or only the aesthetic merit? Can we separate content from aesthetic merit? (The best way to approach this issue probably is to begin by thinking of a strongly political work.)

4. Is it censorship not to award public funds to writers whose work is not approved of, or is it simply a matter of refusing to reward them with taxpayers' dollars?

5. Should decisions about grants to writers be made chiefly by government officials or chiefly by experts in the field? Why?

A CASEBOOK ON LITERATURE AND SOCIETY: What Should Be Our National Anthem?

Caldwell Titcomb

Caldwell Titcomb (b. 1926), a professor emeritus of music at Brandeis University, has composed stage and film music scores. This essay first appeared in The New Republic, 1985.

Star-Spangled Earache: What So Loudly We Wail

Not long ago Representative Andrew Jacobs, Jr., of Indiana filed a bill to replace "The Star-Spangled Banner" with "America the Beautiful" as our national anthem. Many people have long advocated just such a change, and for a number of reasons the bill deserves wide support.

"The Star-Spangled Banner" has been the official national anthem only since March 3, 1931. Most people assume that it has been the anthem virtually from time immemorial and that it is thus now sacrosanct. But clearly there is nothing wrong with supplanting something that has been in effect for only fifty-odd years.

The music is by an Englishman, John Stafford Smith (1750–1836), who wrote it as a drinking song for a London social club, the Anacreontic Society. Is our nation so poverty-stricken that we must rule out homegrown music?

The tune is a constant stumbling block. Technically, it covers a span of a twelfth—that is, an octave plus a perfect fifth. Not only is it difficult for the general public to sing, but it has repeatedly caused trouble even for professional opera singers. Some people assert that this problem could be solved by selecting the right key for performance. But the point is that *all* twelve possible keys are poor. No matter what the key, the tune goes either too high or too low (and both, for some people). What's more, the tune is irregular in its phrasing, and does not always fit the text well. In "Whose broad stripes," for instance, assigning "broad" to a tiny sixteenth note is bad.

Finally, Francis Scott Key's poem (1814) is not suitable. It is of low quality as poetry, and its subject matter is too specific and too militaristic, dealing with a one-day incident in a war. Are glaring rockets and bursting bombs the essence of the nation? I wonder how many people have really read through all four stanzas and thought about the words. The third stanza is particularly offensive: "Their blood has wash'd out their foul footsteps' pollution. / No refuge could save the hireling and slave / From the terror of flight or the gloom of the grave." When a bank celebrated the last Independence Day by buying a full page in the *New York Times* to print the tune and text of the anthem, not surprisingly the dreadful third stanza was entirely omitted. The poem has little to recommend it except for the single line, "The land of the free and the home of the brave."

Why choose "America the Beautiful" in its place?

Both the text and music are by citizens of the United States. And now that we have overcome the notion that this is mainly a man's world, it is additionally fitting that the poem was written by a woman, Katharine Lee Bates (1859–1929), and the music by a man, Samuel Augustus Ward (1848–1903).

The music (composed in 1882) is simple and dignified, and exhibits balanced phrasing. The tune has a range of only a ninth—that is, an octave plus one step—which means that almost anyone, trained or untrained, can sing it. For the musically sophisticated, there is also a neat touch in the four-voice harmonization that has been standard since its first publication in 1888: The soprano tune of the first line becomes the bass part of the third line.

The poem—originally written in 1893, and by a happy coincidence first printed in the Fourth of July issue of a periodical in 1895 (and twice somewhat revised by its author)—is in its final form an admirable text of broad scope. It is not bellicose or geographically restricted, and all four stanzas can be sung without embarrassment. It was inspired by a trip taken by an Easterner through the Midwest (with a visit to the Chicago World's Columbian Exposition: "alabaster cities gleam") and on across "the fruited plain" and "amber waves of grain" to the Rocky Mountains (Pikes Peak in Colorado: "purple mountain majesties").

It acknowledges both urban and rural life. It pays homage to our nation's past and to those who have sacrificed themselves for their country (without glorifying war), it points to present virtues, and it voices a goal that our nation should aspire to ("brotherhood / From sea to shining sea"). Even a celebrated foreign historian was impelled to comment: "Few patriotic songs breathe such broad, humane idealism as this."

This joining of words and music has stood the test of time. The piece is taught and learned in school throughout the country, and is known and loved by the populace at large, which can sing it effectively, confidently, and with pride.

There has long been widespread advocacy for making it our national anthem. When the selection of an anthem was before Congress in 1931, several organizations, acting independently, took a strong stand in favor of "America the Beautiful" and against "The Star-Spangled Banner," including the National Federation of Music Clubs, the National Hymn Society, the Music Supervisors National Conference, and education experts at Columbia Teachers College.

When the controversy resurfaced in Boston in 1977 (as it periodically does here and there), a poll of *Boston Globe* readers revealed that they favored "America the Beautiful" over "The Star-Spangled Banner" by a vote of 493 to 220. And it has already been adopted as the official song of the National Federation of Women's Clubs.

From time to time people have expressed a preference for other choices, but these can easily be shown unsuitable. "The Battle Hymn of the Republic" (1861), like "The Star-Spangled Banner," is too warlike, and its tune belongs to "John Brown's Body Lies A-Mould'ring in the Grave." The music of Irving Berlin's "God Bless America" (1918) is insufficiently dignified, and the text setting is faulty. "My Country 'Tis of Thee" uses the music of the British national anthem, and thus cannot be seriously considered. John Philip Sousa's "The Stars and Stripes Forever" (1897) is as great a march as anyone has ever composed, but it lacks a text and only its refrain would lend itself to singing. The idea of having a nationwide contest for a new anthem has been tried, without success. If tried again, there would surely be no agreement.

When one takes all factors into account, "America the Beautiful" is 15 by far the outstanding candidate. It would indeed be fortunate if the entire country could sing "America the Beautiful" as the official national anthem when it celebrates the two-hundredth anniversary of the Constitution on September 17, 1987. We have less than two years to accomplish this worthy task.

Topics for Critical Thinking and Writing

1. Evaluate Titcomb's title and first paragraph. How effective do you think they are? How would you defend (or criticize) them?

2. List, in order, Titcomb's arguments for replacing the anthem. Do you think the sequence is reasonable and effective? Why, or why not?

3. Suppose someone were to argue, by analogy, that since the national bird is the bald eagle, not exactly a gentle creature, it is appropriate that the national anthem be similarly vigorous and even warlike. Write a 100-word essay supporting or attacking the analogy.

4. Titcomb asserts in paragraph 5 that "The poem has little to recommend it except for the single line, 'The land of the free and the home of the brave.'" Do you agree with his evaluation? And, whether you agree or not, do you think he should have *argued* that Key's poem is weak rather than merely asserting that it is?

5. As his final paragraph indicates, Titcomb wrote the essay in 1985, two years before the two-hundredth anniversary of the Constitution. We have now passed that landmark, and so his final paragraph is no longer appropriate. Regardless of the merits of Titcomb's position, write a new concluding paragraph for his essay.

Hendrik Hertzberg

Hendrik Hertzberg (b. 1943) is the editorial director of The New Yorker, *where this essay originally appeared in 1997.*

Star-Spangled Banter

Ted Turner set off a firecracker of his own this Fourth of July. Speaking in front of Independence Hall, in Philadelphia, he argued that it's time to dump "The Star-Spangled Banner." Over the years, Mr. Turner has had many capital ideas — CNN, Turner Classic Movies, and interrupting Jane Fonda's career as a serial monogamist, to name three. Now he has come up with another, and one cannot but agree with him. By all means, let us ease the old chestnut into well-deserved retirement. But not for the reason he offers, and not to make way for the alternative he recommends.

Mr. T notes that the national anthem is warlike, whereas the age we live in is (relatively) peaceful. He is right on both counts, but his second point makes his first less compelling. Just as gun control is more urgent in Detroit than in Lausanne, bellicose songs are more worrying in bellicose times than in times of tranquillity. "The Star-Spangled Banner" is warlike, yes. But so are a lot of first-rate national anthems. ("The Marseillaise," with its ghoulish call to "drench our fields" in "impure blood," makes its American counterpart sound like a Joni Mitchell ditty.) In any case, there are plenty of better reasons for getting rid of "The Star-Spangled Banner." Its tonal range corresponds to that of the electric guitar, as Jimi Hendrix proved, but not to that of the human voice. The lyrics include some fine phrases — "the twilight's last gleaming," "the ramparts we watched"—that are a reliable source of titles for the type of potboiler novel that goes in for raised lettering on the jacket, but on the whole the words don't convey what politicians call core American values. Francis Scott Key's poem was written to immortalize the siege of Fort McHenry, Maryland, during the War of 1812—a silly war, a minor war, a war that ended in what was at best a tie. (The British torched the White House and smashed our hopes of gobbling up Canada. We got to keep our independence.) The poem lends itself to mishearing, from the traditional "José, can you see" opening, through "O, sadists that stars spank," to the closing "Orlando D. Free and Homer D. Brave."

Congress designated "The Star-Spangled Banner" our national anthem during the Hoover Administration, when the country's judgment was impaired by clinical depression. The relevant bill—whose sponsor hoped to promote the tourist trade in his district, which included Fort McHenry—was rejected three times by the House before it finally passed, on a slow day. It was supported by the "Americanism" busybodies of the Daughters of the American Revolution and the American Legion but opposed by music teachers—an important group at a time when pianos were more common than phonographs. The complaints then were identical to the complaints now: too martial, too irritating, too hard to sing.

What's the alternative? Mr. T suggests "America the Beautiful"—the music teachers' choice back in 1930, by the way. It's nice, but, like so many nice things, it's also wimpy. The best that can be said for it is that it's more singable than the incumbent. A third contender—"America (My Country, 'Tis of Thee)"—has O.K. words, but the tune is the same as that of "God Save the Queen." This would make for an unusually severe "Is there an echo in here?" problem during joint appearances by Bill Clinton and Tony Blair. How about "This Land Is Your Land"? Plenty of progressive-school pupils already think Woody Guthrie's populist jingle is the national anthem, but the tune is a little too Barney the Dinosaurish, and the lyrics have a musty, Popular Front feeling about them.

Our country has at hand what is perhaps the greatest patriotic hymn   5
ever written: "The Battle Hymn of the Republic." But secularists would object that it is too God-filled, and Southerners—white Southerners, at least—would complain that the vineyards it advocates trampling were their vineyards. ("The Star-Spangled Banner" was also popular with the Union Army, but never mind.) Perhaps "The Battle Hymn of the Republic" could be twinned with "Dixie," as in the Elvis Presley version, but "Dixie" has its own problems. Anyhow, serious countries do not have national medleys.

This space would like to offer a recommendation of its own: "Lift Ev'ry Voice and Sing." James Weldon Johnson, a poet of the Harlem Renaissance, wrote it, in 1900, for a Lincoln's Birthday celebration. It is already a national anthem of sorts; its alternative title, in fact, is "The Negro National Anthem." Its tune (by J. Rosamond Johnson, the poet's brother) is stirring, and so are its words. The opening verse, the one that would be sung at ballgames, goes, in part:

> Lift ev'ry voice and sing,
> Till earth and heaven ring,
> Ring with the harmonies of liberty . . .
> Sing a song full of the faith that the dark past has taught us,
> Sing a song full of the hope that the present has brought us;
> Facing the rising sun of our new day begun,
> Let us march on till victory is won.

No bombast, no boasting, no wimpishness—just good, solid values that are both American and universal. How about it, Ted?

Topics for Critical Thinking and Writing

1. List the reasons that Hertzberg gives for replacing "The Star-Spangled Banner" with "Lift Ev'ry Voice and Sing." (We give the full text of "The Star-Spangled Banner" on p. 377, and of "Lift Ev'ry Voice and Sing" on pp. 380–81.) Which of his reasons (if any) seem especially strong? Which (if any) seem especially weak? Explain your evaluations.

2. In paragraph 2 Hertzberg says that the French national anthem is first-rate even though it includes a "ghoulish call to 'drench our fields' in 'impure blood.'" If you are familiar with "The Marseillaise," evaluate Hertzberg's view of it. Even if you are not familiar with the anthem, indicate whether you think such phrases ought to disqualify the song from high praise as a national anthem.

3. Read or reread Caldwell Titcomb's essay (p. 371). In 500 words, write Titcomb's imagined response to Hertzberg. Might Titcomb be convinced by Hertzberg's argument? Or would Titcomb reject Hertzberg's nomination? In any case, write a response that you can imagine Titcomb offering.

Francis Scott Key

Francis Scott Key (1779–1843), a lawyer who practiced in Washington, wrote "The Star-Spangled Banner" while aboard a British ship, seeking the release of an American who had been taken prisoner during the War of 1812. After Key boarded the ship, the British force began bombarding Fort McHenry, in Baltimore Harbor, and Key was forced to remain on the ship throughout the night of September 13, 1814. Released the next morning, he drafted the poem while being taken ashore, and revised it in his Baltimore hotel on the night of September 14. It was published anonymously on September 20. The tune is that of a popular drinking song by John Stafford Smith whose first words are "To Anacreon in Heaven." In 1916 President Wilson issued an executive order designating "The Star-Spangled Banner" as the national anthem, but it did not officially achieve this status until Congress confirmed Wilson's order in 1931.

The Star-Spangled Banner

O say, can you see, by the dawn's early light,
  What so proudly we hailed at the twilight's last gleaming?
Whose broad stripes and bright stars, through the perilous fight,
  O'er the ramparts we watched, were so gallantly streaming!
And the rockets' red glare, the bombs bursting in air,   5
Gave proof through the night that our flag was still there:
  O say, does that star-spangled banner yet wave
  O'er the land of the free and the home of the brave?

On the shore, dimly seen through the mists of the deep,
  Where the foe's haughty host in dread silence reposes,   10
What is that which the breeze, o'er the towering steep,
  As it fitfully blows, now conceals, now discloses?
Now it catches the gleam of the morning's first beam,
In full glory reflected now shines on the stream:
  'Tis the star-spangled banner! O long may it wave   15
  O'er the land of the free and the home of the brave!

And where is the band who so vauntingly swore
  That the havoc of war and the battle's confusion
A home and a country would leave us no more?
  Their blood has washed out their foul footsteps' pollution.   20
No refuge could save the hireling and slave
From the terror of flight, or the gloom of the grave:
  And the star-spangled banner in triumph doth wave
  O'er the land of the free and the home of the brave!

Oh! thus be it ever, when freemen shall stand   25
  Between their loved homes and the war's desolation!
Blest with victory and peace, may the heaven-rescued land
  Praise the Power that hath made and preserved us a nation.
Then conquer we must, for our cause it is just,
And this be our motto: "In God is our trust."   30
  And the star-spangled banner in triumph shall wave
  O'er the land of the free and the home of the brave!

Samuel Francis Smith

Samuel Francis Smith (1808–1895), a Boston Baptist clergyman, wrote "America" in 1831, when he was a student at Andover Theological Seminary. It was first sung on July 4, 1931, to the tune of the British "God Save the King."

America

My country! 'tis of thee,
Sweet land of liberty!
Of thee I sing;
Land where my fathers died,
Land of the pilgrim's pride,   5
From ev'ry mountain side
Let freedom ring.

My native country! thee,
Land of the noble free,
Thy name I love;   10
I love thy rocks and rills,
Thy woods and templed hills,
My heart with rapture thrills,
Like that above.

Our Father's God! to thee,   15
Author of liberty!
To thee we sing;
Long may our land be bright,
With freedom's holy light,
Protect us by Thy might,   20
Great God, our King.

Katharine Lee Bates

Katharine Lee Bates (1859–1929), a professor of English at Wellesley College, Massachusetts, wrote children's books and scholarly works as well as poems. "America the Beautiful," first published on July 4, 1895, was later set to music by Samuel Ward.

America the Beautiful

Oh beautiful for spacious skies,
For amber waves of grain,
For purple mountain majesties
Above the fruited plain.
America! America!   5
God shed His grace on thee,
And crown thy good with brotherhood
From sea to shining sea.

Oh beautiful for pilgrim feet
Whose stern impassioned stress   10
A thoroughfare for freedom beat
Across the wilderness.
America! America!
God mend thine ev'ry flaw,
Confirm thy soul in self-control,   15
Thy liberty in law.

Oh beautiful for heroes proved
In liberating strife,
Who more than self their country loved,
And mercy more than life.   20
America! America!
May God thy gold refine,
Till all success be nobleness,
And every gain divine.

Oh beautiful for patriot dream   25
That sees beyond the years,
Thine alabaster cities gleam,
Undimmed by human tears.
America! America!
God shed His grace on thee,   30
And crown thy good with brotherhood
From sea to shining sea.

James Weldon Johnson

James Weldon Johnson (1871–1938), born in Jacksonville, Florida, was the first African American lawyer to be admitted to the Florida bar, the founder in 1895 of the first black daily newspaper (the Daily American*), and a diplomat of distinction. He was also an accomplished poet, novelist, and essayist. "Lift Ev'ry Voice and Sing," written in 1900 to celebrate Lincoln's birthday, is well known among African Americans but not among other Americans. Johnson's poem was set to music composed by his brother, J. Rosamond Johnson.*

Lift Ev'ry Voice and Sing

1 Lift ev-ery voice and sing, till earth and heav-en ring, ring with the
2 Ston-y the road we trod, bit-ter the chas-tening rod, felt in the
3 God of our wea - ry years, God of our si - lent tears, God who has

har - mo - nies of lib - er - ty; Let our re - joic - ing
days when hope un - born had died; Yet with a stead - y
brought us thus, far on the way; God, who by your

rise, high as the lis - tening skies, let it re - sound loud as the
beat, have not our wea - ry feet, come to the place for which our
might, led us in - to the light, keep us for - ev - er in the

roll - ing sea. Sing a song full of the
peo - ple sighed? We have come o - ver a
path, we pray. Lest our feet stray from the

Topics for Critical Thinking and Writing

1. Which song do you consider the best as a poem, and which the weakest? Compare the two, indicating the reasons for your preference. *Suggestion*: You may want to begin by finding lines in each poem that you consider especially memorable or quotable. For instance, some students have cited, in "The Star-Spangled Banner," "The land of the free and the home of the brave." Which phrases particularly appeal to you? Try to explain *why* certain lines appeal. Probably your answers will have to do not only with the subject matter but also with the distinctive *way* in which it is expressed. For instance, do you agree that "The land of the free and the home of the brave" owes some of its effectiveness to the parallelism? Test this assertion by comparing it with "The land of the free, and brave people's home," or "The land of the free, where brave people live," or some such formulation.

2. Next turn to the overall content of the two poems you chose and discuss it in terms of suitability for the national anthem. If you are discussing "The Star-Spangled Banner," how much weight do you give to the argument that it is militaristic (especially in the third and fourth stanzas), too much so to be our anthem?

3. "The Star-Spangled Banner" asserts that "In God is our trust." It also says that our nation is "heaven-rescued" and it speaks of "the Power that hath made and preserved us a nation." Smith's "America" ends by referring to "Great God, our King"; Bates's "America the Beautiful" and Johnson's "Lift Ev'ry Voice and Sing" also speak of God. Americans hold a variety of faiths, and some Americans do not believe in God. Are the quoted expressions inappropriate in the anthem of a nation that does not have a national church? Explain your reasoning.

4. If you are familiar with a national anthem other than "The Star-Spangled Banner," evaluate it (1) as a poem or song, and (2) as a national anthem. (Bring at least a few copies of the work to class.)

Part Four

A CASEBOOK
ON THE STATE
AND THE INDIVIDUAL

12

How Much Obedience to the State Does Conscience Demand?

Sophocles

One of the three great tragic dramatists of ancient Greece, Sophocles (496?–406 B.C.) was born in Colonus, near Athens. He is said to have written 120 plays, but only 7 tragedies are extant.

Antigone, probably written about 441 B.C., is one play in Sophocles' so-called Theban Trilogy, three plays about the family of Oedipus, King of Thebes. In fact, however, the three plays were written at widely separated intervals; King Oedipus *is usually dated about 430 B.C., and the third play,* Oedipus at Colonus, *written at the very end of Sophocles' life, was not produced until 401 B.C., five years after his death. Further, although* Antigone *is the first in terms of date of composition, in terms of the narrative it is the last, taking place after the death of Oedipus.*

Just as today someone writing a novel, play, or film script on the Civil War can assume that we know the roles of characters with the names of Lincoln, Grant, Lee, Jackson, and Booth and yet can still offer fresh characterizations of these figures, so Sophocles could assume that his audience knew the outlines of the story of Oedipus and his family, and yet he could to some degree make it his own story. The gist is this: When Oedipus, King of Thebes, learned that he had unknowingly killed his father and married his mother, he blinded himself and left Thebes. Ultimately he died in Colonus. His sons, Polyneices and Eteocles, quarreled; Polyneices was driven out, went to Argos, and returned with the Argive army to assault Thebes, and in the battle each brother killed the other. Creon became king (this is the situation in Antigone) *and ordered that Polyneices' body be left to rot unburied on the battlefield because he attacked his own city.*

Antigone

An English Version by Dudley Fitts and Robert Fitzgerald

LIST OF CHARACTERS
ANTIGONE
ISMENE
EURYDICE

CREON
HAIMON
TEIRESIAS
A SENTRY
A MESSENGER
CHORUS

SCENE: *Before the palace of Creon, King of Thebes. A central double door, and two lateral doors. A platform extends the length of the façade, and from this platform three steps lead down into the "orchestra," or chorus-ground.*

TIME: *Dawn of the day after the repulse of the Argive army from the assault on Thebes.*

Prologue

Antigone and Ismene enter from the central door of the palace.

ANTIGONE. Ismene, dear sister,
    You would think that we had already suffered enough
    For the curse on Oedipus.°
    I cannot imagine any grief
    That you and I have not gone through. And now—   5
    Have they told you of the new decree of our King Creon?
ISMENE. I have heard nothing: I know
    That two sisters lost two brothers, a double death
    In a single hour; and I know that the Argive army
    Fled in the night; but beyond this, nothing.   10
ANTIGONE. I thought so. And this is why I wanted you
    To come out here with me. There is something we must do.
ISMENE. Why do you speak so strangely?
ANTIGONE. Listen, Ismene:
    Creon buried our brother Eteocles   .   15
    With military honors, gave him a soldier's funeral,
    And it was right that he should; but Polyneices,
    Who fought as bravely and died as miserably,—
    They say that Creon has sworn
    No one shall bury him, no one mourn for him,   20
    But his body must lie in the fields, a sweet treasure
    For carrion birds to find as they search for food.
    That is what they say, and our good Creon is coming here

---

3 Oedipus once King of Thebes, was the father of Antigone and Ismene, and of their brothers Polyneices and Eteocles. Oedipus unwittingly killed his father, Laïos, and married his own mother, Iocaste. When he learned what he had done, he blinded himself and left Thebes. Eteocles and Polyneices quarreled; Polyneices was driven out but returned to assault Thebes. In the battle each brother killed the other; Creon became king and ordered that Polyneices be left to rot unburied on the battlefield as a traitor. [All notes are the editors'.]

To announce it publicly; and the penalty—
Stoning to death in the public square!
                                        There it is, 25
And now you can prove what you are:
A true sister, or a traitor to your family.
ISMENE. Antigone, you are mad! What could I possibly do?
ANTIGONE. You must decide whether you will help me or not.
ISMENE. I do not understand you. Help you in what? 30
ANTIGONE. Ismene. I am going to bury him. Will you come?
ISMENE. Bury him! You have just said the new law forbids it.
ANTIGONE. He is my brother. And he is your brother, too.
ISMENE. But think of the danger! Think what Creon will do!
ANTIGONE. Creon is not strong enough to stand in my way. 35
ISMENE. Ah sister!
    Oedipus died, everyone hating him
    For what his own search brought to light, his eyes
    Ripped out by his own hand; and Iocaste died,
    His mother and wife at once: she twisted the cords 40
    That strangled her life; and our two brothers died,
    Each killed by the other's sword. And we are left:
    But oh, Antigone,
    Think how much more terrible than these
    Our own death would be if we should go against Creon 45
    And do what he has forbidden! We are only women,
    We cannot fight with men, Antigone!
    The law is strong, we must give in to the law
    In this thing, and in worse. I beg the Dead
    To forgive me, but I am helpless: I must yield 50
    To those in authority. And I think it is dangerous business
    To be always meddling.
ANTIGONE.   If that is what you think,
    I should not want you, even if you asked to come.
    You have made your choice, you can be what you want to be.
    But I will bury him; and if I must die, 55
    I say that this crime is holy: I shall lie down
    With him in death, and I shall be as dear
    To him as he to me.
                        It is the dead,
    Not the living, who make the longest demands:
    We die for ever. . . .
                        You may do as you like. 60
    Since apparently the laws of the gods mean nothing to you.
ISMENE. They mean a great deal to me; but I have no strength
    To break laws that were made for the public good.
ANTIGONE. That must be your excuse, I suppose. But as for me,
    I will bury the brother I love.

ISMENE.   Antigone,   65
    I am so afraid for you!
ANTIGONE.   You need not be:
    You have yourself to consider, after all.
ISMENE. But no one must hear of this, you must tell no one!
    I will keep it a secret, I promise!
ANTIGONE.   O tell it! Tell everyone!
    Think how they'll hate you when it all comes out   70
    If they learn that you knew about it all the time!
ISMENE. So fiery! You should be cold with fear.
ANTIGONE. Perhaps. But I am doing only what I must.
ISMENE. But can you do it? I say that you cannot.
ANTIGONE. Very well: when my strength gives out, I shall do no more.   75
ISMENE. Impossible things should not be tried at all.
ANTIGONE. Go away, Ismene:
    I shall be hating you soon, and the dead will too,
    For your words are hateful. Leave me my foolish plan:
    I am not afraid of the danger; if it means death,   80
    It will not be the worst of deaths — death without honor.
ISMENE. Go then, if you feel that you must.
    You are unwise,
    But a loyal friend indeed to those who love you.

    Exit into the palace. Antigone goes off, left. Enter the Chorus.

Parodos

CHORUS. Now the long blade of the sun, lying   *Strophe° 1*
    Level east to west, touches with glory
    Thebes of the Seven Gates. Open, unlidded
    Eye of golden day! O marching light
    Across the eddy and rush of Dirce's stream,°   5
    Striking the white shields of the enemy
    Thrown headlong backward from the blaze of morning!
CHORAGOS.° Polyneices their commander
    Roused them with windy phrases,
    He the wild eagle screaming   10
    Insults above our land,
    His wings their shields of snow,
    His crest their marshalled helms.

CHORUS. Against our seven gates in a yawning ring   *Antistrophe° 1*
    The famished spears came onward in the night: 15

----

1 Strophe Literally, "turn," a stanza of a choral song, sung as the chorus moves in one direction.   **5 Dirce's stream** A stream west of Thebes.   **8 Choragos** Leader of the Chorus.
14 Antistrophe Sung as the chorus moves in the opposite direction.

But before his jaws were sated with our blood,
Or pine fire took the garland of our towers,
He was thrown back; and as he turned, great Thebes—
No tender victim for his noisy power—
Rose like a dragon behind him, shouting war.   20

CHORAGOS. For God hates utterly
The bray of bragging tongues;
And when he beheld their smiling,
Their swagger of golden helms,
The frown of his thunder blasted   25
Their first man from our walls.

CHORUS. We heard his shout of triumph high in the air   *Strophe 2*
Turn to a scream; far out in a flaming arc
He fell with his windy torch, and the earth struck him.
And others storming in fury no less than his   30
Found shock of death in the dusty joy of battle.

CHORAGOS. Seven captains at seven gates
Yielded their clanging arms to the god
That bends the battle-line and breaks it.
These two only, brothers in blood,   35
Face to face in matchless rage,
Mirroring each the other's death,
Clashed in long combat.

CHORUS. But now in the beautiful morning of victory   *Antistrophe 2*
Let Thebes of the many chariots sing for joy!   40
With hearts for dancing we'll take leave of war:
Our temples shall be sweet with hymns of praise,
And the long nights shall echo with our chorus.

Scene I

CHORAGOS. But now at last our new King is coming:
Creon of Thebes, Menoikeus' son.
In this auspicious dawn of his reign
What are the new complexities
That shifting Fate has woven for him?   5
What is his counsel? Why has he summoned
The old men to hear him?

Enter Creon from the palace, center. He addresses the Chorus from the top step.

CREON. Gentlemen: I have the honor to inform you that our Ship of State, which recent storms have threatened to destroy, has come safely to harbor at last, guided by the merciful wisdom of Heaven. I have sum- 10 moned you here this morning because I know that I can depend upon you: your devotion to King Laïos was absolute; you never hesitated in your duty to our late ruler Oedipus; and when Oedipus died, your

loyalty was transferred to his children. Unfortunately, as you know, his two
sons, the princes Eteocles and Polyneices, have killed each other in 15
battle; and I, as the next in blood, have succeeded to the full power of
the throne.

I am aware, of course, that no Ruler can expect complete loyalty
from his subjects until he has been tested in office. Nevertheless, I say to
you at the very outset that I have nothing but contempt for the kind of 20
Governor who is afraid, for whatever reason, to follow the course that
he knows is best for the State; and as for the man who sets private
friendship above the public welfare,—I have no use for him, either. I
call God to witness that if I saw my country headed for ruin, I should not
be afraid to speak out plainly; and I need hardly remind you that I would 25
never have any dealings with an enemy of the people. No one values
friendship more highly than I: but we must remember that friends made
at the risk of wrecking our Ship are not real friends at all.

These are my principles, at any rate, and that is why I have made the
following decision concerning the sons of Oedipus: Eteocles, who died as 30
a man should die, fighting for his country, is to be buried with full military honors, with all the ceremony that is usual when the greatest heroes die; but his brother Polyneices, who broke his exile to come back
with fire and sword against his native city and the shrines of his fathers'
gods, whose one idea was to spill the blood of his blood and sell his own 35
people into slavery—Polyneices, I say, is to have no burial: no man is to
touch him or say the least prayer for him; he shall lie on the plain, unburied; and the birds and the scavenging dogs can do with him whatever
they like.

This is my command, and you can see the wisdom behind it. As long 40
as I am King, no traitor is going to be honored with the loyal man. But
whoever shows by word and deed that he is on the side of the State—
he shall have my respect while he is living and my reverence when he
is dead.

CHORAGOS. If that is your will, Creon son of Menoikeus,   45
You have the right to enforce it: we are yours.

CREON. That is my will. Take care that you do your part.

CHORAGOS. We are old men: let the younger ones carry it out.

CREON. I do not mean that: the sentries have been appointed.

CHORAGOS. Then what is it that you would have us do?   50

CREON. You will give no support to whoever breaks the law.

CHORAGOS. Only a crazy man is in love with death!

CREON. And death it is; yet money talks, and the wisest
Have sometimes been known to count a few coins too many.

Enter Sentry from left.

SENTRY. I'll not say that I'm out of breath from running, King, because 55
every time I stopped to think about what I have to tell you, I felt like
going back. And all the time a voice kept saying, "You fool, don't you

know you're walking straight into trouble?"; and then another voice:
"Yes, but if you let somebody else get the news to Creon first, it will be
even worse than that for you!" But good sense won out, at least I hope it   60
was good sense, and here I am with a story that makes no sense at all;
but I'll tell it anyhow, because, as they say, what's going to happen's
going to happen and —

CREON. Come to the point. What have you to say?

SENTRY. I did not do it. I did not see who did it. You must not punish me   65
   for what someone else has done.

CREON. A comprehensive defense! More effective, perhaps,
   If I knew its purpose. Come: what is it?

SENTRY. A dreadful thing . . . I don't know how to put it —

CREON. Out with it!

SENTRY.   Well, then;   70
   The dead man —
                      Polyneices —

Pause. The Sentry is overcome, fumbles for words. Creon waits impassively.

                      out there —
                              someone, —
New dust on the slimy flesh!

Pause. No sign from Creon.

Someone has given it burial that way, and
Gone . . .

Long pause. Creon finally speaks with deadly control.

CREON. And the man who dared do this?

SENTRY.   I swear I   75
   Do not know! You must believe me!
                              Listen:
The ground was dry, not a sign of digging, no,
Not a wheeltrack in the dust, no trace of anyone.
It was when they relieved us this morning: and one of them,
The corporal, pointed to it.
                      There it was,   80
   The strangest —
             Look:
The body, just mounded over with light dust: you see?
Not buried really, but as if they'd covered it
Just enough for the ghost's peace. And no sign
Of dogs or any wild animal that had been there.   85

And then what a scene there was! Every man of us
Accusing the other: we all proved the other man did it,
We all had proof that we could not have done it.
We were ready to take hot iron in our hands,

Walk through fire, swear by all the gods,   90
It was not I!
I do not know who it was, but it was not I!

*Creon's rage has been mounting steadily, but the sentry is too intent upon his
story to notice it.*

And then, when this came to nothing, someone said
A thing that silenced us and made us stare
Down at the ground: you had to be told the news,   95
And one of us had to do it! We threw the dice,
And the bad luck fell to me. So here I am,
No happier to be here than you are to have me:
Nobody likes the man who brings bad news.

CHORAGOS. I have been wondering, King: can it be that the gods have 100
done this?

CREON (*furiously*). Stop!
Must you doddering wrecks
Go out of your heads entirely? "The gods"!
Intolerable!   105
The gods favor this corpse? Why? How had he served them?
Tried to loot their temples, burn their images,
Yes, and the whole State, and its laws with it!
Is it your senile opinion that the gods love to honor bad men?
A pious thought! —
                            No, from the very beginning   110
There have been those who have whispered together,
Stiff-necked anarchists, putting their heads together,
Scheming against me in alleys. These are the men,
And they have bribed my own guard to do this thing.
(*Sententiously.*) Money!   115
There's nothing in the world so demoralizing as money.
Down go your cities,
Homes gone, men gone, honest hearts corrupted.
Crookedness of all kinds, and all for money!
(*To Sentry.*)   But you —!
I swear by God and by the throne of God,   120
The man who has done this thing shall pay for it!
Find that man, bring him here to me, or your death
Will be the least of your problems: I'll string you up
Alive, and there will be certain ways to make you
Discover your employer before you die;   125
And the process may teach you a lesson you seem to have missed:
The dearest profit is sometimes all too dear:
That depends on the source. Do you understand me?
A fortune won is often misfortune.

SENTRY. King, may I speak?

CREON.   Your very voice distresses me.   130
SENTRY. Are you sure that it is my voice, and not your conscience?
CREON. By God, he wants to analyze me now!
SENTRY. It is not what I say, but what has been done, that hurts you.
CREON. You talk too much.
SENTRY.   Maybe; but I've done nothing.
CREON. Sold your soul for some silver: that's all you've done.   135
SENTRY. How dreadful it is when the right judge judges wrong!
CREON. Your figures of speech
    May entertain you now; but unless you bring me the man,
    You will get little profit from them in the end.

    Exit Creon into the palace.

SENTRY. "Bring me the man" — !   140
    I'd like nothing better than bringing him the man!
    But bring him or not, you have seen the last of me here.
    At any rate, I am safe!

    (Exit Sentry.)

Ode I

CHORUS. Numberless are the world's wonders, but none   *Strophe 1*
    More wonderful than man; the stormgray sea
    Yields to his prows, the huge crests bear him high;
    Earth, holy and inexhaustible, is graven
    With shining furrows where his plows have gone   5
    Year after year, the timeless labor of stallions.

    The lightboned birds and beasts that cling to cover,   *Antistrophe 1*
    The lithe fish lighting their reaches of dim water,
    All are taken, tamed in the net of his mind;
    The lion on the hill, the wild horse windy-maned,   10
    Resign to him; and his blunt yoke has broken
    The sultry shoulders of the mountain bull.

    Words also, and thought as rapid as air,   *Strophe 2*
    He fashions to his good use; statecraft is his,
    And his the skill that deflects the arrows of snow,   15
    The spears of winter rain: from every wind
    He has made himself secure — from all but one:
    In the late wind of death he cannot stand.

    O clear intelligence, force beyond all measure!   *Antistrophe 2*
    O fate of man, working both good and evil!   20
    When the laws are kept, how proudly his city stands!
    When the laws are broken, what of his city then?

Never may the anarchic man find rest at my hearth,
Never be it said that my thoughts are his thoughts.

Scene II

Reenter Sentry leading Antigone.

CHORAGOS. What does this mean? Surely this captive woman
    Is the Princess, Antigone. Why should she be taken?
SENTRY. Here is the one who did it! We caught her
    In the very act of burying him. — Where is Creon?
CHORAGOS. Just coming from the house.

Enter Creon, center.

CREON.   What has happened?   5
    Why have you come back so soon?
SENTRY (*expansively*).   O King,
    A man should never be too sure of anything:
    I would have sworn
    That you'd not see me here again: your anger
    Frightened me so, and the things you threatened me with;   10
    But how could I tell then
    That I'd be able to solve the case so soon?
    No dice-throwing this time: I was only too glad to come!
    Here is this woman. She is the guilty one:
    We found her trying to bury him.   15
    Take her, then; question her; judge her as you will.
    I am through with the whole thing now, and glad of it.
CREON. But this is Antigone! Why have you brought her here?
SENTRY. She was burying him, I tell you!
CREON (*severely*).   Is this the truth?
SENTRY. I saw her with my own eyes. Can I say more?   20
CREON. The details: come, tell me quickly!
SENTRY.   It was like this:
    After those terrible threats of yours, King,
    We went back and brushed the dust away from the body.
    The flesh was soft by now, and stinking,
    So we sat on a hill to windward and kept guard.   25
    No napping this time! We kept each other awake.
    But nothing happened until the white round sun
    Whirled in the center of the round sky over us:
    Then, suddenly,
    A storm of dust roared up from the earth, and the sky   30
    Went out, the plain vanished with all its trees
    In the stinging dark. We closed our eyes and endured it.
    The whirlwind lasted a long time, but it passed;
    And then we looked, and there was Antigone!

I have seen   35
A mother bird come back to a stripped nest, heard
Her crying bitterly a broken note or two
For the young ones stolen. Just so, when this girl
Found the bare corpse, and all her love's work wasted,
She wept, and cried on heaven to damn the hands   40
That had done this thing.
                                    And then she brought more dust
And sprinkled wine three times for her brother's ghost.

We ran and took her at once. She was not afraid,
Not even when we charged her with what she had done.
She denied nothing.
                                    And this was a comfort to me,   45
And some uneasiness: for it is a good thing
To escape from death, but it is no great pleasure
To bring death to a friend.
                                    Yet I always say
There is nothing so comfortable as your own safe skin!
CREON (*slowly, dangerously*).   And you, Antigone,   50
    You with your head hanging, — do you confess this thing?
ANTIGONE.   I do. I deny nothing.
CREON (*to Sentry*).   You may go.

    (*Exit Sentry.*)

    (*To Antigone.*) Tell me, tell me briefly:
Had you heard my proclamation touching this matter?
ANTIGONE.   It was public. Could I help hearing it?   55
CREON.   And yet you dared defy the law.
ANTIGONE.   I dared.
    It was not God's proclamation. That final Justice
    That rules the world below makes no such laws.

Your edict, King, was strong.
But all your strength is weakness itself against   60
The immortal unrecorded laws of God.
They are not merely now: they were, and shall be,
Operative for ever, beyond man utterly.
I knew I must die, even without your decree:
I am only mortal. And if I must die   65
Now, before it is my time to die,
Surely this is no hardship: can anyone
Living, as I live, with evil all about me,
Think Death less than a friend? This death of mine
Is of no importance; but if I had left my brother   70
Lying in death unburied, I should have suffered.

Now I do not.
              You smile at me. Ah Creon,
Think me a fool, if you like; but it may well be
That a fool convicts me of folly.
CHORAGOS. Like father, like daughter: both headstrong, deaf to reason!   75
    She has never learned to yield.
CREON.   She has much to learn.
    The inflexible heart breaks first, the toughest iron
    Cracks first, and the wildest horses bend their necks
    At the pull of the smallest curb.
                   Pride? In a slave?
    This girl is guilty of a double insolence,   80
    Breaking the given laws and boasting of it.
    Who is the man here,
    She or I, if this crime goes unpunished?
    Sister's child, or more than sister's child,
    Or closer yet in blood—she and her sister   85
    Win bitter death for this!
    (*To Servants.*)   Go, some of you,
    Arrest Ismene. I accuse her equally.
    Bring her: you will find her sniffling in the house there.

    Her mind's a traitor: crimes kept in the dark
    Cry for light, and the guardian brain shudders;   90
    But how much worse than this
    Is brazen boasting of barefaced anarchy!
ANTIGONE. Creon, what more do you want than my death?
CREON.   Nothing.
    That gives me everything.
ANTIGONE.   Then I beg you: kill me.
    This talking is a great weariness: your words   95
    Are distasteful to me, and I am sure that mine
    Seem so to you. And yet they should not seem so:
    I should have praise and honor for what I have done.
    All these men here would praise me
    Were their lips not frozen shut with fear of you.   100
    (*Bitterly.*) Ah the good fortune of kings,
    Licensed to say and do whatever they please!
CREON. You are alone here in that opinion.
ANTIGONE. No, they are with me. But they keep their tongues in leash.
CREON. Maybe. But you are guilty, and they are not.   105
ANTIGONE. There is no guilt in reverence for the dead.
CREON. But Eteocles—was he not your brother too?
ANTIGONE. My brother too.
CREON.   And you insult his memory?
ANTIGONE (*softly*). The dead man would not say that I insult it.

CREON. He would: for you honor a traitor as much as him.   110
ANTIGONE. His own brother, traitor or not, and equal in blood.
CREON. He made war on his country. Eteocles defended it.
ANTIGONE. Nevertheless, there are honors due all the dead.
CREON. But not the same for the wicked as for the just.
ANTIGONE. Ah Creon, Creon,   115
    Which of us can say what the gods hold wicked?
CREON. An enemy is an enemy, even dead.
ANTIGONE. It is my nature to join in love, not hate.
CREON (*finally losing patience*). Go join them then; if you must have your love,
    Find it in hell!   120
CHORAGOS. But see, Ismene comes:

Enter Ismene, guarded.

    Those tears are sisterly, the cloud
    That shadows her eyes rains down gentle sorrow.
CREON. You too, Ismene,
    Snake in my ordered house, sucking my blood   125
    Stealthily—and all the time I never knew
    That these two sisters were aiming at my throne!

                                          Ismene,
    Do you confess your share in this crime, or deny it?
    Answer me.
ISMENE. Yes, if she will let me say so. I am guilty.   130
ANTIGONE (*coldly*). No, Ismene. You have no right to say so.
    You would not help me, and I will not have you help me.
ISMENE. But now I know what you meant; and I am here
    To join you, to take my share of punishment.
ANTIGONE. The dead man and the gods who rule the dead   135
    Know whose act this was. Words are not friends.
ISMENE. Do you refuse me, Antigone? I want to die with you:
    I too have a duty that I must discharge to the dead.
ANTIGONE. You shall not lessen my death by sharing it.
ISMENE. What do I care for life when you are dead?   140
ANTIGONE. Ask Creon. You're always hanging on his opinions.
ISMENE. You are laughing at me. Why, Antigone?
ANTIGONE. It's a joyless laughter, Ismene.
ISMENE.   But can I do nothing?
ANTIGONE. Yes. Save yourself. I shall not envy you.
    There are those who will praise you; I shall have honor, too.   145
ISMENE. But we are equally guilty!
ANTIGONE.   No more, Ismene.
    You are alive, but I belong to Death.
CREON (*to the Chorus*). Gentlemen, I beg you to observe these girls:
    One has just now lost her mind; the other,
    It seems, has never had a mind at all.   150

ISMENE. Grief teaches the steadiest minds to waver, King.

CREON. Yours certainly did, when you assumed guilt with the guilty!

ISMENE. But how could I go on living without her?

CREON.   You are.

  She is already dead.

ISMENE.   But your own son's bride!

CREON. There are places enough for him to push his plow.   155

  I want no wicked women for my sons!

ISMENE. O dearest Haimon, how your father wrongs you!

CREON. I've had enough of your childish talk of marriage!

CHORAGOS. Do you really intend to steal this girl from your son?

CREON. No; Death will do that for me.

CHORAGOS.   Then she must die?   160

CREON (*ironically*). You dazzle me.

                    —But enough of this talk!

(*To Guards.*) You, there, take them away and guard them well:

For they are but women, and even brave men run

When they see Death coming.

Exeunt Ismene, Antigone, and Guards.

Ode II

CHORUS. Fortunate is the man who has never tasted God's

   vengeance!   *Strophe 1*

Where once the anger of heaven has struck, that house is shaken

For ever: damnation rises behind each child

Like a wave cresting out of the black northeast,

When the long darkness under sea roars up   5

And bursts drumming death upon the windwhipped sand.

I have seen this gathering sorrow from time long past   *Antistrophe 1*

Loom upon Oedipus' children: generation from generation

Takes the compulsive rage of the enemy god.

So lately this last flower of Oedipus' line   10

Drank the sunlight! but now a passionate word

And a handful of dust have closed up all its beauty.

What mortal arrogance   *Strophe 2*

Transcends the wrath of Zeus°?

Sleep cannot lull him nor the effortless long months   15

Of the timeless gods: but he is young for ever,

And his house is the shining day of high Olympos.

All that is and shall be,

And all the past, is his.

14 Zeus Chief Greek deity.

No pride on earth is free of the curse of heaven. 20

The straying dreams of men *Antistrophe 2*
   May bring them ghosts of joy:
But as they drowse, the waking embers burn them;
Or they walk with fixed eyes, as blind men walk.
But the ancient wisdom speaks for our own time: 25
   Fate works most for woe
   With Folly's fairest show.
Man's little pleasure is the spring of sorrow.

Scene III

CHORAGOS. But here is Haimon, King, the last of all your sons.
   Is it grief for Antigone that brings him here,
   And bitterness at being robbed of his bride?

Enter Haimon.

CREON. We shall soon see, and no need of diviners.
                         —Son,
   You have heard my final judgment on that girl: 5
   Have you come here hating me, or have you come
   With deference and with love, whatever I do?
HAIMON. I am your son, father. You are my guide.
   You make things clear for me, and I obey you.
   No marriage means more to me than your continuing wisdom. 10
CREON. Good. That is the way to behave: subordinate
   Everything else, my son, to your father's will.
   This is what a man prays for, that he may get
   Sons attentive and dutiful in his house,
   Each one hating his father's enemies, 15
   Honoring his father's friends. But if his sons
   Fail him, if they turn out unprofitably,
   What has he fathered but trouble for himself
   And amusement for the malicious?
                     So you are right
   Not to lose your head over this woman. 20
   Your pleasure with her would soon grow cold, Haimon,
   And then you'd have a hellcat in bed and elsewhere.
   Let her find her husband in Hell!
   Of all the people in this city, only she
   Has had contempt for my law and broken it. 25

Do you want me to show myself weak before the people?
Or to break my sworn word? No, and I will not.

The woman dies.
I suppose she'll plead "family ties." Well, let her.
If I permit my own family to rebel,   30
How shall I earn the world's obedience?
Show me the man who keeps his house in hand,
He's fit for public authority.

                     I'll have no dealings
With lawbreakers, critics of the government:
Whoever is chosen to govern should be obeyed—   35
Must be obeyed, in all things, great and small,
Just and unjust! O Haimon,
The man who knows how to obey, and that man only,
Knows how to give commands when the time comes.
You can depend on him, no matter how fast   40
The spears come: he's a good soldier, he'll stick it out.

Anarchy, anarchy! Show me a greater evil!
This is why cities tumble and the great houses rain down,
This is what scatters armies!
No, no: good lives are made so by discipline.   45
We keep the laws then, and the lawmakers,
And no woman shall seduce us. If we must lose,
Let's lose to a man, at least! Is a woman stronger than we?
CHORAGOS. Unless time has rusted my wits,
What you say, King, is said with point and dignity.   50
HAIMON (*boyishly earnest*). Father:
Reason is God's crowning gift to man, and you are right
To warn me against losing mine. I cannot say—
I hope that I shall never want to say!—that you
Have reasoned badly. Yet there are other men   55
Who can reason, too; and their opinions might be helpful.
You are not in a position to know everything
That people say or do, or what they feel:
Your temper terrifies—everyone
Will tell you only what you like to hear.   60
But I, at any rate, can listen; and I have heard them
Muttering and whispering in the dark about this girl.
They say no woman has ever, so unreasonably,
Died so shameful a death for a generous act:
"She covered her brother's body. Is this indecent?   65
She kept him from dogs and vultures. Is this a crime?
Death?—She should have all the honor that we can give her!"

This is the way they talk out there in the city.

You must believe me:

Nothing is closer to me than your happiness.   70
What could be closer? Must not any son
Value his father's fortune as his father does his?
I beg you, do not be unchangeable:
Do not believe that you alone can be right.
The man who thinks that,   75
The man who maintains that only he has the power
To reason correctly, the gift to speak, the soul—
A man like that, when you know him, turns out empty.

It is not reason never to yield to reason!
In flood time you can see how some trees bend,   80
And because they bend, even their twigs are safe,
While stubborn trees are torn up, roots and all.
And the same thing happens in sailing:
Make your sheet fast, never slacken,—and over you go,
Head over heels and under: and there's your voyage.   85
Forget you are angry! Let yourself be moved!
I know I am young; but please let me say this:
The ideal condition
Would be, I admit, that men should be right by instinct;
But since we are all too likely to go astray,   90
The reasonable thing is to learn from those who can teach.
CHORAGOS. You will do well to listen to him, King,
    If what he says is sensible. And you, Haimon,
    Must listen to your father.—Both speak well.
CREON. You consider it right for a man of my years and experience   95
    To go to school to a boy?
HAIMON.   It is not right
    If I am wrong. But if I am young, and right,
    What does my age matter?
CREON. You think it right to stand up for an anarchist?
HAIMON. Not at all. I pay no respect to criminals.   100
CREON. Then she is not a criminal?
HAIMON. The City would deny it, to a man.
CREON. And the City proposes to teach me how to rule?
HAIMON. Ah. Who is it that's talking like a boy now?
CREON. My voice is the one voice giving orders in this City!   105
HAIMON. It is no City if it takes orders from one voice.
CREON. The State is the King!
HAIMON.   Yes, if the State is a desert.

    Pause.

CREON. This boy, it seems, has sold out to a woman.
HAIMON. If you are a woman: my concern is only for you.
CREON. So? Your "concern"! In a public brawl with your father!   110

HAIMON. How about you, in a public brawl with justice?
CREON. With justice, when all that I do is within my rights?
HAIMON. You have no right to trample on God's right.
CREON (completely out of control). Fool, adolescent fool! Taken in by
    a woman!
HAIMON. You'll never see me taken in by anything vile.   115
CREON. Every word you say is for her!
HAIMON. (quietly, darkly).   And for you.
    And for me. And for the gods under the earth.
CREON. You'll never marry her while she lives.
HAIMON. Then she must die.—But her death will cause another.
CREON. Another?   120
    Have you lost your senses? Is this an open threat?
HAIMON. There is no threat in speaking to emptiness.
CREON. I swear you'll regret this superior tone of yours!
    You are the empty one!
HAIMON.   If you were not my father,
    I'd say you were perverse.   125
CREON. You girlstruck fool, don't play at words with me!
HAIMON. I am sorry. You prefer silence.
CREON.   Now, by God—!
    I swear, by all the gods in heaven above us,
    You'll watch it, I swear you shall!
    (To the Servants.)   Bring her out!
    Bring the woman out! Let her die before his eyes!   130
    Here, this instant, with her bridegroom beside her!
HAIMON. Not here, no; she will not die here, King.
    And you will never see my face again.
    Go on raving as long as you've a friend to endure you.

    (Exit Haimon.)

CHORAGOS. Gone, gone.   135
    Creon, a young man in a rage is dangerous!
CREON. Let him do, or dream to do, more than a man can.
    He shall not save these girls from death.
CHORAGOS.   These girls?
    You have sentenced them both?
CREON.   No, you are right.
    I will not kill the one whose hands are clean.   140
CHORAGOS. But Antigone?
CREON (somberly).   I will carry her far away
    Out there in the wilderness, and lock her
    Living in a vault of stone. She shall have food,
    As the custom is, to absolve the State of her death.
    And there let her pray to the gods of hell: 145
    They are her only gods:

Perhaps they will show her an escape from death,
Or she may learn,
                    though late,
That piety shown the dead is piety in vain.

(Exit Creon.)

Ode III

CHORUS. Love, unconquerable   *Strophe*
        Waster of rich men, keeper
        Of warm lights and all-night vigil
        In the soft face of a girl:
        Sea-wanderer, forest-visitor!   5
        Even the pure Immortals cannot escape you,
        And mortal man, in his one day's dusk,
        Trembles before your glory.

        Surely you swerve upon ruin   *Antistrophe*
        The just man's consenting heart,   10
        As here you have made bright anger
        Strike between father and son—
        And none has conquered but Love!
        A girl's glance working the will of heaven:
        Pleasure to her alone who mocks us,   15
        Merciless Aphrodite.°

Scene IV

CHORAGOS (*as Antigone enters guarded*). But I can no longer stand in awe of this,
        Nor, seeing what I see, keep back my tears.
        Here is Antigone, passing to that chamber
        Where all find sleep at last.

ANTIGONE. Look upon me, friends, and pity me   *Strophe 1*   5
        Turning back at the night's edge to say
        Good-by to the sun that shines for me no longer;
        Now sleepy Death
        Summons me down to Acheron,° that cold shore:
        There is no bridesong there, nor any music.   10
CHORUS. Yet not unpraised, not without a kind of honor,
        You walk at last into the underworld;
        Untouched by sickness, broken by no sword.

16 Aphrodite Goddess of love.   **Scene IV 9 Acheron** A river of the underworld,
which was ruled by Hades.

What woman has ever found your way to death?

ANTIGONE. How often I have heard the story of Niobe,°   *Antistrophe 1* 15
    Tantalos' wretched daughter, how the stone
    Clung fast about her, ivy-close: and they say
    The rain falls endlessly
    And sifting soft snow; her tears are never done.
    I feel the loneliness of her death in mine.   20
CHORUS. But she was born of heaven, and you
    Are woman, woman-born. If her death is yours,
    A mortal woman's, is this not for you
    Glory in our world and in the world beyond?

ANTIGONE. You laugh at me. Ah, friends, friends,   *Strophe 2* 25
    Can you not wait until I am dead? O Thebes,
    O men many-charioted, in love with Fortune,
    Dear springs of Dirce, sacred Theban grove,
    Be witnesses for me, denied all pity,
    Unjustly judged! and think a word of love   30
    For her whose path turns
    Under dark earth, where there are no more tears.
CHORUS. You have passed beyond human daring and come at last
    Into a place of stone where Justice sits.
    I cannot tell   35
    What shape of your father's guilt appears in this.
ANTIGONE. You have touched it at last: that bridal bed   *Antistrophe 2*
    Unspeakable, horror of son and mother mingling:
    Their crime, infection of all our family!
    O Oedipus, father and brother!   40
    Your marriage strikes from the grave to murder mine.
    I have been a stranger here in my own land:
    All my life
    The blasphemy of my birth has followed me.
CHORUS. Reverence is a virtue, but strength   45
    Lives in established law: that must prevail.
    You have made your choice,
    Your death is the doing of your conscious hand.
ANTIGONE. Then let me go, since all your words are bitter,   *Epode*°
    And the very light of the sun is cold to me.   50
    Lead me to my vigil, where I must have
    Neither love nor lamentation; no song, but silence.

---

15 Niobe Niobe boasted of her numerous children, provoking Leto, the mother of Apollo, to destroy them. Niobe wept profusely, and finally was turned to stone on Mount Sipylus, whose streams are her tears.   **49 Epode** The third unit of a triad following the strophe and antistrophe.

Creon interrupts impatiently.

CREON. If dirges and planned lamentations could put off death,
　　Men would be singing for ever.
　　(*To the Servants.*)　　　　　　　　Take her, go!
　　You know your orders: take her to the vault   55
　　And leave her alone there. And if she lives or dies,
　　That's her affair, not ours: our hands are clean.

ANTIGONE. O tomb, vaulted bride-bed in eternal rock,
　　Soon I shall be with my own again
　　Where Persephone° welcomes the thin ghosts underground: 60
　　And I shall see my father again, and you, mother,
　　And dearest Polyneices—
　　　　　　　　　　　　　　　　dearest indeed
　　To me, since it was my hand
　　That washed him clean and poured the ritual wine:
　　And my reward is death before my time!   65

And yet, as men's hearts know, I have done no wrong,
　　I have not sinned before God. Or if I have,
　　I shall know the truth in death. But if the guilt
　　Lies upon Creon who judged me, then, I pray,
　　May his punishment equal my own.
CHORAGOS.　　　　　　　　　　　　　　O passionate heart,   70
　　Unyielding, tormented still by the same winds!
CREON. Her guards shall have good cause to regret their delaying.
ANTIGONE. Ah! That voice is like the voice of death!
CREON. I can give you no reason to think you are mistaken.
ANTIGONE. Thebes, and you my fathers' gods,   75
　　And rulers of Thebes, you see me now, the last
　　Unhappy daughter of a line of kings,
　　Your kings, led away to death. You will remember
　　What things I suffer, and at what men's hands,
　　Because I would not transgress the laws of heaven.   80
　　(*To the Guards, simply.*) Come: let us wait no longer.

(*Exit Antigone, left, guarded.*)

Ode IV

CHORUS. All Danae's° beauty was locked away   *Strophe 1*
　　In a brazen cell where the sunlight could not come:

---

60 Persephone Queen of the underworld.　　**1 Danae** In Greek mythology, she was imprisoned in a tower, but Zeus so lusted for her that he visited in a shower of gold.

A small room still as any grave, enclosed her.
Yet she was a princess too,
And Zeus in a rain of gold poured love upon her.   5
O child, child,
No power in wealth or war
Or tough sea-blackened ships
Can prevail against untiring Destiny!

And Dryas' son° also, that furious king,   *Antistrophe 1* 10
Bore the god's prisoning anger for his pride:
Sealed up by Dionysos in deaf stone,
His madness died among echoes.
So at the last he learned what dreadful power
His tongue had mocked: 15
For he had profaned the revels,
And fired the wrath of the nine
Implacable Sisters° that love the sound of the flute.

And old men tell a half-remembered tale   *Strophe 2*
Of horror where a dark ledge splits the sea   20
And a double surf beats on the gray shores:
How a king's new woman,° sick
With hatred for the queen he had imprisoned,
Ripped out his two sons' eyes with her bloody hands
While grinning Ares° watched the shuttle plunge   25
Four times: four blind wounds crying for revenge,

Crying, tears and blood mingled. — Piteously born,   *Antistrophe 2*
Those sons whose mother was of heavenly birth!
Her father was the god of the North Wind
And she was cradled by gales,   30
She raced with young colts on the glittering hills
And walked untrammeled in the open light:
But in her marriage deathless Fate found means
To build a tomb like yours for all her joy.

Scene V

Enter blind Teiresias, led by a boy. The opening speeches of Teiresias should be in singsong contrast to the realistic lines of Creon.

---

10 Dryas' son Lycurgus, King of Thrace.   **18 Sisters** The Muses.   **22 king's new woman** Eidothea, second wife of King Phineus, blinded her stepsons. Their mother, Cleopatra, had been imprisoned in a cave. Phineus was the son of a king, and Cleopatra, his first wife, was the daughter of Boreas, the North Wind, but this illustrious ancestry could not protect his sons from violence and darkness.   **25 Ares** God of war.

TEIRESIAS. This is the way the blind man comes, Princes, Princes,
    Lock-step, two heads lit by the eyes of one.
CREON. What new thing have you to tell us, old Teiresias?
TEIRESIAS. I have much to tell you: listen to the prophet, Creon.
CREON. I am not aware that I have ever failed to listen.   5
TEIRESIAS. Then you have done wisely, King, and ruled well.
CREON. I admit my debt to you. But what have you to say?
TEIRESIAS. This, Creon: you stand once more on the edge of fate.
CREON. What do you mean? Your words are a kind of dread.
TEIRESIAS. Listen, Creon: 10
    I was sitting in my chair of augury, at the place
    Where the birds gather about me. They were all a-chatter,
    As is their habit, when suddenly I heard
    A strange note in their jangling, a scream, a
    Whirring fury; I knew that they were fighting,   15
    Tearing each other, dying
    In a whirlwind of wings clashing. And I was afraid.
    I began the rites of burnt-offering at the altar,
    But Hephaistos° failed me: instead of bright flame,
    There was only the sputtering slime of the fat thigh-flesh   20
    Melting: the entrails dissolved in gray smoke,
    The bare bone burst from the welter. And no blaze!

    This was a sign from heaven. My boy described it,
    Seeing for me as I see for others.

    I tell you, Creon, you yourself have brought   25
    This new calamity upon us. Our hearths and altars
    Are stained with the corruption of dogs and carrion birds
    That glut themselves on the corpse of Oedipus' son.
    The gods are deaf when we pray to them, their fire
    Recoils from our offering, their birds of omen   30
    Have no cry of comfort, for they are gorged
    With the thick blood of the dead.
                     O my son,
    These are no trifles! Think: all men make mistakes,
    But a good man yields when he knows his course is wrong,
    And repairs the evil. The only crime is pride.   35

    Give in to the dead man, then: do not fight with a corpse—
    What glory is it to kill a man who is dead?
    Think, I beg you:

19 Hephaistos God of fire.

It is for your own good that I speak as I do.
You should be able to yield for your own good.   40
CREON. It seems that prophets have made me their especial province.
   All my life long
   I have been a kind of butt for the dull arrows
   Of doddering fortune-tellers!
                            No, Teiresias:
   If your birds—if the great eagles of God himself   45
   Should carry him stinking bit by bit to heaven,
   I would not yield. I am not afraid of pollution:
   No man can defile the gods.
                    Do what you will,
   Go into business, make money, speculate
   In India gold or that synthetic gold from Sardis,   50
   Get rich otherwise than by my consent to bury him.
   Teiresias, it is a sorry thing when a wise man
   Sells his wisdom, lets out his words for hire!
TEIRESIAS. Ah Creon! Is there no man left in the world—
CREON. To do what?—Come, let's have the aphorism!   55
TEIRESIAS. No man who knows that wisdom outweighs any wealth?
CREON. As surely as bribes are baser than any baseness.
TEIRESIAS. You are sick, Creon! You are deathly sick!
CREON. As you say: it is not my place to challenge a prophet.
TEIRESIAS. Yet you have said my prophecy is for sale.   60
CREON. The generation of prophets has always loved gold.
TEIRESIAS. The generation of kings has always loved brass.
CREON. You forget yourself! You are speaking to your King.
TEIRESIAS. I know it. You are a king because of me.
CREON. You have a certain skill; but you have sold out.   65
TEIRESIAS. King, you will drive me to words that—
CREON.   Say them, say them!
   Only remember: I will not pay you for them.
TEIRESIAS. No, you will find them too costly.
CREON.   No doubt. Speak:
   Whatever you say, you will not change my will.
TEIRESIAS. Then take this, and take it to heart!   70
   The time is not far off when you shall pay back
   Corpse for corpse, flesh of your own flesh.
   You have thrust the child of this world into living night,
   You have kept from the gods below the child that is theirs:
   The one in a grave before her death, the other,   75
   Dead, denied the grave. This is your crime:
   And the Furies and the dark gods of Hell
   Are swift with terrible punishment for you.

   Do you want to buy me now, Creon?

Not many days,
And your house will be full of men and women weeping,   80
And curses will be hurled at you from far
Cities grieving for sons unburied, left to rot
Before the walls of Thebes.

These are my arrows, Creon: they are all for you.

(*To Boy.*) But come, child: lead me home.   85
Let him waste his fine anger upon younger men.
Maybe he will learn at last
To control a wiser tongue in a better head. (*Exit Teiresias.*)
CHORAGOS. The old man has gone, King, but his words
Remain to plague us. I am old, too,   90
But I cannot remember that he was ever false.
CREON. That is true. . . . It troubles me.
Oh it is hard to give in! but it is worse
To risk everything for stubborn pride.
CHORAGOS. Creon: take my advice.
CREON.   What shall I do?   95
CHORAGOS. Go quickly: free Antigone from her vault
And build a tomb for the body of Polyneices.
CREON. You would have me do this!
CHORAGOS.   Creon, yes!
And it must be done at once: God moves
Swiftly to cancel the folly of stubborn men.   100
CREON. It is hard to deny the heart! But I
Will do it: I will not fight with destiny.
CHORAGOS. You must go yourself, you cannot leave it to others.
CREON. I will go.
                    —Bring axes, servants:
Come with me to the tomb. I buried her, I   105
Will set her free.
                    Oh quickly!
My mind misgives—
The laws of the gods are mighty, and a man must serve them
To the last day of his life!

(*Exit Creon.*)

Paean°

CHORAGOS. God of many names   *Strophe 1*

Paean A hymn (here dedicated to Iacchos, also called Dionysos. His father was Zeus, his mother was Semele, daughter of Kadmos. Iacchos's worshipers were the Maenads, whose cry was "*Evohe evohe*").

CHORUS.   O Iacchos
                                        son
        of Kadmeian Semele
                        O born of the Thunder!
        Guardian of the West
                        Regent
        of Eleusis' plain
                        O Prince of maenad Thebes
        and the Dragon Field by rippling Ismenos:°   5
CHORAGOS. God of many names   *Antistrophe 1*
CHORUS.   the flame of torches
        flares on our hills
                        the nymphs of Iacchos
        dance at the spring of Castalia:°
        from the vine-close mountain
                                come ah come in ivy:
        Evohe evohe! sings through the streets of Thebes   10
CHORAGOS. God of many names   *Strophe 2*
CHORUS.   Iacchos of Thebes
        heavenly Child
                        of Semele bride of the Thunderer!
        The shadow of plague is upon us:
                                come
        with clement feet
                        oh come from Parnassos
        down the long slopes
                        across the lamenting water   15
CHORAGOS. Io Fire! Chorister of the throbbing stars!   *Antistrophe 2*
        O purest among the voices of the night!
        Thou son of God, blaze for us!
CHORUS. Come with choric rapture of circling Maenads
        Who cry *Io Iacche!*
                        God of many names!   20

                        Exodos°

Enter Messenger from left.

MESSENGER. Men of the line of Kadmos,° you who live
        Near Amphion's citadel,°
                        I cannot say

---

5 Ismenos A river east of Thebes. From a dragon's teeth, sown near the river, there
sprang men who became the ancestors of the Theban nobility.   **8 Castalia** A spring on
Mount Parnassos.   **Exodos** The final scene in a Greek tragedy.   **1 Kadmos,** who
sowed the dragon's teeth, was founder of Thebes.   **2 Amphion's citadel** Amphion
played so sweetly on his lyre that he charmed stones to form a wall around Thebes.

Of any condition of human life "This is fixed.
This is clearly good, or bad." Fate raises up,
And Fate casts down the happy and unhappy alike: 5
No man can foretell his Fate.
                              Take the case of Creon:
Creon was happy once, as I count happiness:
Victorious in battle, sole governor of the land,
Fortunate father of children nobly born.
And now it has all gone from him! Who can say   10
That a man is still alive when his life's joy fails?
He is a walking dead man. Grant him rich,
Let him live like a king in his great house:
If his pleasure is gone, I would not give
So much as the shadow of smoke for all he owns.   15

CHORAGOS. Your words hint at sorrow: what is your news for us?

MESSENGER. They are dead. The living are guilty of their death.

CHORAGOS. Who is guilty? Who is dead? Speak!

MESSENGER.   Haimon.
Haimon is dead; and the hand that killed him
Is his own hand.

CHORAGOS. His father's? or his own?   20

MESSENGER. His own, driven mad by the murder his father had done.

CHORAGOS. Teiresias, Teiresias, how clearly you saw it all!

MESSENGER. This is my news: you must draw what conclusions you can
    from it.

CHORAGOS. But look: Eurydice, our Queen:
Has she overheard us?   25

Enter Eurydice from the palace, center.

EURYDICE. I have heard something, friends:
As I was unlocking the gate of Pallas'° shrine,
For I needed her help today, I heard a voice
Telling of some new sorrow. And I fainted
There at the temple with all my maidens about me.   30
But speak again: whatever it is, I can bear it:
Grief and I are no strangers.

MESSENGER.   Dearest Lady,
I will tell you plainly all that I have seen.
I shall not try to comfort you: what is the use,
Since comfort could lie only in what is not true?   35
The truth is always best.
                         I went with Creon

---

27 Pallas' Pallas Athene, goddess of wisdom.

To the outer plain where Polyneices was lying,
No friend to pity him, his body shredded by dogs.
We made our prayers in the place to Hecate
And Pluto,° that they would be merciful. And we bathed   40
The corpse with holy water, and we brought
Fresh-broken branches to burn what was left of it,
And upon the urn we heaped up a towering barrow
Of the earth of his own land.

> When we were done, we ran
To the vault where Antigone lay on her couch of stone.   45
One of the servants had gone ahead,
And while he was yet far off he heard a voice
Grieving within the chamber, and he came back
And told Creon. And as the King went closer,
The air was full of wailing, the words lost,   50
And he begged us to make all haste. "Am I a prophet?"
He said, weeping, "And must I walk this road,
The saddest of all that I have gone before?
My son's voice calls me on. Oh quickly, quickly!
Look through the crevice there, and tell me   55
If it is Haimon, or some deception of the gods!"

We obeyed: and in the cavern's farthest corner
We saw her lying:
She had made a noose of her fine linen veil
And hanged herself. Haimon lay beside her,   60
His arms about her waist, lamenting her,
His love lost under ground, crying out
That his father had stolen her away from him.
When Creon saw him the tears rushed to his eyes
And he called to him: "What have you done, child? Speak to me.   65
What are you thinking that makes your eyes so strange?
O my son, my son, I come to you on my knees!"
But Haimon spat in his face. He said not a word,
Staring—

> And suddenly drew his sword
And lunged. Creon shrank back, the blade missed; and the boy,   70
Desperate against himself, drove it half its length
Into his own side, and fell. And as he died
He gathered Antigone close in his arms again,
Choking, his blood bright red on her white cheek.
And now he lies dead with the dead, and she is his   75

39–40 Hecate / And Pluto Hecate and Pluto (also known as Hades) were deities of the underworld.

At last, his bride in the house of the dead.

Exit Eurydice into the palace.

CHORAGOS. She has left us without a word. What can this mean?

MESSENGER. It troubles me, too; yet she knows what is best,
Her grief is too great for public lamentation,
And doubtless she has gone to her chamber to weep   80
For her dead son, leading her maidens in his dirge.

Pause.

CHORAGOS. It may be so: but I fear this deep silence.

MESSENGER. I will see what she is doing. I will go in.

Exit Messenger into the palace.

Enter Creon with attendants, bearing Haimon's body.

CHORAGOS. But here is the king himself: oh look at him,
Bearing his own damnation in his arms.   85

CREON. Nothing you say can touch me any more.
My own blind heart has brought me
From darkness to final darkness. Here you see
The father murdering, the murdered son—
And all my civic wisdom!   90

Haimon my son, so young, so young to die,
I was the fool, not you; and you died for me.

CHORAGOS. That is the truth; but you were late in learning it.

CREON. This truth is hard to bear. Surely a god
Has crushed me beneath the hugest weight of heaven,   95
And driven me headlong a barbaric way
To trample out the thing I held most dear.

The pains that men will take to come to pain!

Enter Messenger from the palace.

MESSENGER. The burden you carry in your hands is heavy,
But it is not all: you will find more in your house.   100

CREON. What burden worse than this shall I find there?

MESSENGER. The Queen is dead.

CREON. O port of death, deaf world,
Is there no pity for me? And you, Angel of evil,
I was dead, and your words are death again.   105
Is it true, boy? Can it be true?
Is my wife dead? Has death bred death?

MESSENGER. You can see for yourself.

The doors are opened and the body of Eurydice is disclosed within.

CREON. Oh pity!
All true, all true, and more than I can bear!   110

O my wife, my son!
MESSENGER. She stood before the altar, and her heart
   Welcomed the knife her own hand guided,
   And a great cry burst from her lips for Megareus° dead,
   And for Haimon dead, her sons; and her last breath   115
   Was a curse for their father, the murderer of her sons.
   And she fell, and the dark flowed in through her closing eyes.
CREON. O God, I am sick with fear.
   Are there no swords here? Has no one a blow for me?
MESSENGER. Her curse is upon you for the deaths of both.   120
CREON. It is right that it should be. I alone am guilty.
   I know it, and I say it. Lead me in,
   Quickly, friends.
   I have neither life nor substance. Lead me in.
CHORAGOS. You are right, if there can be right in so much wrong.   125
   The briefest way is best in a world of sorrow.
CREON. Let it come,
   Let death come quickly, and be kind to me.
   I would not ever see the sun again.
CHORAGOS. All that will come when it will; but we, meanwhile,   130
   Have much to do. Leave the future to itself.
CREON. All my heart was in that prayer!
CHORAGOS. Then do not pray any more: the sky is deaf.
CREON. Lead me away. I have been rash and foolish.
   I have killed my son and my wife.   135
   I look for comfort; my comfort lies here dead.
   Whatever my hands have touched has come to nothing.
   Fate has brought all my pride to a thought of dust.

As Creon is being led into the house, the Choragos advances and speaks directly to the audience.

CHORAGOS. There is no happiness where there is no wisdom;
   No wisdom but in submission to the gods.   140
   Big words are always punished,
   And proud men in old age learn to be wise.

Topics for Critical Thinking and Writing

1. In the prologue, on page 386, Ismene insists, "we must give in to the law" (line 48), and Antigone replies, "apparently the laws of the gods mean nothing to you" (line 61). Can you reconcile this apparent contradiction?

2. In scene II Ismene says that she and Antigone are "equally guilty," but Antigone coldly (nastily?) refuses to let Ismene share her martyrdom.

114 Megareus Megareus, brother of Haimon, had died in the assault on Thebes.

What do you make of her behavior? In a 500-word essay write on Ismene's assertion that the two are equally guilty, and on Antigone's response.

3. The play includes several references to Fate or Destiny. At the beginning of scene IV, Ode IV, for example, the chorus, speaking of Danae, says that nothing "can prevail against untiring Destiny" (p. 406, line 9). How seriously are we to take these references to Fate? Do you think they reflect the dominant theme of the play, or are they to be explained as merely the utterances of this or that dramatic character? As instances of a human tendency to blame ill fortune on some mysterious external force? Do you think that, as we see them in the play, Antigone and Creon act of their own free will? Explain.

4. Throughout the play, Creon bewails the risk of "anarchy." What is anarchy? Is it reasonable for Creon to condemn Antigone's behavior for its anarchistic tendencies?

5. When the Chorus in scene IV declares "strength Lives in established law" (p. 404, lines 45–46), is this said in support of Creon, Antigone, both, or neither? Which law should be enforced, do you think— Creon's edict or the customary law of Thebes, on which Antigone relies? In a 500-word essay support your view.

6. At the end of the play Creon says, "I alone am guilty" (p. 414, line 121). Do you share his view? Or do you think that in some ways Antigone too is guilty? Are the words *hero* and *villain* of some use in talking about this play, or should they be discarded? In an essay of 500 words discuss some aspect of these related issues.

7. In scene V, p. 407, line 35, Teiresias says, "The only crime is pride." Is Antigone as guilty of this crime as Creon? How much of the terrible harms done throughout the play can be explained by excessive pride?

8. The play obviously deals with a clash between a citizen who feels she has familial and religious duties and a political leader who believes it is his duty to govern the state. Do you think that in addition to the conflict between feeling and law there are also significant conflicts between a male and a female? Between an old person and a young one?

9. If you were staging the play today, would you use modern dress? What might be gained, and what might be lost, by using modern dress?

Plato

Plato (427–347 B.C.), an Athenian aristocrat by birth, was the student of one great philosopher (Socrates) and the teacher of another (Aristotle). His legacy of more than two dozen dialogues—imaginary discussions between Socrates and one or more other speakers, usually young Athenians—has been of such influence that the whole of Western philosophy can be characterized, A. N. Whitehead wrote, as "a series of footnotes to Plato." Plato's interests encompassed the full range of topics in philosophy: ethics, politics, logic, metaphysics, epistemology, aesthetics, psychology, and education.

The selection reprinted here, Crito, *is the third of four dialogues telling the story of the final days of Socrates (469–399 B.C.). The first in the sequence,* Euthyphro, *portrays Socrates in his typical role, questioning someone about his beliefs (in this case, the young aristocrat, Euthyphro). The discussion is focused on the nature of piety, but the conversation breaks off before a final answer is reached—perhaps none is possible—because Socrates is on his way to stand trial before the Athenian assembly. He has been charged with "preaching false gods" (heresy) and "corrupting the youth" by causing them to doubt or disregard the wisdom of their elders. (How faithful to any actual event or discussion* Euthyphro *and Plato's other Socratic dialogues really are, scholars cannot say with assurance.)*

In Apology, *the second dialogue in the sequence, Plato (who remains entirely in the background, as he does in all the dialogues) recounts Socrates' public reply to the charges against him. During the speech, Socrates explains his life, reminding his fellow citizens that if he is (as the oracle had pronounced) "the wisest of men," then it is only because he knows that he doesn't know what others believe or pretend they do know. The dialogue ends with Socrates being found guilty and duly sentenced to death.*

The third in the series is Crito, *but we will postpone comment on it for a moment, and glance at the fourth dialogue,* Phaedo, *in which Plato portrays Socrates' final philosophical discussion. The topic, appropriately, is whether the soul is immortal. It ends with Socrates, in the company of his closest friends, bidding them a last farewell and drinking the fatal cup of hemlock.*

Crito, *the whole text of which is reprinted here, is the debate provoked by Crito, an old friend and admirer of Socrates. He visits Socrates in prison and urges him to escape while he still has the chance. After all, Crito argues, the guilty verdict was wrong and unfair, few Athenians really want to have Socrates put to death, his family and friends will be distraught, and so forth. Socrates will not have it. He patiently but firmly examines each of Crito's arguments and explains why it would be wrong to follow his advice.*

Plato's Crito *thus ranks with Sophocles' tragedy* Antigone *as one of the first explorations in Western literature of the perennial theme of our responsibility for obeying laws that challenge our conscientious moral convictions.* Antigone *concludes that she must disobey the law of Creon, tyrant of Thebes; Socrates concludes that he must obey the law of democratic Athens.*

In Crito, *we have not only a superb illustration of Socratic dialogue and argument, but also a portrait of a virtuous thinker at the end of a long life, reflecting on its course and on the moral principles that have guided him. We see Socrates living an "examined life," the only life he thought was worth living.*

Crito

(**SCENE:** *A room in the State prison at Athens in the year 399 B.C. The time is half an hour before dawn, and the room would be almost dark but for the light of a little oil lamp. There is a pallet bed against the back wall. At the head of it a small table supports the lamp; near the foot of it Crito is sitting patiently on a stool. He is an old man, kindly, practical, simple-minded; at present he is suffering from acute* *emotional strain. On the bed lies Socrates asleep. He stirs, yawns, opens his eyes and sees Crito.)*

SOCRATES: Here already, Crito? Surely it is still early?

CRITO: Indeed it is.

SOCRATES: About what time?

CRITO: Just before dawn.

SOCRATES: I wonder that the warder paid any attention to you.   5

CRITO: He is used to me now, Socrates, because I come here so often; besides, he is under some small obligation to me.

SOCRATES: Have you only just come, or have you been here for long?

CRITO: Fairly long.

SOCRATES: Then why didn't you wake me at once, instead of sitting by my bed so quietly?

CRITO: I wouldn't dream of such a thing, Socrates. I only wish I were 10 not so sleepless and depressed myself. I have been wondering at you, because I saw how comfortably you were sleeping; and I deliberately didn't wake you because I wanted you to go on being as comfortable as you could. I have often felt before in the course of my life how fortunate you are in your disposition, but I feel it more than ever now in your present misfortune when I see how easily and placidly you put up with it.

SOCRATES: Well, really, Crito, it would be hardly suitable for a man of my age to resent having to die.

CRITO: Other people just as old as you are get involved in these misfortunes, Socrates, but their age doesn't keep them from resenting it when they find themselves in your position.

SOCRATES: Quite true. But tell me, why have you come so early?

CRITO: Because I bring bad news, Socrates; not so bad from your point of view, I suppose, but it will be very hard to bear for me and your other friends, and I think that I shall find it hardest of all.

SOCRATES: Why, what is this news? Has the boat come in from Delos— 15 the boat which ends my reprieve when it arrives?[1]

CRITO: It hasn't actually come in yet, but I expect that it will be here today, judging from the report of some people who have just arrived from Sunium and left it there. It's quite clear from their account that it will be here today; and so by tomorrow, Socrates, you will have to—to end your life.

SOCRATES: Well, Crito, I hope that it may be for the best; if the gods will it so, so be it. All the same, I don't think it will arrive today.

CRITO: What makes you think that?

[1]**Delos . . . arrives** Ordinarily execution was immediately carried out, but the day before Socrates' trial was the first day of an annual ceremony that involved sending a ship to Delos. When the ship was absent—in this case for about a month—executions could not be performed. As Crito goes on to say, Socrates could easily escape, and indeed he could have left the country before being tried. [All notes are the editors'.]

SOCRATES: I will try to explain. I think I am right in saying that I have to die on the day after the boat arrives?

CRITO: That's what the authorities say, at any rate.   20

SOCRATES: Then I don't think it will arrive on this day that is just beginning, but on the day after. I am going by a dream that I had in the night, only a little while ago. It looks as though you were right not to wake me up.

CRITO: Why, what was the dream about?

SOCRATES: I thought I saw a gloriously beautiful woman dressed in white robes, who came up to me and addressed me in these words: "Socrates, to the pleasant land of Phthia on the third day thou shalt come."

CRITO: Your dream makes no sense, Socrates.

SOCRATES: To my mind, Crito, it is perfectly clear.   25

CRITO: Too clear, apparently. But look here, Socrates, it is still not too late to take my advice and escape. Your death means a double calamity for me. I shall not only lose a friend whom I can never possibly replace, but besides a great many people who don't know you and me very well will be sure to think that I let you down, because I could have saved you if I had been willing to spend the money; and what could be more contemptible than to get a name for thinking more of money than of your friends? Most people will never believe that it was you who refused to leave this place although we tried our hardest to persuade you.

SOCRATES: But my dear Crito, why should we pay so much attention to what "most people" think? The really reasonable people, who have more claim to be considered, will believe that the facts are exactly as they are.

CRITO: You can see for yourself, Socrates, that one has to think of popular opinion as well. Your present position is quite enough to show that the capacity of ordinary people for causing trouble is not confined to petty annoyances, but has hardly any limits if you once get a bad name with them.

SOCRATES: I only wish that ordinary people *had* unlimited capacity for doing harm; then they might have an unlimited power for doing good; which would be a splendid thing, if it were so. Actually they have neither. They cannot make a man wise or stupid; they simply act at random.

CRITO: Have it that way if you like; but tell me this, Socrates. I hope 30 that you aren't worrying about the possible effects on me and the rest of your friends, and thinking that if you escape we shall have trouble with informers for having helped you to get away, and have to forfeit all our property or pay an enormous fine, or even incur some further punishment? If any idea like that is troubling you, you can dismiss it altogether. We are quite entitled to run that risk in saving you, and even worse, if necessary. Take my advice, and be reasonable.

SOCRATES: All that you say is very much in my mind, Crito, and a great deal more besides.

CRITO: Very well, then, don't let it distress you. I know some people who are willing to rescue you from here and get you out of the country for quite a moderate sum. And then surely you realize how cheap these informers are to buy off; we shan't need much money to settle them; and I think you've got enough of my money for yourself already. And then even supposing that in your anxiety for my safety you feel that you oughtn't to spend my money, there are these foreign gentlemen staying in Athens who are quite willing to spend theirs. One of them, Simmias of Thebes, has actually brought the money with him for this very purpose; and Cebes and a number of others are quite ready to do the same. So as I say, you mustn't let any fears on these grounds make you slacken your efforts to escape; and you mustn't feel any misgivings about what you said at your trial, that you wouldn't know what to do with yourself if you left this country. Wherever you go, there are plenty of places where you will find a welcome; and if you choose to go to Thessaly, I have friends there who will make much of you and give you complete protection, so that no one in Thessaly can interfere with you.

Besides, Socrates, I don't even feel that it is right for you to try to do what you are doing, throwing away your life when you might save it. You are doing your best to treat yourself in exactly the same way as your enemies would, or rather did, when they wanted to ruin you. What is more, it seems to me that you are letting your sons down too. You have it in your power to finish their bringing up and education, and instead of that you are proposing to go off and desert them, and so far as you are concerned they will have to take their chance. And what sort of chance are they likely to get? The sort of thing that usually happens to orphans when they lose their parents. Either one ought not to have children at all, or one ought to see their upbringing and education through to the end. It strikes me that you are taking the line of least resistance, whereas you ought to make the choice of a good man and a brave one, considering that you profess to have made goodness your object all through life. Really, I am ashamed, both on your account and on ours your friends'; it will look as though we had played something like a coward's part all through this affair of yours. First, there was the way you came into court when it was quite unnecessary—that was the first act; then there was the conduct of the defense—that was the second; and finally, to complete the farce, we get this situation, which makes it appear that we have let you slip out of our hands through some lack of courage and enterprise on our part, because we didn't save you, and you didn't save yourself, when it would have been quite possible and practicable, if we had been any use at all.

There, Socrates; if you aren't careful, besides the suffering there will be all this disgrace for you and us to bear. Come, make up your mind. Really it's too late for that now; you ought to have it made up already. There is no alternative; the whole thing must be carried through during this coming night. If we lose any more time, it can't be done, it will be too late. I appeal to you, Socrates, on every ground; take my advice and please don't be unreasonable!

SOCRATES: My dear Crito, I appreciate your warm feelings very 35 much—that is, assuming that they have some justification; if not, the stronger they are, the harder they will be to deal with. Very well, then; we must consider whether we ought to follow your advice or not. You know that this is not a new idea of mine; it has always been my nature never to accept advice from any of my friends unless reflection shows that it is the best course that reason offers. I cannot abandon the principles which I used to hold in the past simply because this accident has happened to me; they seem to me to be much as they were, and I respect and regard the same principles now as before. So unless we can find better principles on this occasion, you can be quite sure that I shall not agree with you; not even if the power of the people conjures up fresh hordes of bogies to terrify our childish minds, by subjecting us to chains and executions and confiscations of our property.

Well, then, how can we consider the question most reasonably? Suppose that we begin by reverting to this view which you hold about people's opinions. Was it always right to argue that some opinions should be taken seriously but not others? Or was it always wrong? Perhaps it was right before the question of my death arose, but now we can see clearly that it was a mistaken persistence in a point of view which was really irresponsible nonsense. I should like very much to inquire into this problem, Crito, with your help, and to see whether the argument will appear in any different light to me now that I am in this position, or whether it will remain the same; and whether we shall dismiss it or accept it.

Serious thinkers, I believe, have always held some such view as the one which I mentioned just now: that some of the opinions which people entertain should be respected, and others should not. Now I ask you, Crito, don't you think that this is a sound principle?—You are safe from the prospect of dying tomorrow, in all human probability; and you are not likely to have your judgment upset by this impending calamity. Consider, then; don't you think that this is a sound enough principle, that one should not regard all the opinions that people hold, but only some and not others? What do you say? Isn't that a fair statement?

CRITO: Yes, it is.

SOCRATES: In other words, one should regard the good ones and not the bad?

CRITO: Yes.   40

SOCRATES: The opinions of the wise being good, and the opinions of the foolish bad?

CRITO: Naturally.

SOCRATES: To pass on, then: What do you think of the sort of illustration that I used to employ? When a man is in training, and taking it seriously, does he pay attention to all praise and criticism and opinion indiscriminately, or only when it comes from the one qualified person, the actual doctor or trainer?

CRITO: Only when it comes from the one qualified person.

SOCRATES: Then he should be afraid of the criticism and welcome the 45 praise of the one qualified person, but not those of the general public.

CRITO: Obviously.

SOCRATES: So he ought to regulate his actions and exercises and eating and drinking by the judgment of his instructor, who has expert knowledge, rather than by the opinions of the rest of the public.

CRITO: Yes, that is so.

SOCRATES: Very well. Now if he disobeys the one man and disregards his opinion and commendations, and pays attention to the advice of the many who have no expert knowledge, surely he will suffer some bad effect?

CRITO: Certainly. 50

SOCRATES: And what is this bad effect? Where is it produced?—I mean, in what part of the disobedient person?

CRITO: His body, obviously; that is what suffers.

SOCRATES: Very good. Well now, tell me, Crito—we don't want to go through all the examples one by one—does this apply as a general rule, and above all to the sort of actions which we are trying to decide about: just and unjust, honorable and dishonorable, good and bad? Ought we to be guided and intimidated by the opinion of the many or by that of the one—assuming that there is someone with expert knowledge? Is it true that we ought to respect and fear this person more than all the rest put together; and that if we do not follow his guidance we shall spoil and mutilate that part of us which, as we used to say, is improved by right conduct and destroyed by wrong? Or is this all nonsense?

CRITO: No, I think it is true, Socrates.

SOCRATES: Then consider the next step. There is a part of us which is 55 improved by healthy actions and ruined by unhealthy ones. If we spoil it by taking the advice of nonexperts, will life be worth living when this part is once ruined? The part I mean is the body; do you accept this?

CRITO: Yes.

SOCRATES: Well, is life worth living with a body which is worn out and ruined by health?

CRITO: Certainly not.

SOCRATES: What about the part of us which is mutilated by wrong actions and benefited by right ones? Is life worth living with this part ruined? Or do we believe that this part of us, whatever it may be, in which right and wrong operate, is of less importance than the body?

CRITO: Certainly not. 60

SOCRATES: It is really more precious?

CRITO: Much more.

SOCRATES: In that case, my dear fellow, what we ought to consider is not so much what people in general will say about us but how we stand with the expert in right and wrong, the one authority, who represents the actual truth. So in the first place your proposition is not correct when you say that we should consider popular opinion in questions of what is right and honorable and good, or the opposite. Of course one might object "All the same, the people have the power to put us to death."

CRITO: No doubt about that! Quite true, Socrates; it is a possible objection.

SOCRATES: But so far as I can see, my dear fellow, the argument 65 which we have just been through is quite unaffected by it. At the same time I should like you to consider whether we are still satisfied on this point: that the really important thing is not to live, but to live well.

CRITO: Why, yes.

SOCRATES: And that to live well means the same thing as to live honorably or rightly?

CRITO: Yes.

SOCRATES: Then in the light of this agreement we must consider whether or not it is right for me to try to get away without an official discharge. If it turns out to be right, we must make the attempt; if not, we must let it drop. As for the considerations you raise about expense and reputation and bringing up children, I am afraid, Crito, that they represent the reflections of the ordinary public, who put people to death, and would bring them back to life if they could, with equal indifference to reason. Our real duty, I fancy, since the argument leads that way, is to consider one question only, the one which we raised just now: Shall we be acting rightly in paying money and showing gratitude to these people who are going to rescue me, and in escaping or arranging the escape ourselves, or shall we really be acting wrongly in doing all this? If it becomes clear that such conduct is wrong, I cannot help thinking that the question whether we are sure to die, or to suffer any other ill effect for that matter, if we stand our ground and take no action, ought not to weigh with us at all in comparison with the risk of doing what is wrong.

CRITO: I agree with what you say, Socrates; but I wish you would 70 consider what we ought to *do*.

SOCRATES: Let us look at it together, my dear fellow; and if you can challenge any of my arguments, do so and I will listen to you; but if you can't, be a good fellow and stop telling me over and over again that I ought to leave this place without official permission. I am very anxious to obtain your approval before I adopt the course which I have in mind; I don't want to act against your convictions. Now give your attention to the starting point of this inquiry—I hope that you will be satisfied with my way of stating it—and try to answer my questions to the best of your judgment.

CRITO: Well, I will try.

SOCRATES: Do we say that one must never willingly do wrong, or does it depend upon circumstance? Is it true, as we have often agreed before, that there is no sense in which wrongdoing is good or honorable? Or have we jettisoned all our former convictions in these last few days? Can you and I at our age, Crito, have spent all these years in serious discussions without realizing that we were no better than a pair of children? Surely the truth is just what we have always said. Whatever the popular view is, and whether the alternative is pleasanter than the present one or even harder to bear, the fact remains that to do wrong is in every sense bad and dishonorable for the person who does it. Is that our view, or not?

CRITO: Yes, it is.

SOCRATES: Then in no circumstances must one do wrong.   75

CRITO: No.

SOCRATES: In that case one must not even do wrong when one is wronged, which most people regard as the natural course.

CRITO: Apparently not.

SOCRATES: Tell me another thing, Crito: Ought one to do injuries or not?

CRITO: Surely not, Socrates.   80

SOCRATES: And tell me: Is it right to do an injury in retaliation, as most people believe, or not?

CRITO: No, never.

SOCRATES: Because, I suppose, there is no difference between injuring people and wronging them.

CRITO: Exactly.

SOCRATES: So one ought not to return a wrong or an injury to any 85
person, whatever the provocation is. Now be careful, Crito, that in making these single admissions you do not end by admitting something contrary to your real beliefs. I know that there are and always will be few people who think like this; and consequently between those who do think so and those who do not there can be no agreement on principle; they must always feel contempt when they observe one another's decisions. I want even you to consider very carefully whether you share my views and agree with me, and whether we can proceed with our discussion from the established hypothesis that it is never right to do a wrong or return a wrong or defend one's self against injury by retaliation; or whether you dissociate yourself from any share in this view as a basis for discussion. I have held it for a long time, and still hold it; but if you have formed any other opinion, say so and tell me what it is. If, on the other hand, you stand by what we have said, listen to my next point.

CRITO: Yes, I stand by it and agree with you. Go on.

SOCRATES: Well, here is my next point, or rather question. Ought one to fulfill all one's agreements, provided that they are right, or break them?

CRITO: One ought to fulfill them.

SOCRATES: Then consider the logical consequence. If we leave this place without first persuading the State to let us go, are we or are we not doing an injury, and doing it in a quarter where it is least justifiable? Are we or are we not abiding by our just agreements?

CRITO: I can't answer your question, Socrates; I am not clear in my mind. 90

SOCRATES: Look at it in this way. Suppose that while we were preparing to run away from here (or however one should describe it) the Laws and Constitution of Athens were to come and confront us and ask this question: "Now, Socrates, what are you proposing to do? Can you deny that by this act which you are contemplating you intend, so far as you have the power, to destroy us, the Laws, and the whole State as well? Do you imagine that a city can continue to exist and not be turned upside down, if the legal judgments which are pronounced in it have no force but are nullified and destroyed by private persons?" — how shall we answer this question, Crito, and others of the same kind? There is much that could be said, especially by a professional advocate, to protest against the invalidation of this law which enacts that judgments once pronounced shall be binding. Shall we say "Yes, I do intend to destroy the laws, because the State wronged me by passing a faulty judgment at my trial"? Is this to be our answer, or what?

CRITO: What you have just said, by all means, Socrates.

SOCRATES: Then what supposing the Laws say, "Was there provision for this in the agreement between you and us, Socrates? Or did you undertake to abide by whatever judgments the State pronounced?" If we expressed surprise at such language, they would probably say: "Never mind our language, Socrates, but answer our questions; after all, you are accustomed to the method of question and answer. Come now, what charge do you bring against us and the State, that you are trying to destroy us? Did we not give you life in the first place? Was it not through us that your father married your mother and begot you? Tell us, have you any complaint against those of us Laws that deal with marriage?" "No, none," I should say. "Well, have you any against the laws which deal with children's upbringing and education, such as you had yourself? Are you not grateful to those of us Laws which were instituted for this end, for requiring your father to give you a cultural and physical education?" "Yes," I should say. "Very good. Then since you have been born and brought up and educated, can you deny, in the first place, that you were our child and servant, both you and your ancestors? And if this is so, do you imagine that what is right for us is equally right for you, and that whatever we try to do to you, you are justified in retaliating? You did not have equality of rights with your father, or your employer (supposing that you had had one), to enable you to retaliate; you were not allowed to answer back when you were scolded or to hit back when you were beaten, or to do a great many other things of the same kind. Do you expect to have such license against your country and its laws that if we try to put you to death in the belief that it is right to do so, you on your part will try your hardest to destroy your country and us its Laws in return? And will you, the true devotee of goodness, claim that you are justified in doing so? Are you so wise as to have forgotten that compared with your mother and father and all the rest of your ancestors your country is something far more precious, more venerable, more sacred, and held in greater honor both among gods and among all reasonable men? Do you not realize that you are even more bound to respect and placate the anger of your country than your father's anger? That if you cannot persuade your country you must do whatever it orders, and patiently submit to any punishment that it imposes, whether it be flogging or imprisonment? And if it leads you out to war, to be wounded or killed, you must comply, and it is right that you should do so; you must not give way or retreat or abandon your position. Both in war and in the law courts and everywhere else you must do whatever your city and your country commands, or else persuade it in accordance with universal justice; but violence is a sin even against your parents, and it is a far greater sin against your country" — What shall we say to this, Crito? — that what the Laws say is true, or not?

CRITO: Yes, I think so.

SOCRATES: "Consider, then, Socrates," the Laws would probably con- 95 tinue, "whether it is also true for us to say that what you are now trying to do to us is not right. Although we have brought you into the world and reared you and educated you, and given you and all your fellow citizens a share in all the good things at our disposal, nevertheless by the very fact of granting our permission we openly proclaim this principle: that any Athenian, on attaining to manhood and seeing for himself the political organization of the State and us its Laws, is permitted, if he is not satisfied with us, to take his property and go away wherever he likes. If any of you chooses to go to one of our colonies, supposing that he should not be satisfied with us and the State, or to emigrate to any other country, not one of us Laws hinders or prevents him from going away wherever he likes, without any loss of property. On the other hand, if any one of you stands his ground when he can see how we administer justice and the rest of our public organization, we hold that by so doing he has in fact undertaken to do anything that we tell him; and we maintain that anyone who disobeys is guilty of doing wrong on three separate counts: first because we are his parents, and secondly because we are his guardians; and thirdly because, after promising obedience, he is neither obeying us nor persuading us to change our decision if we are at fault in any way; and although all our orders are in the form of proposals, not of savage commands, and we give him the choice of either persuading us or doing what we say, he is actually doing neither. These are the charges, Socrates, to which we say that you will be liable if you do what you are contemplating; and you will not be the least culpable of your fellow countrymen, but one of the most guilty." If I said "Why do you say that?" they would no doubt pounce upon me with perfect justice and point out that there are very few people in Athens who have entered into this agreement with them as explicitly as I have. They would say "Socrates, we have substantial evidence that you are satisfied with us and with the State. You would not have been so exceptionally reluctant to cross the borders of your country if you had not been exceptionally attached to it. You have never left the city to attend a festival or for any other purpose, except on some military expedition; you have never traveled abroad as other people do, and you have never felt the impulse to acquaint yourself with another country or constitution; you have been content with us and with our city. You have definitely chosen us, and undertaken to observe us in all your activities as a citizen; and as the crowning proof that you are satisfied with our city, you have begotten children in it. Furthermore, even at the time of your trial you could have proposed the penalty of banishment, if you had chosen to do so; that is, you could have done then with the sanction of the State what you are now trying to do without it. But whereas at that time you made a noble show of indifference if you had to die, and in fact preferred death, as you said, to banishment, now you show no respect for your earlier professions, and no regard for us, the Laws, whom you are trying to destroy; you are behaving like the lowest type of menial, trying to run away in spite of the contracts and undertakings by which you agreed to live as a member of our State. Now first answer this question: Are we or are we not speaking the truth when we say that you have undertaken, in deed if not in word, to live your life as a citizen in obedience to us?" What are we to say to that, Crito? Are we not bound to admit it?

CRITO: We cannot help it, Socrates.

SOCRATES: "It is a fact, then," they would say, "that you are breaking covenants and undertakings made with us, although you made them under no compulsion or misunderstanding, and were not compelled to decide in a limited time; you had seventy years in which you could have left the country, if you were not satisfied with us or felt that the agreements were unfair. You did not choose Sparta or Crete—your favorite models of good government—or any other Greek or foreign state; you could not have absented yourself from the city less if you had been lame or blind or decrepit in some other way. It is quite obvious that you stand by yourself above all other Athenians in your affection for this city and for us its Laws;—who would care for a city without laws? And now, after all this, are you not going to stand by your agreement? Yes, you are, Socrates, if you will take our advice; and then you will at least escape being laughed at for leaving the city.

"We invite you to consider what good you will do to yourself or your friends if you commit this breach of faith and stain your conscience. It is fairly obvious that the risk of being banished and either losing their citizenship or having their property confiscated will extend to your friends as well. As for yourself, if you go to one of the neighboring states, such as Thebes or Megara, which are both well governed, you will enter them as an enemy to their constitution[2] and all good patriots will eye you with suspicion as a destroyer of law and order. Incidentally you will confirm the opinion of the jurors who tried you that they gave a correct verdict; a destroyer of laws might very well be supposed to have a destructive influence upon young and foolish human beings. Do you intend, then, to avoid well governed states and the higher forms of human society? And if you do, will life be worth living? Or will you approach these people and have the impudence to converse with them? What arguments will you use, Socrates? The same which you used here, that goodness and integrity, institutions and laws, are the most precious possessions of mankind? Do you not think that Socrates and everything about him will appear in a disreputable light? You certainly ought to think so. But perhaps you will retire from this part of the world and go to Crito's friends in Thessaly? That is the home of indiscipline and laxity, and no doubt they would enjoy hearing the amusing story of how you managed to run away from prison by arraying yourself in some costume or putting on a shepherd's smock or some other conventional runaway's disguise, and altering your personal appearance. And will no one comment on the fact that an old man of your age, probably with only a short time left to live, should dare to cling so greedily to life, at the price of violating the most stringent laws? Perhaps not, if you avoid irritating anyone. Otherwise, Socrates, you will hear a good many humiliating comments. So you will live as the toady and slave of all the populace, literally 'roistering in Thessaly,' as though you had left this country for Thessaly to attend a banquet there; and where will your discussions about goodness and uprightness be then, we should like to know? But of course you want to live for your children's sake, so that you may be able to bring them up and educate them. Indeed! by first taking them off to Thessaly and making foreigners of them, so that they may have that additional enjoyment? Or if that is not your intention, supposing that they are brought up here with you still alive, will they be better cared for and educated without you, because of course your friends will look after them? Will they look after your children if you go away to Thessaly, and not if you go away to the next world? Surely if those who profess to be your friends are worth anything, you must believe that they would care for them.

[2]**as an enemy to their constitution** As a lawbreaker.

"No, Socrates; be advised by us your guardians, and do not think more of your children or of your life or of anything else than you think of what is right; so that when you enter the next world you may have all this to plead in your defense before the authorities there. It seems clear that if you do this thing, neither you nor any of your friends will be the better for it or be more upright or have a cleaner conscience here in this world, nor will it be better for you when you reach the next. As it is, you will leave this place, when you do, as the victim of a wrong done not by us, the Laws, but by your fellow men. But if you leave in that dishonorable way, returning wrong for wrong and evil for evil, breaking your agreements and covenants with us, and injuring those whom you least ought to injure—yourself, your friends, your country, and us—then you will have to face our anger in your lifetime, and in that place beyond when the laws of the other world know that you have tried, so far as you could, to destroy even us their brothers, they will not receive you with a kindly welcome. Do not take Crito's advice, but follow ours."

That, my dear friend Crito, I do assure you, is what I seem to hear 100 them saying, just as a mystic seems to hear the strains of music; and the sound of their arguments rings so loudly in my head that I cannot hear the other side. I warn you that, as my opinion stands at present, it will be useless to urge a different view. However, if you think that you will do any good by it, say what you like.

CRITO: No, Socrates, I have nothing to say.

SOCRATES: Then give it up, Crito, and let us follow this course, since God points out the way.

Topics for Critical Thinking and Writing

1. State as precisely as you can all the arguments Crito uses to try to convince Socrates that he ought to escape. Which of these arguments seems to you to be the best? The worst? Why?

2. Socrates says to Crito, "I cannot abandon the principles which I used to hold in the past simply because this accident [the misfortune of being convicted by the Athenian assembly and then sentenced to death] has happened to me" (para. 35). Does this remark strike you as self-righteous? Stubborn? Smug? Stupid? Explain.

3. Socrates declares that "serious thinkers" have always held the view that "some of the opinions which people entertain should be respected, and others should not" (para. 37). There are two main alternatives to this principle: (a) One should respect *all* the opinions that others hold, and (b) one should respect *none* of the opinions of others. Socrates attacks (a) but he ignores (b).What are his objections to (a)? Do you find them convincing? Can you think of any convincing arguments against (b)?

4. As Socrates shows in his reply to Crito, he seems ready to believe (para. 63) that there are "expert[s] in right and wrong"—that is, persons with

expert opinion or even authoritative knowledge on matters of right and wrong conduct—and that their advice should be sought and followed. Do you agree? Consider the thesis that there are no such experts, and write a 500-word essay defending or attacking it.

5. Socrates, as he comments to Crito, believes that "it is never right to do a wrong or return a wrong or defend one's self against injury by retaliation" (para. 85). He does not offer any argument for this thesis in the dialogue (although he does elsewhere). It was a very strange doctrine in his day, and even now it is not generally accepted. Write a 1,000-word essay defending or attacking this thesis.

6. Socrates seems to argue: Because (a) no one ought to do wrong, and because (b) it would injure the state for someone in Socrates' position to escape, because (c) this act would break a "just agreement" between the citizen and his state, therefore (d) no one in Socrates' position should escape. Do you think this argument is valid? If not, what further assumptions would be needed to make it valid? Do you think the argument is sound (that is, both valid and true in all its premises)? If not, explain. If you had to attack premise (b) or (c), which do you think is the more vulnerable, and why?

7. In the imaginary speech by the Laws of Athens to Socrates, especially in paragraph 93, the Laws convey a picture of the supremacy of the state over the individual—and Socrates seems to assent to this picture. Do you? Why, or why not?

8. The Laws (para. 95) claim that if Socrates were to escape, he would be "guilty of doing wrong on three separate counts." What are they? Do you agree with all or any? Why, or why not? Read the essay by Martin Luther King, Jr., "Letter from Birmingham Jail" (p. 430), and decide how King would have responded to the judgment of the Laws of Athens.

9. At the end of their peroration (para. 99), the Laws of Athens say to Socrates: Take your punishment as prescribed, and at your death "you will leave this place . . . as the victim of wrong done not by us, the Laws, but by your fellow men." To what wrong do the Laws allude? Do you agree that it is men and not laws who perpetrated this wrong? If you were in Socrates' position, would it matter to you if you were being wronged not by laws but only by men? Explain.

Martin Luther King, Jr.

Martin Luther King, Jr. (1929–1968) was born in Atlanta and educated at Morehouse College, Crozer Theological Seminary, and Boston University. In 1954 he was called to serve as a Baptist minister in Montgomery, Alabama. During the next two years he achieved national fame when, using a policy of nonviolent resistance, he successfully led the boycott against segregated bus lines in Montgomery. He then organized the Southern Christian Leadership Conference, which furthered civil rights, first in the South and then nationwide. In

1964 he was awarded the Nobel Peace Prize. Four years later he was assassinated in Memphis, Tennessee, while supporting striking garbage workers.

In 1963 Dr. King was arrested in Birmingham, Alabama, for participating in a march for which no parade permit had been issued by the city officials. In jail he wrote a response to a letter that eight local clergymen had published in a newspaper. Their letter, titled "A Call for Unity," is printed here, followed by King's response.

Letter from Birmingham Jail

A CALL FOR UNITY

April 12, 1963

We the undersigned clergymen are among those who, in January, issued "An Appeal for Law and Order and Common Sense," in dealing with racial problems in Alabama. We expressed understanding that honest convictions in racial matters could properly be pursued in the courts, but urged that decisions of those courts should in the meantime be peacefully obeyed.

Since that time there had been some evidence of increased forebearance and a willingness to face facts. Responsible citizens have undertaken to work on various problems which cause racial friction and unrest. In Birmingham, recent public events have given indication that we all have opportunity for a new constructive and realistic approach to racial problems.

However, we are now confronted by a series of demonstrations by some of our Negro citizens, directed and led in part by outsiders. We recognize the natural impatience of people who feel that their hopes are slow in being realized. But we are convinced that these demonstrations are unwise and untimely.

We agree rather with certain local Negro leadership which has called for honest and open negotiation of racial issues in our area. And we believe this kind of facing of issues can best be accomplished by citizens of our own metropolitan area, white and Negro, meeting with their knowledge and experience of the local situation. All of us need to face that responsibility and find proper channels for its accomplishment.

Just as we formerly pointed out that "hatred and violence have no 5
sanction in our religious and political traditions," we also point out that such actions as incite to hatred and violence, however technically peaceful those actions may be, have not contributed to the resolution of our local problems. We do not believe that these days of new hope are days when extreme measures are justified in Birmingham.

We commend the community as a whole, and the local news media and law enforcement officials in particular, on the calm manner in which these demonstrations have been handled. We urge the public to continue to show restraint should the demonstrations continue, and the law enforcement officials to remain calm and continue to protect our city from violence.

We further strongly urge our own Negro community to withdraw support from these demonstrations, and to unite locally in working peacefully for a better Birmingham. When rights are consistently denied, a cause should be pressed in the courts and in negotiations among local leaders, and not in the streets. We appeal to both our white and Negro citizenry to observe the principles of law and order and common sense.

C.C.J. Carpenter, D.D., L.L.D., Bishop of Alabama; Joseph A. Durick, D.D., Auxiliary Bishop, Diocese of Mobile-Birmingham; Rabbi Milton L. Grafman, Temple Emanu-El, Birmingham, Alabama; Bishop Paul Hardin, Bishop of the Alabama–West Florida Conference of the Methodist Church; Bishop Nolan B. Harmon, Bishop of the North Alabama Conference of the Methodist Church; George M. Murray, D.D., L.L.D., Bishop Coadjutor, Episcopal Diocese of Alabama; Edward V. Ramage, Moderator, Synod of the Alabama Presbyterian Church in the United States; Earl Stallings, Pastor, First Baptist Church, Birmingham, Alabama.

LETTER FROM BIRMINGHAM JAIL

April 16, 1963

My Dear Fellow Clergymen:

While confined here in the Birmingham city jail, I came across your recent statement calling my present activities "unwise and untimely."[1] Seldom do I pause to answer criticism of my work and ideas. If I sought to answer all the criticisms that cross my desk, my secretaries would have little time for anything other than such correspondence in the course of the day, and I would have no time for constructive work. But since I feel that you are men of genuine good will and that your criticisms are sincerely set forth, I want to try to answer your statement in what I hope will be patient and reasonable terms.

I think I should indicate why I am here in Birmingham, since you have been influenced by the view which argues against "outsiders coming in." I have the honor of serving as president of the Southern Christian Leadership Conference, an organization operating in every southern state, with headquarters in Atlanta, Georgia. We have some eighty-five

---

[1]This response to a published statement by eight fellow clergymen from Alabama (Bishop C.C.J. Carpenter, Bishop Joseph A. Durick, Rabbi Milton L. Grafman, Bishop Paul Hardin, Bishop Nolan B. Harmon, the Reverend George M. Murray, the Reverend Edward V. Ramage, and the Reverend Earl Stallings) was composed under somewhat constricting circumstances. Begun on the margins of the newspaper in which the statement appeared while I was in jail, the letter was continued on scraps of writing paper supplied by a friendly Negro trusty, and concluded on a pad my attorneys were eventually permitted to leave me. Although the text remains in substance unaltered, I have indulged in the author's prerogative of polishing it for publication. [King's note.]

affiliated organizations across the South, and one of them is the Alabama Christian Movement for Human Rights. Frequently we share staff, educational, and financial resources with our affiliates. Several months ago the affiliate here in Birmingham asked us to be on call to engage in a nonviolent direct-action program if such were deemed necessary. We readily consented, and when the hour came we lived up to our promise. So I, along with several members of my staff, am here because I was invited here. I am here because I have organizational ties here.

But more basically, I am in Birmingham because injustice is here. Just as the prophets of the eighth century B.C. left their villages and carried their "thus saith the Lord" far beyond the boundaries of their home towns, and just as the Apostle Paul left his village of Tarsus and carried the gospel of Jesus Christ to the far corners of the Greco-Roman world, so am I compelled to carry the gospel of freedom beyond my own home town. Like Paul, I must constantly respond to the Macedonian call for aid.

Moreover, I am cognizant of the interrelatedness of all communities and states. I cannot sit idly by in Atlanta and not be concerned about what happens in Birmingham. Injustice anywhere is a threat to justice everywhere. We are caught in an inescapable network of mutuality; tied in a single garment of destiny. Whatever affects one directly, affects all indirectly. Never again can we afford to live with the narrow, provincial "outside agitator" idea. Anyone who lives inside the United States can never be considered an outsider anywhere within its bounds.

You deplore the demonstrations taking place in Birmingham. But your statement, I am sorry to say, fails to express a similar concern for the conditions that brought about the demonstrations. I am sure that none of you would want to rest content with the superficial kind of social analysis that deals merely with effects and does not grapple with underlying causes. It is unfortunate that demonstrations are taking place in Birmingham, but it is even more unfortunate that the city's white power structure left the Negro community with no alternative.

In any nonviolent campaign there are four basic steps: collection of the facts to determine whether injustices exist; negotiation; self-purification; and direct action. We have gone through all these steps in Birmingham. There can be no gainsaying the fact that racial injustice engulfs this community. Birmingham is probably the most thoroughly segregated city in the United States. Its ugly record of brutality is widely known. Negroes have experienced grossly unjust treatment in the courts. There have been more unsolved bombings of Negro homes and churches in Birmingham than in any other city in the nation. These are the hard, brutal facts of the case. On the basis of these conditions, Negro leaders sought to negotiate with the city fathers. But the latter consistently refused to engage in good-faith negotiation.

Then, last September, came the opportunity to talk with leaders of Birmingham's economic community. In the course of the negotiations, certain promises were made by the merchants—for example, to remove the stores' humiliating racial signs. On the basis of these promises, the Reverend Fred Shuttleworth and the leaders of the Alabama Christian Movement for Human Rights agreed to a moratorium on all demonstrations. As the weeks and months went by, we realized that we were the victims of a broken promise. A few signs, briefly removed, returned; the others remained.

As in so many past experiences, our hopes had been blasted, and the shadow of deep disappointment settled upon us. We had no alternative except to prepare for direct action, whereby we would present our very bodies as a means of laying our case before the conscience of the local and the national community. Mindful of the difficulties involved, we decided to undertake a process of self-purification. We began a series of workshops on nonviolence, and we repeatedly asked ourselves: "Are you able to accept blows without retaliating?" "Are you able to endure the ordeal of jail?" We decided to schedule our direct-action program for the Easter season, realizing that except for Christmas, this is the main shopping period of the year. Knowing that a strong economic-withdrawal program would be the by-product of direct action, we felt that this would be the best time to bring pressure to bear on the merchants for the needed change.

Then it occurred to us that Birmingham's mayoralty election was coming up in March, and we speedily decided to postpone action until after election day. When we discovered that the Commissioner of Public Safety, Eugene "Bull" Connor, had piled up enough votes to be in the run-off, we decided again to postpone action until the day after the run-off so that the demonstrations could not be used to cloud the issues. Like many others, we waited to see Mr. Connor defeated, and to this end we endured postponement after postponement. Having aided in this community need, we felt that our direct-action program could be delayed no longer.

You may well ask: "Why direct action? Why sit-ins, marches, and so 10 forth? Isn't negotiation a better path?" You are quite right in calling for negotiation. Indeed, this is the very purpose of direct action. Nonviolent direct action seeks to create such a crisis and foster such a tension that a community which has constantly refused to negotiate is forced to confront the issue. It seeks so to dramatize the issue that it can no longer be ignored. My citing the creation of tension as part of the work of the nonviolent-resister may sound rather shocking. But I must confess that I am not afraid of the word "tension." I have earnestly opposed violent tension, but there is a type of constructive, nonviolent tension which is necessary for growth. Just as Socrates felt that it was necessary to create a tension in the mind so that individuals could rise from the bondage of myths and half-truths to the unfettered realm of creative analysis and objective appraisal, so must we see the need for nonviolent gadflies to create the kind of tension in society that will help men rise from the dark depths of prejudice and racism to the majestic heights of understanding and brotherhood.

The purpose of our direct-action program is to create a situation so crisis-packed that it will inevitably open the door to negotiation. I therefore concur with you in your call for negotiation. Too long has our beloved Southland been bogged down in a tragic effort to live in monologue rather than dialogue.

One of the basic points in your statement is that the action that I and my associates have taken in Birmingham is untimely. Some have asked: "Why didn't you give the new city administration time to act?" The only answer that I can give to this query is that the new Birmingham administration must be prodded about as much as the outgoing one, before it will act. We are sadly mistaken if we feel that the election of Albert Boutwell as mayor will bring the millennium to Birmingham. While Mr. Boutwell is a much more gentle person than Mr. Connor, they are both segregationists, dedicated to maintenance of the status quo. I have hope that Mr. Boutwell will be reasonable enough to see the futility of massive resistance to desegregation. But he will not see this without pressure from devotees of civil rights. My friends, I must say to you that we have not made a single gain in civil rights without determined legal and nonviolent pressure. Lamentably, it is an historical fact that privileged groups seldom give up their privileges voluntarily. Individuals may see the moral light and voluntarily give up their unjust posture; but as Reinhold Niebuhr[2] has reminded us, groups tend to be more immoral than individuals.

We know through painful experience that freedom is never voluntarily given by the oppressor; it must be demanded by the oppressed. Frankly, I have yet to engage in a direct-action campaign that was "well timed" in the view of those who have not suffered unduly from the disease of segregation. For years now I have heard the word "Wait!" It rings in the ear of every Negro with piercing familiarity. This "Wait" has almost always meant "Never." We must come to see, with one of our distinguished jurists, that "justice too long delayed is justice denied."[3]

We have waited for more than 340 years for our constitutional and God-given rights. The nations of Asia and Africa are moving with jetlike speed toward gaining political independence, but we still creep at horse-and-buggy pace toward gaining a cup of coffee at a lunch counter. Perhaps it is easy for those who have never felt the stinging darts of segregation to say, "Wait." But when you have seen vicious mobs lynch your mothers and fathers at will and drown your sisters and brothers at whim; when you

---

[2]**Reinhold Niebuhr** Niebuhr (1892–1971) was a minister, political activist, author, and professor of applied Christianity at Union Theological Seminary. [All notes are the editors' unless otherwise specified.]

[3]**justice . . . denied** A quotation attributed to William E. Gladstone (1809–1898), British statesman and prime minister.

have seen hate-filled policemen curse, kick, and even kill your black brothers and sisters; when you see the vast majority of your twenty million Negro brothers smothering in an airtight cage of poverty in the midst of an affluent society; when you suddenly find your tongue twisted and your speech stammering as you seek to explain to your six-year-old daughter why she can't go to the public amusement park that has just been advertised on television, and see tears welling up in her eyes when she is told that Funtown is closed to colored children, and see ominous clouds of inferiority beginning to form in her little mental sky, and see her beginning to distort her personality by developing an unconscious bitterness toward white people; when you have to concoct an answer for a five-year-old son who is asking: "Daddy, why do white people treat colored people so mean?"; when you take a cross-country drive and find it necessary to sleep night after night in the uncomfortable corners of your automobile because no motel will accept you; when you are humiliated day in and day out by nagging signs reading "white" and "colored"; when your first name becomes "nigger," your middle name becomes "boy" (however old you are) and your last name becomes "John," and your wife and mother are never given the respected title "Mrs."; when you are harried by day and haunted by night by the fact that you are a Negro, living constantly at tiptoe stance, never quite knowing what to expect next, and are plagued with inner fears and outer resentments; when you are forever fighting a degenerating sense of "nobodiness" — then you will understand why we find it difficult to wait. There comes a time when the cup of endurance runs over, and men are no longer willing to be plunged into the abyss of despair. I hope, sirs, you can understand our legitimate and unavoidable impatience.

You express a great deal of anxiety over our willingness to break 15 laws. This is certainly a legitimate concern. Since we so diligently urge people to obey the Supreme Court's decision of 1954 outlawing segregation in the public schools, at first glance it may seem rather paradoxical for us consciously to break laws. One may well ask: "How can you advocate breaking some laws and obeying others?" The answer lies in the fact that there are two types of laws: just and unjust. I would be the first to advocate obeying just laws. One has not only a legal but a moral responsibility to obey just laws. Conversely, one has a moral responsibility to disobey unjust laws. I would agree with St. Augustine that "an unjust law is no law at all."

Now, what is the difference between the two? How does one determine whether a law is just or unjust? A just law is a man-made code that squares with the moral law or the law of God. An unjust law is a code that is out of harmony with the moral law. To put it in the terms of St. Thomas Aquinas: An unjust law is a human law that is not rooted in eternal law and natural law. Any law that uplifts human personality is just. Any law that degrades human personality is unjust. All segregation statutes are unjust because segregation distorts the soul and damages the personality. It gives the segregator a false sense of superiority and the segregated a false sense of inferiority. Segregation, to use the terminology of the Jewish philosopher Martin Buber, substitutes an "I-it" relationship for an "I-thou" relationship and ends up relegating persons to the status of things. Hence segregation is not only politically, economically, and sociologically unsound, it is morally wrong and sinful. Paul Tillich[4] has said that sin is separation. Is not segregation an existential expression of man's tragic separation, his awful estrangement, his terrible sinfulness? Thus it is that I can urge men to obey the 1954 decision of the Supreme Court, for it is morally right; and I can urge them to disobey segregation ordinances, for they are morally wrong.

Let us consider a more concrete example of just and unjust laws. An unjust law is a code that a numerical or power majority group compels a minority group to obey but does not make binding on itself. This is *difference* made legal. By the same token, a just law is a code that a majority compels a minority to follow and that it is willing to follow itself. This is *sameness* made legal.

Let me give another explanation. A law is unjust if it is inflicted on a minority that, as a result of being denied the right to vote, had no part in enacting or devising the law. Who can say that the legislature of Alabama which set up that state's segregation laws was democratically elected? Throughout Alabama all sorts of devious methods are used to prevent Negroes from becoming registered voters, and there are some counties in which, even though Negroes constitute a majority of the population, not a single Negro is registered. Can any law enacted under such circumstances be considered democratically structured?

Sometimes a law is just on its face and unjust in its application. For instance, I have been arrested on a charge of parading without a permit. Now, there is nothing wrong in having an ordinance which requires a permit for a parade. But such an ordinance becomes unjust when it is used to maintain segregation and to deny citizens the First Amendment privilege of peaceful assembly and protest.

I hope you are able to see the distinction I am trying to point out. In 20 no sense do I advocate evading or defying the law, as would the rabid segregationist. That would lead to anarchy. One who breaks an unjust law must do so openly, lovingly, and with a willingness to accept the penalty. I submit that an individual who breaks a law that conscience tells him is unjust, and who willingly accepts the penalty of imprisonment in order to arouse the conscience of the community over its injustice, is in reality expressing the highest respect for law.

Of course, there is nothing new about this kind of civil disobedience. It was evidenced sublimely in the refusal of Shadrach, Meshach, and

[4]**Paul Tillich** Tillich (1886–1965), born in Germany, taught theology at several German universities, but in 1933 he was dismissed from his post at the University of Frankfurt because of his opposition to the Nazi regime. At the invitation of Reinhold Niebuhr, he came to the United States and taught at Union Theological Seminary.

Abednego to obey the laws of Nebuchadnezzar, on the ground that a higher moral law was at stake. It was practiced superbly by the early Christians, who were willing to face hungry lions and the excruciating pain of chopping blocks rather than submit to certain unjust laws of the Roman Empire. To a degree, academic freedom is a reality today because Socrates practiced civil disobedience. In our own nation, the Boston Tea Party represented a massive act of civil disobedience.

We should never forget that everything Adolf Hitler did in Germany was "legal" and everything the Hungarian freedom fighters did in Hungary was "illegal." It was "illegal" to aid and comfort a Jew in Hitler's Germany. Even so, I am sure that, had I lived in Germany at the time, I would have aided and comforted my Jewish brothers. If today I lived in a Communist country where certain principles dear to the Christian faith are suppressed, I would openly advocate disobeying that country's anti-religious laws.

I must make two honest confessions to you, my Christian and Jewish brothers. First, I must confess that over the past few years I have been gravely disappointed with the white moderate. I have almost reached the regrettable conclusion that the Negro's great stumbling block in his stride toward freedom is not the White Citizen's Counciler or the Ku Klux Klanner, but the white moderate, who is more devoted to "order" than to justice; who prefers a negative peace which is the absence of tension to a positive peace which is the presence of justice; who constantly says: "I agree with you in the goal you seek, but I cannot agree with your methods or direct action"; who paternalistically believes he can set the timetable for another man's freedom; who lives by a mythical concept of time and who constantly advises the Negro to wait for a "more convenient season." Shallow understanding from people of good will is more frustrating than absolute misunderstanding from people of ill will. Lukewarm acceptance is much more bewildering than outright rejection.

I had hoped that the white moderate would understand that law and order exist for the purpose of establishing justice and that when they fail in this purpose they become the dangerously structured dams that block the flow of social progress. I had hoped that the white moderate would understand that the present tension in the South is a necessary phase of the transition from an obnoxious negative peace, in which the Negro passively accepted his unjust plight, to a substantive and positive peace, in which all men will respect the dignity and worth of human personality. Actually, we who engage in nonviolent direct action are not the creators of tension. We merely bring to the surface the hidden tension that is already alive. We bring it out in the open, where it can be seen and dealt with. Like a boil that can never be cured so long as it is covered up but must be opened with all its ugliness to the natural medicines of air and light, injustice must be exposed, with all the tension its exposure creates, to the light of human conscience and the air of national opinion before it can be cured.

In your statement you assert that our actions, even though peaceful, 25 must be condemned because they precipitate violence. But is this a logical assertion? Isn't this like condemning a robbed man because his possession of money precipitated the evil act of robbery? Isn't this like condemning Socrates because his unswerving commitment to truth and his philosophical inquiries precipitated the act by the misguided populace in which they made him drink hemlock? Isn't this like condemning Jesus because his unique God-consciousness and never-ceasing devotion to God's will precipitated the evil act of crucifixion? We must come to see that, as the federal courts have consistently affirmed, it is wrong to urge an individual to cease his efforts to gain his basic constitutional rights because the quest may precipitate violence. Society must protect the robbed and punish the robber.

I had also hoped that the white moderate would reject the myth concerning time in relation to the struggle for freedom. I have just received a letter from a white brother in Texas. He writes: "All Christians know that the colored people will receive equal rights eventually, but it is possible that you are in too great a religious hurry. It has taken Christianity almost two thousand years to accomplish what it has. The teachings of Christ take time to come to earth." Such an attitude stems from a tragic misconception of time, from the strangely irrational notion that there is something in the very flow of time that will inevitably cure all ills. Actually, time itself is neutral; it can be used either destructively or constructively. More and more I feel that the people of ill will have used time much more effectively than have the people of good will. We will have to repent in this generation not merely for the hateful words and actions of the bad people but for the appalling silence of the good people. Human progress never rolls in on wheels of inevitability; it comes through the tireless efforts of men willing to be co-workers with God, and without this hard work, time itself becomes an ally of the forces of social stagnation. We must use time creatively, in the knowledge that the time is always ripe to do right. Now is the time to make real the promise of democracy and transform our pending national elegy into a creative psalm of brotherhood. Now is the time to lift our national policy from the quicksand of racial injustice to the solid rock of human dignity.

You speak of our activity in Birmingham as extreme. At first I was rather disappointed that fellow clergymen would see my nonviolent efforts as those of an extremist. I began thinking about the fact that I stand in the middle of two opposing forces in the Negro community. One is a force of complacency, made up in part of Negroes who, as a result of long years of oppression, are so drained of self-respect and a sense of "somebodiness" that they have adjusted to segregation; and in part of a few middle-class Negroes who, because of a degree of academic and economic security and because in some ways they profit by segregation, have become insensitive to the problems of the masses. The other force is one of bitterness and hatred, and it comes perilously close to advocating violence. It is expressed in the various black nationalist groups that are springing up across the nation, the largest and best-known being Elijah Muhammad's Muslim movement. Nourished by the Negro's frustration over the continued existence of racial discrimination, this movement is made up of people who have lost faith in America, who have absolutely repudiated Christianity, and who have concluded that the white man is an incorrigible "devil."

I have tried to stand between these two forces, saying that we need emulate neither the "do-nothingism" of the complacent nor the hatred and despair of the black nationalist. For there is the more excellent way of love and nonviolent protest. I am grateful to God that, through the influence of the Negro church, the way of nonviolence became an integral part of our struggle.

If this philosophy had not emerged, by now many streets of the South should, I am convinced, be flowing with blood. And I am further convinced that if our white brothers dismiss as "rabble-rousers" and "outside agitators" those of us who employ nonviolent direct action, and if they refuse to support our nonviolent efforts, millions of Negroes will, out of frustration and despair, seek solace and security in black-nationalist ideologies—a development that would inevitably lead to a frightening racial nightmare.

Oppressed people cannot remain oppressed forever. The yearning 30 for freedom eventually manifests itself, and that is what has happened to the American Negro. Something within has reminded him of his birthright of freedom, and something without has reminded him that it can be gained. Consciously or unconsciously, he has been caught up by the *Zeitgeist*,[5] and with his black brothers of Africa and his brown and yellow brothers of Asia, South America, and the Caribbean, the United States Negro is moving with a sense of great urgency toward the promised land of racial justice. If one recognizes this vital urge that has engulfed the Negro community, one should readily understand why public demonstrations are taking place. The Negro has many pent-up resentments and latent frustrations, and he must release them. So let him march; let him make prayer pilgrimages to the city hall; let him go on freedom rides—and try to understand why he must do so. If his repressed emotions are not released in nonviolent ways, they will seek expression through violence; this is not a threat but a fact of history. So I have not said to my people: "Get rid of your discontent." Rather, I have tried to say that this normal and healthy discontent can be channeled into the creative outlet of nonviolent direct action. And now this approach is being termed extremist.

But though I was initially disappointed at being categorized as an extremist, as I continued to think about the matter I gradually gained a

---

[5]*Zeitgeist* German for "spirit of the age."

measure of satisfaction from the label. Was not Jesus an extremist for love: "Love your enemies, bless them that curse you, do good to them that hate you, and pray for them which despitefully use you, and persecute you." Was not Amos an extremist for justice: "Let justice roll down like waters and righteousness like an ever-flowing stream." Was not Paul an extremist for the Christian gospel: "I bear in my body the marks of the Lord Jesus." Was not Martin Luther an extremist: "Here I stand; I cannot do otherwise, so help me God." And John Bunyan: "I will stay in jail to the end of my days before I make a butchery of my conscience." And Abraham Lincoln: "This nation cannot survive half slave and half free." And Thomas Jefferson: "We hold these truths to be self-evident, that all men are created equal. . . ." So the question is not whether we will be extremists, but what kind of extremists we will be. Will we be extremists for hate or for love? Will we be extremists for the preservation of injustice or for the extension of justice? In that dramatic scene on Calvary's hill three men were crucified. We must never forget that all three were crucified for the same crime—the crime of extremism. Two were extremists for immorality, and thus fell below their environment. The other, Jesus Christ, was an extremist for love, truth, and goodness, and thereby rose above his environment. Perhaps the South, the nation, and the world are in dire need of creative extremists.

I had hoped that the white moderate would see this need. Perhaps I was too optimistic; perhaps I expected too much. I suppose I should have realized that few members of the oppressor race can understand the deep groans and passionate yearnings of the oppressed race, and still fewer have the vision to see that injustice must be rooted out by strong, persistent, and determined action. I am thankful, however, that some of our white brothers in the South have grasped the meaning of this social revolution and committed themselves to it. They are still all too few in quantity, but they are big in quality. Some—such as Ralph McGill, Lillian Smith, Harry Golden, James McBride Dabbs, Ann Braden, and Sarah Patton Boyle—have written about our struggle in eloquent and prophetic terms. Others have marched with us down nameless streets of the South. They have languished in filthy, roach-infested jails, suffering the abuse and brutality of policemen who view them as "dirty nigger-lovers." Unlike so many of their moderate brothers and sisters, they have recognized the urgency of the moment and sensed the need for powerful "action" antidotes to combat the disease of segregation.

Let me take note of my other major disappointment. I have been so greatly disappointed with the white church and its leadership. Of course, there are some notable exceptions. I am not unmindful of the fact that each of you has taken some significant stands on this issue. I commend you, Reverend Stallings, for your Christian stand on this past Sunday, in welcoming Negroes to your worship service on a nonsegregated basis. I commend the Catholic leaders of this state for integrating Spring Hill College several years ago.

But despite these notable exceptions, I must honestly reiterate that I have been disappointed with the church. I do not say this as one of those negative critics who can always find something wrong with the church. I say this as a minister of the gospel, who loves the church; who was nurtured in its bosom; who has been sustained by its spiritual blessings and who will remain true to it as long as the cord of life shall lengthen.

When I was suddenly catapulted into the leadership of the bus 35 protest in Montgomery, Alabama, a few years ago, I felt we would be supported by the white church. I felt that the white ministers, priests, and rabbis of the South would be among our strongest allies. Instead, some have been outright opponents, refusing to understand the freedom movement and misrepresenting its leaders; all too many others have been more cautious than courageous and have remained silent behind the anesthetizing security of stained-glass windows.

In spite of my shattered dreams, I came to Birmingham with the hope that the white religious leadership of this community would see the justice of our cause and, with deep moral concern, would serve as the channel through which our just grievances could reach the power structure. I had hoped that each of you would understand. But again I have been disappointed.

I have heard numerous southern religious leaders admonish their worshipers to comply with a desegregation decision because it is the law, but I have longed to hear white ministers declare: "Follow this decree because integration is morally right and because the Negro is your brother." In the midst of blatant injustices inflicted upon the Negro, I have watched white churchmen stand on the sideline and mouth pious irrelevancies and sanctimonious trivialities. In the midst of a mighty struggle to rid our nation of racial and economic injustice, I have heard many ministers say: "Those are social issues, with which the gospel has no real concern." And I have watched many churches commit themselves to a completely otherworldly religion which makes a strange, unbiblical distinction between body and soul, between the sacred and the secular.

I have traveled the length and breadth of Alabama, Mississippi, and all the other southern states. On sweltering summer days and crisp autumn mornings I have looked at the South's beautiful churches with their lofty spires pointing heavenward. I have beheld the impressive outlines of her massive religious-education buildings. Over and over I have found myself saying: "What kind of people worship here? Who is their God? Where were their voices when the lips of Governor Barnett dripped with words of interposition and nullification? Where were they when Governor Wallace gave a clarion call for defiance and hatred? Where were their voices of support when bruised and weary Negro men and women decided to rise from the dark dungeons of complacency to the bright hills of creative protest?"

Yes, these questions are still in my mind. In deep disappointment I have wept over the laxity of the church. But be assured that my tears have been tears of love. There can be no deep disappointment where there is not deep love. Yes, I love the church. How could I do otherwise? I am in the rather unique position of being the son, the grandson, and the great-grandson of preachers. Yes, I see the church as the body of Christ. But, Oh! How we have blemished and scarred that body through social neglect and through fear of being nonconformists.

There was a time when the church was very powerful—in the time 40 when the early Christians rejoiced at being deemed worthy to suffer for what they believed. In those days the church was not merely a thermometer that recorded the ideas and principles of popular opinion; it was a thermostat that transformed the mores of society. Whenever the early Christians entered a town, the people in power became disturbed and immediately sought to convict the Christians for being "disturbers of the peace" and "outside agitators." But the Christians pressed on, in the conviction that they were "a colony of heaven," called to obey God rather than man. Small in number, they were big in commitment. They were too God-intoxicated to be "astronomically intimidated." By their effort and example they brought an end to such ancient evils as infanticide and gladiatorial contests.

Things are different now. So often the contemporary church is a weak, ineffectual voice with an uncertain sound. So often it is an archdefender of the status quo. Far from being disturbed by the presence of the church, the power structure of the average community is consoled by the church's silent—and often even vocal—sanction of things as they are.

But the judgment of God is upon the church as never before. If today's church does not recapture the sacrificial spirit of the early church, it will lose its authenticity, forfeit the loyalty of millions, and be dismissed as an irrelevant social club with no meaning for the twentieth century. Every day I meet young people whose disappointment with the church has turned into outright disgust.

Perhaps I have once again been too optimistic. Is organized religion too inextricably bound to the status quo to save our nation and the world? Perhaps I must turn my faith to the inner spiritual church, the church within the church, as the true *ekklesia* and the hope of the world. But again I am thankful to God that some noble souls from the ranks of organized religion have broken loose from the paralyzing chains of conformity and joined us as active partners in the struggle for freedom. They have left their secure congregations and walked the streets of Albany, Georgia, with us. They have gone down the highways of the South on tortuous rides for freedom. Yes, they have gone to jail with us. Some have been dismissed from their churches, have lost the support of their bishops and fellow ministers. But they have acted in the faith that right defeated is stronger than evil triumphant. Their witness has been the spiritual salt that has preserved the true meaning of the gospel in these troubled times. They have carved a tunnel of hope through the dark mountain of disappointment.

I hope the church as a whole will meet the challenge of this decisive hour. But even if the church does not come to the aid of justice, I have no despair about the future. I have no fear about the outcome of our struggle in Birmingham, even if our motives are at present misunderstood. We will reach the goal of freedom in Birmingham and all over the nation, because the goal of America is freedom. Abused and scorned though we may be, our destiny is tied up with America's destiny. Before the pilgrims landed at Plymouth, we were here. Before the pen of Jefferson etched the majestic words of the Declaration of Independence across the pages of history, we were here. For more than two centuries our forebears labored in this country without wages; they made cotton king; they built the homes of their masters while suffering gross injustice and shameful humiliation — and yet out of a bottomless vitality they continue to thrive and develop. If the inexpressible cruelties of slavery could not stop us, the opposition we now face will surely fail. We will win our freedom because the sacred heritage of our nation and the eternal will of God are embodied in our echoing demands.

Before closing I feel impelled to mention one other point in your 45 statement that has troubled me profoundly. You warmly commended the Birmingham police force for keeping "order" and "preventing violence." I doubt that you would have so warmly commended the police force if you had seen its dogs sinking their teeth into unarmed, nonviolent Negroes. I doubt that you would so quickly commend the policemen if you were to observe their ugly and inhumane treatment of Negroes here in the city jail; if you were to watch them push and curse old Negro women and young Negro girls; if you were to see them slap and kick old Negro men and young boys; if you were to observe them, as they did on two occasions, refuse to give us food because we wanted to sing our grace together. I cannot join you in your praise of the Birmingham police department.

It is true that the police have exercised a degree of discipline in handling the demonstrators. In this sense they have conducted themselves rather "nonviolently" in public. But for what purpose? To preserve the evil system of segregation. Over the past few years I have consistently preached that nonviolence demands that the means we use must be as pure as the ends we seek. I have tried to make clear that it is wrong to use immoral means to attain moral ends. But now I must affirm that it is just as wrong, or perhaps even more so, to use moral means to preserve immoral ends. Perhaps Mr. Connor and his policemen have been rather nonviolent in public, as was Chief Pritchett in Albany, Georgia, but they used the moral means of nonviolence to maintain the immoral end of racial injustice. As T. S. Eliot has said: "The last temptation is the greatest treason: To do the right deed for the wrong reason."

I wish you had commended the Negro sit-inners and demonstrators of Birmingham for their sublime courage, their willingness to suffer, and their amazing discipline in the midst of great provocation. One day the South will recognize its real heroes. They will be the James Merediths, with the noble sense of purpose that enables them to face jeering and hostile mobs, and with the agonizing loneliness that characterizes the life of the pioneer. They will be old, oppressed, battered Negro women, symbolized in a seventy-two-year-old woman in Montgomery, Alabama, who rose up with a sense of dignity and with her people decided not to ride segregated buses, and who responded with ungrammatical profundity to one who inquired about her weariness: "My feets is tired, but my soul is at rest." They will be the young high school and college students, the young ministers of the gospel and a host of their elders, courageously and nonviolently sitting in at lunch counters and willingly going to jail for conscience' sake. One day the South will know that when these disinherited children of God sat down at lunch counters, they were in reality standing up for what is best in the American dream and for the most sacred values in our Judaeo-Christian heritage, thereby bringing our nation back to those great wells of democracy which were dug deep by the founding fathers in their formulation of the Constitution and the Declaration of Independence.

Never before have I written so long a letter. I'm afraid it is much too long to take your precious time. I can assure you that it would have been much shorter if I had been writing from a comfortable desk, but what else can one do when he is alone in a narrow jail cell, other than write long letters, think long thoughts, and pray long prayers?

If I have said anything in this letter that overstates the truth and indicates an unreasonable impatience, I beg you to forgive me. If I have said anything that understates the truth and indicates my having a patience that allows me to settle for anything less than brotherhood, I beg God to forgive me.

I hope this letter finds you strong in the faith. I also hope that circumstances will soon make it possible for me to meet each of you, not as an integrationist or a civil-rights leader but as a fellow clergyman and a Christian brother. Let us all hope that the dark clouds of racial prejudice will soon pass away and the deep fog of misunderstanding will be lifted from our fear-drenched communities, and in some not too distant tomorrow the radiant stars of love and brotherhood will shine over our great nation with all their scintillating beauty.

Yours for the cause of Peace and Brotherhood,
Martin Luther King, Jr.

Topics for Critical Thinking and Writing

1. In his first five paragraphs, how does King assure his audience that he is not a meddlesome intruder but a man of good will?

2. In paragraph 3 King refers to Hebrew prophets and to the Apostle Paul, and later (para. 10) to Socrates. What is the point of these references?

3. In paragraph 11 what does King mean when he says that "our beloved Southland" has long tried to "live in monologue rather than dialogue"?

4. King begins paragraph 23 with "I must make two honest confessions to you, my Christian and Jewish brothers." What would have been gained or lost if he had used this paragraph as his opening?

5. King's last three paragraphs do not advance his argument. What do they do?

6. Why does King advocate breaking unjust laws "openly, lovingly" (para. 20)? What does he mean by these words? What other motives or attitudes do these words rule out?

7. Construct two definitions of "civil disobedience," and explain whether and to what extent it is easier (or harder) to justify civil disobedience, depending on how you have defined the expression.

8. If you feel that you wish to respond to King's letter on some point, write a letter nominally addressed to King. You may, if you wish, adopt the persona of one of the eight clergymen whom King initially addressed.

9. King writes (para. 46) that "nonviolence demands that the means we use must be as pure as the ends we seek." How do you think King would evaluate the following acts of civil disobedience: (a) occupying a college administration building in order to protest the administration's unsatisfactory response to a racial incident on campus, or in order to protest the failure of the administration to hire minority persons as staff and faculty; (b) sailing on a collision course with a whaling ship to protest against whaling; (c) trespassing on an abortion clinic to protest abortion? Set down your answer in an essay of 500 words.

Appendix:
World Wide Web Sources
for Current Issues

If you use the Internet for research, you may have difficulty knowing where to begin. The following list can help by pointing you toward some useful sources of information on the World Wide Web covering many of the current issues in this book. Many of these topics have hundreds, even thousands, of Web pages dedicated to them, pages of highly varied quality and reliability. This list is hardly complete or definitive; it is merely a place to start, so you are not overwhelmed by the available choices. Many of the sources listed should be useful for the early stages of your research because they often contain extensive links and pointers to other sources of information: further Web sites, newsgroups and discussion lists, archived electronic documents, and traditional print sources. We have tried to indicate whether the author or sponsoring organization for a Web site takes sides in the debate.

Please note that although we tried to include only stable and up-to-date sources, the Internet changes from day to day. It is possible that some of these sources are no longer available at the specified address, or that the content of the pages has changed significantly.

General Information/Current Events

CNN Interactive and the *New York Times Online* are two excellent sources of late-breaking information on current topics, essentially any story that would be covered in print or broadcast news. Of course, there are many other reputable news organizations with online components, and if you are researching a very timely topic, you may want to expand your search or use another source (such as the newspaper for a particular city) that seems appropriate.

CNN Interactive. <http://www.cnn.com>
A very elaborate site, with many visuals, audio and video clips, and user-friendly site navigation. Its extensive coverage of current news is revised several times daily, as news breaks, and it also includes features, commentaries, and related stories.

New York Times Online. <http://www.nytimes.com>
Contains text and pictures from the day's edition of the *Times*, the nation's "newspaper of record." You must register the first time you use the site, but registration is free for users within the United States.

Alcohol Abuse

Rutgers University Center of Alcohol Studies.
<http://www.rci.rutgers.edu/~cas2>
Site maintained by a multidisciplinary research institute. Includes fact sheets on topics such as drunk driving, the effects of alcohol, alcohol and domestic violence, and women and alcohol. Also provides links to pages of other major organizations and government agencies.

Animal Rights

People for the Ethical Treatment of Animals (PETA).
<http://www.peta-online.org>
A comprehensive site run by the largest animal rights organization in America. Includes answers to frequently asked questions on PETA philosophy, links to news articles on animal rights, and an "activists library" pointing to publications, videos, images of animal research labs, and so on.

Critiques of Animal Rights. <http://www.animalrights.net>
A site favoring animal use. The "Links" section connects to the pages of antianimal rights groups, as well as to online articles on "animal rights terrorism," animal testing, hunting, and education.

Bilingual Education

"Bilingual Education." *Education Week.*
<http://www.edweek.org/context/topics/biling.htm>
Provides an overview of the debate on bilingual education in the United States. Discusses various theories of and methods for bilingual education and gives links to articles from the *Education Week* archives on various aspects of bilingual education — legal, financial, and social.

Bilingual Education Resources on the Internet.
<http://www.edb.utexas.edu/coe/depts/ci/bilingue/resources.html>
Although this site favors bilingual education, it gives links to broadly useful sources, including government documents, journals, and an online discussion list.

Divorce

Divorce Reform Page. <http://adams.patriot.net/~crouch/divorce.html>
Although page has a bias in favor of making divorce more difficult, it includes links to both pro- and antireform articles and editorials in reputable online periodicals as well as to divorce statistics and news about laws in various states.

Euthanasia

Euthanasia World Directory. <http://www.efn.org/~ergo>

Generally advocating the right to die, the site includes many links to groups favoring that perspective, as well as texts of euthanasia-related laws. The "news" link is updated daily and points to sources of world news on all aspects of euthanasia and assisted suicide.

First Amendment

"Some Freedom of Expression WWW Sources." *MIT Student Association for Freedom of Expression (SAFE) Home Page.*
<http://www.mit.edu:8001/activities/safe/resources.html>

Provides an annotated list of links to many reliable sites and sources, including the American Civil Liberties Union Archive, the Electronic Frontier Foundation, and the text of Supreme Court decisions.

Fourth Amendment

The Privacy Pages. <http://www.2020tech.com/maildrop/privacy.html>

Includes links to breaking news, privacy organizations, and articles from worldwide periodicals. Provides much information on privacy issues online, including encryption, anonymous servers, and privacy software.

Gun Control

Handgun Control, Inc. and The Center To Prevent Handgun Violence.
<http://www.handguncontrol.org>

Provides useful information on state and national laws, as well as links to pro-gun control articles (the site's bias).

Immigration

Yahoo! News.
<http://headlines.yahoo.com/Full_Coverage/US/Immigration>

Part of the *Yahoo!* Web search "Full Coverage" series. Provides links to recent immigration-related stories in major U.S. newspapers and magazines as well as additional Web sites screened for reliability.

Siskind, Susser, Haas & Chang Documents Collection.
<http://www.telalink.net/~gsiskind/docs>

Site of large immigration law firm. The collection includes text of recent and pending state and national immigration legislation, reports, and related documents.

Internet Censorship

"Internet Censorship." *Electronic Privacy Information Center.*
<http://www.epic.org/free_speech/censorship>

Links to text of current Internet censorship legislation and to other groups interested in free speech on the Net, including the Electronic Freedom Forum and the American Civil Liberties Union.

Juvenile Justice

Juvenile Justice Center.
<http://www.abanet.org/crimjust/juvjus/home.html>

The American Bar Association's Juvenile Justice Center exists "to monitor and influence juvenile justice policy and practice." Web site provides links to information on state and national law and the full text of articles from law journals.

Pornography

Computer Mediate Communications Magazine.
<http://sunsite.unc.edu/cmc/mag/1995/aug/toc.html>

The August 1995 issue of this online magazine is dedicated to an analysis of the debate over pornography on the Internet. Several thoughtful articles are included, many with links to other sources. Links from "Editor's Page" are especially useful.

Racist Speech

"Internet Resources on Hate Speech." *University of Iowa Libraries Gateway to the Internet.*
<http://www.arcade.uiowa.edu:80/gw/journalism/mediaLaw/hateSpeech.html>

Links to a number of reputable articles on racist and other forms of hate speech, especially emphasizing speech online and on college campuses.

Smokers' Rights

CDC's Tobacco Information and Prevention Source.
<http://www.cdc.gov/tobacco>

Part of the U.S. Centers for Disease Control's antismoking education effort, this site includes the text of Surgeon General's reports, research and statistics, and information on smoking and tobacco legislation in the news.

Fight Ordinances & Restrictions to Control and Eliminate Smoking (FORCES).
<http://forces.org>

Site demonstrates a strong bias in favor of smokers' rights. Provides links to the pages of like-minded groups, the text of recent antismoking legislation, and articles downplaying the dangers of smoking and arguing against restrictions.

Teenage Pregnancy

Boston University Community Outreach Health Information System.
<http://web.bu.edu:80/COHIS/teenpreg/teenpreg.htm>
Part of a clearinghouse of information on public health issues. Provides general statistics about teen pregnancy and information on risks, pregnancy prevention, maternal and infant health, and related topics.

National Campaign to Prevent Teen Pregnancy.
<http://www.teenpregnancy.org>
The stated goal of the sponsoring organization is "to reduce the teen pregnancy rate by one-third by the year 2005." The site provides recent statistics and facts, as well as an annotated page of "related sites," linking to other organizations with an interest in teen pregnancy.

ries Current Today We Shall Have to Reject" from *The Republic*, translated by Desmond Lee. Copyright © 1955, 1974 by H. D. P. Lee. Reprinted with the permission of Penguin Books Ltd.

Katha Pollitt, "It Takes Two: A Modest Proposal for Holding Fathers Equally Accountable" from *The Nation* (January 30, 1995). Originally appeared in *The Boston Globe* (January 27, 1995). Copyright © 1995 The Nation Company, L.P. Reprinted with the permission of *The Nation*.

Diane Ravitch, "First Teach Them English" from *The New York Times* (September 5, 1997). Copyright © 1997 by The New York Times Company. Reprinted with the permission of *The New York Times*.

Jean Rhys, "I Used to Live Here Once" from *The Collected Stories of Jean Rhys* (New York: W. W. Norton & Company, 1987). Copyright © 1976 by Jean Rhys. Reprinted with the permission of The Wallace Agency.

Janet Radcliffe Richards, "Thinking Straight and Dying Well" from *Newsletter of the Voluntary Euthanasia Society of Scotland* (September 1994). Copyright © 1994. Reprinted with the permission of the publishers.

Patrick G. D. Riley, "A Contract to Be Kept" from *The New York Times* (February 21, 1996), "Letters to the Editor." Reprinted with the permission of the author.

Carl R. Rogers, "Communication: Its Blocking and Its Facilitation." Reprinted with the permission of the author.

Rebecca Sawyer-Fay, "Letter to the Editor" from *The New York Times* (February 24, 1996). Reprinted with the permission of the author.

Stanley S. Scott, "Smokers Get a Raw Deal" from *The New York Times* (December 29, 1984). Copyright © 1984 by The New York Times Company. Reprinted with the permission of *The New York Times*.

Max Shulman, "Love is a Fallacy" from *Love is a Fallacy* (New York: Doubleday, 1951). Copyright 1951 and renewed © 1979 by Max Shulman. Reprinted with the permission of Harold Matson Agency.

John Silber, "Students Should Not Be Above the Law" from *The New York Times* (May 9, 1996). Copyright © 1996 by The New York Times Company. Reprinted with the permission of *The New York Times*.

Peter Singer, "Animal Liberation" from *The New York Review of Books* (April 15, 1973). Copyright © 1973 by Peter Singer. Reprinted with the permission of the author.

Sophocles, "Antigone," translated by Dudley Fitts and Robert Fitzgerald, from *The Oedipus Cycle: An English Version*. Copyright 1939 by Dudley Fitts and Robert Fitzgerald. Reprinted with the permission of Harcourt Brace & Company.

Ronald Takaki, "The Harmful Myth of Asian Superiority" from *The New York Times* (June 16, 1990). Copyright © 1990 by The New York Times Company. Reprinted with the permission of *The New York Times*.

Caldwell Titcomb, "Star-Spangled Earache: What So Loudly We Wail" from *The New Republic* (1985). Copyright © 1985 by The New Republic, Inc. Reprinted with the permission of *The New Republic*.

Judith D. Wallach, "We Strive to Be Insular" from *The New York Times* (September 9, 1997), "Letters to the Editor." Reprinted with the permission of the author.

Elizabeth M. Whelan, "Perils of Prohibition" from *Newsweek* (May 29, 1995). Copyright © 1995 by Newsweek, Inc. Reprinted with the permission of *Newsweek*.

James Q. Wilson, "Just Take Away Their Guns" from *The New York Times* (March 20, 1994). Copyright © 1994 by The New York Times Company. Reprinted with the permission of *The New York Times*. "The Paradox of Cloning" from *The Weekly Standard* (May 26, 1997). Copyright © 1997 by James Q. Wilson. Reprinted with the permission of the author.

Index of Authors
and Titles

Index of Terms

DIRECTORY TO DOCUMENTATION MODELS IN MLA FORMAT

In-Text or Parenthetical Citations, 210

List of Works Cited, 216

Books

Anthologies

Periodical Articles